PHILOSOLIFE

Re-inventing Philosophy as a Way of Life

Series editors: Keith Ansell-Pearson, Matthew Sharpe and Michael Ure

For the most part, academic philosophy is considered a purely theoretical discipline that aims at systematic knowledge; contemporary philosophers do not, as a rule, think that they or their audience will lead better lives by doing philosophy. Recently, however, we have seen a powerful resurgence of interest in the countervailing ancient view that philosophy facilitates human flourishing. Philosophy, Seneca famously stated, teaches us doing, not saying. It aims to transform how we live. This ancient ideal has continually been reinvented from the Renaissance through to late modernity and is now central to contemporary debates about philosophy's role and future.

This series is the first synoptic study of the re-inventions of the idea of philosophy as an ethical pursuit or 'way of life'. Collectively and individually, the books in this series will answer the following questions:

1. How have philosophers re-animated the ancient model of philosophy? How have they revised ancient assumptions, concepts and practices in the light of wider cultural shifts in the modern world? What new ideas of the good life and new arts, exercises, disciplines and consolations have they formulated?
2. Do these re-inventions successfully re-establish the idea that philosophy can transform our lives? What are the standard criticisms of this philosophical ambition and how have they been addressed?
3. What are the implications for these new versions of philosophy as a way of life for contemporary issues that concern the nature of philosophy, its procedures, limits, ends, and its relationship to wider society?

Other titles in the series include:
The Selected Writings of Pierre Hadot, trans. Matthew Sharpe and Federico Testa
Effort and Grace, Simone Kotva
The Late Foucault, ed. Marta Faustino and Gianfranco Ferraro

PHILOSOPHY AS A WAY OF LIFE

HISTORY, DIMENSIONS, DIRECTIONS

Matthew Sharpe and Michael Ure

BLOOMSBURY ACADEMIC
LONDON • NEW YORK • OXFORD • NEW DELHI • SYDNEY

BLOOMSBURY ACADEMIC
Bloomsbury Publishing Plc
50 Bedford Square, London, WC1B 3DP, UK
1385 Broadway, New York, NY 10018, USA
29 Earlsfort Terrace, Dublin 2, Ireland

BLOOMSBURY, BLOOMSBURY ACADEMIC and the Diana logo are
trademarks of Bloomsbury Publishing Plc

First published in Great Britain 2021

Series design by Charlotte Daniels
Cover image: *Logic and Dialectic* (represented by Plato and
Aristotle): Lucca della Robbia, (1437–39) Florence, Museo dell'
Opera del Duomo, (© Peter Horree / Alamy Stock Photo)

A catalogue record for this book is available from the British Library.

A catalog record for this book is available from the Library of Congress.

ISBN: HB: 978-1-3501-0215-6
         PB: 978-1-3501-0214-9
         ePDF: 978-1-3501-0213-2
         eBook: 978-1-3501-0216-3

Series: Re-inventing Philosophy as a Way of Life

Typeset by Integra Software Solutions Pvt. Ltd.
Printed and bound in Great Britain

To find out more about our authors and books visit www.bloomsbury.com
and sign up for our newsletters.

M. Sharpe dedication: to my kids, from the past, for your future

M. Ure dedication: to Jules & Louie, there's more to life than is dreamt

of in these philosophies

CONTENTS

Contents

LIST OF ILLUSTRATIONS

ACKNOWLEDGEMENTS

We would like to acknowledge the Australian Research Council and the Monash Prato Centre for generously supporting this project. We would also like to thank our editor Liza Thompson for her support and patience. We are indebted to the following friends and scholars: Keith Ansell-Pearson, David Cartwright, Christopher Celenza, Ian Hunter, Michael Janover, David Konstan, John Sellars and Matteo Stettler. An earlier version of Chapter 11 appeared in The Late Foucault, edited by Marta Faustino & Gianfranco Ferraro (London: Bloomsbury Academic, an imprint of Bloomsbury Publishing Plc, 2020)

INTRODUCTION

To undertake to write a synoptic historical study is in one sense the humblest of tasks. To set out to analyse, summarize and synthesize the works of other philosophers is, indeed, so diminutive an endeavour as to risk not being considered 'research' in today's novelty-hungry ideas marketplace. In another sense, though, someone could interject that it is hybris itself to attempt an intellectual history, however basic, to retrace for the first time the history of a specific but major, mostly-forgotten conception of philosophy in the West. What any such project cedes in depth it takes back in scope, and in spades. At every moment, the attempt of such a Primer to achieve such wide historical scope flirts with making its treatments of any one philosopher or philosophy too superficial by half.

Both considerations are valid. We have felt acutely these competing risks in the long process of putting together this book. In response to anxieties about both depth and scope, we can only provide our own version of the famous Newtonian *bon mot*. Whatever success our endeavour can claim, and whatever insights we may have achieved, comes from how we have been able to stand on the shoulders of giants. First and foremost amongst the giants is the French philosopher and historian of ideas, Pierre Hadot, whose work we will introduce specifically in a moment. But he is accompanied by many others, each of whom, like Hadot himself in our chapters on the Epicureans, Stoics, Platonists and Christians, has been our close interlocutor in the studies of the different figures we undertake in this book: W.K. C. Guthrie and Gregory Vlastos on Socrates; Julia Annas, Diskin Clay and Catherine Wilson on the Epicureans [2]; Ilsetraut Hadot, Pierre's wife, on Seneca and the Stoics [esp. 3.4]; John Sellars on the Stoics [3.1] and then again, Justus Lipsius [6.4]; Juliusz Domański on the medievals [4] and the renaissance *humanisti* [5.1–2]; Ruedi Imbach on the medievals [5.3–4]; Christopher Celenza, Gur Zak and James Siegel on what counted as philosophy in the Italian renaissance [5.1]; Sorana Corneanu, Stephen Gaukroger and Peter Harrison on Bacon [7.2]; Amelie Rorty and Zeno Vendler on Descartes [7.3]; Ira Wade, Calas Duflo and Peter Gay on the *lumières*; David Cartwright, Christopher Janaway and Julian Young's dissections of Schopenhauer's metaphysics and ethics [9]; and scholars who have recently rediscovered Nietzsche as a student, teacher and exponent of philosophy as a way of life such as Keith Ansell-Pearson and Alexander Nehamas [10].

And all this is not to suggest that all of our interpretations of these philosophies are wholly 'unoriginal'. Readers will see that our own critical perspectives never entirely disappear behind the accounts of the different thinkers and movements presented in this book; Socrates, the Epicureans, the Stoics, the Sceptics, the Neoplatonists, the Christian monastics, Scholastics and Averroists; the renaissance *humanisti* led by Petrarch, then Montaigne, Lipsius, Bacon, Descartes, the *virtuosi* and the *lumières*, Schopenhauer, Nietzsche and Foucault. The venture to open such a wide purview, and cover so many alternative ideas and practices of philosophy, also opens new, original synthetic vistas, and casts new framing light on individual philosophers. As we shall see, the very inventory of figures we have considered, with its inclusion of Hellenistics and Romans, monastics and humanists, as well as enlightenment *philosophes*, also reflects the originality of the 'philosophy as a way of life' (or PWL) approach that shapes and orients this study.

This much then by way of Socratic apology for *Philosophy as a Way of Life: History, Dimensions and Directions*. We need now to address just what is PWL, as we conceive it, and then introduce the key methodological and substantive claims of the book.

Pierre Hadot, PWL and spiritual exercises

If the idea of PWL is today emerging as its own subfield within metaphilosophy and the history of philosophy, it is above all because of the work of Pierre Hadot. Hadot begun his intellectual life in training as a Catholic priest. However, as he has frankly disclosed in interviews, his life was transformed by a series of extraordinary 'mystical' or 'unitive' experiences which he had in his early life, which he found could not be accommodated within his childhood faith (Hadot, 2009: 5–6). Hadot began to work on late ancient Neoplatonic as well as Christian thinkers, and in 1963 (1998), wrote a groundbreaking study on Plotinus, which we draw upon directly in **Chapter 4.3** below.

Hadot's work, *Plotinus, or the Simplicity of Vision* (1998) is unusual for the attention Hadot pays to Plotinus's life and experiences, as well as to his philosophical discourse concerning the different metaphysical levels

Plotinus postulates, of the One, the Platonic Ideas, the Soul and material reality. Hadot claims that we cannot fully understand Plotinus's philosophical discourse if we do not conceive of these metaphysical postulations as the expressions and corollaries of certain transformative experiences Plotinus had undergone. This holds not only concerning Plotinus's claims about the civic or 'purificatory' virtues (courage, moderation, justice). It holds in particular for his seemingly 'abstract' claims concerning the Intellect and Ideas, and the One beyond being and language. Plotinus's claims regarding these putatively higher realities, for Hadot, are the reflections of different 'levels of inner life':

> Within this framework, the experience Plotinus describes for us consists in a movement by which the soul lifts itself up to the level of divine intelligence, which creates all things and contains within itself, in the form of a spiritual world, all the eternal Ideas or immutable models of which the things of this world are nothing but images. (Hadot, 1998: 25–6)

In other words, philosophy for the Hadot of 1963 is already envisaged as something that one does or even undergoes. It is not just something one thinks, or teaches to others, or writes. Plotinus, in fact, like Socrates and Epictetus, himself wrote nothing. We owe the work called the *Enneads* to his pupil, Porphyry. Philosophy involves in addition a kind of spiritual itinerary. Plotinus describes the task of philosophy as a process of self-transformation, in which one chips away at the unshaped rock of one's character in order to shape a new, more beautiful form. It is also for him, in an abiding metaphor, the process of an ethical or spiritual ascent, in which the philosopher gradually comes ideally both to see and know new things, and to become thereby an ultimately wiser person.

In this early work, Hadot does not systematically use the key term 'spiritual exercises' that he will later coin. If we are not mistaken, the term appears first in 1973 in a piece on Marcus Aurelius's conception of physics, the study of non-human nature, as one way that the Stoic can transform their ways of seeing and experiencing the world. Arguably the single most decisive text in Hadot's evolution towards 'becoming Hadot' however is his 1962 piece (still untranslated, as of May 2020), 'Jeux de langage et philosophie' (Hadot, 2004). Hadot here argues that the famous philosopher Wittgenstein's later conception of 'language games' could be used to develop a new understanding of ancient philosophy, one which would challenge the predominant focus (then as now) on reasoning and argumentation alone.

Hadot begun to ask in this paper about the puzzling differences between different ancient philosophical texts and the texts in which we write philosophy in later modernity. Some of these texts, like Aristotle's lecture courses, are more or less like today's papers, chapters or books. Yet others are consolations, meditations, dialogues, aphorisms, even poems. These would not make it past the editors of a philosophical journal today, let alone a team of reviewers. This is where Hadot boldly proposes to adapt Wittgenstein's idea that everyone plays different 'language games' in the space of almost any ordinary day: we make promises, teach our toddlers, banter with colleagues, type emails, or bark or follow orders in the workplace. What if the differences of ancient from modern philosophical texts reflect the ways that the ancient philosophers were playing different language games than we do?, Hadot began to ask. What if the literary texts of ancient philosophy, with all their different genres, were the legacy of an older, quite different and wider conception of philosophical activity than our own?

The idea of PWL was then born, in Hadot's work, from a hermeneutic programme. It responds to an attempt to make sense of the different kinds of philosophical text bequeathed to us the ancient philosophers. Hadot's claim was that large parts of some texts (for instance, the *Enneads*), and the entirety of some others (for instance, Marcus Aurelius's *Meditations*) make no sense if we hold our own metaphilosophical assumptions constant, and try to read these philosophers as only interested in what we do today as scholars: making arguments, discovering new knowledges or attracting external funding. By contrast, these texts do make sense if we suppose that many of those parts we find most strange, 'merely literary' or supplementary, involve the staging, prescribing or performance of what Hadot calls 'spiritual exercises' (1995: 79–125).

What are spiritual exercises? Hadot addresses this question in a 1976 presentation that profoundly affected Michel Foucault, and which became the paradigmatic 'Spiritual Exercises' chapter in *Philosophy as a Way of Life* (1995). They are not philosophical arguments, inductive or deductive. But they can involve restating and recollecting such arguments, their conclusions or implications, and applying them to new situations. Nor are they physical exercises, like training to run distances. Yet they can include a physical component, and some exercises involve consciously chosen physical hardships. Nor are they, despite some anxiety from critics, necessarily religious or wholly rhetorical. Yet, many such exercises draw upon the artful use of language to frame philosophical claims in the most striking, and therefore the most *memorable*, forms. Hadot gives different definitions of 'spiritual exercises' across different texts, and Foucault in his wake proposes a variant term, 'technologies of (the) self' (Foucault, 2005). In each case, what is at issue is a cognitive, mnemonic, imaginative, rhetorical or physical exercise *consciously chosen and undertaken by an agent with a view to the transformative effects the undertaking of this exercise will have upon the practitioner's way of experiencing, desiring, emoting, or thinking.*

To repeat, the ancient philosophers didn't undertake or write down such exercises to discover new knowledge, publicize arguments or advertise conclusions. They prescribed and practised them in order to transform themselves with a view to approaching the wisdom and virtues of the sage (*sophos* or *sapiens*). For Hadot (2020a: 185–206), the ancient philosophical discourses concerning the wonderful attributes of the fully wise or enlightened person (the figure of the sage) are therefore another genre of ancient philosophical writing attesting to the ancients' conception of PWL. Even when wisdom was conceived theoretically, as knowledge of the first principles of the sciences, including metaphysics (as in Aristotle's *Metaphysics* I), the text still asks about its attributes by considering the qualities of the wise man. Many ethical texts, for instance Cicero's *Tusculan Disputations* (especially book V), address ethical questions concerning the virtues, happiness and the good life by dialoguing concerning the persona of the sage.

Hadot himself, and commentators working in his wake, give different categorizations of the spiritual exercises (Harter, 2018; Sharpe & Kramer, 2019). For our purposes here, acknowledging that different possible divisions are present in the literature, let us say that there are twelve species of exercises. Our list includes three more or less purely 'intellectual exercises', a term Hadot sometimes introduces (2020: 35, 58–9) to describe pedagogical exercises which are still widely promoted in philosophy courses today:

1. There are practices of meditation, wherein the exercitant undertakes not to free their mind of all content, as on one Buddhist model, but to recollect specific metaphysical, ethical, physical or logical precepts so as to apply them in their daily lives or, in Epicureanism, to recall pleasant and forget unpleasant experiences;

2. There are practices to cultivate philosophically informed kinds of attention to the present moment, to the different features of things,

to the distinction between what is and is not dependent on us, or to the task at hand;

3. There are contemplative exercises wherein one is enjoined to call to mind and savour the wonders of the cosmos, nature, the Ideas, the One or God;

4. There are practices of *pre*meditation, in which the exercitant prepares themselves in advance for difficulties, and for the inevitability of their own and loved ones' deaths;

5. On the other hand, there are exercises of *retrospective self-examination* of one's conscience, thoughts and actions, for instance at the end of the day, as in Pythagoreanism and some Stoics;

6. There are also exercises of reframing one's way of seeing, neither to focus on what is immediately present nor on the cosmos as a whole, but to recontextualize one's particular concerns and experience in the context of the larger cosmos or whole:

   a. whether in space, by envisaging oneself and one's surrounds as if from above (what Hadot [1995] calls 'the view from above');

   b. or in time, by depicting what one experiences *sub specie aeternitatis*, as a passing minute in eternity or the eternal recurrence of all things.

7. There are exercises to tame one's passions, including meditative recollection of calming precepts (1), practices of self-examination (5), but also including (in some philosophers like Aristotle and Bacon) conscious practices of opposing a tempting passion (say anger) with its opposite (gratitude, generosity, serenity or sadness). As an important subset of these exercises, philosophical texts of consolation for grief such as those of Seneca, Cicero and Plutarch should be mentioned here;

8. There are exercises in training oneself to fortitude, or training the mind to deal with pain or quell desire, including prescribed abstinences and fasting, but also some of the more spectacular public exercises of Diogenes the Cynic (like begging for money in the open from inanimate statues [DL VI, 23, 49]);

9. There are established practices concerning students' relationships with teachers who are also, in Ilsetraut Hadot's term (2014), 'spiritual guides'; these include forms of counselling, confession,

frank speaking and writing (as, for instance, in Marcus Aurelius's letters to his teacher Fronto) as well as, in the Epicurean school, practices of examining oneself in the presence of a friend, who doubles as a critic and counsellor.

In addition to these 'spiritual exercises', which engage what Hadot calls 'the entire psychism' of the philosopher (1995: 82), Hadot sometimes talks of more purely 'intellectual exercises' (2020: 35, 58–9; cf. 1995: 89–93, 101–9). By these, he means specifically:

10. dialogic exercises, from the Socratic elenchus aiming to refute and change interlocutors' views to highly codified rules governing 'dialectical' exchanges (notably in Platonism and Aristotle) between interlocutors, in order to discover independent truths, but also to train the intellects of inquirers;

11. prescriptions concerning how to listen to spoken discourses, how to read written texts and also how to remember what one reads or hears, including forms of what Michel Foucault (1983) called 'self-writing';

12. exercises also taught in the rhetorical schools concerning how to develop different kinds of discourses, with different goals, to different audiences (rhetoric being considered one of what became, following Plato and Augustine, the 'liberal arts' befitting the educated person), as well as – significantly – how to memorize ideas.

As a result of the practice of these exercises, in conjunction with the education in the technical philosophical discourses of the schools, ancient philosophers were throughout antiquity a distinctly recognizable, somewhat 'edgy' cultural type (Hadot, 1995: 97). Many ancient texts of philosophy, starting from Plato's dialogues, have a strongly biographical component. They are portraits of the philosopher in dialogue with different people and highlight what in Socrates's case is called his strangeness or *atopia* (Hadot, 1995: 58; Domański, 1996: 19–22). Or else, they are collections of salutary or salacious anecdotes and sayings of philosophers (like Diogenes Laertius) interspersed with summaries of philosophical doctrines. The aim of these texts is to inspire emulation, as well as to edify and inform readers about technical dogmata. From Aristophanes to Lucian, the philosophers were subject to lampooning because of their manners of dress, their tell-tale beards, their unusual habits and exercises, their ways of talking, as well as because of their pretentions to wisdom and virtue. Whilst anti-intellectualism, like the poor, will probably always be with us, it is fair to say that after the eighteenth century [8.1], the 'philosopher' has ceased being such a distinct and influential cultural type as to attract its own genre of parody.

A key distinction Hadot recurs to in order to assist readers in grasping the idea of PWL is the distinction between philosophical discourse and philosophy itself. Philosophical discourse involves codified, more or less systematized teachings, which may be written down (2002: 172–236). Philosophy itself is the ongoing practice or way of life of a philosopher, involving spiritual exercises to shape a manner of living in light of the tenets of different philosophical teachings. For long periods of antiquity, it was undertaken by students within competing, recognized schools (Academy, Lyceum, Stoic porch, Epicurean garden), under the pedagogical and spiritual guidance of teachers. Philosophy as such an exercise in the art of living, to use a Stoic term, requires training in philosophical discourse, since the content and justification of different spiritual exercises turns on such knowledge. Yet to only learn philosophical discourses, and the arts of speaking and arguing skilfully, holds a permanent danger. This is the temptation of sophistry, as Hadot mostly presents it: the ability to win friends, fame and power by impressing people with one's rhetorical and argumentative skills, with no commitment to living according to a systematic, normative philosophical teaching.

Hadot's historical works on ancient philosophy therefore increasingly involve a criticism, not of modern philosophy or 'modernity' per se, but of the way that philosophy since the medieval period has in his view forgotten its ancient calling, as the cultivation of a *bios* or way of life. This critique is made explicit in the final part of Hadot's long study, *What Is Ancient Philosophy?*, but it is developed in a number of other places (2002: 253–70). Modern academic philosophy, Hadot suggests, has become solely the learning, teaching and writing of philosophical discourse, wherein closed groups of professionals, most working on texts closed to all except other such professionals, discuss these texts with each other in fora closed to outsiders. If a philosopher chooses to live according to some *ethos*, this will usually be an *ethos* unrelated to his professional work. Moreover, according to an anecdote from Kant with which Hadot concludes a public lecture on his work on PWL:

To an old man, who told him that he attended lessons on virtue, Plato responded: 'and when will you begin to live virtuously?' One cannot always theorise. One must finally aim at passing from thought to exercise. But today we take someone who lives what he teaches to be a dreamer. (at Hadot, 2020: 42)

It is remarkable that Hadot's work has become popular in a period wherein the marginal utility of philosophical discourse is widely questioned, as universities increasingly reconceive their educational mission according to corporate imperatives. The rise of PWL is certainly in part due to Foucault's uptake of Hadot's work on the ancients in Foucault's last lectures and books on the history of sexuality and 'technologies of the self' (Chapter 11). The advent of modern Stoicism is unthinkable without the internet. But this rise also speaks to a hunger amongst students and the educated public for something like Hadot's more humanistic (as against scholastic or academic) vision of philosophy (see Chapter 6). The recovery of the ancient sense of PWL speaks to concerns of life, death and the everyday as well as to perplexities of the mind in the theoretical empyrean.

Our approach in this book would be impossible without Hadot's work.

PWL as historiographical approach

PWL thus begun its career as the response to a hermeneutic conundrum. How can we understand the seeming inconsistencies and strange literary features of ancient philosophical texts, without dismissing whole parts of (or entire) texts, as well as many figures the ancients considered philosophers, from Diogenes the Cynic to statesmen like Cato of Utica (cf. Cooper, 2012)? In a revealing Preface to Richard Goulet's *Dictionnaire des philosophes antiques*, as well as his February 1983 inaugural address at the Collège de France, Hadot makes the claim that if we are to understand the intentions of an ancient text, we must situate it within three interesting contexts:

In the context [*cadre*] *of the school* in which and for which it is composed, the perspective of the students for whom it could have been addressed. Moreover, it is in the school after all that the writing has been conserved, classed in a corpus and commented upon with the aid of traditional rules of interpretation. One must also consider that this form and content could be determined *by political concerns*: for example, one could draw a portrait of the ideal king in order to advise or criticise a sovereign ... And finally, one must never forget that *theory is never totally separated from the spiritual practice*, that philosophical works aimed above all to form as well as to inform, and that philosophical discourse is only a means intended to lead to a mode of life which is not different from philosophy itself. (Hadot, 2020: 51–2 [trans. & italics ours])

As readers can appreciate, the combined effect of:

1. PWL's expanded willingness to consider forms of writing as philosophical which today we might dismiss as merely literary or inconsequential; and

2. Hadot's post-Wittgensteinian directives to consider texts (2004) not as self-standing artefacts, but practices and cultures

means that Hadot's work has opened an entire set of new vistas for understanding the history of Western philosophy. (This purview indeed does not exclude new comparative philosophical vistas, on the contrary [see: Fiordalis ed., 2018; Sharpe & Kramer, 2019].) To use a metaphor we will recur to below (see Figure 0.1), this methodological approach to reading philosophical texts opens up *a new grid of visibility*, relative to other ways of understanding the history of philosophy. The idea here is simple: if how we understand philosophy, and what can count as philosophy changes, then what we will include and exclude in any history of philosophy will also change.

The term 'philosophy' today still carries a normative, as well as a descriptive charge, if only amongst career professionals. Like everybody else, as Montaigne would advise, we are inclined to understand the philosophy of different times on the model of how we presently understand what 'we' are doing. There are nevertheless potential problems associated with this metaphilosophical assumption, whether one begins with 'analytic' or 'continental' expectations. Ruedi Imbach has commented upon these problems in connection with the philosophical texts of the medieval period. But Imbach's comments can be applied more widely, to include the texts of the Hellenistic and Roman periods, the Italian and European renaissance, and the French enlightenment. Imbach notes that we tend today to think of philosophy as a body of impersonal, conceptual discourses, embodied in written texts, to be interpreted in more or less complete abstraction from their social, institutional and biographical preconditions. To ask questions about where and when any 'great philosopher' was situated, how the author might have understood his work in relation to contemporaries and how his contemporaries understood it is a task to be assigned to intellectual historians, historians of philosophy or historians of ideas. Imbach calls this a kind of 'Platonist' image of philosophical activity, as if philosophies spring from disembodied minds, if not gods (Imbach, 1996: 87; Plato, *Soph.* 216a). The texts that are worth mentioning in the history of philosophy, on this model, are the great texts that contribute something 'original', at the level of discourse or argumentation. So, we leap, very often, from Aristotle to Aquinas or to Descartes, then to Kant and Hegel, omitting all others. This 'imperialism of originality' (Imbach, 1996: 87) might also today be termed a para-Heideggerian image of philosophy, with debts to Nietzsche's idea of monumental history in the second *Untimely Meditation* [see **10.2**].

The PWL research programme initiated by the Hadots and others however challenges these Platonic or Heideggerian images of the history of *philosophia*. If philosophy is conceived as implicating a way or ways of life, as we have been seeing, then its history will involve more than 'the great thinkers', their books, arguments and myriad imitators. Alongside the great innovators, Plato, Aristotle, Augustine, Aquinas, Bacon, Descartes etc., there are the lives and histories of schools, commentators and revivers of old ideas, the development of teaching and writing cultures, and the ongoing philosophical pedagogy and practice of less well-known figures (Hadot, 2020b, 43–54).

To adopt such an expanded perspective is not to give way to a nominalist relativism, or so we will argue (**Conclusion**). A PWL approach need not, although it may, accept that whatever anyone at any time thought to call 'philosophy' should be considered equally philosophical. Nor is a PWL position committed to the idea that all 'philosophy' is equally good, important, serious, rigorous or influential. Nevertheless, to entertain a PWL approach is to be open to the ways in which what people have called philosophy at different periods in the history of Western thought has changed. Accordingly, it is to be awake to how much of what thinkers in other cultures and historical periods counted as philosophical challenges our present institutional, pedagogical and intellectual presuppositions, even as these periods disappear from visibility in many contemporary syllabi.

It is to be open therefore to the reality that what we presently count as philosophical will change in future periods.

Adopting a PWL perspective also enables the historian of philosophy, or the student of philosophy, to ask different questions concerning this history than other approaches can so much as frame. When, for instance, did the conception of PWL cease to be the predominant one in the West? Because of what reason or combination of intellectual, institutional, social, political or religious conditions did this change occur? Did this 'fall' occur all at once, or are we rather dealing with a complex, staged, contingent, reversible history or histories? How did philosophy as PWL inherit from, transform, anticipate, cross-pollinate with, and critique different forms of religion and religious practices at different points in philosophical history? What transformations and modulations of the idea of PWL are possible, and have been embodied, in the history of Western thought? What possibilities does the intellectual recovery of the very idea of PWL present for contemporary philosophy, faced with the increasing marginalization of the discipline within the corporatized university?

For now, let us say that one of the greatest potential boons of the research programme opened up by PWL hails from the way that it opens us to the plurality of forms in which philosophy has been conceived, written, institutionalized and undertaken. PWL as an historiographical approach also enables us to open and read anew, as philosophical, the works of profoundly influential authors in several crucial periods that most later modern histories of Western philosophy pass over. There is first of all the Hellenistic and Roman periods, whose philosophies exerted continuous cultural influence until the eighteenth century. These have widely been the victim of a 'classical' prejudice hailing from nineteenth-century German scholarship, which reads these periods as periods of philosophical derivativeness and decline [see **9.1, 10.1**]. The contrast here is usually with the putatively more systematic thought of Plato and Aristotle, despite the difficulties posed by these two thinkers' unusual (by our lights) written outputs.

Then there is the period of the Italian and Northern renaissances (*c.* 1400–1600), in which the works of antiquity, principally including those of the Sceptics, Epicureans and Stoics, were recovered, and thinkers like Petrarch, Montaigne and Lipsius undertook to reanimate (and renovate) their conceptions of the philosophical life. Finally, there is the period of the enlightenment (*c.* 1720–90), known under one of its monikers as the 'age of philosophy' (Wade, 1977a), yet now almost completely sidelined (excepting the university-based, critical philosopher, Immanuel Kant) in understandings of philosophy today (Wilson, 2008).

The present book accordingly contains chapters on each of these periods, and one of its claims to originality consists in this profile of inclusions. Other philosophers, of course, could have been considered, and it is worth mentioning several giants: the humanist Erasmus (cf. Dealy, 2017), the sage-like Spinoza (1982), Lord Shaftesbury (cf. Sellars, 2016; Gill, 2018), and the poet-philosophers Goethe (cf. Hadot, 2008) and Camus (cf. Sharpe, 2015a), in this place.[1] We should also add one further qualification under this heading of PWL as historiographical approach.

The contextualist dimension of Hadot's conception of PWL, its emphasis on the need to understand the institutional, political and ethical conditions of different ways of philosophising means that it can in principle be applied to any and all forms of philosophy (Hunter, 2007). This could include forms of philosophy that most certainly do *not* conceive of their activities as taking aim at transforming students, except intellectually, and at shaping particular ways of living, beyond the language of 'career pathways' which we today apply to any and all professions. Intellectual historian Ian Hunter (2007, 2016) has done the most to promote such a research programme. In our conclusion, we will return to engage with the questions posed by Hunter's provocative work, but it should be clear from the start that the choices of which philosophers we have included in this Primer is limited to those who directly avow some vision of PWL, or form of therapy, or self- or other-cultivation.

Our analytic 'tennead'

In order to introduce a continuity of analytic approach in a work covering such diverse philosophers as Socrates and Nietzsche, Epictetus and Descartes, Seneca and Voltaire, we have developed the following 'grid' or 'table', to which we will be recurring throughout this Primer. Drawing from Hadot and those who have worked in his wake, the table isolates some ten features of philosophical activity which a PWL approach casts into visibility. Isolating these ten, numbered features of philosophical activity has allowed us to generate a series of discrete comparisons and contrasts between the metaphilosophies of the different figures and schools we analyse. Here as in our listing of the spiritual and intellectual exercises above, we acknowledge that this division is contestable, and that other tabulations are possible.

Figure 0.1 'Tennead', ten features of philosophy in our PWL approach.

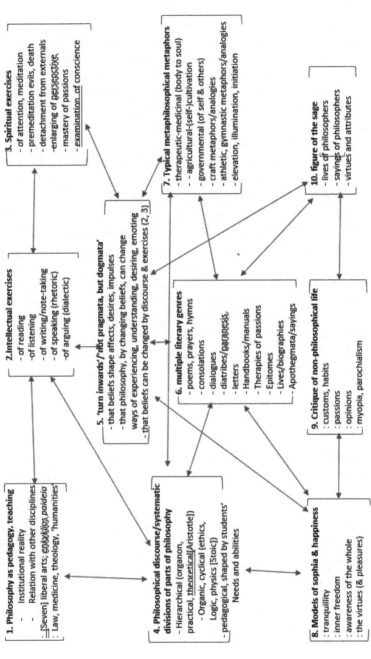

1. Philosophy as pedagogy, teaching
- Institutional reality
- Relation with other disciplines
- [Seven] liberal arts; *enkyklios paideia*
- Law, medicine, theology, 'humanities'

2. Intellectual exercises
- of reading
- of listening
- of writing/note-taking
- of speaking (rhetoric)
- of arguing (dialectic)

3. Spiritual exercises
- of attention, meditation
- premeditation evils, death
- detachment from externals
- enlarging of perception
- mastery of passions
- examination of conscience

5. 'turn inwards'/'not pragmata, but dogmata'
- that beliefs shape affects, desires, impulses
- that philosophy, by changing beliefs, can change ways of experiencing, understanding, desiring, emoting
- that beliefs can be changed by discourse & exercises (2, 3)

4. Philosophical discourse/systematic divisions of parts of philosophy
- Hierarchical (organon, practical, theoretical[Aristotle])
- Organic, cyclical (ethics, Logic, physics [Stoic])
- pedagogical, shaped by students' Needs and abilities

6. multiple literary genres
- poems, prayers, hymns
- consolations
- dialogues
- diatribes/*paraenesis*
- letters
- Handbooks/manuals
- Therapies of passions
- Epitomes
- Lives/biographies
- Apothegmata/sayings

7. Typical metaphilosophical metaphors
- therapeutic-medicinal (body to soul)
- agricultural-(self-)cultivation
- governmental (of self & others)
- craft metaphors/analogies
- athletic, gymnastic metaphors/analogies
- elevation, illumination, initiation

8. Models of sophia & happiness
: tranquillity
: inner freedom
: awareness of the whole
: the virtues (& pleasures)

9. Critique of non-philosophical life
: customs, habits
: passions
: opinions
: myopia, parochialism

10. figure of the sage
- lives of philosophers
- sayings of philosophers
- virtues and attributes

The joints where one cuts between different features of PWL, and so their enumeration, might differ. Nevertheless, there is heuristic value in working with this tabulation of ten features of philosophical activity a PWL approach focuses us upon as we proceed, and then in the summative Appendix which closes this Primer.

Numbers placed in brackets and typed in bold (**1, 2** …) in the text refer to these ten features of PWL (by contrast, bolded numbers in square brackets and with decimal points [**3.1, 4.3** …] refer to the book chapters and sections). The three levels of the tennead diagram (1, 2, 3; then 4, 6, 7; then 8, 9, 10) respectively represent the pedagogical-practical level of philosophy, the level of philosophical writing and communication, and the normative level.

Standing alone and central is number **5**. It describes the founding premise for any conception of PWL, insofar as the latter maintains that philosophical discourse, through teaching and intellectual exercises, can change people's deep-set beliefs. This change in turn enables lasting ethical or spiritual transformation, insofar as philosophers maintain that human beings are rational animals. This is to say that humans act on the basis of reasons. Even when we act irrationally, we seek justifications for our actions. Even when we emote, our passions are based on beliefs about the world and our place within it.

It is on the basis of such reasoning that Socrates famously announced in his defence speech in the *Apology* that all he had aimed to do was to ask Athenians to cease caring so much about fame, power, money and wealth, and to care for their own *psychai* (*Apo.* 29e-30c). Such a 'turn inwards' (to use a provisional description which would need careful qualification) towards a focused philosophical attention on one's own beliefs, attitudes and affects is basic to any and all conceptions of PWL. The Epicureans, for example, did not avow Socrates as one of their inspirations, looking rather to the pre-Socratic atomists and to Democritus. Nevertheless, the same conception of the dependence of our desires and perceived needs on our beliefs, or empty beliefs (*kenodoxia*), enables Epicurus to present his philosophy as medicinal and eudaimonistic, and Lucretius to celebrate Epicurus as a deity who had not simply conquered external monsters, like Hercules, but internal or ethical monsters, which pose a much more immediate threat to many more people's well-being (*De rer. nat.*, V, 39–59).

Some version or analogue of this Socratic call for the philosopher to attend as much or more to his own beliefs about things, as to things themselves (as in Epictetus's famous claim that it is not things [*pragmata*] but our opinions about things [*dogmata*] which trouble us [*Ench.* 5]), seems to us minimally constitutive of any PWL approach. We find it carried out in a variety of different, at times competing theoretical vocabularies.

The pedagogical-practical level

1. **Philosophy as pedagogy:** a PWL approach stands back from looking only at the textual achievements of philosophical writing by qualified experts, to see philosophy as a pedagogical reality. Before philosophers are qualified, someone teaches them. The devaluation of teaching, in contrast to 'metricizable' or saleable research which institutional pressures today enshrine is from a PWL perspective a deeply unhappy development. To understand philosophy in any given school or period, a PWL approach counsels that we should ask about the institutional settings in which it is undertaken. We should ask: What are the explicit or implicit aims of this teaching? How is it taught, to and by whom, in what relations of authority, friendship, correspondence etc.? What role do writing and other exercises play in the instruction? Also, is the teaching of philosophy considered as just one, or the privileged part of a larger pedagogical programme which includes other disciplines, especially the 'liberal arts' that dominated university syllabi in 'Arts' from the twelfth until the eighteenth century [**5.3** below]? Does philosophy lay claim to primacy, as 'science of sciences', on ground of its putative objects and scope, or is it conceived as a kind of 'organon' giving students argumentative and related skills to move to higher or other faculties like theology, medicine or law? What effect does the emergence of new sciences in the seventeenth to nineteenth centuries have on how philosophy conceives itself at different points, and today?

2. **Intellectual exercises:** as above, to the extent that we consider philosophy as something that people teach others, we confront the reality of intellectual exercises prescribed to students to train them in how to read, speak, write and remember. Today, although we may not primarily think of what we do in these terms, we train students how to read books of philosophy, to discuss ideas and write academic papers for assessment. There is a long history of philosophical thinkers prescribing norms and exercises concerning how students should read, reason, dialogue and write. There is also a

long history of learned discourse about how we should take notes so as to be able to internalize and recall ethical, philosophical, biblical or theological notions at need;

3. **Spiritual exercises:** as above, does the philosophy prescribe exercises of meditation, recollection, contemplation, premeditation, examination of conscience, transformation of vision, taming the passions and pedagogical relations to others? Which such exercises, if any, does a philosophy prescribe? What are the ends of these exercises? How are they understood in relation to each other, and are they ordered into sequential regimens, like the staged meditations in the Christian tradition and Descartes's *Meditations on First Philosophy* [**7.3**]?

The level of philosophical discourse

4. **The internal divisions within a philosophy:** How does a philosophy, if at all, engage with the questions surrounding how many different parts or divisions there are in philosophical discourse? How does it formulate the division of philosophy into parts? Does it proceed in a hierarchical way, as in Plato and Aristotle, with metaphysics or theology at the pinnacle, on the basis of the generality, immutability and immateriality of their putative objects? Or, like the Stoics, are the different parts of philosophy (for the Porch, logic, ethics, physics) conceived as thoroughly interdependent and interpenetrating, without any one necessarily having a strong pedagogical or ontological priority? Or again, as in Bacon, is the division undertaken instead on the basis of the different human faculties pre-eminently engaged in the different disciplines (memory, imagination, the will or the intellect), and if so, with what relationship to pedagogical considerations concerning ordering of teachings?[2]

6. **Literary genres:** What literary genres do philosophers write in? And what is the avowed and discernible purpose of philosophers writing in such different discourses in antiquity or the renaissance as poetry, mythology, epitomes, inventories of sayings, fables, treatises, dialogues, consolations, therapeutic or exhortatory texts, and more? How do these forms of writing relate to the intellectual exercises (**2**) or spiritual exercises (**3**) recommended by the philosopher

or his doctrinal school? How do they relate to the conceptions of wisdom (8) and the sage (10) of different philosophers? What different pedagogical and psychagogic effects can be intended (1) by adopting different forms of literary method or presentation?

7. **Metaphilosophical metaphors:** how is philosophy described, according to what metaphors or analogies? Is it compared to other crafts, for instance medicine? Or to bodily exercises like training in athletics, wrestling, archery or gymnastics? Is it compared to non-human things, like the Stoics' eggs or gardens, and with what implications? Is the agricultural language of cultivation predominant, and why? Or is it the ancient political metaphor, comparing parts of the soul (as in Plato [*Rep.* III–IV]) to parts of a regime, or self-government to government of others (*Alc. Maj.*; Foucault, 2005: 65–80)? Finally, are 'illumination' or 'elevation' metaphors employed, and in what relation to the prescription and ordering of different spiritual and intellectual exercises (**2, 3**)?

The normative level

8. **Notions of wisdom and happiness:** how does the philosophy describe its normative goals? Does it contain a robust conception of wisdom? Does it distinguish theoretical from practical modes of wisdom, and with what effect on how philosophy is conceived? Is the philosophy explicitly eudaimonistic, which is to say, concerned with engendering or cultivating the happiness or flourishing of its students? If so, how is happiness conceived, with what attributes? Is it described in terms of serenity, self-mastery, self-overcoming, self-transformation or spiritual ascent? Does it involve the attempt to enhance one's bodily, transient, this-worldly existence, or does it take aim at a putative transcendence of this existence?

9. **Critique[s] of non-philosophers:** the philosophies we examine in this book all nominate ways of life and conceptions of wisdom and happiness which challenge ordinary conventions and norms. But how is this challenge and critique of 'average everydayness' carried out, and how are non-philosophers represented? Should the philosopher withdraw into a contemplative existence, or take his philosophy back down into the streets and agoras? What makes the views of non-philosophers putatively problematic? Are 'ordinary'

human beings deemed 'beneath' philosophers, and in what terms, more or less scornful or sympathetic? Is it rather the beliefs of non-philosophers which are problematic, and which lead them into avoidable forms of suffering, discord and unhappiness? What is the philosopher's responsibility, if any, towards non-philosophers and how is the socio-political scope of the philosophy conceived?

10. **Conceptions of the sage:** philosophies which conceive of philosophy as eudaimonistic, the means to attain putative wisdom and happiness each present more or less developed portraits of the ideal individual: the sage, the well-educated person, the *gentilhomme*, even the philosopher-king. What claims does the philosophy make about these idealized figures? Is such a figure possible, beyond operating as a kind of counterfactual ideal to inspire emulation? How does the sage relate to non-philosophers? How does s/he relate to political power, the lures of money and fame, and the political and religious mythologies of her/his tribe? Does s/he experience passions and pleasures, and if so, are these of the same order as those available to non-sages?

Not all of the philosophies we study in this text exhibit all ten of these features, although the Epicureans and Stoics in particular do so. Where one or more features disappear, however, keeping these ten features in view allows us to remark and, as it were, chart these changes. The utility of the table also consists in how it can allow us to hone in on cases wherein different philosophies preserve versions of one or more of the ten features, but they also change the ways in which the relevant subjects are framed or approached. For instance, in the early modern period, the Royal Society *virtuosi* working in Francis Bacon's wake [7.4] clearly conceive of philosophy as a kind of pedagogy (1), involving intellectual exercises (2), challenging contemporary university divisions of knowledge (4), inventing new forms of writing to enable the fostering of a collective experimental culture of inquiry (5). Their texts use therapeutic metaphors to describe experimental philosophy as a *medicina animi* (7), and they most certainly develop ideas concerning wisdom and the ideal inquirer, if not the sage (8, 10). There is a political background to their changed conception of philosophy, which includes (following Bacon) a great elevation of the place of physics or natural philosophy (4), as against their medieval predecessors. Their work is animated by the desire to create a more peaceable culture and new conceptions of gentlemanly sociability, after centuries of sectarian, religious division in England and Europe (9).

However, the *virtuosi*'s conceptions of wisdom and the ideal inquirer (**8, 10**) are more exclusively concerned with how this person will form their theoretical opinions, in particular about natural philosophy, than is the case with the Stoics or Epicureans, or even Socrates. Although the *virtuosi*'s intellectual exercises (**2**), one basis for the experimental sciences, are founded on a post-Baconian sense that the life of the mind is distempered and even distorted by the passions (whence philosophical *medicina* is needed (**6, 7**)), nevertheless the *virtuosi* do not prescribe spiritual exercises (**3**) of meditation, contemplation or premeditation; nor do they console, wrestle with anger or exhort directly to the civic virtues.

Given this grid or table of ten features of PWL, we will be able to address one question, raised above, which haunts the PWL literature. This is the question as to when, how and why PWL ceased to be the predominant understanding of philosophy in the West. As we shall see, different thinkers propose different solutions:

i. That Aristotle already, within classical philosophy, proposes a solely discursive conception of philosophy, and a wholly theoretical concept of *sophia* (Sellars, 2017);

ii. That, with some telling exceptions, the medieval period saw the end of PWL, as the spiritual exercises were Christianized and philosophical discourse was dissevered from all connections to living any way of life, instead serving as handmaiden to the ascendant discipline of theology (Domański, 1996; Hadot, 2002: 237–52);

iii. That the early modern philosophies of Bacon or Descartes put an end to PWL, by proposing new forms of almost-mechanical methodologies in which practitioners could pursue and share knowledge without transforming themselves, and subordinating contemplation to the pursuit of utility (Gaukroger, 2001; Foucault, 2005; Harrison, 2015);

iv. That the 'fall' was with the enlightenment, the last period in which there is public debate about the figure of 'the philosopher' as someone worth reckoning with (**10**), in which ancient Roman ethical and political philosophy especially is central, but in which spiritual exercises only appear within philosophical literature (**4**) untied to any explicit programme of spiritual self-formation (Wilson, 2008).

v. That the advent of the modern research university, and of systematic philosophy in its modern form in Kant and the German idealists

(Ferry & Renaut, 1979), has seen the end of PWL, except as an object of historical inquiry. The Humboldtian university gives philosophy a post-theological status as Queen of the Sciences. But this is a philosophy conceived as pre-eminently embodied in written, printed discourse, abstracted from any way of life beyond that of a civil servant and career professional (Hadot, 2002; 253–70).

Faced with such a complex history, our ten-featured grid responds to a felt need to begin to treat PWL not as one 'block', which would either be wholly present and predominant or wholly absent or subordinate at any one time. Rather, it is a multidimensional philosophical paradigm, with different aspects or features. Some of these may endure at a given moment, when others go into decline or are forgotten. Just so, the history of PWL's eclipse or end as the predominant way of seeing and doing philosophy in the West may not be one, more or less dramatic, more or less eschatological 'fall' narrative. What we might be tempted to consider this 'fall', if we are sympathetic with the idea of PWL, may have been a long, uneven, halting and staged process. And we can make visible these halting step, rather than straining our eyes to see one great leap, by dividing PWL's conceptions of the relations between the disciplines, its intellectual and spiritual exercises, its forms of writing and predominant metaphors, its critiques of non-philosophers and ideals of Sagehood and Wisdom, so we can understand how each of these is transformed at different moments of the history.

The path ahead

Let us map out the path ahead, to use our own metaphor. We begin by examining Socrates (Chapter 1), the teacher of Plato, and inspiration of all of the ancient schools, excepting the Epicureans and, differently, the Peripatetics. Chapter 2, following chronology, addresses the Epicureans, and their conception of PWL leading to the stable (*katastêmatic*) pleasures and absence of anxiety (*ataraxia*) ultimately characteristic of their serene but indifferent gods. Chapter 3 examines the Stoics, starting from their conception of wisdom, then looking successively at Musonius Rufus, Epictetus and Marcus Aurelius to develop their vision of philosophy as an 'art of life'. Chapter 4 turns from the Stoic Porch to the Platonic Academy. We track the evolution of sceptical forms of Platonism into Pyrrhonian scepticism, the eclecticism of Marcus Tullius Cicero, the philosophical mysticism of Plotinus and Boethius's *Consolation of Philosophy*, the last book of ancient philosophy.

From the ancients, in Chapter 5, we move to the medievals. Here, we trace and examine Pierre Hadot's claim that the spiritual exercises developed within the pagan philosophies were Christianized in the first centuries of the common era, and integrated into the monastic regimens for living, which many of the Church fathers conceived as the truest form of *philosophia*. We then qualify Hadot's claims that the advent of university scholasticism saw the end of all features of PWL, arguing (with Domański and Imbach) that some dissident figures kept alive different ancient conceptions of philosophy. We also submit that, even within scholasticism, the intellectual exercise of the disputation (2) as well as the aspiration towards Christian *beatitude* (8) transform, but do not absolutely break with ancient philosophical conceptions.

Chapter 6 turns to the renaissance and examines how philosophy was conceived in this period, in particular in relationship to rhetoric ((1) Siegel, 1968; Celenza, 2013). We see that, whilst the *humanisti* acerbically critiqued the university philosophy of the time, and the predominance of dialectic in curricula (4), their recovery of ancient sources inspired attempts to reanimate PWL. Petrarch and Montaigne are examined here, as two exemplary figures in this metaphilosophical renaissance. Then, we turn to Justus Lipsius's avowed neo-Stoicism as it shapes the form and content of his dialogue, *On Constancy*.

Chapter 7 examines Francis Bacon and René Descartes from a PWL perspective. Like the scholastics, these figures have been charged by some historians of ideas with ending the ancient notion of PWL, in their development of forms of putatively impersonal method, enabling the refiguring of inquiry into the cumulative, collective endeavours which after the nineteenth century would be known as 'the sciences'. In Chapter 7, as in chapter 5, we qualify claims about the simple end of PWL in the early modern period, examining how Bacon's conception of philosophy is deeply indebted to the ancients (especially including his moral philosophy), and how Descartes's *Discourse on Method* and *Meditations on First Philosophy* both transform and inherit older literary paradigms tied to conceptions of inquiry as an ethically or spiritually transformative process.

Chapter 8 looks at that 'age of philosophy', the enlightenment, which has somewhat ironically all-but disappeared from today's philosophy syllabi, instead becoming the *bête noire* for many polemical, but demonstrably problematic critiques (cf. Rasmussen, 2013). Our opening section is dedicated to examining the conception of the *philosophe*, focusing on the famous portrait of this figure in Du Marsais's entry on the subject in Diderot and D'Alembert's *Encyclopaedia*. We then look, firstly, at Voltaire's nuanced relationship with ancient eudaimonistic philosophies, and his adoption of sceptical and Stoic conceptions of the therapeutic power of philosophy in his quest to combat religious sectarianism and fanaticism; then, secondly, to Diderot's ongoing critical engagements with ancient Scepticism, Cynicism, the Epicureanism of Lucretius, and above all the Stoic Seneca, on whose life and philosophical works Diderot penned his last work.

Chapter 9 moves from France to Germany, and from the enlightenment to the philosophy of Arthur Schopenhauer. Schopenhauer conducts arguably the most acerbic critique of the new, universitized philosophy [9] since Petrarch's attack on the scholastics. He then develops an account of PWL, involving spiritual exercises, which is also a way *out of life*, conceived of by him in pessimistic vein as a condition to be transcended, not enhanced, in ways which echo earlier Christianizations of philosophical discourse and practices.

Chapter 10 addresses Friedrich Nietzsche's conception of PWL, especially in his middle period. Nietzsche shares Schopenhauer's hostility to academic philosophy and takes from his early philological work a deep appreciation of ancient philosophy as PWL. His own philosophy is, in one register, an exercise in exploring different possibilities in living, one in which he becomes increasingly sceptical about ancient Hellenistic models as involving the forms of life-denial he decries in his teacher, Schopenhauer. In the eternal recurrence, Nietzsche develops a spiritual exercise which at once has ancient Stoic bases, and goes beyond the ancients, embracing a dynamic and tragic vision of existence, in which the best life is one of passion-filled experimentation and suffering, as against one characterized by ancient serenity.

Chapter 11 focuses on Foucault's explorations of ancient spiritual exercises or technologies of the self, as he called them. It suggests that Foucault conceived genealogy as a spiritual exercise that aims to create radical discontinuities between the self and itself so that it can ceaselessly experiment with new ways of living rather than return the self to its true, universal form or being so that it can realize divine self-sufficiency. In doing so, we suggest, Foucault's genealogy serves to illuminate an ethical tension between ancient and modern versions of PWL.

In the conclusion, we cast aside the mask of the commentator to address the different philosophical and other issues that are raised by PWL as a conception of philosophy and of its history:

- Does any conception of philosophy as PWL require that the specifically rational, argumentative dimensions of philosophy be devalued, collapsing any distinction between philosophy and rhetoric or religion?

- Does any approach to philosophy which considers its institutional, socio-political and literary-rhetorical aspects commit us to a form of contextualist relativism?

- Is the project of philosophical self-transformation intrinsically narcissistic or egotistical, nothing more intellectually reputable than glorified 'self-help'?

- Does PWL prescribe and rationalize an elevated withdrawal from public life, or a script or scripts for turning away from socio-political struggles and the fortification of one's 'inner citadel'?

- Just when or how do we see PWL as the predominant metaphilosophical paradigm coming to an end, if we do dispute other leading scholars' claims on this historical question (in Chapters 5, 7, 8)? What role did the 'universitization' of philosophy or what Frodeman and Briggle (2016) call its 'disciplinary capture' in the late nineteenth-century play in this story?

- Finally, what prospects does the recovery of this alternative metaphilosophy and history of philosophy open up for philosophers today, within and outside of universities? Can PWL be reanimated, and if so, what could that mean?

PART I
THE ANCIENTS

CHAPTER 1
SOCRATES AND THE INCEPTION OF
PHILOSOPHY AS A WAY OF LIFE

1.1 The *atopia* of Socrates

The fifth-century Athenian philosopher Socrates (470–399 BCE) is widely acknowledged as the founder of the tradition of philosophy as a way of life (PWL). Unlike the pre-Socratic philosophers, on most reckonings, he focused exclusively on ethics rather than natural philosophy. Socrates's ethical philosophy marked a significant cultural and intellectual shift away from pre-Platonic natural philosophy, which was widely conceived as 'irrelevant to the good life' (Cicero, *Ac.* 1. 4.15). For Socrates, philosophy's most important topic was the conduct of human life. Socrates in Cicero's words 'was the first who called philosophy down from heaven, and placed it in cities, and introduced it even in homes, and drove it to inquire about life and customs and things good and evil' (*TD* 5.4.10–11).[1]

That is to say, Socrates made the central philosophical question: 'how can we live a good human life?' Plato, whose written dialogues immortalized Socrates, depicted him engaged in discussions focused exclusively on this question. As Plato's Socrates asserts, 'There can be no finer subject for discussion than the question of what a man should be like and what occupation he should engage in and how far he should pursue it' (*G.* 487e-488a). As we shall stress in this chapter, Socrates defined PWL *against* the dominant values of his Greek compatriots (**9**). The conception of PWL is borne from a conflict with the ancient Homeric ideal of the good life and what we might call the Periclean and sophistic sublimations of this ideal that shaped fifth-century Athenian democracy. Socrates's bold, controversial claim is that *only* the philosophical way of life can deliver eudaimonia. In addressing the question of the good life, Socrates suggested that Athenians must choose between two incompatible alternatives: namely the philosophical *or* the political way of life, the practice of citizenship *or* the care of the soul. Plato's Socrates spells out these alternatives in his dialogue with the fictional character Callicles[2]:

Is he to adopt the life, to which you invite me ... speaking in the assembly and practising oratory and engaging in politics ... or should he follow my example and lead the life of a philosopher; and in what is the latter life superior to the former? (*G.* 500c)

The central issue at stake in Socrates's philosophy is the choice between the life of the philosopher and that of other non-philosophical citizens, including rhetoricians, sophists and even natural philosophers. Socrates maintains that to lead the philosophical way of life necessarily requires criticizing the norms and practices of Athenian citizenship. To borrow Nietzschean terminology, Socrates undertook a revaluation of all hitherto dominant values.[3] Of course, we know from the trial and execution of Socrates (399 BCE) that his criticism of the moral failings and limits of Athenian citizenship and political practices incurred the contempt and displeasure of many fellow citizens who praised the virtues of civic participation.[4] For the harshest of his critics, indeed, Socrates was not merely a voluntary exile, but a dangerous enemy of the people (*misodemos*). 'What kind of wisdom can we call it,' Callicles in the *Gorgias* reproves Socrates, 'that "takes a man of parts and spoils his gifts" so that he cannot defend himself or another from mortal danger, but lets his enemies rob him of his goods, and lives to all intents and purposes the life of an outlaw in his own city' (*G.* 486b-c). Socrates's fellow Athenians valued 'external' goods like fame, honour, reputation and wealth above all else, and they identified active, agonistic citizenship as the principal means of acquiring these goods. From this perspective, Socrates's philosophical way of life seemed to corrupt rather than educate citizens.

Socrates by contrast admonished Athenians that 'the unexamined life is not worth living' (*Ap.* 38a; **1.3** below). At issue is what has long been called the *atopia* of Socrates, his 'strangeness' in the eyes of his contemporaries, a strangeness which will continue to confound, fascinate or irritate commentators throughout the history of Western ideas. A veritable cottage industry of *Sokratikoi logoi*, mostly lost, emerged in the wake of his execution in 399 BCE, one feature of which involved recounting and celebrating Socrates's odd ways of conduct, down to his rather fraught relationship with his formidable wife Xanthippe (**10**). The most famous, almost mythological dimension of Socrates's *atopia* concerns what he calls his *daimon* or 'inner spirit', one which he tells us would counsel him against certain actions – perhaps a kind of semi-deity perceived by nobody else, perhaps Socrates's way of describing what would later be called the conscience (*Ap.* 31c-d). Another dimension of this *atopia* are the famous Socratic paradoxes, which are as close to what we could term a literary genre that we can get when it comes to Socrates ((5) see 1.7 below). Plato also allows us to glimpse Socrates's unusual conduct at the beginning of the *Protagoras* and *Symposium*, where his teacher is depicted as literally arrested by meditation on some thought. There is also Plato's Alcibiades's famous description of Socrates's endurance, and seeming practice of some kind of contemplative spiritual exercises (3) on military campaign, in the later dialogue:

> I remember, among his many marvellous feats, how once there came a frost about as awful as can be: we all preferred not to stir abroad, or if any of us did, we wrapped ourselves up with prodigious care, and after putting on our shoes we muffled up our feet with felt and little fleeces. But he walked out in that weather, clad in just such a coat as he was always wont to wear, and he made his way more easily over the ice unshod than the rest of us did in our shoes .... Immersed in some problem at dawn, he stood in the same spot considering it; and when he found it a tough one, he would not give it up but stood there trying. The time drew on to midday, and the men began to notice him, and said to one another in wonder: 'Socrates has been standing there in a study ever since dawn!' The end of it was that in the evening some of the Ionians after they had supped – this time it was summer – brought out their mattresses and rugs and took their sleep in the cool; thus they waited to see if he would go on standing all night too. He stood till dawn came and the sun rose; then walked away, after offering a prayer to the Sun. (*Symp.* 220b-d)

In this chapter, we analyse the key parameters of Socrates's revolutionary invention of the persona of the philosopher, and of PWL. This includes his signature dialogic practice of the elenchus (3), his foundational call for philosophers to 'turn inwards' (5), paying primary attention to themselves as against externals (6), his description of philosophy as a care of the soul (7), its attendant ethical paradoxes (6), as well as his embodiment and advertisement of the new ideal of the philosophical sage (10). We can begin to understand the basic characteristics of Socrates's mode of philosophical living, however [1.2], by comparing it with modern university philosophy (what is 'first for us', as Aristotle might say), and then with Socrates' own rivals, the sophists [1.3].

1.2 A founding exception

For contemporary philosophers, Socrates cuts a very strange figure (see Frodeman & Briggle, 2016). Socrates's philosophy consists exclusively of his way of life. Unlike modern philosophers, he did not write books formulating, systematizing or defending theoretical doctrines. All that we know of Socrates's philosophy derives exclusively from the writings of others, including the popular genre of Socratic dialogue or *logoi sokratoi* that arose among his disciples after his death. The principal ancient sources of our knowledge of Socrates are Xenophon's *Memorabilia*, Plato's Socratic dialogues and Aristophanes's satire *The Clouds*.[5] Rather than writing philosophical treatises, Socrates spent his life in the streets and marketplaces of Athens engaging in ethical dialogue with any persons willing to submit their lives and values to examination. We might visualize this difference by contrasting conventional portraits of two modern professional philosophers (Figures 1.1 and 1.2) with Jacques-Louis David's famous neo-classical representation of Socrates (Figure 1.3):

The conventional representations of Professors Jacques Derrida and G. E. Moore, founding figures of so-called 'postmodern' and 'analytic'

Figure 1.1 J. Derrida. Jacques Derrida Portrait Session. RIS-ORANGIS, FRANCE – JANUARY 25. Jacques Derrida, French philosopher, poses during a portrait session held on 25 January 1988 in Ris-Orangis, France (Photo by Ulf Andersen/Getty Images). Source: Getty Images.

Figure 1.2 G.E. Moore, Reproduced with the kind permission of the Faculty of Philosophy, University of Cambridge.

philosophy respectively, picture them as solitary, study-bound masters of book learning. If we judge by portraiture, how they live is irrelevant to their philosophy. Apart from a faint hint of the philosophical 'seer' in their penetrating, fixed gaze, neither portrait suggests that how these two professors live beyond the study has any philosophical significance. By contrast, already in antiquity, Plutarch, the first-century Greek biographer and moralist, nicely captures the figure of Socrates as the antithetical to 'academic', armchair philosophers:

Figure 1.3 Jacques-Louis David's Socrates. Public domain. Sourced from The Metropolitan Museum of Art, https://www.metmuseum.org/art/collection/search/436105

> Most people think ... those are philosophers who sit in a chair and converse and prepare their lectures over their books; but the continuous practice of ... philosophy, which is every day alike seen in acts and deeds, they fail to perceive ... Socrates ... was a philosopher, although he did not set out benches or seat himself in an armchair or observe a fixed hour for conversing or promenading with his pupils, but jested with them, when it so happened, and drank with them, served in the army or lounged in the market-place with some of them, and finally was imprisoned and drank the poison. He was the first to show that life at all times and in all parts, in all experiences and activities, universally admits philosophy. (Plutarch, 'Whether an Old Man Should Engage in Public Affairs', 26)

For Socrates, philosophy was a comprehensive mode of living that expressed itself in every facet of experience. 'Through the centuries ...,' as Hadot observes, 'and first of all in antiquity, particularly for the Stoics and the Cynics, Socrates was the model of the philosopher, and precisely the model of the philosopher whose life and death are his main teaching'

(Hadot, 2009: 121–2). For the Renaissance Neoplatonist Ficino, Socrates was 'the antischolastic, a man who taught philosophy by his life and death, not *de haut en bas* from a professorial chair' (Hankins, 2006: 348). In the nineteenth century, both Soren Kierkegaard and Friedrich Nietzsche would each be fascinated and vexed by Socrates, exactly as the avatar of a new form of life which each felt they needed to contest (Hadot, 1995: 148–51, 155–7, 165–70). However we assess the fact, Socrates exemplified the courage to live truthfully, and the serenity to die without fear or bitterness. David's 1787 painting, *The Death of Socrates* dramatizes Socrates's extraordinary self-mastery by sharply contrasting his philosophical composure in the face of his own death with the emotional agitation of his friends, disciples and even his guard (whom Socrates tells us that he had befriended).[6] David's portrait underscores that for Socrates's followers it was his sage-like elevation above the ordinary fear of mortality that distinguished his way of life. 'The image of the dying Socrates,' as the young Nietzsche puts it (see Chapter 10), 'the man freed by insight and reason from the fear of death, became the emblem over the portals of science' (*BT* 15).

We cannot overemphasize the sharp contrast with contemporary professional, disciplinary philosophy which is represented by the fact that Socrates did not aim to formulate, teach or interpret theoretical doctrines. He instead aimed to exemplify the philosophical mode of life and engage his interlocutors in a particular spiritual exercise, namely the famous Socratic elenchus. By means of this spiritual exercise, as we shall see [**1.4**], Socrates sought not to inculcate theoretical doctrine, but to convert their souls or psyche. Socrates's discourse, as Hadot explains, 'disturbed them so much that they were eventually led to question their entire lives ... Socrates sows disquiet in the soul ... leading to a heightened self-consciousness which may go so far as a philosophical conversion' (Hadot, 1995: 148). And this action of conversion, enabling and exemplifying it, just *was* the pre-eminent business of Socratic philosophy.

1.3 Socrates contra the Sophists

However, in inaugurating the new paradigm of PWL, Socrates's main target was of course nothing like what we know as academic philosophy, a phenomenon whose first antecedents would only emerge after, and perhaps because of his passing. Socrates's intellectual rival, alongside perhaps the poets of such centrality to ancient Greek education (*Rep.* X, 607a-b), was the highly politicized intellectual movement known as sophistry. We can therefore clarify his ideal of PWL by understanding his objections to sophistry. In order to do this, let us briefly sketch the sophistic political education that rose to cultural prominence in fifth-century Athens before turning to Socrates's alternative philosophical way of life.

In Athenian democracy, rhetoric, or the technical art of speaking well, was a vital skill of citizenship. With the advent of the polis, as Jean-Pierre Vernant explains, 'speech became the political tool *par excellence*, the key to authority in the state, the means of commanding and dominating others ... The art of politics became essentially the management of language' (Vernant, 1982: 49–50). To secure votes in the democratic Assembly or to win cases in the Athenian law courts, citizens had to strive to master the art of rhetorical persuasion. The power of sophistry to enable the trained orator to dominate the popular courts, Assembly and Council, as Plato's Gorgias advertises in the dialogue that bears his name (*G.* 452e). Major sophists like Gorgias, Prodicus, Hippias and Protagoras moved to Athens to serve the educational demands of its flourishing democracy. For those who wished to master the art of rhetoric, Protagoras counselled that 'there are two opposite arguments on every subject'. Protagoras's 'antilogies' (opposing arguments) illustrated how on each question one could make an effective case for either side, and taught young citizens to argue one or other side of a case, depending on which one best served their political ambitions without any regard for the truth of the matter. In this respect, the sophists seemed to assume that there is no such thing as the 'truth', or valid argument; in their purely instrumental use of logos the only thing of importance was to secure victory in a debate or acquittal on conviction in court. At least some of the sophists, certainly as they are presented by Plato, seem to have identified knowledge as power.[7]

In doing so, the sophists transformed the inherited Homeric ideal of virtue or excellence (*arête*) in the new institutions of fifth-century democracy. According to Plato's Gorgias, for example, by teaching citizens the technique of persuasion, sophists aim to confer on all who possess it the 'greatest blessing', 'not only freedom for himself but also the power of ruling his fellow-countrymen' (*G.* 452d). Yet, despite their name deriving from the Greek word 'sophia', Socrates argued that the sophists were not teachers of wisdom, but 'misologists' (*Ph.* 89a). Against the sophists, Socrates made it a point of honour to freely engage his interlocutors in dialogue about how to live better lives rather than receive payment for teaching the art of rhetoric they could use to win legal and political debates in the popular courts and democratic Assembly. Socrates and his pupil Plato maintained that the sophists' political education was both a cause and a symptom of Athens' moral failings. Socrates challenges the sophists for at least three closely related reasons.

In the first place, Socrates suggests that it is because sophists 'spend their time arguing both sides' that, in his judgement, they wrongly 'end by believing that they are wiser than anyone else, because they alone have discovered that there is nothing stable or dependable in either facts or arguments, and that everything fluctuates just like water in a tidal channel, and never stays at any point at any time' (*Ph.* 90b-c). As he sees it, the sophists claim to be the wisest on the grounds that they admit of no single, final, conclusive vision of the true, or the right order of living. Rather like mariners who adjust their sails to suit the weather, sophists shift their 'truths' to suit their practical purposes. Socrates claims that the sophists' shifting between opposing perspectives or arguments is symptomatic of their hatred of logos (reason):

> Supposing that there is an argument which is true or valid and capable of being discovered, if anyone nevertheless, through his experience of these arguments which seem to these same people to be sometime true and sometimes false, attached no responsibility to himself and his lack of technical ability, but was finally content, in exasperation, to shift the blame from himself to the arguments, and spend the rest of his life loathing and decrying them, and so missed the chance of knowing the truth about reality, would it not be a deplorable thing? (*Ph.* 90d)

Second, Socrates as he is presented to us by Plato suggests that the sophists did not bind themselves to the truth of what they said but exercised their rhetorical skills to create convictions and beliefs to serve their own ends. In this sense, the sophists utilized speech as a form of violence. By perfecting the technical skills of persuasion, they taught wealthy young Athenians how to succeed in the agonistic struggle for power and distinction that was conducted in the democratic Assembly and popular courts. As we shall see, in sharp contrast, Socrates sought to identify and exemplify a new way of life that radically overturned the Homeric ethos that the sophists took for granted and transformed, from the battlefields outside the walls of Troy to the *ekklesia* within the walls of Athens.

Third, Socrates maintains that to successfully coerce listeners, sophistic rhetoric appealed to their pleasures and prejudices rather than their reason. In his famous display of rhetorical virtuosity, *In Praise of Helen*, Gorgias characterized the effect of sophistic speech as a drug that charms and bewitches the listener's mind. Sophistic speech, as Gorgias explains, 'pleases a large crowd and persuades by being written with art even though not spoken with truth' (quoted in Colaiaco, 2001: 27). Plato's Socrates argues that sophists cultivate demagogic tyrants who exercise power by pandering to the peoples' irrational pleasures and appetites. He inaugurates the long philosophical tradition of scepticism about the rationality of the passions and intuition, one which we will see again and again in this book. Without being able to govern themselves, *Alcibiades Major* argues, men will be unfit to govern others; inaugurating an abiding metaphilosophical metaphor ((7) *Alc I*, 131a-d, 134c-135e; Foucault, 2006: 33–9, 44–5).

In the *Apology*, Socrates aims to dethrone the sophists and lay claim to the mantle of the truly wisest teacher of the Athenians. His means to do this are however famously paradoxical. In contrast to the boastful sophists, Socrates suggests that his wisdom lies in knowing just how much that he does not know (*Ap.* 21d), whilst remaining committed to the discovery of truth through dialogical inquiry. For Socrates, the philosophical ideal is asymptotic: philosophers strive to attain wisdom, but they never fully attain this end. In the words of Plato's Socrates in the *Phaedo*, as philosophers 'we should recognise that we are still intellectual invalids; but that we should brace ourselves and do our best to become healthy' (*Ph.* 90e). In this sense, as Hadot puts it, Plato's figure of Socrates 'is the portrait of a mediator between the transcendent ideal of wisdom and the concrete human reality … the mediator between the ideal norms and human reality' (Hadot, 1995: 147).

1.4 The elenchus as spiritual exercise

In 399 BCE Athenian democracy's popular court, composed of 500 adult citizens, tried the seventy-year-old Socrates on charges of impiety and corrupting the youth. By a slight majority (approximately 280/220), Socrates's fellow citizens found him guilty and by significantly larger majority (approximately 360/140), the same jurors voted for the death penalty. It is one of the unintended ironies of Socrates's life that many of his fellow Athenians criticized him as a sophist despite his explicit opposition to the teachers of rhetoric, while the sophists clearly saw him as their opponent and rejected his new philosophical way of life. In his defence speech in 399 BCE, therefore, Socrates was compelled to answer his 'conservative' critics by differentiating the philosophical life from sophistic paideia, and challenge his sophistic critics by demonstrating the superiority of this philosophical way of life over the political life devoted to attaining individual or collective glory.

The first criticisms of his philosophical mode of life as the works of his contemporary Aristophanes (446–386 BCE), the celebrated comic playwright, in particular his satirical portrait in *The Clouds*, which was produced at the major Athenian festival of Dionysia in 423 BCE (*Ap.* 17c). Aristophanes's comedy identified Socrates as the supreme sophist, and Aristophanes's satire expressed a widespread Athenian worry that the sophists were responsible for the city's political decline and moral corruption.[8] According to this politically conservative assessment, Socrates's dialectical examination of the 'virtues' clearly risked, if not encouraged, a dangerous disrespect for the law, no less than the rhetorical training youths were receiving at the hands of Protagoras, Gorgias et al.

At his trial, to rebut these charges, Socrates claimed, so far was he from encouraging disbelief in the old ways, that his philosophizing answered to the religious instructions of the oracle of Apollo at Delphi, the holiest of holy pan-Hellenic religious authorities. Socrates relates that his friend Chaerephon had asked the Delphic priestess whether there was anyone wiser than Socrates, to which she answered that there were none. Unable to believe this, Socrates tells us that his philosophical career involved testing the oracle's proposition by setting about examining his fellow Athenians' claims to wisdom. He became, as we might say, a 'street philosopher' widely known in Athens for accosting citizens, resident aliens (or metics) and, at least potentially in Hades, women, and engaging them in discussion according to a method of refutation known as the 'elenchus'.[9]

So what is the elenchus? As Aristotle explains Socrates's method, 'it was the practise of Socrates to ask questions but not to give answers, for he confessed that he did not know' (*Soph. el.* 183b 6–8). Front and centre here is Socrates's famous 'irony'. This involves Socrates's repeated confessions of ignorance, as at his trial, coupled with his claims to desire only to learn from others, and professions to deeply admire his interlocutors' putative wisdom. By positioning himself as the prospective student in this way, Socrates would turn the dialogue towards his interlocutors' answer to the question: 'What is X?': What is virtue (*Meno*)? What is moderation (*Charmides*)? What is piety (*Euthyphro*)? What is courage (*Laches*)? Socrates's questioning hence tested *the others'* claims to moral expertise rather than teaching them *his* own doctrine, as the sophists had accepted money for doing. Through his so-called 'elenctic' conversations he discovered, so he tells his Athenian judges, that true wisdom belongs only to god, and that he himself is wiser than all others only in the sense that he realizes that he lacks wisdom (*Ap.* 21d).

Socrates's account of his philosophical career in the *Apology* is broadly borne out by what we can learn of Socrates from Plato's so-called early dialogues.[10] As Gregory Vlastos stressed, it is vital to Socrates that his interlocutor must commit to only presenting his own opinions. They cannot rely on hearsay or *endoxa*, nor engage in the process in any kind of impersonal way, for instance as a mere dialectical game. In the elenctic method, which Aristotle called 'peirastic' (testing), a thesis is then refuted when its negation is derived 'from the answerer's own beliefs'. As Vlastos (1983) and Robinson (1971) allow us to loosely formalize the procedure:

1. Socrates puts to the other a general question, usually in the field of ethics (e.g. what is courage?);

2. The interlocutor proffers a primary answer, like 'courage is endurance';

3. Next, Socrates asks a series of secondary questions, like: 'what are the different kinds of endurance then? ... can there be good and bad kinds? ... ':

   > These [questions] differ from the primary question in that, whereas that was a matter of real doubt and difficulty, the answers to all these seem obvious and inescapable ... They often seem at first irrelevant to the primary question, and sometimes they seem to fall into two disconnected groups among themselves; (Robinson, 1971: 78)

4. Nevertheless, under Socrates's direction, it soon emerges that, in answering the secondary questions, the interlocutor has been drawn to assent to propositions which contradict the original assertion (2): like 'there are bad kinds of endurance ... yet courage as a virtue can never be bad';

5. Socrates then draws in the threads, or (depending on one's preference in metaphor) snaps the trap shut: 'come now, let us add our admissions together', as he says in *Protagoras* (332d);

6. Thus, the conversation closes with an admission that both Socrates and his interlocutors lack wisdom, and should redouble their efforts to learn.[11]

Socrates used an 'elenctic hammer' to beat out of his fellow their epistemic hubris (Vlastos, 1991: 29). Given the seemingly sceptical dimensions of this procedure [**4.2**], we can see why Socrates's philosophy was easily confused by critics with the sophistic scepticism or relativism. Nevertheless, two further dimensions of the elenchus as what Hadot calls a spiritual exercise need stressing here. Firstly, the elenchus responds to a situation where Socrates's interlocutors not only hold confused ideas about the virtues and subjects of discussion. Like most of us most of the time, they also suppose that they are *not* confused; many interlocutors (for instance, Euthyphro concerning piety) initially brag of their epistemic credentials. As such, any open attempt to change their opinions from the outside would be more likely to provoke a defensive reaction, rather than epistemic and ethical change. By contrast, what Socrates does by showing through questioning that a person *himself* holds contradictory beliefs on a given subject is open up the possibility that they can be brought to acknowledge their own ignorance. A famous passage in Plato's *Sophist*, albeit in the mouth of the enigmatic Eleatic Stranger, describes this perfectly:

> Str. But … some appear to have arrived at the conclusion that all ignorance is involuntary, and that no one who thinks himself wise is willing to learn any of those things in which he is conscious of his own cleverness, and that the admonitory sort of instruction gives much trouble and does little good

> -Theaet. There they are quite right. Str. Accordingly, they set to work to eradicate the spirit of conceit in another way … They cross-examine a man's words, when he thinks that he is saying something and is really saying nothing, and easily convict him of inconsistencies in his opinions; these they then collect by the dialectical process, and placing them side by side, show that they contradict one another about the same things, in relation to the same things, and in the same respect. He, seeing this, is angry with himself, and grows gentle towards others, and thus is entirely delivered from great prejudices and harsh notions, in a way which is most amusing to the hearer, and produces the most lasting good effect on the person who is the subject of the operation. (*Soph.* 230b-d)

Second, at this point of aporia, the interlocutor confronts perhaps for the first time the limitations of their own claims to knowledge. It is a possible moment of conversion, or the transformation of one's beliefs, or of the kind of 'resistance to analysis' a figure like Euthyphro shows, when he hastily concocts an excuse to leave the discussion. If the interlocutor does not get angry at Socrates, but at themselves, Socrates changes gear, going from interrogator to the object of identification for the interlocutor. As Hackforth explains, Socrates 'has no ready-made system of ethics to impart. This is of course, what we should expect from his disclaiming the office of the teacher; he is a fellow searcher only' (1933: 265). In Hadot's words:

> He takes the others' doubt, uneasiness, and discouragement upon himself. He assumes all the risks of the dialectical adventure and carries out a complete switching of roles. If the enterprise fails, it will henceforth be his responsibility. In this way, he shows his interlocutors a projection of their own selves. They can now transfer their personal uneasiness onto Socrates and regain confidence in dialectical research and in the logos itself. (Hadot, 1995: 149; cf. Sharpe, 2016: 417–18)[12]

Socratic irony is hence absolutely vital. It is at the start the necessary means to elicit the interlocutors' opinions: 'this constitutes [Socrates'] ironic self-deprecation'. (PWL: 154) Next, it enables the interlocutor's identification with Socrates in shared ignorance, and invites them to the experience of questioning, so that 'throughout the duration of the discussion, he has experienced what true activity of the mind is' (PWL: 154). Perhaps, again, for the first time, they feel the sting of what Plato calls *eros*, the felt lack of wisdom which is at the same time the impulse to seek it out through dialectical investigation. Plato's Meno in fact describes Socrates as a kind of intellectual stingray; and Socrates himself at his trial (*Apo.* 30e) describes his activities as like those of a gadfly, stinging the somnolent horse of the Athenians, to try to keep it awake. In the *Theaetetus*, perhaps most famously, the elenchus is described as a 'maieutic' method, or intellectual midwifery, through which Socrates helps other discover their own truths:

> I am so far like the midwife that I cannot myself give birth to wisdom, and the common reproach is true, that, though I question others, I can myself bring nothing to light because there is no wisdom in me. The reason is this. Heaven constrains me to serve as a midwife, but has debarred me from giving birth. So of myself I have no sort of wisdom, nor has any discovery ever been born to me as the child of my soul. Those who frequent my company at first appear, some of

them, quite unintelligent, but, as we go further with our discussions, all who are favored by heaven make progress at a rate that seems surprising to others as well as to themselves, although it is clear that they have never learned anything from me. The many admirable truths they bring to birth have been discovered by themselves from within. (*Theaet.* 150 c-d)[13]

Pierre Hadot has argued that we can best understand Socrates's practice if we see as a development of ancient pre-philosophical spiritual exercises (3). Hadot acknowledge that Socrates's exercises were almost certainly 'rooted in traditions going back to immemorial times', having their origins in much older 'magico-religious and shamanistic traditions of respiratory and mnemonic exercises' (Hadot, 1995: 116; see Dodds, 1963, Gernet, 1981, & Vernant, 1982). However, Socrates 'cause[d] them to emerge into Western consciousness' as specifically *philosophical* exercises of self-transformation and self-cultivation (Hadot, 1995: 89). Such philosophical spiritual exercises, as he explains 'are mental processes, which have nothing in common with cataleptic trances, but on the contrary, respond to the rigorous demand for rational control which ... emerges with the figure of Socrates' (Hadot, 1995: 116). On this view, Socrates's spiritual exercises are continuous with the ancient, pre-philosophic tradition insofar as they entail a radical conversion of the self. But they are discontinuous with the same pre-philosophical tradition, insofar as they transform its means, through their recourse to dialectic, argumentation, as well as the shared work of self-examination in presence of the other:

In it, the interlocutors are 'invited' to participate in such inner spiritual exercises as examination of conscience and attention to oneself; in other words, they are urged to comply with the famous dictum, 'Know thyself.' ... it invites us to establish a relationship of the self to the self, which constitutes the foundation of every spiritual exercise. To know oneself means, among other things, to know oneself *qua* non-sage: that is, not as a *sophos,* but as a *philo-sophos,* someone *on the way toward* wisdom. Alternatively, it can mean to know oneself in one's essential being; this entails separating that which we *are not* from that which we *are.* Finally, it can mean to know oneself in one's true moral state: that is, to examine one's conscience. (Hadot, 1995: 90)[14]

1.5 Care of the psyche

If we ask then how did Socrates pre-eminently distinguish his philosophical way of life from the values of the sophists and contemporary Greeks in his *Apology*, the answer is that Socrates conceived of the elenchus as a means to Michel Foucault has termed the 'care of the self'. Hadot himself is fond of citing the ill-fated General Nicias (Alcibiades's rival)'s declaration in the *Laches*, attesting to how the elenchus always turns into an exercise in self-reflection:

> Don't you know that whoever approaches Socrates closely and begins a dialogue with him, even if he begins by talking about something entirely different, nevertheless finds himself forcibly carried around in a circle by this discourse, until he gets to the point of having to give an account of himself-as much with regard to the way he is living now, as to the way he has lived his past existence. When that point is reached, Socrates doesn't let you leave until he has submitted all that to the test of his control, well and thoroughly … He who does not run away from this will necessarily be more prudent in the rest of his life.
> (Plato, *Laches*, 197e)

As Nicias registers here, in contrast alike to both the sophists and more ordinary contemporary values, Socrates insistently exhorted his interlocutors to turn inwards, to pay attention to themselves, and to critically examine their beliefs, desires and actions. In what is arguably the key passage of the *Apology*, Socrates thus professes (5):

> My good friends, are you who are a citizen of Athens, the greatest of cities and the most famous for wisdom and power, not ashamed of caring for money and to how to get as much of it as you can, and for honour and reputation, and not caring or taking thought for wisdom and truth [*aletheia*] and for your soul [*psyche*], and how to make it as good as possible? And if any of you argues the point, and says he does care, I shall not let him go at once, nor shall I go away, but I shall question and examine and cross-examine him, and if I find that he does not possess virtue, but says he does, I shall rebuke him for scorning the things that are of most importance and caring more for what is of less worth … For I go about doing nothing else than urging you, young and old, not to care for your persons or your property

more than for the perfection of your souls, or even so much; and I tell you that virtue does not come from money, but from virtue comes money and all other good things to man, both to the individual and to the state. (*Ap.* 29d-30b)

Socrates recognized the eccentricity of this exhortation that Athenians should care for their souls and treat external goods as matters, if not of indifference (as for the Stoics, see Chapter 3), then of a secondary priority:

I did not care for the things that most people care about: making money, having a comfortable home, high military or civil rank, and all the other activities – political appointments, secret societies, party organisations – which go on in our city .... For I tried to persuade each of you to care for himself and his own perfection in goodness and wisdom rather than for any of his belongings, and for the state itself rather than for its interests, and to follow the same method in his care for other things. (*Ap.* 36b-c)

Taking care of oneself, by the way of the spiritual exercise of the elenchus, constituted a radical redefinition of *eudaimonia* in Greek culture. In questioning his interlocutors, Socrates led them to see that they themselves could not affirm the truth of their intuitive or 'common-sense' moral judgements and beliefs. In the early Socratic dialogues, Plato depicts him as making those he cross-examined, most notably politicians, artists, poets, acutely aware that they lack any knowledge about precisely the matters in which they proclaimed expertise. If we accept Plato's judgement, it would be difficult to underestimate the impact of Socrates's spiritual exercises on Athenian culture and Greek philosophy. In *The Symposium*, Plato shows that for Athenian followers like the young aristocratic General Alcibiades, Socrates's dialectic seemed to have had the same kind of enchantment as the mythical song of the Sirens that lured sailors to their death (*Sym.* 216 a; see *Odyss.* XII). In his relationship to Socrates's dialectic, Alcibiades sees himself as analogous to Odysseus trying to escape the Sirens' song. At the same time, it is important to note that he also confesses at this point that Socrates is the only one able to make him feel shame (*aidos*), and experience the impulse to examine himself, rather than conquering others:

Whenever I listen to him speak, I get more ecstatic than the Corybantes! My heart pounds and tears flood from my eyes under the spell of his words. I've seen him have the same effect on plenty of others too ... I have heard some great speakers, including Pericles, and while I thought they did a good job, they never had the same kind of effect on me and they never *disturbed my mental composure or made me dissatisfied with the slavishness of my life*. This Marsyas here, however, has often changed my outlook, and *made me think that the life I lead isn't worth leading* ... If I allowed myself to listen to him, I wouldn't be able to resist even now ... You see he forces me to admit that I'm busy myself with Athenian politics when *I'm far from perfect and should be doing something about myself instead*. (*Sym.* 215e-216a, emphases added)[15]

1.6 The sage and the Socratic paradoxes

Alcibiades's speech makes it clear that for some Athenians, Socrates's elenctic dialogue compelled them to disdain ordinary life as a form of slavishness that they could only escape by submitting themselves to the demands of the logos. Alcibiades repeatedly states that Socrates's philosophical discourse had an intoxicating, disturbing effect on him observes 'I was in such a state that it does not seem possible to live while behaving as I was behaving ... He forces me to admit to myself that *I do not take care of myself*' (*Sym.* 216a). Socratic dialectic induces in Alcibiades an ecstatic state, a transcendence of his ordinary self, which he conceives as akin to that experienced by the Corybantes who by means of their musical practices sought to attain union with the great goddess. Centuries later, Nietzsche, an admirer of Alcibiades, and deeply ambivalent critic of Socrates, confirms this judgement: 'He who does not hear the continual rejoicing which resounds through every speech and counter-speech of a Platonic dialogue, the rejoicing over the new invention of *rational* thinking, what does he understand ... of the philosophy of antiquity?' (Nietzsche, *D* 544)[16]

Socrates's elenctic method served to circumscribe and legitimate a radically new ethical eudaimonism with a new embodied ideal, that of the sage (**10**). Against the honour code underpinning both archaic Homeric culture and sophistic culture, Socrates's intervention represents nothing short of his formulating a new, specifically *philosophical* heroism, heading up a new form of life.[17] Socrates's philosophical heroism consisted in giving absolute priority to rational self-mastery or 'virtue' over all other principles. Virtue, in its turn, Socrates seems to have identified with some kind of knowledge, at the same time as – in one more of Socrates's famed paradoxes (6) – he resists the sophists' claim that virtue could be taught. The paradox can be resolved, when we recall that the elenchus does not teach definitions of virtues from the outside, so much as elicit such definitions from within the other through question and answer. The midwife is not a teacher, and he cannot pour his knowledge as from a cup into the passive vessel of his pupil (*Symp.* 175d).

For Socrates and the later philosophical schools, in any case, *only* the philosophical sage can realize godlike serenity. The sage hence outranks Homeric heroes like Achilles who seeks 'divinity' through worldly glory by defeating his enemies, as well as Athenian democrats animated by civic pride at their city's victories and beauties. Socrates, we might say, aimed to displace Achilles, the greatest Greek hero, with the philosopher.[18] In the *Apology,* Socrates even identifies himself with Achilles, since he too follows the noble principle of death before dishonour, and that one should never abandon one's post, facing whatever adversities (*Apo.*, 29b).

Several of Socrates's infamous paradoxes all spring from his attempt to best and overcome the Homeric honour code. Socrates argued that the true self is neither the body (*soma*), nor one's name (*onoma*), but the soul (*psyche*), albeit that it is unclear as to whether he (as against Plato) had any developed opinions concerning the soul's immortality. In this Socratic view, which would become common to most of the ancient schools of philosophy, to take care of oneself necessarily requires reconstructing the ordinary or pre-philosophic psyche, through intellectual and spiritual exercises like the elenchus (**2, 3**). In a startlingly original move, Socrates also conceived the psyche as governed by, if not identical with reason, which 'in a properly ordered life is in complete control of the senses and emotions. Its proper virtue is wisdom and thought and to improve the psyche is to take thought for wisdom and truth' (Guthrie, 1971: 150).[19] In F. M. Cornford's well-chosen words, to tell the ordinary Athenian, educated in the Homeric culture of honour, 'that his chief concern was to care for his soul and its perfection, was like telling him to neglect his substance and cherish his shadow' (Cornford, 1965: 50).

Socrates's ethics hence identifies *eudaimonia* as lying in the exercise of rational self-control or self-mastery, *sophrosyne* or *enkrateia*. The sage on this vision has a specific kind of knowledge, wisdom (*phronesis* or *sophia*) which he has attained through reason, hardened by the spiritual and intellectual exercises into a transformed self. This is a knowledge, not necessarily of all things, but certainly of what is truly beneficial for human beings to value, pursue, choose and avoid. This knowledge frees the sage from the distractions and illusions of the bodily senses and the passions, which suggest illusory or immediate satisfiers, and prevent us from keeping in mind the bigger picture, both of the world and of our own larger priorities.

In order to care for the soul, Socrates claimed, reason or virtue must trump all other values. For Socrates, virtue alone is happiness (see *Ap.* 28B5-9, *Ap.* 28d6-1; *Cr.* 48c6-d5). Socrates's ethics therefore entailed rejecting the ancient ethos of achieving excellence through victory in combat. 'If you are serious and what you say is true,' as Callicles caustically observes, 'we shall have human life turned completely upside down; we are doing, apparently, the complete opposite of what we ought to do' (*G.* 481c). Nietzsche nicely captures how Socrates's ethical eudaimonism fundamentally clashed with this heroic ethic:

> But when Socrates went so far as to say 'the virtuous man is the happiest man' they did not believe their ears and fancied they had heard something insane. For when he pictures the happiest man, every man of noble origin included in the picture the perfect ruthlessness and devilry of the tyrant who sacrifices everyone and everything to his arrogance and pleasure. (*D* 199)[20]

For the late Nietzsche, Socrates's mode of living constituted such an outlandish corruption of healthy ancient Greek culture that he felt it required psychological explanation rather than philosophical cogitation:

> Everything in him is exaggerated, buffo, a caricature; everything is at the same time concealed, ulterior, subterranean. I seek to comprehend what idiosyncrasy begot that Socratic equation of reason, virtue, and happiness: that most bizarre of all equations which, moreover, is opposed to all the instincts of the earlier Greeks. (TI, 'The Problem of Socrates')

In the *Crito* and *Gorgias*, Plato's Socrates specifies that his ethics entailed rejecting the basic Homeric (and wider) principle that justice should involve doing good to friends and harming enemies (see *Rep.* I). Against the Homeric principle, Socrates argued we should never commit an injustice even in retaliation for an injustice: indeed, he 'would rather suffer wrong than do wrong' (*G.* 469c):

So one ought not to return a wrong with a wrong or an injury to any person, whatever the provocation ... I know that there are *and always will be* few people who think like this; and, consequently, between those who think so and those who do not there can be no agreement in principle: they must always feel contempt when they observe one another's decisions. (*Cr.* 49d)

To the astonishment of his interlocutors, he insists that we do far more harm to ourselves by committing rather than by doing wrong (see *Cr.* 48 b-c; *G.* 472e-473e). Indeed, on a strict interpretation, Socrates believes that the good or virtuous person can suffer no harm or evil – although they can through bad action bring ethical harm upon themselves. This is because the only true evil, on his view, is moral fault, which is something over which no one else but the sage himself can have control. All those things that people commonly assume are evils – death, sickness, poverty, illness, even persecution or torture – are not evils for Socrates (see esp. Chapter 3). They only become evils, and the source of avoidable distress, if the person does not have the wisdom to accept and respond to them, as best as they are able. 'For the good man', Socrates declares, 'there is no evil, neither during life, nor after he is dead' (*Ap.* 41d).

As we might say, if Homeric heroes led by Achilles were willing to sacrifice everything for the sake of worldly glory, Socrates was willing to renounce everything external to the psyche, but for the sake of a virtue rooted in wisdom. By contrast with the Homeric and tragic heroes whose happiness turns on honour, which is subject to the vagaries of fortune, Socrates's happiness turns on virtue that is entirely independent of fate. As Vlastos comments, 'if you believe what Socrates does,' namely that virtue is happiness, 'you hold the secret of your happiness in your own hands. Nothing the world can do to you can make you unhappy' (Vlastos, 1991: 234–5). On this view, followed through to its ultimate conclusions, then, 'an inmate of Gulag should be as happy as an equally virtuous inmate of a Cambridge college', at least if the former knows and practises philosophy (Vlastos, 1991: 215–16).[21]

We need also to mention here Socrates's austere indifference before the prospect of his own death, which Plato makes clear for us in *The Apology* and *Phaedo* in particular – in the latter of which, as we saw above, he is depicted as comforting his friends, rather than cursing his misfortune. Xenophon depicts Socrates responding deadpan to disciples who lament that he has been put to death by the city of Athens: that they have been put to death by nature (Xen., *Apo.* 27). To the lament that he has been delivered to execution unjustly, he replies by asking whether they would rather that he had been executed justly (Vlastos, 1991: 28). In Plato's *Apology*, the arguments Socrates gives for his 'Achillean' choice of death over dishonour, characteristically, concern the unknowability of death. It would be rational to fear death only if we knew that it was evil. This we cannot know. Either death sees the just rewarded in the afterlife, or it is as a dreamless sleep – the latter an idea that will be taken up within Epicureanism especially (Chapter 3). What matters is that in neither case is it fearful, so the wise person cannot say it is an evil.

1.7 The Socratic legacy

If ancient PWL begins with a choice of life or an existential option, as Hadot maintains, then we can see in Socrates's choice of virtue its fundamental orientation. In arguably somewhat anachronistic Kantian terms, Hadot identifies this as 'the absolute value of moral intent'. In other words, Socrates's ethics grants value *only* to the individual's choices and their reasons. Socrates aims to 'return' his interlocutors to the self that freely chooses the moral good and finds its happiness or completion in nothing other than its freedom to choose the good. 'The content of Socratic knowledge is thus essentially "the absolute value of moral intent", and the certainty provided by the choice of this value' (Hadot, 1995: 34). Socrates's existential option, Hadot claims, lies at the heart of all the ancient philosophical schools, despite the Epicureans' denial of a direct influence of Socrates upon their founder. As we shall see, all these schools practise spiritual exercises to attain a philosophical conversion: namely a state of self-realization or perfection which involves a break from ordinary ways of thinking and of living. In contemporary terms, we can say that Socrates and the Hellenistic schools 'internalized' happiness (**6**). 'All spiritual exercises', Hadot claims:

> are fundamentally a return to the self, in which the self is liberated from the state of alienation into which it has been plunged by worries, passions, and desires. The 'self' liberated in this way is no longer merely egoistic, passionate individuality: it is our *moral* person, open to universality and objectivity and participating in universal nature or thought. (Hadot, 1995: 103)

At its origins, then, as we have been seeing in this chapter, PWL constitutes nothing less than a moral and cultural revolution. Socrates and the ancient schools' spiritual exercises were not minor modifications of the pre-philosophical self's ordinary conventions and practices, but invitations 'to enter an alternative world and acquire a new self' (Long, 2006; 13). Ancient philosophers debated how strictly we should understand Socrates's seemingly paradoxical doctrine that to live well just is to live virtuously, leaving all else to others, fortune, or the gods. For different reasons, philosophers as otherwise opposed as Aristotle and Nietzsche have dismissed Socrates's key claims as exercises in absurdity or even 'life-denial'. 'Those who say that a man who is being tortured and has suffered terrible calamities is happy if he is a good man are willy-nilly talking nonsense,' Aristotle bluntly asserts, with the Socratic conception of the sage in view (*EN* 1153 B 19–21).

However, as we shall see in the following chapters, Socrates' ideal of PWL, as well as his own *atopia* and heroic model of fearless serenity constitutes the red thread running through the Hellenistic schools, and it will continue to inspire later rebirths of PWL. Nietzsche highlights this in his paean to Socrates as a philosophical chameleon:

> The pathways of the most various philosophical modes of life lead back to [Socrates]; at bottom they are the modes of life of the various temperaments confirmed and established by reason and habit and all of them directed towards joy in living and in one's own self, from which one might conclude that Socrates' most personal characteristic was a participation in every temperament. – ... Socrates excels the founder of Christianity in possessing a joyful kind of seriousness and that *wisdom full of roguishness* that constitutes the finest state of the human soul. (*WS* 86)

A. A. Long suggests that what made the post-Socratic schools' modes of living specifically *Socratic* is their sharing his 'particular view of what ethics should be about: the questioning of convention, the removal of fears and desires that lack any rational foundation, a radical reordering of priorities with a view to the soul's health, and, above all, the notion of self-mastery' (Long, 2006: 7). Incisively, he identifies the philosophical foundations of this Socratic legacy with the following propositions concerning happiness or eudaimonia:

1. Happiness is living in agreement with nature.

2. Happiness is something available to any person willing to engage in sufficient physical and mental training.

3. The essence of happiness is self-mastery, which manifests itself in the ability to live happily under even highly adverse circumstances.

4. Self-mastery is equivalent to, or entails, a virtuous character.

5. The happy person, as so conceived, is the only person who is truly wise, kingly and free.

6. Things conventionally deemed necessary for happiness such as wealth, fame and political power have no value in nature.

7. Prime impediments to happiness are false judgements of value together with the emotional disturbances and weakness of character which arise from these false judgements (Long, 1999c: 624).

Of course, though nearly all of them drew on Socrates, the post-Socratic, Hellenistic and Roman philosophers did so in different ways and therefore diverged in their conception of the good life. Ancient comic poets took delight in mocking the philosophers' disagreements over the best life (cf. Lucian, *Herm.*; *Phil. Sale; see* Konstan, 2014). Yet, as Long observes, despite these divergences, 'there is remarkable consensus among the philosophers about the type of character that their ethics seeks to produce ... a new kind of hero, a living embodiment of philosophical power, a figure whose appeal to the Hellenistic world consisted in self-mastery' (Long, 2006: 7). The ancient Cynics claimed that their ascetic practice made it possible for individuals to realize true kingship, or rule over themselves that exposed even the most powerful kings as slaves (see **Chapters 10–11**); similarly, Epicureans promised that their practices allow one to 'live like a god among men' (**Chapter 2**), and the Stoics suggested that only the Stoic sage is truly free, the rest being fools or slaves (**Chapter 3**). We are now ready to turn to the post-Socratic schools of philosophy.

CHAPTER 2
EPICUREANISM: PHILOSOPHY AS A DIVINE WAY OF LIFE

2.1 Introduction

Epicureanism began in the late fourth century BCE when Epicurus (341–270 BCE), an Athenian citizen born on the island of Samos, brought his school to Athens and planted it in a garden outside of the walls of the city, in competition with the already existing Platonic Academy, the Lyceum of Aristotle and later the Stoic Porch, which was founded after the garden. Seneca, the first century CE Roman Stoic, claimed that there was an inscription at the gates to Epicurus's garden: 'Stranger, your time will be pleasant here. Here the highest good is pleasure' (*Ep.* 79.15). (This stood in pointed contrast with the signpost from the nearby Platonic Academy: 'Let no one unversed in geometry enter here'). Epicureanism would become one of the most popular, yet controversial schools of ancient philosophy, from its foundation at the end of the fourth century BCE to the pinnacle of its popularity in the first century BCE Roman Republic. Diogenes Laertius reports that Epicurus's contemporary rival, the sceptical Platonist Arcesilaus (316–241 BCE), the head of the Platonic Academy, was asked why so many schools regularly lost students to the Epicureans, but very few Epicureans switched allegiances to other schools. Arcesilaus replied: 'You can turn a man into a eunuch, but you can't turn a eunuch into a man' (*DL.* 4.43). Arcesilaus's dismissal haunts Epicureanism. Philosophical critics condemn Epicureanism as a cult of personality that excised its students' impartial, critical reason and replaced it with the pursuit of happiness (Nussbaum, 1994: 138–9). On this view Epicureanism trained its students to believe what made them happy, rather than to pursue the truth.[1]

On the other hand, popular criticisms of Epicurus's conception of the highest good as lying in a species of pleasure (*hedônê*) have continued to accompany the philosophy, no less than the Stoics continue to face lay misunderstandings of their claims on behalf of virtue. Horace, the first century BCE Roman lyrical poet captured the popular ancient stereotype of the Epicurean in his ironic self-characterization: 'As for me, when you want a laugh, you will find me in fine fettle, fat and sleek, a hog from Epicurus' herd' (E. I.4.15f). In his polemic against Epicureanism, the Roman Stoic Epictetus [**3.4**] waxed wroth that if you believe that 'the essence of the good' consists in nothing but pleasure, then, 'lie down and sleep, and lead the worm's life, which you have judged yourself worthy of. Eat and drink and copulate and defecate and snore' (*Diss*. 2.20.9–10). As Diogenes Laertius reports:

> Epictetus also attacks him as a most debauched man, and reproaches him most vehemently, and so does Timocrates, the brother of Metrodorus, ... and he says that [Epicurus] used to vomit twice a day, in consequence of his intemperance. (DL X, 6)

In contemporary usage, 'epicureanism' remains a byword for a principle of pleasure that applies mostly to eating and drinking; shallow-minded, amoral pleasure-seeking, and living a life of luxury or debauch, just as 'Stoic' is still used to describe a dour but joyless enduring of Hamlet's 'slings and arrows of outrageous fortune'.

In this chapter, we will illuminate Epicureanism's contribution to the ancient tradition of PWL, in a way which will also show that its most facile criticisms are misplaced. As we shall see, Epicurus's philosophy is both a good deal more subtle and a good deal less vulgar than his critics often imagined. Epicureanism, beneath the surface, turns out to be a rather 'sober and temperate' (Seneca, *Vita Beata*, 12) affair, one which 'spit[s] upon luxurious pleasures' (U 181) (and declares enmity upon 'Venus' [or romantic love]), albeit 'not for their own sake, but because of the inconveniences that follow them' and indeed proposes a revaluation of contemporary values no less radical than that of Socrates (Chapter 1). We begin by looking at Epicurus's and his followers meta-philosophical statements, as they have survived.

2.2 Epicureanism as way of life, therapy and of writing

Like other ancient philosophies, Epicureanism defined itself as way of life that purported to grant its followers happiness (*eudaimonia*) or blessedness (*makaria*). 'By "philosophy,"' as Diskin Clay observes, 'Epicurus means a philosophical way of life and not only a set of doctrines' (Clay, 2009: 15).

For Epicureans as much as for the Stoics (**Chapter 3**), that is, philosophy consisted above all in 'the questioning of convention, the removal of fears and desires that lack any rational foundation, a radical reordering of priorities with a view to the soul's health, and, above all, the notion of self-mastery', in A. A. Long's formulation (2006).

Yet Epicureanism distinguished itself from other ancient philosophies by the extent to which it conceived and practised its way of life on the basis of the medical analogy which was common to Hellenistic thought, and which we will see again especially in Cicero (**7**) (Nussbaum, 1994; Clay, 2007: 20; Sharpe, 2016a; **4.3** below).[2] 'Empty (*kenos*) is the word of a philosopher which does not heal any suffering of man *[pathos anthropou therepeutai]*', U 221 famously reads: 'For just as there is no profit in medicine if it does not expel the diseases of the body, so there is no profit in philosophy either, if it does not expel the suffering of the mind'. Epicurus's *Letter to Menoeceus* likewise commences with this exhortation:

> Let no one be slow to seek wisdom when he is young nor weary in the search of it when he has grown old. For no age is too early or too late for the health of the soul. And to say that the season for studying philosophy has not yet come, or that it is past and gone, is like saying that the season for happiness is not yet or that it is now no more. (DL X, 122)

It is in this light that Epicurus's often-blunt criticisms of the Greek tradition of *paideia*, what we might call a liberal education (**4**), must be conceived. 'Launch your boat, oh blessed youth, and flee at full speed from every form of culture *[paideia]*', Epicurus enjoins (B 33; Cic. *De fin.* II, 4). Likewise, all philosophical concerns for logic or dialectic he shuns, 'for [Epicureans] say that the correspondence of words with things is sufficient for the natural philosopher, so as to enable him to advance with certainty' (DL X, 30).[3] Here as elsewhere, then, it would in fact be hard to imagine a conception of philosophy more distant from those predominant in academic thought today. The start and endpoint of philosophy for Epicurus is a pressing concern for avoidable human suffering:

> Do not think it unnatural that when the flesh cries out, the soul cries too. The flesh cries out to be saved from hunger, thirst, and cold. It is hard for the soul to repress these cries, and dangerous for it to disregard nature's summons. (U 200)

Most people's lives for the Epicureans are characterized by painful stresses and disturbances (9). As the Roman Epicurean Lucretius dramatizes in his long poem, this applies even (if not most of all) to the famous, rich and powerful (RN II, 30–61). It is as if non-philosophers, or non-Epicureans, were suffering from an epidemic which Diogenes of Oeneanda opens by diagnosing in his extraordinary missionary work inscribed into monumental public stone wall in the mountain town:

> The fact is ... that the majority is infected by an epidemic of false opinions concerning the world, as if they were suffering from a plague – and their numbers are increasing, for in their mutual emulation one person catches it from another like sheep, and, since it is right and proper to help those who live after us, for they too belong to us even if they are not yet born to come to the aid of strangers who visit our city – now since the kinds of remedy (I offer) have extended to an large group, I wanted, by making use of this stoa, to set out (the remedies) which bring salvation. (fr. 3 II.7-VI.2 Smith)

Epicurean philosophy hence explicitly describes its doctrines as containing *pharmaka* or remedies to human ailments, as we will see with the most famous of them all, the 'fourfold cure' or *tetrapharmakos*. The formulation or communication of such remedies, as we can imagine, strikingly differs from philosophy as it is written today, even in this book (6).[4] We need to be careful here, since we know that Epicurus wrote over 300 works, including the famous (and partly recovered) treatise *On Nature*, which seems to have been thirty-seven books based on spoken lectures, addressed to Metrodorus (DL X, 25). However, it is important that Epicurus wrote letters to epitomize his philosophy and many sententiae, which were excerpted from his works, have also survived. These involve discrete, almost aphoristic statements for purposes of ready memorization, like U 469, for instance: 'Thanks be to blessed Nature, because she has made necessary things (*ta anankaia*) easy to supply, and what is not easy to get (*ta dysporista*) unnecessary.'[5] In the tenth book of *Lives*, Diogenes Laertius gives us complete versions of three of Epicurus's letters dealing with physics, astronomy and ethics. These relatively brief letters, addressed in the second person, to Herodotus, Pythocles and Menoeceus also epitomize the whole Epicurean system of beliefs.

In a groundbreaking article on Epicurean manners of teaching, Ilsetraut Hadot (1969) has highlighted the pedagogical logic behind Epicurus's use of these literary forms (5). She cites an especially vital passage from the *Letter* to *Herodotus* (DL X, 25 ff.; I. Hadot, 1963: 347–8), wherein he argues that reducing his philosophical discourse into epitomes has value for two different classes of students. For beginners and those who do not have the time to explore all of the aspects of the Epicurean philosophical discourse, such epitomes present a readily digestible summary, which will enable them to recall the key ideas. For more advanced students, such epitomes are necessary:

> To recollect the principles laid down as elements of the whole discussion; for we have still greater need of a correct notion of the whole, than we have even of an accurate understanding of the details. (DL X, 35, Yonge trans.)

Condensing the key principles of the school into maxims, Epicurus appreciated, enables them to be always ready to hand (*procheiron*) (I. Hadot, 1963: 352). More than this, composing rhetorically crafted maxims enables them to be readily memorized. At the end of his 'Letter to Menoeceus', his epitome of Epicurean ethics, Epicurus reminds his addressee (and thereby us readers) that they will need to run through its main points literally 'night and day' (DL X, 135), so that 'they become settled convictions [and] they will drive out the deeply rooted empty opinions which fuel fear of pain and death' (Erler & Schofield, 1999: 670). It is a matter here of a spiritual exercise of meditation (3) involving the very deep processing of core Epicurean tenets: 'A continual meditation on the fundamental philosophical truths, a practice which the philosophical adept can practice alone, or with another' (I. Hadot, 1963: 349). The aim of this exercise, which we will meet again with Marcus Aurelius [**3.4**], is that these tenets will be so deeply integrated into students' characters as to reshape not simply their theoretical beliefs, but their day-to-day impulses, desires and actions (I. Hadot, 1963: 352–3). Epicurus's *Key Doctrines*, Erler and Schofield hence comment, is best read as a kind of philosophical catechism 'designed to be memorised and absorbed into the Epicurean's intellectual and emotional bloodstream' (Erler & Schofield, 1999: 670). Theoretical comprehension of the philosophical discourse, at least of its essential claims, is necessary but not sufficient, if the Epicurean is to live well.

2.3 The turn inwards: against empty opinions, unnatural and unnecessary desires

As in Socrates and the Stoics, if Epicureanism is to make sense as a philosophical therapy, it is on the basis of a specific account of mind and motivation. In particular, what is decisive here as in the other ancient schools is a diagnosis of the role of judgement of or belief in happiness and unhappiness. By themselves, Epicurus maintains that the sensations we have are always right or true to the world (Cic. *De Fin.* I, 30). We see this in what has become known as Epicurus's 'cradle argument', wherein he observes innocent infants and animals, in order to decide what is the true good for human beings (DL X, 137; Cic. *De Fin.* I, 30; I, 71; see Brunschwig, 1986). Nevertheless, human beings interpret their sensations according to beliefs and opinions which can be, and all-too-often are mistaken. Our reason can make inferences from the evidence which lead us to suppose threats and enticements that do not exist, imagination can reimagine what the senses present, shaped by our passions (Nussbaum, 1994: 106–7). Such false, 'empty' (*kenos*), or 'empty-striving' (*kenospoudon*) beliefs are 'productive causes' (*drastikē aitiai*) of unhappiness-producing fears and desires.

Human beings, in short, suffer because of their false beliefs concerning life, death, nature, the good and the gods (e.g.: KD 30; Nussbaum, 1994: 153). It is the same position (**5**), behoving us to 'turn inwards' and examine ourselves, as characterizes Socrates's defence in *The Apology* (see **Chapter 1**). Philosophy then becomes the sober reasoning which, making this turn, will correct these false beliefs, and thus remove the consequent desires. This is how it can be therapeutic (**6**).

But what then are the characteristic shapes of this suffering-inducing *kenodoxia*, according to Epicurean philosophy? As in Stoicism, there are perhaps four species of such beliefs:

Descriptively:

- We can foolishly believe and act as if things are real and relevant to us that, in truth, are neither (the gods, Hades, the afterlife).

- We vainly believe and can act as if things are unreal and not relevant to us that, in fact, really do exist (atomic processes, temporal genesis and death of all living things etc.).

Desideratively:

- We can foolishly desire that things we by nature do not need to be happy (like vast wealth, power, or fame) are necessary for our happiness.

- We can vainly wish that things which are necessary within life (like ageing, pain, dying) could be avoided, or are unnecessary.

Epicurean physics is, famously, a form of atomism looking back to the pre-Socratic philosopher, Democritus, strikingly anticipating the modern scientific worldview of the infinite universe.[6] Nevertheless, for Epicurus, accepting such a view of physics is not anxiety-provoking, nor does it 'rob things of meaning' or order. For him, human nature as we experience it sets limits to what creatures like us actually need in order to be happy. There are hence for Epicureans natural and necessary desires (*orexeis*), to be satisfied without anxiety or stress (food, drink, shelter) (see LM, 127; KD, 15, 26; VS, 21, 23, 35, 59; Cic. *Fin.* II 26 ff.). There are also natural but unnecessary needs, like the desire for sex, which are again to be satisfied in moderation. However, decisively, there are finally also unnatural (*aphysikai*) desires which humans can conceive, for things we don't naturally need. Such desires are the products of empty opinions, and as such even their successful pursuit does not in truth lastingly satisfy (KD 15, 18, 20, 21). There is the fact that, for instance, pursuing wealth knows no limits, so that those who undertake this pursuit rarely seem to be satisfied that they have enough (and convinced that other less deserving folk are draining what is rightfully theirs). This is nature's 'sign' that what we have here is an unnatural desire, based in an empty opinion about what we need to be happy (Nussbaum, 1994: 111–12; LM, 130, KD, 14, Sen. *Ep.* 1 6 9). B 46 thus tells us, in the second person, exactly that 'your anxiety (*taraxia*) is directly proportional to your forgetfulness of nature, for you bring on yourself unlimited fears and desires'. Lucretius laments in book V of *De rerum natura* (lines 1429–31):

> The human race labors constantly, without purpose and in vain, consuming men's lives with empty worries, for clearly they are ignorant about a limit to their possessions and about how far true pleasure can increase.

Unhappiness then is for Epicureanism a kind of fever in the soul, born of errors in the mind; even a kind of inner 'tempest' (DL X, 128). The errors in our opinions (*doxa*) set us craving and chasing after things we don't need, like wealth and most 'status goods'. They likewise put us on the path of worrying about things we cannot change, like death, or which do not in fact exist, like the gods. So, U 471 tells us:

It is rare to find a man who is poor with regard to the aims of nature and rich in groundless desires. For a fool is never satisfied with what he has, but instead is distressed about what he doesn't have. Just as those who are feverish through the evil of their sickness are always thirsty and desiring the opposite of what they should, so those whose souls are in a bad condition are always poor in everything and through their greed fall into ever-changing desires.

Epicurean philosophy, as a therapy, hence works by correcting our false beliefs, and replacing the phantoms of our empty opinions concerning the world and what we truly need with true beliefs concerning what is according to our nature.

2.4 Epicurus's revaluation of happiness, pleasure and the good

In the Epicurean garden as with Socrates, we see again see the extent to which ancient philosophy as a way of life called for a revaluation of the values of the ancient, and modern worlds. Epicureanism in fact gives us some of ancient philosophy's most idyllic images of happiness as resting in the simple life, outside of the cities, with all of their rush and their business, as well as spurs to needlessly multiply our desires and concerns. As Lucretius details, monetary wealth for the Epicureans is not by itself a good. Nor can it make a person truly 'rich', if by this term, we mean truly satisfied:

> Now, although there are also many things which can more agreeably at times provide us many pleasures, for her part nature does not seek them – if houses lack golden statues of young lads with right hands holding flaming torches out … if the home does not glitter with silver or gleam with gold, or if harps do not make gilded panels on the ceiling echo. (RN II, 23–9)

True happiness, as revealed by philosophy, rather asks very little:

> When, in their own company, men lie beside a river on soft grass, under the branches of a towering tree, and, with no great effort, enjoy themselves, they restore their bodies, especially when the weather smiles and annual seasons scatter flowers across the greening turf. If you are tossing on embroidered sheets dyed deep purple, hot fevers

will not leave your body faster than if you are forced to lie on common bedding. That is why, since riches, high rank, and ruling glory are of no advantage to our bodies, it therefore follows that we must assume they also bring no profit to our minds. (Nussbaum, 1994: II, 30–9)

There hence is something definitively 'para-doxical', again, about the Epicurean position, whose turn inwards reconceives true riches as riches of the character, true mastery as mastery over one's own beliefs and passions, and true 'piety' as a philosophical grasp of nature. 'If you wish to make Pythocles rich, do not give him more money, but diminish his desire', Epicurus writes, in a formulation which finds Stoic parallels (U 135; Cic. *Sto. Par.* I). Again, U 207 tells us: 'It is better for you to be free of fear lying upon a bed of straw, than to have a golden couch and a lavish table and be full of trouble.' Concerning the traditional virtue of piety, here is Lucretius, outlining the philosophical reversal and appropriation of received values:

There is no piety in being seen time and again turning towards a stone with one's head covered and approaching close to every altar, and hurling oneself prostrate on the ground, stretching out one's palms before gods' shrines, or spreading lots of blood from four-footed beasts on altars, or piling sacred pledges onto sacred pledges, but rather in being able to perceive all things with one's mind at peace. (*RN* V, 1195–202)

At issue here is a reconception of the goal of life (**8**) which challenges contemporary values no less radically than Socrates, albeit on different bases. 'Happiness and blessedness do not correlate with abundance of riches, exalted positions, or offices or power', Epicurus claims (U 548), 'but with freedom from pain (*alypia*) and gentleness of feeling (*praotês*) and a state of mind that sets limits that are in accordance with nature.' Here is the place to restore Epicurus's high valuation of pleasure, and his signature claim that pleasure represents the highest good. By nature (as above), from earliest childhood, Epicurus believes that human beings naturally aim at pleasure and to avoid pain. What this indicates, Epicurus claims, is that any 'good' like Socrates's or the Stoic's flaunted 'virtue' or Plato's 'Good' that was not the occasion of a pleasure, would not in fact *be* truly good. However, we can and must distinguish between kinds of pleasures, with a view to their wider effects upon us. As *Kyria Doxa* (principal opinions) 8 underlines: 'No pleasure is intrinsically bad: but the effective causes of some pleasures bring with them a great many perturbations of pleasure.' What is intended here are the forms of shame, regret, hang-overs or negative health effects that we all know can follow overindulging in bodily pleasures. 'Every pleasure is therefore a good on account of its own nature, but it does not follow that every pleasure is worthy of being chosen,' Epicurus hence reasons:

> Just as every pain is an evil, and yet every pain must not be avoided. But it is right to estimate all these things by the measurement and view of what is suitable and unsuitable; for at times we may feel the good as an evil, and at times, on the contrary, we may feel the evil as good. (*Letter to Menoeceus*, 129–30)

In this way, what is called a 'hedonic calculus' in fact operates in Epicureanism, rather than a mindless call for hedonic self-indulgence. One must balance short- versus medium- and longer-term pleasures. Reasoning on experience hence suggests an ethic of moderation concerning what Epicurus calls the 'kinetic' or 'dynamic' pleasures afforded us by eating, drinking and making love. U 181 thus reports to us:

> Living on bread and water, I rejoice in the pleasure of my body and spit upon the pleasures of extravagance, not for what they are but because of the difficulties that follow from them.

The 'dynamism' at issue here reflects the way that, for instance, slaking thirst yields pleasure only as long as drinking serves to remedy the pain of thirst. Then it passes. As such, as Aristotle also saw, to pursue such pleasures *ad infinitum* will lead to an unsettled life.

But, for Epicurus, not all pleasures are of this kind.[7] There is a second species of pleasure, which he terms 'stable' or *katastêmatikê*. '[Epicurus] differs from the Cyrenaics about pleasure. For they do not admit that pleasure can exist as a state, but place it wholly in motion,' Diogenes Laertius explains (X, 128). There is some interpretive uncertainty about what exactly the latter kinds of pleasures involve. Some fragments suggest that what is at issue is the kind of pleasure we experience after the dynamic business of sating one's corporeal, remedial, kinetic desires has finished. Other fragments suggest a more negative definition, identifying the stable pleasure with having no unfulfilled desire, and hence no sense of pain or lack. So, for instance, Usener 423 claims:

That which creates insuperable joy is the complete removal of a great evil. And this is the nature of good, if one can once grasp it rightly and then hold by it, rather than walking about tediously babbling about the *good*. [i.e. Plato]

It is significant that the principal terms Epicurus uses to identify what happiness itself involves (**8**) are both privative. These are *ataraxia*, first, the absence of anxiety, worry or inner distress and *aponia*, the absence of physical pain. Usener 2 hence claims that 'freedom from trouble in the mind [*ataraxia*] and from pain in the body [*aponia*] are static pleasures, [as against] joy and exultation … active pleasures involving motion'. Certainly, a claim about duration is in play in the sense that such pleasures are more stable than bodily satisfactions. 'I summon you to continuous pleasures and not to vain and empty virtues which have but a desperate hope for rewards', another fragment (U 116) hence instructs us. This indeed is *ataraxia*: a more or less continuous span of time, ideally extending to the whole of a human life, characterised by a continuous, stable sense of satisfaction, untroubled by anxiety, fear, troubles and pains, because untroubled by false beliefs about what we should desire and fear.

2.5 The gods and the figure of the sage

We see again why Lucretius will picture this existence as rustic or extramural, and indeed why Epicurus doubtless chose to found his school in a garden, outside of the walls of Athens. There can for him be no real eudemonic gain in public service, endlessly preoccupied with unstable demands, or the life of business, accumulating worldly goods which at most we need in moderation, and in some cases, have no real need of at all. If Socrates and the Cynics presented themselves as critics within the polis who nonetheless sought to define and exercise new forms of citizenship, and Plato sought to educate philosopher-kings, Epicurus opposed these ideals and opted instead for a way of life that entailed a withdrawal from politics[8] (Clay, 1998: vii). 'Live unknown (*lathê biôsas*)', is one of Epicurus's most famous injunctions (U 551).

It is vital for us to note here however that, as in the other ancient schools we are examining, Epicurus's descriptions of the goal of life (**8**) take the form of descriptions of the ideal personification of wisdom, the sage. In Epicureanism, in notable contrast with the other schools, Epicurus himself did not baulk from recommending himself to his followers as such a figure.

Reflecting on the striking features of Epicurus's will (*DL* X, 18), Clay observes that 'both he and Metrodorus received honours on the twentieth day of each month ... A monthly cult was reserved for divinities ... The Epicurean cult of the twentieth was, therefore, conceived of as a cult to Epicurus and Metrodorus as divinities' (Clay, 2007: 23). Lucretius goes so far in the proem to Book 5 of his *De rerum natura* as to proclaim Epicurus divine: *deus ille fuit, deus* (RN V, 8). Direct criticism in the garden with any of 'The Men', as Epicurus and his principal followers Metrodorus, Polyaenus and Hermarchus were collectively known, 'was out of the question' (Fish & Sanders, 2011: 2). In the garden, the Stoic Seneca remarks, Epicureans were exhorted to 'act as though Epicurus were watching you' as a kind of spiritual exercise (Seneca, *Ep.* 25, 5). Cicero reports that Epicureans lived with statues and portraits of Epicurus, and even carried his likeness on their rings and drinking cups (*Fin.* 5, 1, 3; Pliny *NH* 35, 5). 'The basic and most important [principle] is that we will obey Epicurus, according to whom we have chosen to live,' reads *Kyria doxa* 45, 8–11 (cf. De Witt, 1936: 205).

There are very good reasons for philosophers and others to be critical of what we might today call such a cult of personality. But it is important also to understand its philosophical bases. These lie in that turn inwards we saw above [**2.2**]. In *De rerum natura*, Lucretius hence notes that non-philosophers in Greece and Rome worship divine figures who have provided bodily goods like wheat (Ceres) or wine (Bacchus), or else who were their protectors from physical threats (Hercules) (RN V, 1–56). Philosophers however understand that the goods of peace of mind, and the means to stave of the spiritual threats posed by false beliefs and unnatural desires are far greater than those afforded by the traditional pagan deities. Hence, Lucretius writes:

As it is, the earth is full, even nowadays, of savage creatures, crammed with alarming terror in the woods, immense mountains, and deep forests, but we, for the most part, have the power to shun such places. However, unless our hearts are purified, what battles and dangers must then insinuate themselves in us, against our will! What bitter cares then tear men disturbed by passion! What other fears do just the same! What of arrogance, filth, depravity? What ruin they produce! What of luxuriousness and indolence? And so the man who has overpowered all these and driven them out of his mind – not by weapons but by words – should this man not be rightly found worthy of inclusion among the gods, especially because it was his custom to say many things, in an elegant and inspired manner, concerning the immortal gods themselves, and in his teachings to elucidate the entire nature of things? (RN V, 54–75)

The life of the sage, in any event, will be for the Epicureans as for the Stoics alike to that of the gods themselves, as the Epicureans conceive them. Famously touted and reviled as an atheist, Epicurus nevertheless includes a theological discourse in his account of nature. It is just that these gods (a) are not creator gods, (b) are not interventionist, and (c) have no concern for human affairs, salvation or damnation (Cic. *De nat. deo.*, I, 16–21). 'This is one of Epicurus' great intuitions,' Hadot claims: 'He does not imagine divinity as a power of creating, dominating, or imposing one's will upon the less powerful. Instead it is perfection of the supreme being: happiness, indestructibility, beauty, pleasure, and tranquillity' (Hadot, 1995: 121). Epicurus's key argument for these unusual claims is indeed what we might call a pious one. The gods, all agree, are the most self-sufficient beings. But such beings could *not need* or *desire* to create the world. Nor could they be troubled by the affairs and requests of such un-self-sufficient beings as we. 'What is blessed and indestructible has no troubles itself, nor does it give trouble to anyone else, so that it is not affected by feelings of anger or gratitude. For all such things are a sign of weakness' (KD 1). Instead, the Epicurean deities dwell in the *intermundia* between the worlds, untouched alike by chance and care, but 'gazing down and smiling, as far and wide the light spreads out'. As Lucretius explains:

> For the whole nature of gods, in itself, must for all time enjoy the utmost peace – far removed and long cut off from us and our affairs, and free from any pain, free from dangers, strong in its own power, and needing nothing from us, such nature will not give in to those good things we do nor will it be moved by our resentment. (RN II, 647–52; cf. Nietzsche, *WS* 7)

Likewise, the mortal sage (**10**) will live as freely as possible from fortune. We can see why when we appreciate how little he desires so little beyond his own control. 'I have gotten ahead of you, *O Tuchē*, and I have built up my fortifications against all your stealthy attacks,' *Vatican Sayings* 47 boasts. *The Letter to Menoeceus* relays the position in these terms (DL X, 134–5):

> And [the sage] does not consider fortune a goddess, as most men esteem her … for he thinks that good or evil is not given by her to men

so as to make them live happily ... ; thinking it better to be unfortunate in accordance with reason, than to be fortunate irrationally; for that those actions which are judged to be the best, are rightly done in consequence of reason.

As per the Stoics, the Epicureans maintained that 'even if the wise man were to be put to the torture, he would still be happy', in ways that have not failed to attract ancient and modern criticisms – since if pleasure is the good, being stretched on the wheel seems a strong candidate for its privation (Cic. *De fin.* II, 19 cf. II, 5; *TD* V, 5). Beyond this, Diogenes Laertius's summary (X, 117–21b) gives us a fairly exacting picture of the Epicurean sage's extramural, as it were 'intermundial' existence. The sage will have friends, and even die for his friends (although critics again have questioned the consistency of such claims). He will be kind to and even pity his slaves; but he will not usually marry, and be satisfied if sexual intercourse causes him no troubles, rather than pursuing what we call a 'rich sex life'. The sage will never engage in drunkenness, here in contrast with Socrates and Cato the Younger, amongst figures otherwise widely upheld as *sophoi*. He will take care of his property and mind of his future; but, as we know, he will not engage in public affairs unless he has little choice and will prefer to live in the country. His withdrawal from ordinary human affairs is, nevertheless, not complete. The Epicurean sage will participate in many activities non-philosophers indulge in. But he will do so with a kind of philosophical reserve which we will see in Chapter 3 has clear Stoic parallels. Thus, we are informed that this sage 'will show a regard for a fair reputation, *to such an extent as to avoid being despised*'; he will, 'if he is in need, earn money, *but only by his wisdom*'. Accordingly, like Epicurus himself, he may teach, '*but not on such a system as to draw a crowd about him*'. Likewise, he may give speeches, '*but that will be against his inclination*', which will instead be to live quietly with his friends, his Epicurean tenets always at hand and in practice. 'A little garden, some figs, a piece of cheese, plus three or four good friends', as Nietzsche observed, 'was the sum of Epicurus' extravagance' (*WS* 192; see *DL* 10.11), and the full extent of his sage's ascetic riches.

2.6 The fourfold cure, and physics as spiritual exercise

How exactly though are we to secure the goal of living like a sage in *ataraxia*, this life of continuous stable pleasure and absence of the distresses that otherwise plague human lives (**8**)? We have already glimpsed some of these means, as recommended by Epicurus: firstly, through the meditative internalization and commemoration of Epicurus's principal doctrines; and secondly, in the ways that these doctrines serve to correct our empty beliefs about what to desire, and what to avoid. The most famous Epicurean remedy, hence, is the so-called fourfold cure or *tetrapharmakos*. In line with Epicurus's bent for epitomizing his key precepts in striking curt formulations, the *tetrapharmakos* consists of four injunctions:

> God presents no fears (*aphobon ô theos*);
> death no cause for alarm (*anypopton ô thanatos*);
> it is easy to procure what is good (*kai tagathon men euktêton*);
> it is also easy to endure what is evil (*to de deinon eukarterêton*).
> (Philodemus, *Herculaneum Papyrus*, 1005, 4.9–14).

The bases of the claims that what is good or necessary is easy to acquire (U 469) we have seen; at issue here is the natural and necessary desires, of food, drink and shelter, all of which are readily available in all but the most exceptional circumstances. However, the claims concerning the gods and mortality, as Michael Erler and Malcolm Schofield remark, 'can be established only by physics, not by ethical inquiry narrowly conceived' (1999: 645). Indeed, Epicurus claimed that *only* physics can dispel the profoundest fears that haunt the lives of mortal creatures:

> There is no way to dispel being afraid about matters of supreme importance if someone does not know what the nature of the universe is but is anxious about some of the things retailed in myths. Hence without natural philosophy it is impossible to secure the purity of our pleasures. (*KD* 12)

As Epicurus stresses in his *Letter to Pythocles*, there is no 'other goal to be achieved by the knowledge of meteorological phenomena' or of 'physics' more broadly, 'than freedom from disturbance and a secure conviction' (DL X, 85). 'Were we not upset by the worries that celestial phenomena and death might matter to us, and also by failure to appreciate the limits of pains and desires, we would have no need for natural philosophy,' he contends (*KD* 11). Like the other ancient schools, then, Epicureanism also conceived physics as a spiritual exercise necessary to the realization of the happy, blessed life. 'Physics', as Hadot explains, 'is conceived as a spiritual exercise, which particularly among the Epicureans, was intended to ensure peace of mind by suppressing fear of the gods and of death' (Hadot, 2006: 162).

The full details of Epicurean physics can only be glimpsed here. As Lucretius's *De rerum natura* makes clear, Epicurus believes that the only way we can quiet the human fear that interventionist, potentially punishing gods exist – on top of the theological reflections we introduced in **2.4** – is by expounding a wholly physical worldview which can explain the striking and disturbing phenomena that underlie people's susceptibility to belief in such deities. The claim that natural disasters represent punishments for impiety, for instance, is refuted by the calm observation that such disasters befall good and bad people alike. Natural causes for happenings like earthquakes must instead be assumed, even if we cannot presently see or understand them (RN VI, 535–607). The claim that gods created the world supposes that things could come from nothing (RN II 287–307). But if this were the case, there would be no basis for the dynamic but relative order of things we experience, in which observable natural effects follow natural causes, and in which plants and animals can only engender others of their own kind: 'humans could spring up from the sea, races of fish arise from land, and birds burst from the sky' (RN I, 160–4). What we do experience instead suggests that beings are shaped within, and by their environing causes:

> Why could nature not have created men so big that they could make their way on foot across the sea, with their own hands tear down great mountains, and in life expectancy outlast many human generations, unless the reason is that certain stuff has been designed to make specific things, and that determines what can be produced? (RN I, 199–203)

According to the Epicureans, that is, founding a tradition of materialist criticism of revealed religion leading into Marx and Freud in modernity, ignorance of causes pushes human beings to assign responsibility for inexplicable natural events to mysterious supernatural deities (cf. RN I, 67–70). For this reason, Lucretius spends Books V and VI of *De rerum natura* providing naturalistic-philosophical explanations of the creation of the world, plants and animals which strikingly anticipate post-Darwinian accounts of natural selection (see Wilson, 2019: 83–123); the creation of language, law, religion, war and the arts; the orderly circuits of the heavenly bodies; as well as startling natural events, like lightning strikes, earthquakes, but also culminating in diseases, like the plagues which can blindly strike down even great cities like Athens (V Proem). The central books (III–IV) of the poem, comparably, are dedicated to overcoming the bases of fears surrounding the survival of the soul after death, and its possible suffering there. Such beliefs, the Epicureans contend, are drawn from our experience of dreams, in particular, wherein (for instance) bereaved people meet and converse with the deceased. Again, Epicureanism proposes that 'keen reasoning ... to look into what makes up the soul', from a wholly naturalistic perspective, can allay these fears. If we observe animals, Lucretius argues, we see that they clearly dream and about their waking concerns. Dogs, for instance, dream of cats or birds or foxes to chase (RN IV 989 ff.). Just so, human beings evidently dream of what preoccupies their waking lives (RN IV 962–9; 1010–36). Lucretius's most vivid example of this (which serves a specific argumentative purpose) is an adolescent boy's wet dream, provoked by his encountering a beauty who had piqued his desire on the dream day. For himself, Lucretius charmingly confides that his dreams are filled with visions and arguments about the nature of things (RN IV, 967–9). The decisive consideration is that, in order to explain mourners who dream of their dead loved ones, we need only posit their natural longing for the departed, not any supernatural realm of the afterlife.

To move to the fear of death: 'someone born must wish to stay alive as long as enticing pleasure [*blanda voluptas*] holds him', Lucretius avows (RN V, 177–8). As Martha Nussbaum has argued, Epicureanism enshrines the deepest ancient appreciation of the way this fear of mortality underlies and can inform other forms of human malaise (RN III, 37–40; DL X, 125; Nussbaum, 1994: 195; Konstan 2008: x–xiv). The Epicureans present three readily memorable arguments to combat this intransigent fear.[9] The first is the famous *aesthêsis* argument. 'When death is, we are not, and when we are there, death is not' (DL X, 125; cf. *Kyr. Dog.* II). Suffering alone is bad, and reasonably to be feared, the argument goes. But suffering requires consciousness and sensation (*aesthêsis*). However, death ends consciousness and *aesthêsis*. Thus, there is nothing to be feared in death. We must 'accustom [ourselves] to believing that death is nothing to us, since all good and evil reside in sensation [*aesthêsis*], and death is the privation of sensation' (DL X, 124).[10]

Secondly, there is the so-called symmetry argument (cf. Nussbaum, 1994: 203). Being dead will be as fearful or pleasurable as the time before we were born, the argument runs.[11] But we have no memory of any experience of the time before we were born to either lament or celebrate. Thus, death is as little to be feared as the time before we were born.[12] Or, as Lucretius dramatizes the argument:

> Just as in the past we felt no pain when Carthaginian troops, massing for battle, advanced from every side, when all things, disturbed by war's fearful noise, shook with dread under high heavenly skies, in doubt on which of the two sides would fall power to rule all men on sea and land, so, when we cease to be, when soul and body, whose union makes us one single being, part company, it is clear nothing at all can happen to us or rouse our feelings, not even if earth is mixed in with sea and sea with sky – for then we won't exist. (RN III, 832–42)

The third argument features in Lucretius's *De rerum natura*. At a certain moment, the philosopher-poet has Nature Herself rebuke an aged man, greedy for more life (either he has lived well, and should be content; or has not, so should not fear his life's end). If humans could ever become immortal, she contends, the world would soon become unlivably overpopulated. Each generation must instead accept the need to pass away, in order to make room for the next – and also, according to Epicurean physics, to provide the material in order to form later peoples. As Lucretius praises Nature's counsel:

> She would be right, in my view, to say this – right to rebuke and criticize the man. For old things, driven out by what is new, always yield, and one must renew one thing with something else. So no one is sent down into the abyss and black Tartarus. Material is needed for the growth of later generations – yet all of them, once their life is over, will follow you. Men have died before and will die again, just like you. Thus, one thing will never cease being born from something else. Life is given to no man as a permanent possession – instead, all men receive it as a loan. (RN III, 965–73)

2.7 Spiritual exercises within the garden

The individual Epicurean was to confront the sources of their own avoidable suffering in their empty beliefs concerning the world, and what is desirable within it. Epicurus's writings were to be memorized, in both their more systematic expressions and above all in their concentrated summaries, so that the cures the philosophy offers to fears of god, death and pain could be readily adduced when needed. Insofar as such fears and false desires are not readily to be overcome, these teachings were to be returned to again and again, becoming the object of the spiritual exercise of meditation. As Hadot writes:

> Above all, Epicureans believed that it is necessary to practice the discipline of desire. We must learn to be content with what is easy to obtain and what satisfies the organism's fundamental needs, while renouncing what is superfluous. A simple formula, but one that cannot but imply a radical upheaval of our lives. It means being content with simple foods and simple clothes; renouncing wealth, honours, and public positions; and living in retreat. (2002: 123)

Nevertheless, Epicurus himself, like the idealized figure of the sage [2.4], founded his own school, albeit one not open to large crowds. In doing so, he seems to have been moved by the sense that such ascesis cannot readily be practised in solitude. It best flourishes within small communities of like-minded friends. It is well known that Epicurus waxed lyrical about the significance of friendship for the Epicurean way of life: 'Friendship dances around the world announcing to all of us that we must wake up to blessedness' (VS 52). 'Of all the things wisdom prepares for the blessedness of life as a whole', he asserted, 'much the greatest is the possession of friendship' (KD 27). Controversially, and in some contrast with other ancient philosophical discourses surrounding friendship, Epicurus's principal claim to the value of friendship is instrumental, at least initially. 'All friendship is choice-worthy for its own sake, but it takes its origin from benefit,' he claims (VS 23). Having friends helps us achieve the stable pleasures of ataraxia.

Twentieth-century scholarship has in fact given us a clearer picture of the way Epicureanism transformed friendship into a therapeutic means to enable the curing of individual souls (esp. De Witt, 1936; 1954). The rediscovery and translation of some texts of Philodemus of Gadara (110/100–40/35 BCE), especially *On Frank Criticism*, have shed new light on the Epicurean garden as a therapeutic community[13] originally under the direction of Epicurus, but later his successors, as leaders (or 'scholarchs') (Tsouna, 2007). 'As in the Platonic school, friendship, in the Epicurean school, was the privileged path toward and means for the transformation of one's self. Masters and disciples helped one another closely in order to obtain a cure for their souls,' Hadot writes (2002: 123). As Cicero informs us:

> Epicurus says that of all the things which wisdom provides in order for us to live happily, there is nothing better, more fruitful, or more pleasant than friendship. Nor did he merely declare this; he confirmed it in his actions and habits. In Epicurus' one little house, what a troop of friends there was, all gathered together by him! What a conspiracy of love united their feelings! (*De fin.* I, 25, 65; Hadot, 2002: 125)

Epicurus and his successors hence functioned less as teachers of doctrine, than as spiritual directors who took charge of curing students through instituting a whole range of practices, including examination of conscience, confession, correction and above all frank speech or *parrhesia*. Recognizing the difficulty of living wholly according to the Epicurean ideals, in the garden, students were enjoined to confess their errors to others, disclose the faults of their fellows and submit themselves to their teachers' criticism, which might range in severity from gentle admonition to sharp rebuke. 'For the masters', as Hadot explains, 'free self-expression meant not being afraid to hand out reproaches; for the disciple, it meant not hesitating to admit one's faults, and even not being afraid to tell friends about their own faults' (2002: 124). In this way, as Clay concurs, in the Epicurean community, frank speech served 'a therapeutic purpose: self-disclosure was a means towards correction and improvement, as well as a barrier to dissension within the group' (Clay, 2007: 7). For a post-Christian readership, it is impossible not to think here of the later Christian institution of confession, albeit in this apparently most non-theological of contexts [5.2].

Epicureanism was also characterized by a series of practices more specifically directed to the goal of achieving stable pleasures. These include the cultivation of discussion amongst friends as a source of great pleasures; and, notably enough given some criticisms, the pleasures of learning, since 'pleasure goes hand in hand with knowledge; for we do not obtain enjoyment after we learn, but learn and enjoy simultaneously' (*VS*, 27). These exercises also include practices in the mastery of one's thought and attention. The Epicurean needs to monitor his or her own thoughts, so that they can learn not to dwell on unpleasant subjects. Instead, they need to cultivate the ability to revive memories of past pleasures in times of difficulty, and to savour present pleasures without anxiety or stress. Facing his own mortal illness, Epicurus thus tells his disciple Idomeneus that 'to these pains, I have opposed the joy I feel in my soul when I recall our philosophical conversations' (at Hadot, 2002: 124; cf. Cic. *De fin.*, II, 30; Marcus Aurelius, *Med.* IX, 4, 1). As in Stoicism, the premeditation of one's mortality was also enjoined in

Epicureanism, but precisely as a means to 'seize the day!', in the Epicurean-influenced poet Horace's famous injunction. 'Persuade yourself that each new day that dawns will be your last; then you will receive each unexpected hour with gratitude. Recognize all the value of each moment of time which is added on as if it were happening by an incredible stroke of luck,' Epicurus instructs (Horace, *Epistles*, I, 4, 13; Philodemus, *On Death* IV, cols. 38, 24).

Above all, despite what the therapeutic bent of Epicurus's meta-philosophy can lead us to imagine, there is a sense which again finds parallels within Stoicism and other schools in which achieving a perspective deeply shaped by Epicurean philosophy opens up a transformed, expanded vision of things. 'How pleasant it is, when windstorms lash the mighty seas, to gaze out from the land upon another man in great distress – not because you feel delightful pleasure when anyone is forced to suffer pain, but because it brings you joy to witness misfortunes you yourself do not live through,' Lucretius thus writes: 'It is also sweet to watch great armies, opposing forces in a war, drawn upon the field, when you are in no danger. But nothing brings more joy than to live well in serene high sanctuaries fortified by wise men's learning' (RN II, 1–10). It is a matter here, directly, of that spiritual exercise Hadot has identified as the view from above, tied in the Epicurean spirit to a sense of pleasure at existence itself. In another famous passage, Lucretius describes Epicurus's physics as breaking open the walls of the world, within which our vision is usually enclosed, as follows:

> For once that philosophy which arose in your godlike mind has begun to speak about the nature of things, then terrors in the mind disperse, world's walls fall open, I see what is going on in all the void, the majesty and calm habitations of the gods reveal themselves in places where no winds disturb, no clouds bring showers, no white snow falls, congealed with bitter frost, to harm them, the always cloudless aether vaults above, and they smile, as far and wide the light spreads out … and earth presents no barrier to a full view of all events going on throughout the void lying underfoot. Godlike pleasure and awe [*horror*] take hold of me up there with these things. (RN III, 12–31)

2.8 Criticisms

The extent of Epicurus's influence on subsequent philosophy, mediated through his disciple Lucretius's extraordinary philosophical poem *De rerum natura*, can hardly be overstated. Epicureanism went into decline in late antiquity. Early Christian thinkers took umbrage at Epicurus's purely naturalistic philosophy and its vindication of the pleasure of existence.[14] For the entire medieval period, Epicurus's and Lucretius's texts were lost to wider culture, those surviving stored away (ironically) in the Vatican and in monastery libraries. According to Stephen Greeblatt's claim in *The Swerve* (2011), it was the recovery of Lucretius's poem by papal secretary Poggio Bracciolini in 1417 that marked the beginning of the modern age. Certainly, in the work of figures like Pierre Gassendi, Epicurean physics – albeit largely dissevered from its ancient function in spiritual therapy – was to exercise a lasting influence on the development of modern natural philosophy (Wilson, 2009). The Epicurean criticism of revealed religion, including the dangers that uncritical adherence to beliefs in vengeful deities can do, was celebrated by Karl Marx:

> Philosophy, as long as a drop of blood shall pulse in its world-subduing and absolutely free heart, will never grow tired of answering its adversaries with the cry of Epicurus: 'The truly impious man is not he who denies the gods worshipped by the multitude, but he who affirms of the gods what the multitude believes about them.' (Marx, 2000, Preface)[15]

Nietzsche, one of the moderns who, as we shall see (**Chapter 10**), sought to reinvent PWL, was convinced that after the death of God, ancient ethical optimism including that characterizing Epicureanism must revive. At the height of his own brief enthusiasm for ancient eudaimonistic ethics, Nietzsche sets himself the task of 'renewing the garden of Epicurus' and of living 'philosophically' in the manner of the Epicureans (Young, 2010: 278; see Ansell-Pearson, 2013). In her recent, popular book, historian of philosophy Catherine Wilson has agreed that Epicurean philosophy is 'the most interesting and relevant of the ancient philosophical systems' that might prove 'compelling and useful in working out [our] own ideas about how to live … cheerfully and ethically as mortals' (Wilson, 2019).

Nevertheless, Epicureanism from its inception has faced strident criticisms, as we opened this chapter by signalling. Beyond the facile misrepresentation of the philosophy as providing a high-end rationalization for indulging in sensuous license, there are real questions posed by advocating for any form of pleasure as the goal of life. The Epicurean notion of stable pleasure, which would be identical with the absence of all pains is railed at by Cicero as being incoherent, and in no way a viable goal for human existence (Cic. *TD* II, 6–7). 'If we are happy by achieving a condition of ataraxia', modern critic Julia Annas concurs, 'then our happiness resides not in what we actually do or produce, but in our condition of being untroubled about it. There is this much to ancient criticisms that for Epicurus our final end is too passive; it is located not in what we actually do, but in how we feel about what we do' (Annas, 1993: 347).[16] Surely happiness should not be without its pleasures; but whether it is reducible to these is the rub.

If the stable pleasure of *ataraxia* is the goal, moreover, this makes the virtues, led by courage and justice, mere instruments to this goal. This is a position which the Stoics, Cicero and Aristotelians each contest amongst the ancients (e.g.: Cic. *De fin.* II, 16–29). Can the Epicurean, for instance, be trusted to uphold justice when no one is looking, if secret unjust action can maximize his own stable pleasures? The same thought applies to the valorization of friendship as a means to our *ataraxia*. Critics charge that this seems to mandate letting friends go when times get tough, a profoundly dishonourable option.

At another, more fundamental level for the entire conception of PWL, modern critics in particular have raised important questions about the relationship between Epicureanism's therapeutic aims, and its claims *as a philosophy* to uncovering the truth. The question here is whether such a position must sacrifice scientific investigation on the altar of happiness, or of what we call 'mental health'. 'One can see', as Karl Marx put it, 'that there is [in Epicurus] no interest in investigating the real causes of objects. All that matters is the tranquillity of the explaining subject' (Marx, 2000, see also Lange, 1925: 95–6, 103). Or, as Nietzsche put it more strongly, 'Epicurus denied the possibility of knowledge, in order to retain moral (or hedonistic) values as the highest values' (*WP* 578). One of the fundamental meta-philosophical questions concerning PWL (see **Conclusion**) is whether it is legitimate to connect truth and flourishing, or whether in doing so, we necessarily sacrifice truth for the sake of happiness. This criticism is, for example, at the heart of Martha Nussbaum's assessment of Epicureanism. If the purpose of physics is to alleviate our fears and anxieties, as Epicurus maintained, then 'this means that a science of nature that delivered disturbing rather than calming stories of how things are would not have fulfilled the purpose for which we need a science of nature, and would justly be dismissed as empty' (Nussbaum, 1994: 124). Epicureans would at this point have to choose between therapy and *ataraxia* and the love of *sophia*, presuming the latter necessarily entails trying to see things steadily, as they are, and as a whole:

> For it is always possible, and in fact all too easy, to turn from calm critical discourse to some form of therapeutic procedure … But once immersed in therapy it is much more difficult to return to the values of … critical discourse. (Nussbaum, 1994: 139)

In Chapter 3, we turn from the garden to the porch, and from Epicureanism to its great Hellenistic rival, Stoicism.

CHAPTER 3
THE STOIC ART OF LIVING

3.1 Wisdom, knowledge of things human and divine, and an art of living

In this period of remarkable flourishing of online communities of self-describing 'modern' or 'traditional' Stoics, when people mention PWL, they will most often be thinking of the Stoics. The Stoic school (also known as the 'Stoa' or 'the porch') was founded in late fourth century BCE by Zeno of Kition (modern-day Larnaka in Cyprus). As Diogenes Laertius relays the foundation story, Zeno was a merchant who lost all his goods in a shipwreck near Athens. He made his way to the Athenian agora, where he picked up and began reading a copy of Xenophon's *Memorabilia of Socrates*. 'Where can I find a man like this?', he asked, and the bookseller pointed him to the Cynic, Crates. Zeno followed Crates for nearly a decade, before breaking away to found the Stoic school, named after the *Stoa Poikilê* (Painted Stoa) where Zeno would give his lectures to the public and discuss the philosophy (DL VII, 1–3).

Yet what is known as late or 'Roman Stoicism' is that which is today best known.[1] This is due almost entirely to the vicissitudes surrounding the survival and transmission of the ancient texts. The Roman Imperial period from the first to second century CE gives us four key figures, some or all of whose writings have survived, unlike their Hellenistic predecessors': Musonius Rufus, Seneca the Younger, the slave-turned-philosopher Epictetus and the Stoic philosopher-emperor Marcus Aurelius. During this time, there was no formal Stoic school in Rome, although Musonius delivered lectures for a time. Epictetus's school in Nikopolis seems to have been one of only a few in the wider Roman imperium. Stoic philosophers (like philosophers from the other Hellenistic and classical schools) were instead often housed by leading Romans as philosophical advisors or, in Ilsetraut Hadot's term, 'spiritual directors' (I. Hadot, 2014).[2]

The importance of Socrates in inspiring Zeno is significant. There is considerable ancient evidence attesting to the fact that all the Stoics, who called themselves 'Socratics' (Sellars, 2014: 72), followed Socrates in defining philosophy as a business of both *erga* (works) and *logoi* (words). Seneca in the first century CE tells us that philosophy 'tells us how to live, not how to talk' (Ep. 20.2), and distinguishes it as a guide for life (Ep. 16.1). Both Epictetus and the second-century sceptic, Sextus Empiricus, attest that for the Stoics of this time, philosophy is a *technê peri ton bion* or 'art of living' (Sextus Empiricus *Adv. math.* 11.170 [= SVF 3.598]; Epictetus, *Disc.* 1.15.2; Sellars, 2014: 22).[3] As René Brouwer has examined in *The Stoic Sage*, both of the extant Stoic definitions of wisdom stress that what is at stake is not simply a body of systematic, true beliefs concerning 'things both human and divine' (Brouwer, 2014: 8).[4] Wisdom will also involve a 'fitting expertise' (*technê*) whose goal is either 'the virtues', in a passage reported by the first century CE Platonist Plutarch, or 'the best life for human beings', per pseudo-Galen's *History of Philosophy* (Brouwer, 2014: 47).[5]

Philosophy then, the love of such wisdom, is the exercise (*askêsis*) of the *technê* of the best life for human beings.[6] It will involve the training of a person's *psychê*, both to acquire a systematic understanding of the world and to embody that knowledge in their lives. The large Stoic literature devoted to thinking through the attributes of the *Sophos* or *Sapiens*, the wise man, makes sense against the background of these larger conceptions of philosophy (**9**) (Annas, 2008; Hadot, 2020a: 185–206). For the Stoics, as for the other schools, the sage was the embodiment of wisdom itself. To imagine what this 'omni-virtuous' figure would say, think and do was to make vividly present, in personified form, the goal of philosophy. This goal, Zeno had famously defined as 'the life in harmony with nature' (DL VII, 86) characterized by a 'good flow' of experiences (Stobaeus 2.77).

Before we turn in detail to the key Roman Stoics, let us say something more concerning the specifically Socratic dimension of the Stoics' conception of philosophy.

3.2 The Socratic lineage: dialectic, the emotions and the sufficiency of virtue

According to Epictetus, 'God counselled Socrates to undertake the office of refutation *(elenktikên)*; Diogenes, that of reproving men in a kingly manner *(basilikên kai epiplēktikên)*; Zeno, that of doctrinal instruction' (*Disc.*, III 21, 18–20). On the one hand, the Stoics greatly admired Socrates's personal conduct, in particular his fearlessness in the face of death. Socrates's refusal to compromise on his philosophical principles, demonstrated in his defiant conduct at his trial, then his equanimity before drinking the hemlock, set up a paradigm for later Stoic conceptions of the good death. Thus, for instance, we are told that Cato the Younger read Plato's *Phaedo* before committing suicide (Plutarch, *Cato Min.*, 79–81). A century later, Seneca's suicide at the behest of Nero was also consciously modelled on the *atopos* Greek sage (Tacitus, *Annals* XV, 60–64; Ker, 2009).

On the other hand, as per Epictetus's assessment, the Stoics were also legatees to Socrates's conception of the role of dialectic and reasoning in shaping the good life. As Epictetus explains: 'Socrates knew that, if a rational soul be moved by anything, the scale must turn, whether it will or no. Show the governing faculty of reason a contradiction, and it will renounce it; but until you have shown it, rather blame yourself than him who remains unconvinced' (*Disc.* II, 26). For the Stoics as for Socrates, that is, error – whether epistemic or ethical – is involuntary:

> Every error implies a contradiction; for, since he who errs does not wish to err, but to be in the right, it is evident, that he acts contrary to his wish. What does a thief desire to attain? His own interest. If, then, thieving be really against his interest he acts contrary to his own desire. (*Disc.* II, 26, 1–2)

While denying the Platonic conception of *anamnêsis,* the Stoics maintained that people are each endowed by nature with correct starting points or 'preconceptions' (*prolêpseis, emphytos ennoia* [*Disc.* III, 12, 15]) about good and bad, the advantageous, the virtues etc.: 'for which of us does not admit, that good is advantageous and eligible, and in all cases to be pursued and followed? Who does not admit that justice is fair and becoming?' (*Disc* I, 22, 1–2; cf. IV 1, 44–5; Long, 2002: 25–6) It follows that, as A. A. Long (2002: 82) has expressed it, 'whoever has a false moral belief will always have at the same time true moral beliefs entailing the negation of the false belief'. To live philosophically involves a fundamental commitment to the examination of one's various opinions. It also entails a willingness to let go of those opinions that are shown to contradict the better-founded beliefs that Stoic philosophical discourse aimed to codify. Epictetus, as ever, condenses the thought powerfully (*Disc.* III, 12–15), by way of an analogy with the Socrates of the *Apology*:

Just as Socrates used to say we should not live an unexamined life, so we should not accept an unexamined impression (*anazêtaton phantasian*), but should say: 'Wait, let me see who you are and where you are coming from ... Do you have your guarantee from nature, which every impression that is to be accepted should have.'

This work of the examination of one's beliefs is what Pierre Hadot has called the 'discipline of logic' [see **3.4**]. In the pedagogical analogies which Diogenes Laertius tells us that the Stoics used to explain the interdependency of the different parts of philosophy, it is significant that 'logic' is depicted as the sinews and bones of the organism; or else the shell encompassing the egg, or as the wall encompassing the field or city of the whole (DL VII, 41). The full ethical force of the Socratic discipline of logic however rests upon the Stoics' 'cognitivist' or 'intellectualist' account of the emotions, to use modern terms (Frede, 1986: 93–110; Inwood & Dononi, 1999: 699–717; Graver, 2007). For the Stoics as for the Epicureans, what people think about the world and themselves is decisively important in understanding the causes of suffering. 'Men are not disturbed by things which happen (*ta pragmata*), but by the opinions (*dogmata*) about the things,' Epictetus's *Encheiridion* states aphoristically (§5). The emotions, according to the Stoics, embody specific kinds of pathogenic opinions about the world, and about what we imperatively need in order to be happy. Stoic tabulations of the passions (*pathê*), as in Cicero's *Tusculan Disputations* IV, 6–7 hence reduce the range of human emotions to four headers. These are divided according to whether the things that people suppose to be beneficial or harmful to them, and as such necessary to pursue or avoid, are present or in prospect.

These *pathê* are to be extirpated, not simply moderated, for the Stoics (as against the peripatetics). The reason is that, in each case, the shaping belief of the emotion is demonstrably false. Each emotional response reflects an evaluative claim: that we imperatively *need* the things in question, say to avoid someone, or to possess something. This evaluation justifies the directive impulse that the emotion gives body to: that it is 'appropriate'

Figure 2.1 Stoic emotions, from Cicero, *Tusculan Disputations*, book IV, 6–7.

	Present	Future (in prospect)
Things taken to be good	Delight (*hêdonê, gaudium*)	Desire (*epithymia, spez*)
Things taken to be bad	Distress (*lupê, dolor*)	Fear (*phobos, metus*)

(*kathêkon*) for us to respond with anger, or with tears, frustration, envy, desire etc. But if it can be philosophically demonstrated that we do not need the things in question, it follows that the tendency of a person to remain subject to the corresponding emotion both should and can be removed.

That such philosophical demonstration, for the Stoics, is forthcoming points to the third, clear Socratic debt of the Porch. As A. A. Long (1999; 2002, 67–96), William O. Stephens (2002: 59–62) and Gisela Striker (1994) have pointed out, the Stoics' central ethical claim concerning what human beings need to be happy is deeply Socratic. It echoes Socrates's famous claim to the Athenians in the *Apology* (29d-30b) that all he had ever tried to convince anyone of was of the need to make their first and chief concern the care of their souls, rather than external goods, like wealth, fame and power. Socrates's argument for this paradoxical claim is defended directly in Plato's *Euthydemus* 278c-281e, and can be formulated heuristically as follows:

1. Everyone wishes to fare well.

2. Faring well involves the possession or use or enjoyment of good things.

3. These include, according to accepted opinion:
    (a) external goods: wealth, health, beauty, strength, noble birth, power, honour etc.;
    (b) temperance, justice and courage (the virtues);
    (c) wisdom;
    (d) good fortune.

4. But wisdom [c] *is* good fortune [d], since it always makes men act well (so to aim for wisdom is to aim for good fortune, and [d] is identified with [c]).

5. All truly good things benefit their possessor, enjoyer or user (this is what it means for them to be 'good').

6. Good things benefit their possessor by being used or enjoyed, not simply possessed.

7. The correct use of external goods [a] is the wisdom [c] which guides choice and actions concerning how to use or enjoy these.

8. Thus, wisdom [c] provides men both with good fortune [d], *and* also ensures that the external 'goods' [a] are actually *good* for their possessor. By contrast:

9. without such wisdom [c], these goods [a] may harm people, not benefit them.

10. Hence, contra unexamined *endoxa*, wisdom [c] is the only true good, alongside the virtues [b] which embody that wisdom in different concerns of life.

11. As for external goods [a], they are properly speaking neither good nor evil, but 'indifferent' (*ta adiaphora*) or 'intermediary' things (*ta mesa*).

It follows from 11, directly, that it is false to believe that any external thing, outside of the inner character of peoples' psyches, is good or evil: which is to say that we could imperatively need to possess or avoid it in order to flourish. The Stoics delight in reminding people, by example, of how beauty, riches, fame and power do not necessarily bring satisfaction:

Why do you seek this possession [*eudaimonia*] without? It lies not in the body; if you do not believe me, look at Myro, look at Ophellius. It is not in wealth; if you do not believe me, look upon Crœsus; look upon the rich of the present age, how full of lamentation their life is. It is not in power; for otherwise, they who have been twice and thrice consuls must be happy; but they are not. (Epictetus, *Disc.* III, 22, 26)

Nevertheless, it is just this kind of false belief that fuels humans' delights, desires, distresses and fears in their different manifestations. The sage will experience no such emotions. In this sense his inner state will be characterized by *apatheia,* a deep inner tranquillity or serenity. His only imperative attachments will be to the pursuit of wisdom and virtue. Yet these are both within the reach of his own ruling faculty (*hêgemonikon*) to achieve, hostage to neither fortune nor others' vices. In place of the *pathê,* that is, the Stoic sage will feel only what are called the *eupatheia*: a caution to avoid evil, the wish to attain virtue and joy, the 'elation of a spirit that trusts in its own goods and truths' (Seneca, *Ep. 59*; Graver, 2007: 57–60)

We turn now to what the key Roman Stoics each tell us about the 'exercise' of philosophy as the art of living.

3.3 From Musonius Rufus to Seneca

The first two Stoics from whom we have relatively complete works both hail from the early imperial period: Gaius Musonius Rufus (*c.* 30–101 CE) and Lucius Annaeus Seneca (Seneca the Younger [4 BCE–65 CE]). Both philosophers were active in the reign of Nero. Musonius was exiled by in 65 CE, and Seneca was compelled by his former pupil to commit suicide in the same year.

Twenty-one of Gaius Musonius Rufus's *logoi* ('lectures', 'discourses' or 'speeches on philosophy bearing his name') survive, courtesy of a student, one Lucius, and the compiler Stobaeus. These discourses span what we would call meta-ethical subjects, such as 'That Man Is Born with an Inclination toward Virtue' into more immediate, prescriptive considerations: 'That One Should Disdain Hardships', 'On Sexual Indulgence' or 'Must One Obey One's Parents Under All Circumstances?' There are also a series which directly concern themselves with the figure of the philosopher (10), and what is appropriate to him (or indeed *her*), such as 'That Women Too Should Study Philosophy', 'That Kings Also Should Study Philosophy', 'Will the Philosopher Prosecute Anyone for Personal Injury?', 'What Means of Livelihood Is Appropriate for a Philosopher?', and 'Is Marriage a Handicap for the Pursuit of Philosophy?' Of particular interest for us here are the fifth and sixth *logoi*, directly given over to considering 'Which Is more Effective, Character (*Ethos*) or Theory (*Logos*)?', and 'On Exercise (*Peri Askêseôs*)'.

'The problem arose among us whether, for the acquisition of virtue, character (*êthos*) or theory is more effective', Musonius's fifth discourse begins (V, 1). Musonius's position is that ethical cultivation is more important. Echoing Socrates, Musonius asks his pupils to consider whether they would place their faith in a doctor who could discourse well on healing, or a doctor who could heal patients effectively, and so on? 'Well then', Musonius draws in the analogy, the same should apply concerning moderation (*sôphrosyne*) and self-control (*enkrateia*). It is clearly superior for someone to *be* self-controlled and moderate, not to be able to speak well concerning these things (V, 2–4). Theoretical understanding of such subjects is necessary for correct or skilful action. But the *ethos* takes precedence (*proteroi*), when it comes to affecting peoples' actions (V, 4).

Indeed, in 'Of Exercise', it becomes clear that Musonius thinks that teaching the virtues will require students to undertake practical tests. Theory alone will always fall short. Once a student has learned what a virtue is, Musonius counsels, *askêsis* of different kinds must follow, if benefit is to be yielded from the teachings (VI, 3). Usually, even after we have learned the theoretical tenets of Stoic ethics – that pleasure is not to be desired, death or poverty or pain feared; that virtue is the only good, and so on – when actual hardship comes, or some prospect of pleasure, we act as if we somehow did *not* know these things. What is required, accordingly, since human beings are at once souls and bodies, are different forms of *askêsis*: one form, directed to the soul alone, which is pre-eminent; but another, aimed at the body as well as the *psyché* (VI, 4):

> We use the training common to both when we discipline ourselves to cold, heat, thirst, hunger, meagre rations, hard beds, avoidance of pleasures, and patience under suffering. For by these things and others like them the body is strengthened and becomes capable of enduring hardship, sturdy and ready for any task; the soul too is strengthened since it is trained for courage by patience under hardship and for self-control by abstinence from pleasures. (VI, 5)

Here as we will see in Marcus Aurelius, the training which aims solely at the psyche involves the deep internalization of the Stoics' theoretical tenets, beginning from the *Euthydemus* argument we have seen. Such a philosophical *askêsis*

> consists first of all in seeing that the proofs pertaining to apparent goods as not being real goods are always ready at hand and likewise those pertaining to apparent evils as not being real evils, and in learning to recognize the things which are truly good and in becoming accustomed to distinguish them from what are not truly good. In the next place it consists of practice in not avoiding any of the things which only seem evil, and in not pursuing any of the things which only seem good; in shunning by every means those which are truly evil and in pursuing by every means those which are truly good. (VI, 6)

Unlike Musonius, Seneca the younger wrote at least fourteen philosophical works. Almost all of these have survived since antiquity: these were in fact the only extant Stoic texts available for much of the Middle Ages (Verbeke, 1983). The texts include works of ethics, describing 'The Constancy of the Sage', 'On the Happy Life', 'On Leisure', 'On Tranquillity of Mind', 'On Benefits', and two works on Stoic physics, 'On Providence' and 'Natural Questions'. Each of these texts (5) is framed as an epistolary response to a named interlocutor. Seneca's most renowned work, *The Moral Epistles to Lucilius*, is an extended correspondence of the philosopher with this Lucilius, a Roman equestrian and procurator of Sicily with sympathetic leanings towards Epicureanism. Finally, there are three extant Senecan works of consolation, including one written to his own mother to console her for his exile from Rome.

In an important study, Ilsetraut Hadot (2014; cf. Sharpe, 2018) has argued for the need to conceive of Seneca's philosophical *persona* as that of what she calls a 'spiritual director', if we are to understand his philosophical production. According to her, this figure of the philosophical persona stands in a genealogy looking back in antiquity to divine or semi-guides in the Homeric and Hesiodic poems, like Phoenix for Achilles in the *Iliad* (I. Hadot, 2014: 36), as well as idealized Greek and Roman norms of friendship as the vehicle for 'counsel, conversation, encouragement, consolation, and sometimes even reproof' (Cicero, *De off.* I, 58).

Ilsetraut Hadot's groundbreaking reading of Seneca places great emphasis on the 94th and 95th *Letters to Lucilius* (2014: 19–21, 25–8). In the two letters, Seneca counters the scepticism of Aristo of Chios about the idea that the philosopher could do more than generate general teachings (*placita* or *decreta*) about ethical subjects of the kind we find, for instance, in Aristotle's *Nicomachean Ethics*. In response, Seneca invokes the authority of the second Stoic scholarch, Cleanthes, who commented that to produce a set of ethical teachings without specific precepts to assist students in attaining to the virtues is like 'merely … showing the sick man what he ought to do if he were well, instead of making him well' (*Ep.* 95, 5).

The philosopher interested in shaping practice by philosophical reasoning must also cultivate what Hadot calls a 'paranetic' dimension of philosophy (I. Hadot, 2014: 27). Such *parénésis* presupposes and applies Stoic theoretical claims. It involves forms of persuasive speaking and writing to assist people in attaining to the goods described by theoretical discourses. Paranetic philosophizing hence adds specific precepts addressing particular situation-types and cases to general *decreta*, and forms of exhortative rhetoric to inspire change in students' ways of acting in the world (5) (I. Hadot, 2014: 318). As Seneca underlines:

> If the other arts are content with precepts, wisdom will also be content therewith; for wisdom itself is an art of living. And yet the pilot is made by precepts which tell him thus and so to turn the tiller, set his sails, make use of a fair wind, tack, make the best of shifting and variable breezes – all in the proper manner. Other craftsmen also are drilled by precepts; hence precepts will be able to accomplish the same result in the case of our craftsman in the art of living. (*Ep.* 95, 7)

Seneca's paranetic spiritual direction is clearly manifest in the three consolations for grief which he penned to different, specific addressees. The first thing to note about these texts is that they belong to a venerated ancient literary genre. Hellenistic handbooks of letter-writing list *logoi paramuthikoi,* 'exhortatory' or 'consolatory discourses' as an established epistolary form (Hughes, 1991: 246–8). The sophist Antiphon, a contemporary of Socrates, seems to have already advertised his skill in the genre of 'assuaging grief' through *logoi,* and the Homeric funeral oration provides an even more ancient poetic precedent.[7]

When Seneca turned his mind to these consolatory works, then, he was neither undertaking a counselling task specific to the Stoic philosophers, nor undertaking anything *de novo* (cf. Cicero, *TD* III, 31). Near the beginning of the *Ad Helvium* (**1**), Seneca confesses that he has been 'turning over all the works which the greatest geniuses have composed, for the purpose of soothing and pacifying grief'. Han Baltussen (2009: 71–81; cf. Hope, 2017) has shown the common argument types or topics that span the different sophistic, Platonic, Cynical and Stoic consolations: the reminders that time heals; that others, including noble figures, have suffered worse; that death has delivered the beloved one from the hands of misfortune; that we do not grieve the dead, but for our own loss, which is irrational and not what the beloved would want for us; coupled with exhortations to courage, to study as a noble distraction, and for the grieving one not to neglect their duties, nor to complain against the unchangeable unfolding of providence or fate. Seneca's *Consolation to Marcia* moreover concludes with one of the more extraordinary examples of what Pierre Hadot has called 'the view from above' (**3**). This is a spiritual exercise in reconceiving one's own affairs, which we tend to take as all-consuming, as one miniscule part of a larger order.[8] Seneca uses proposopeia, enjoining Marcia through the mouth of her dead father to reconceive her sorrow in the perspective of an eternity in whose light they appear as very small:

> Imagine then, Marcia, that your father, … in a mood as much more joyful as his abode now is higher than of old, is saying, as he looks down from the height of heaven, 'My daughter, why does this sorrow possess you for so long? Why do you live in such ignorance of the truth, as to think that your son has been unfairly dealt with because he has returned to his ancestors in his prime, without decay of body or mind, leaving his family flourishing? Do you not know with what storms Fortune unsettles everything? … I used to take pleasure in

compiling the history of what took place in one century among a few people in the most out-of-the-way corner of the world: here I enjoy the spectacle of all the centuries ... I may view kingdoms when they rise and when they fall, and behold the ruin of cities and the new channels made by the sea, If it will be any consolation to you in your bereavement to know that it is the common lot of all, be assured that nothing will continue to stand in the place in which it now stands.' (Seneca, *ad Marcia*, 26)

The Moral Epistles to Lucilius remain Seneca's most widely read text, in which we find many arresting statements concerning PWL (esp. *Ep.* 16, 3). The Stoic philosopher aspires to wisdom, so as to achieve a life in harmony with nature. To the extent that philosophy aims to identify and overcome the causes of unhappiness and disharmony, like excessive grief, it is therapeutic (7):

The old Romans had a custom which survived even into my lifetime. They would add to the opening words of a letter: 'If you are well, it is well; I also am well.' Persons like ourselves would do well to say. 'If you are studying philosophy, it is well.' For this is just what 'being well' means. Without philosophy the mind is sickly, and the body, too, though it may be very powerful, is strong only as that of a madman or a lunatic is strong. (*Ep.* 15, 1)

Letter 33 in particular makes clear Seneca's distance from today's conception of philosophical activity, and his own distance from being a mere commentator on others' texts: 'there is nothing of eminence in all such men as these, who never create anything themselves, but always lurk in the shadow of others, playing the role of interpreters, never daring to put once into practice what they have been so long in learning' (*Ep.* 33, 7–8). According to Seneca, the kind of 'all books and no practice' of a figure such as Didymus, reputed to have written some 4,000 tomes, make for a 'boring, wordy, insensitive, and self-satisfied' man. *Letter 88* contains Seneca's famous critique of encyclopaedic learning as 'puny and puerile', to the extent that it is not undertaken as preliminary to the truly liberal 'study of wisdom ... that is lofty, brave, and great-souled' (*Ep.* 88, 37) In this vein, as John Cooper (2004) has criticized, Seneca anticipates later passages in Epictetus, wherein the study of logic is attacked as a distraction: 'Do we really have so much time? Do we already know how to live, and how to die?' (*Ep.* 45, 5; 48, 12; 44,

7) The therapeutic calling of philosophy, Seneca sees, demands the variety of paranetic speech-acts to which Ilsetraut Hadot draws our attention:

> Our master Zeno uses a syllogism like this: 'No evil is glorious; but death is glorious; therefore death is no evil'. A cure, Zeno! ... Will you not utter sterner words instead of rousing a dying man to laughter? Indeed, Lucilius, I could not easily tell you whether he who thought that he was quenching the fear of death by setting up this syllogism was the more foolish, or he who attempted to refute it! (*Ep.* 82, 9; 82, 22; 83, 4; 94, 27)

In these lights, Ilsetraut Hadot reads the *Letters to Lucilius* as a master work of spiritual direction (2014: 116–17). This text, she claims, operates in two complementary dimensions as the 124 letters proceed. In a 'centrifugal' movement, Seneca patiently introduces his pupil to different, more complex elements of the Stoic philosophical discourse, gradually expanding his understanding. *Letters* 1–30 are thus by far the briefest, full of ethical *decreta* in striking, memorable sentences, alongside many from Epicurus, whilst not yet confronting his charge with the porch's 'hard' teachings (*Ep.* 14, 4). In *Letters 31–80*, a second pedagogical stage. Seneca cautions Lucilius concerning rote learning of others' teachings without making ideas truly one's own. Recourse to Epicurus decreases, and Seneca reports sending Lucilius notes, epitomes or summaries of philosophical texts (*Ep.* 39, 1). In the culminating pedagogical stage, *Letters 80–124*, Seneca sends Lucilius full theoretical treatises (notably, the *Naturales Questiones* and *De Providentia*) and promises his student an ethical treatise (I. Hadot, 2014: 116–17). For the first time, he engages in lengthy criticisms of the claims of the Epicureans and other philosophical schools.

As this centrifugal theoretical education unfolds, it is punctuated at every stage by a contrary, centripetal movement 'of concentration, ... reduction to the essential, ... [the] unification of all [Lucilius's] knowledges' around the key principles of the Stoic *regula vitae*. In 'all the most subtle letters as in the treatises', Seneca beckons his addressee back 'to the essential' Stoic principles (I. Hadot, 2014: 117):

> 'But,' you reply, 'I wish to dip first into one book and then into another.' I tell you that it is the sign of an overnice appetite to toy with many dishes ... So you should always read standard authors; and when you crave a change, fall back upon those whom you read before. Each day

acquire something that will fortify you against poverty, against death, indeed against other misfortunes as well; and after you have run over many thoughts, select one to be thoroughly digested that day. (*Ep.* 2, 4)

It is precisely this simultaneous unfolding of a gradually expanded theoretical purview, with a concentrated, ever-renewed understanding of the Stoics' key ethical principles, that Hadot (2014: 117) suggests 'has led modern commentators to believe that the [textual] developments of Seneca lack any coherence'. Once the pedagogical dimension is introduced, this incoherence disappears.

3.4 Epictetus's paranetic discourses, and his handbook

The philosopher Epictetus (*c*.50–*c*.135 CE) was born near Hieropolis, a province of Roman Turkey. The lame slave was acquired by one Epaphroditus, secretary of Emperor Nero. While in Rome, he attended Musonius's lectures, and after manumission, himself began teaching, until he was exiled by Domitian in 96 CE. Epictetus next set up his own school at Nikopolis, the Greek city established by Augustus at Actium. By the end of his life, this provincial school had become famous, attracting students and dignitaries from around the empire, including Emperor Hadrian. Yet, like his heroes Socrates and Diogenes, Epictetus wrote nothing. The writings that today bear his name, like Musonius's lectures, are recorded for us by his student, Arrian. Arrian recorded eight books of *Diatribai*, 'Discourses' or 'Conversations', of which four survive. 'I tried to write down whatever I heard him say, in his own words as far as possible,' Arrian tells us in the epistolary 'Preface': 'to keep notes (*hypomnêmata*) of his thought and frankness (*parrêsia*) for my own future use' (Arrian, 1925).

The results, as with many other texts we are examining, seem to lack a clear ordering principle. The 'discourses' the philosopher deliver respond to questions from students, or to the concerns of visitors to his school. Epictetus employs a host of rhetorical techniques, including acerbic humour. The subject matter of the *Discourses* passes freely between theoretical, methodological, polemical, psychological, social and ethical topics. It is clear that Epictetus's classes devoted considerable time to analysing Chrysippus's texts. Nevertheless, like Seneca, he also stresses that philosophy cannot be identified either with textual exegesis, or the mastery of logic.[9] Philosophy as Epictetus conceives it has an ethical intentionality. 'If you could analyse syllogisms like Chrysippus, what is to prevent you from being wretched, sorrowful, envious, and in a word, being distracted and miserable? Not a single thing,' *Discourses* II, 23, 44 declaims. 'The goal of philosopher's principles is to enable us, whatever happens, to have our *hēgemonikon* [governing faculty] in harmony with nature and to keep it so' (*Disc.* III, 9, 11). Again, we are told that 'philosophising is virtually this – inquiry into how it is possible to apply desire and aversion without impediment' (*Disc.* III, 14, 10; IV, 5, 7). Echoing Socrates's criticisms of Gorgias, Prodicus, Hippias and others, Epictetus reserves some of his harshest criticisms for the orators of the 'second sophistic' of his time, who aspired to win popular fame (Long, 2002: 5–6, 62–3). Unless the discourse of a philosopher, like Musonius Rufus's, prompts its addressees to confront 'that you are in a bad way, and that you take care of everything but what you ought; that you knew not what is good or evil, and are unfortunate and unhappy', then as far as Epictetus is concerned, it has failed (*Disc.* III, 23, 30). 'The school of a philosopher is a surgery *(iatreion)*,' Epictetus instead explains, using the medical meta-philosophical analogy (7):

> You are not to go out of it with pleasure, but with pain; for you do not come there in health; but one of you has a dislocated shoulder; another, an abscess; a third, a fistula; a fourth, the headache. And am I, then, to sit uttering pretty, trifling thoughts and little exclamations, that, when you have praised me, you may each of you go away with the same dislocated shoulder, the same aching head, the same fistula, and the same abscess that you brought? (*Disc.*, III, 23, 30)

It was Pierre Hadot who first showed how we can discern a hidden structuring unity underlying Epictetus's *Discourses* and the *Encheiridion* (or *Handbook*) by recognizing three species of philosophical exercises. Epictetus himself points us in this direction in two key discourses (III, 2; III, 12) in which he aligns three 'topics' of *askêsis* that the '*prokopton*' (one who would make progress) should occupy themselves with three activities of the soul:

> There are three topics in philosophy, in which he who would be wise and good must be exercised. That of the *desires* and *aversions* (*tas orezeis kai ta ekkliseis*), that he may not be disappointed of the one, nor incur the other. That of the *impulses* and *avoidances* (*tas hormas kai aphormas*), and, in general, the duty of life (*to kathêkon*); that he may act with order and consideration, and not carelessly. The third

includes integrity of mind and prudence, and, in general, whatever belongs to assents (*synkatatheseis*). (*Disc.*, III, 2)

Hadot's further claim is that these three practical *topoi* correspond to the three parts of Stoic theoretical discourse we mentioned above: logic, physics and ethics (P. Hadot, 2001: 82–98).[10] So what we think and believe corresponds, in practical life, to the field which theoretical logic analyses. What we do clearly corresponds to what ethicists study. But what we desire and despise, Hadot suggests, corresponds in our practical lives to what physics (the understanding of nature) studies in theory, since our desires involve evaluative assessments of which things in the world are beneficial or harmful.

We see the operation of these three topics, and their connection with Stoic philosophical discourse, by paying specific attention to Epictetus's *Encheiridion*. This little book (the *–idion* is diminutive) has been called by the early modern Neostoic Justus Lipsius 'the soul of Stoic philosophy' (at Sellars, 2014: 129). Compiled by Arrian, and addressed to his friend C. Ulpias Prastina Messalanos, governor of Numidia, it is small enough to be carried around 'in hand', as the title also suggests. The text is divided into fifty-two sections condensing small, memorable formulations epitomizing Epictetus's wider philosophy. Simplicius, a sixth-century Neoplatonic commentator explains the intentionality of the text in the following terms: 'It is called *Encheiridion* because all persons who are desirous to live as they ought, should be perfect in this book, and have it ready to hand (*procheiron*): a book of as constant and necessary use as a sword is to a soldier.'[11]

The task of this text, as a 'manual' for a *prokopton*, is signalled in the opening two sections. Here, advice is proffered to the student in a provisional way, 'for the moment' (*para ta paron/epi tou parantos*), pending

Figure 2.2 The three fields of Stoic practice, using Hadot's idea.

Practical physics: concerning desire (*orezis*) and aversion (*ekklisis*); the relation between what we want and don't want, and the way the world really is (thus 'physics').

Practical ethics: concerning the impulses (*hormai*) to act and not to act, regarding others, and appropriate actions (*kathêkonta*).

Practical logic: concerning our judgements, thoughts and "assents" (*synkatatheseis*): namely, what we accept as true, good or appropriate.

their further advancement. In sections 12-13, 22–25, 29 and 46–52, again, the text addresses itself to someone who 'desires (*epithymeis*) philosophy' (§22). As Seneca's conception of the paranetic calling of the spiritual director would suggest, so the *Encheiridion* is riddled with imperatives: *memnêso* (remember (**2**, **3**)), *epimimnêske seauton* (remind yourself (**4**)). Section 50 in particular stresses the urgency of starting *now* to pay attention (*prosezeis*) to yourself. Section 33 opens with the injunction to take on a rule for conduct of life, and abide by this rule as if it was a law *(nomos)*. There is almost no point of detail about mundane social life that the text fails to consider: whether speaking, laughing, clothing, sexual relations, gossip or meeting different people. In short, the text proffers perhaps the best ancient example of a prescriptive regimen of 'spiritual exercises'. As Simplicius again comments, this time drawing on the old Socratic parallel between training of body and the mind:

> For as the body (*soma*) gathers strength by exercise (*gymnazetai*) and frequently repeating such motions as are natural to it; so the *psyche* too, by exerting its powers, and the practice of such things as are agreeable to nature, conforms itself in habits, and strengthens its own constitution. (cf. Sellars, 2014: 129–31)[12]

There are inescapable difficulties about precisely identifying each individual section of the *Encheirdion* with one of the three exercise disciplines. According to the Stoics, all considerations concerning physical things, and what to desire or avoid, will involve selections amongst perceptions or cognitions: and hence, the exercise of 'logical' vigilance, in examining each representation in the way we have seen Epictetus enjoining above. The same consideration applies to the ethical impulses or *hormai* we form concerning others, and how to respond to their speeches and actions. 'Men are not disturbed by things which happen *(ta pragmata)*, but by the opinions (*dogmata*) about the things' (§5). So the path to either reforming our desires, or treating others ethically passes through the logical reform of our opinions It is no mistake then that the *Manual* opens with the robust articulation of what, in Epictetus, represents a kind of master rule, binding all three topics. 'Of things, some depend upon us [*eph'hêmin*]', Epictetus begins (§1):

> And others do not. In our power are opinion [*hypolêpsis*, topic 3, logic], movement toward a thing [impulse, topic 2], desire, aversion, [topic 1, 'physics'], and in a word, whatever are our own acts. Not in

our power are the body, property, reputation, offices, and in a word, whatever are not our own acts.

Epictetus then continues to articulate his own version of the Stoic 'master argument' from Plato's *Euthydemus*, aiming to show that wisdom or self-mastery alone, not external goods, is the key to happiness:

1. Happiness or tranquillity is the fulfilment of all our desires, not wishing for anything we don't or can't have; and not despising anything we do have or can't avoid;

2. But external goods, including political power, wealth, even bodily health, are never fully or lastingly within our control;

3. Thus, if you take these eternals to be necessary to our happiness, 'you will be hindered, you will lament, you will be disturbed, you will blame both gods and men'; 'perhaps you will not gain even these very things (power and wealth) ... '

The end of this opening section of the *Encheiridion* gives us a leading example of what Hadot intends when he talks about Stoic 'practical logic'. If we follow Epictetus, we will need to actively train ourselves morning and night (*Disc.* III, 16) to distinguish everything we encounter according to whether or not it depends upon us, so we can avoid all unnecessary inner tumults. 'Straightway then practice saying to every harsh appearance, "You are an appearance, and in no manner what you appear to be"', Epictetus exhorts:

Then examine it by the rules which you possess, and by this first and chiefly, whether it relates to the things which are in our power (*eph'hêmin*) this is used above, why repeat the Greek term? or to the things which are not in our power: and if it relates to anything which is not in our power, be ready to say that it does not concern you.

Section 44 gives another example of practical logic, the dispassionate analysis of our beliefs, awake to the kinds of *non sequiturs* that habit and custom can naturalize:

These reasons do not cohere: I am richer than you, therefore I am better than you; I am more eloquent than you, therefore I am better than you. On the contrary these rather cohere, I am richer than you, therefore my possessions are greater than yours: I am more eloquent than you, therefore my speech is superior to yours. But you are neither possession nor speech. (cf. §13, §32)

What Hadot calls, literally, 'lived' (*veçu*) physics is at first glance the hardest idea in Stoic practical philosophy to get a sense of. There seems no manifest link between the disciplining of our desires and aversions and a study of physical things. The operative Stoic idea is simply that such 'externals' in the natural world are the things we typically desire, together with the further psychological observation that often our desires paint these things in illusory lights. Indeed, the Stoics claim, when we desire something – particularly if the desire is strong – the desire presents it for us as what in fact it can never be: necessary or sufficient to secure *our* happiness. The urgency of emotions like desire or fear comes from the ensuing sense of an unconditional need for some external thing or event to occur – or to *last* – or not. The key to practical physics in Epictetus's *Encheiridion*, then, is the famous opening injunction of section 8: 'Seek not that the things which happen should happen as you wish; but wish the things which do happen to be as they are, and you will have a tranquil flow of life.'[13] This injunction reflects the fundamental rule for practical logic, dividing what is and is not in our control. But it also points to how the exercises in practical physics are at base exercises in attempting to see things for what they are, as independently as possible of how we wish or fear them to be. *Encheiridion* section 3 hence directs us:

In everything which pleases the soul, or supplies a want, or is loved, remember to add this to its description: what is the nature of each thing, beginning from the smallest? If you love an earthen vessel, say it is an earthen vessel which you love; for when it has been broken, you will not be so disturbed.

The goal of Stoic practical physics is thus to cultivate – as here, by repeating the exercise with 'everything' we love – the famous inner reservation (*hypexairêsis*) about externals. It is not that we could ever cease encountering externals (money, fame, status symbols etc.). It is just that we should always pursue or avoid them, awake to the way they remain beyond our full possession and control, as someone who in effect says to themselves on each occasion, as soon as their desire is prompted: 'I want my friend to love me, but respect that this is at his discretion,' and so on. 'If you have received the impression of any pleasure, guard yourself against being carried away by it,' we are advised: 'but let the thing wait for you, and allow yourself a certain delay on your own part' (*Ench.* §34; cf. §20). For Epictetus, we will never be able to achieve lasting tranquillity until we learn to see things steadily, in the context of the whole of which they each form transient parts, rather than through the lens of our egoistic fears or desires. It is against this background that sections of the *Handbook* stress the transience of the objects of our desire: 'If you would have your children and your wife and your friends to live forever, you are a fool; for you would have the things which are not in your power to be in your power, and the things which belong to others to be yours' (§14).

The therapy of desire is difficult. So, Epictetus advises (§12) to 'begin then from little things. Is the oil spilled? Is a little wine stolen? Say on the occasion, at such price is sold freedom from perturbation; at such price is sold tranquillity, but nothing is got for nothing' [see **5.2**]. These fragments urging reservation cross over into Stoic prescriptions to premeditate accidents that may happen, and one's death, which certainly will. Section 21 advises the student to 'let death and exile and every other thing which appears dreadful be daily before your eyes (*pro opthalmôn estô soi kath'êmeran*) but most of all death'. Section 17 uses the theatrical metaphor of life as a play, in order to awaken a sense of the urgency of ethical reform. We are but players on the stage, and even if the director has chosen that this performance be brief, it is in our power to perform well.

The sobriety of the Epictetan life is especially clear in those sections concerning the third topic: our ethical comportment and 'duties' (*kathêkonta*) towards others. Sections 22 and 46 warn students not to call themselves philosophers, 'vomiting up theorems' rather than attending quietly to one's conduct. Boasting, flattery and gossip alike are decried as inconsistent with dignity, since they involve untruth and reflect envy at the fortune of others (§§ 25, 33, 46, 49). Section 20 asks us to distinguish any insult we suspect ourselves to have received from our assessment of the insult, and attend to the latter, so as to 'gain time, so as to master yourself'. It is an ethical application of section 5's distinction between things, and our judgments concerning them. 'When any person treats you ill or speaks ill of you, remember that he does this or says this because he thinks that it is appropriate for him', section 44 reminds us. If his opinion is wrong, the fault and damage is his. If he is right, one should try to change. Section 33 advises: 'If a man has reported to you, that a certain person speaks ill of you, do not make any defence (answer) to what has been told you: but reply, "The man did not know the rest of my faults, for he would not have mentioned these only."'

We see each of these exercises carried out with interesting variations in Epictetus's most famous pupil, the philosopher-emperor Marcus Aurelius.

3.5 Marcus Aurelius's *Meditations* (*Ta Eis Heauton*)

Ernst Renan writes movingly of the strange fate that saw the *Meditations* of Marcus Aurelius saved from oblivion, lifted like some Stoic ring of power from the river Gran:

> There came out of it this incomparable book, in which Epictetus was surpassed: this manual of the resigned life, this Gospel of those who do not believe in the supernatural, which has not been able to be understood until our own time. A true eternal Gospel, the *Meditations* will never grow old, for it affirms no dogma ... The religion of Marcus Aurelius is, like that of Jesus was at times, absolute religion: that which speaks from the simple fact of a high moral conscience faced with the universe. It is not of one race, nor of one country, no revolution, no progress, no discovery will be able to change it. (at Hadot, 2001: 307–8)

The author of this Stoic gospel was born in 121 CE. He rose to become the emperor of Rome from 161 to 178 CE. His reign was riven with troubles: the flooding of the Tiber and famine in 161 CE, earthquakes in 161 then 178, constant warring in the eastern provinces, an insurrection in 173 and a devastating plague in 166 which took up to 18 million lives. Nevertheless, Marcus is widely accounted as the last of the five, 'good' Nerva-Antonine Emperors (Cassius Dio, 71, 36, 3–4).[14]

Marcus seems to have undertaken to become a philosopher, adopting the signature philosopher's cloak and electing to sleep on hard boards as young as age twelve. He was taught philosophy in late adolescence by Quintius Junius Rusticus and by Apollonius of Chalcedon, whom Marcus's adoptive father, Antoninus Pius, seems to have paid to come to Rome (*Meds.* I, 8). By 146, Marcus's letters to his rhetoric teacher, Fronto, indicate his conversion to philosophy. Marcus reports reading the Cynicizing Stoic Aristo which 'show me to what extent my inner dispositions (*ingenium*) are distant from these better things, then all too often your disciple blushes and is angry with himself'.[15]

The importance of the fact that these 'notes to himself' were never intended for publication cannot be overstressed.[16] The text's literary form

(5), by contemporary lights, is again confusing. From the seventeenth century onwards, it has been divided into some 473 numbered fragments or sections and twelve books, each containing between sixteen and seventy-five such sections. Yet the originals had no such numbering, and the divisions between the books were not always marked (Hadot, 2001: 28). At the end of our books II and III, we read that the forgoing text has been 'written in the land of the Quades ... at Canratum'. This allows us to date these parts of the text in the last decade of Marcus's life, when he was on campaign. The sections of the text are of varying length. Some are mere aphorisms: 'receive wealth without arrogance and be ready to let it go' (*Meds.* VIII, 33); 'consider that benevolence is invincible' (IX, 18); and 'the best revenge is to not become like he who has harmed you' (VI, 6). Many have literary beauty, whilst others feature more impersonal philosophical reflections spanning pages. There is a great deal of repetition, with no single argumentative arc spanning beginning, middle, to end.[17]

Where other commentators have not known how to understand this text, Pierre Hadot in *The Inner Citadel* and elsewhere has presented a compelling PWL interpretation, comparable in vision to that of his wife concerning Seneca's *oeuvre*. In several fragments of Epictetus's *Discourses*, which Marcus admired, Epictetus enjoins students to write down, every day, the principles and prescriptions of Stoic philosophy: 'These are the thoughts that those who pursue philosophy should ponder, these are the lessons they should write down day by day, in these they should exercise themselves' (*Disc.* I, 1, 25).[18] Marcus's *Meditations*, Hadot contends, represent a Stoic set of *hypomnêmata* (literally, aids to memory) answering to Epictetus's exhortation: a kind of writing as spiritual exercise (3). As Michel Foucault has written of this kind of ancient text in *The Hermeneutics of the Subject*:

> *Hypomnêmata,* in the technical sense, could be account books, public registers, or individual notebooks serving as memory aids. Their use as books of life, as guides for conduct, seems to have become a common thing for a whole cultivated public. One wrote down quotes in them, extracts from books, examples, and actions that one had witnessed or read about, reflections or reasonings that one had heard or that had come to mind ... They also formed a raw material for the drafting of more systematic treatises, in which one presented arguments and means for struggling against some weakness (such as anger, envy, gossip, flattery) or for overcoming some difficult circumstance (a grief, an exile, ruin, disgrace). (Foucault, 1983)

Hyopmnêmata were, in Ilsetraut Hadot's formulation (I. Hadot, 2014: 116–17), writings enabling the centripetal concentration and internalization of core philosophical tenets. Their aim is what is sometimes described in the ancient texts through the analogy of a 'dyeing' (*baptizein*) of the soul (*Meds.* V, 16; III, 4; cf. Sellars, 2014, 120–2;), or its 'digestion' of philosophical tenets, as in Seneca's 84th *Letter*.[19] Marcus uses the metaphor of a fire which needs ongoing tending if it is not to flicker out:

> How can our principles become dead, unless the impressions [thoughts] which correspond to them are extinguished? But it is in your power continuously to fan these thoughts into a flame. I can have that opinion about anything, which I ought to have. If I can, why am I disturbed? (*Meds.* VII, 2; cf. IV, 3, 1)

The Stoic practice of writing *hypomnemata*, to deeply internalize Stoic principles, closely relates to the Stoic exercise of the examination of conscience (**3**) which Seneca in *On Anger*, for instance, prescribes as an exercise to be undertaken at the end of each day (*De ira* III, 36). The link of this practice with writing, as a means to prompt this examination, is explicit in Seneca's *Epistle 83*. Here, Seneca responds to Lucilius's request to 'give [him] an account of each separate day, and of the whole day too'. Again, as in Epictetus's *Encheiridion*, we should not be surprised at the frequency with which Marcus addresses himself in the second person imperative, effectively exhorting himself: 'remember (*memnêso*) how long you have been putting off these things' (II, 4); 'remember that it is a shame to be surprised if fig trees produce figs ' (VIII, 15); 'It is necessary then to (*Chrê men oun*) ... ' (III, 4, 2)[20] As Hadot has memorably claimed of the *Meditations*:

> if this book [the *Meditations*] is still so attractive to us, it is because when we read it we get the impression of encountering not the Stoic system ... but a man of good will, who does not hesitate to criticise and to examine himself, who constantly takes up again the task of exhorting and persuading himself, and of finding the words which will help him to live, and to live well ... In world literature, we find lots of preachers, lesson-givers, and censors, who moralise to others with complacency, irony, cynicism, or bitterness, but it is extremely rare to find a person training himself to live and to think like a human being ... the personal effort appears ... in the repetitions, the multiple variations developed around the same theme and the stylistic effort

as well, which always seeks for a striking, effective formula. (Hadot, 2001: 312–13)

Hadot contends that many of the sections of Marcus's *Meditations* represent the writing down, as in a condensed shorthand, of the key Stoic precepts or *kephalaia*. Thus, we find a series of one-line aphorisms, denuded of all justificatory reasoning:

Pleasure and pain are not true goods or evils (IV, 3, 6; XII, 8).
That the only shameful thing is ethical failure (II, 1, 3).
That harms committed against us cannot harm us (II, 1, 3; XII, 26; IV, 26, 3).

Other fragments read more like rapid-fire lists of such *Kephalaia*, written down as a mnemonic exercise, like XII, 26:

When you are troubled about anything, you have forgotten this: that all things happen according to the universal nature; ... that a man's wrongful act is nothing to thee; and further ... that everything which happens, always happened so and will happen so, and now happens so everywhere; ... how close is the kinship between a man and the whole human race, for it is a community, not of a little blood or seed, but of intelligence. And you have forgotten this too, that every man's intelligence is a god, and is an efflux of the deity; and ... that nothing is a man's own, but that his child and his body and his very soul came from the deity; ... that everything is opinion; and lastly ... that every man lives the present time only, and loses only this. (Cf. *Meds.* II.1; IV.3; VII.22.2; VIII.21.2; XI.18; XII.7; XII.8)

A third species of fragment sees Marcus returning to a single exercise theme, in order to imaginatively and rhetorically vary its presentation to make it especially vivid. Perhaps the best example of this is an exercise in practical physics for recalling the universality and constancy of change or *metabolê*, and the transience of all things (cf. Stephen, 2002: 101–24). In IV, 32, Marcus compares his times with those of Vespasian, to remind himself *by examples* that all of its concerns and protagonists are now gone:

Consider, for example, the times of Vespasian. You will see all these things, people marrying, bringing up children, sick, dying, warring, feasting, trafficking, cultivating the ground, flattering, obstinately arrogant, suspecting, plotting, wishing for some to die, grumbling about the present, loving, heaping up treasure, desiring consulship, kingly power. Well then, that life of these people no longer exists at all. (cf. *Meds*. V, 32; VIII, 31; VI, 47; IV, 50; VI, 24; VII, 19, 2; VII, 48; VIII, 25; VIII, 37; IX, 30; XII, 27)

The same three Epictetan exercise topics of physics (the discipline of desire), logic (of thought), and ethics (of impulses) nevertheless run like a red thread through the *Meditations*, Hadot shows us (cf. *Meds*. VII, 54; IX, 6; IV, 33; VIII, 7; IX, 7). This is not to say that Marcus does not bring anything new to these exercises. In particular, Marcus returns to several apparently 'pessimistic' exercises in practical physics, aimed at the chastening of desire, which either do not appear in Epictetus, or are not emphasized (Stephens, 2002: 125–34). In one such exercise, for instance, Marcus enjoins himself to look objectively and analytically at those objects or human beings that provoke his desire:

Make for yourself a definition (*poieisthai horon*) or description of the thing which is presented to you, so as to see distinctly what kind of a thing it is in its substance, in its nudity (*gymnon*), in its complete entirety (*holon*), and tell yourself its proper name (*onoma*), and the names of the things of which it has been compounded, and into which it will be resolved. (*Meds*. III, 11)

As most famously in VI, 13, the aim here is precisely to calm irrational desire by restoring a larger sense to the things which captivate us, viewed in light of the larger whole:

When we have meat before us and such foods, we receive the impression, that this is the dead body of a fish, and this is the dead body of a bird or of a pig; and again, that this Falernian [wine] is only a little grape juice, and this purple robe some sheep's wool dyed with the blood of a shell-fish: or, sexual intercourse, a rubbing together of guts followed by the spasmodic excretion of sticky fluid–such then are these impressions, and they reach the things themselves and penetrate them, and so we see what kind of things they are. Just in the same way ought we to act all through life, and where there are things which appear most worthy of our approbation, we ought to lay them bare and look at their worthlessness, and strip them of all the words by which they are exalted.

On the other hand, the *Meditations* include remarkable sections which less 'focus in' upon the prosaic details of captivating impressions, so much as 'pan out' from these particulars, towards what Hadot has called the 'view from above': 'Look down from above on the countless herds of men and their countless solemnities, and the infinitely varied voyagings in storms and calms, and the differences among those who are born, who live together, and die' (*Meds.* IX, 30). While this exercise appears in Seneca, and infrequently in Epictetus, Marcus returns to and varies it in his own ways. It is not simply the minuteness of human concerns, in a spatial scale, that Marcus stresses, as it, for instance, is in Seneca's *Consolation to Marcia* or his *Natural Questions*. Adopting the historical optic we have already seen, it is more often the lack of novelty or *sameness* that looking at human events in a larger perspective opens to Marcus's purview which emerges:

If you should suddenly be raised up above the earth, and should look down on human beings, and observe the variety of them how great it is, and at the same time also should see at a glance how great is the number of beings who dwell all around in the air and the ether, consider that as often as you should be raised up, you would see the same things, sameness of form and shortness of duration. Are these things to be proud of? (*Meds.* XII, 27; VII, 48)

We thus see palpably how to live as a Stoic, for Marcus, is to call into question many of the customarily received understandings of what things are, and which have selective value (**9**). But none of this is idiosyncratic (Hadot, 1973; 2020c). Hadot notes that in several sections Marcus calls upon himself to divide things exactly according to the four basic categories of Stoic physics: their matter; form and/or cause; duration; and role in the wider cosmos (*Meds.* II.4; III.11; IV.21; VIII.11; IX.25; IX.37; X.9; XII.10; Hadot, 1973, 155, n. 1). The aim of Stoic practical physics is to engender 'greatness of soul' (*megalopsychia*), the ability to metaphorically 'look down upon' (*kataphronêsin*) (XI, 2) what others take to be vital – external goods and affairs, subject to fortune:

For nothing is so productive of elevation of mind (*megalophrosynê*) as to be able to examine methodically and truly every object which is presented to you in life, and always to look at things so as to see at the same time what kind of universe this is, and what kind of use everything performs in it, and what value everything has with reference to the whole, and what with reference to man ... ; what each thing is [form], and of what it is composed [matter], and how long it is the nature of this thing to endure [duration] which now makes an impression on me, and what virtue I have need of with respect to it [relation to self], such as gentleness, manliness, truth, fidelity, simplicity, contentment, and the rest. (*Meds.* III, 11)

What Marcus is aiming at is that 'good flow' of life, 'in agreement with nature' that Zeno had announced as the Stoics' aim (DL VII, 88–9). In the famous section from book IV (*Meds.* IV, 3) from whence Hadot takes his title for *The Inner Citadel*, Marcus gives his own compelling image of this goal (7). The exercise of the *technê* that aims at wisdom is the construction of an 'inner citadel', a place of tranquillity closed off from fortune and its vicissitudes:

Men seek retreats (*anachôreseis*) for themselves, houses in the country, seashores, and mountains; and thou too art wont to desire such things very much. But this is altogether a mark of the most common sort of men, for it is in your own power whenever you shall choose to retire into yourself. For nowhere, either with more quiet or more freedom from trouble, does a man retire than into his own soul, particularly when he has within him such thoughts that by looking into them he is immediately in perfect tranquillity ... This then remains: remember to retire into this little territory of your own, and, above all, do not distract or strain yourself, but be free, and look at things as a man, as a human being, as a citizen, as a mortal. (*Meds.* IV, 3)

From this Stoic elevation, we turn next to examine the competing visions of the philosophical life we find in the Platonists.

CHAPTER 4
PLATONISMS AS WAYS OF LIFE

4.1 Introduction: Platonisms

The Platonic Academy was the first ancient school. It survived in different forms until being finally shut by Emperor Justinian in 529 CE, a date often cited as the definitive end of antiquity. But there was not 'one' Platonism, any more than the literary and pedagogical resources bequeathed to posterity by Plato are unequivocal. Plato authored thirty-five dialogues and fourteen letters, several of whose authenticity remains contested. Yet he was also an outspoken critic, in writing, of the efficacy of writing for practising philosophy.[1] Many of the Platonic dialogues are *aporetic*, like the *Laches, Charmides, Lysis, Ion* or *Euthyphro*. Socrates proceeds dialectically, challenging others' opinions concerning some virtue, like moderation in the *Charmides* or piety in the *Euthyphro*. He ends by professing his own ignorance. Other Platonic dialogues, like the *Republic* or *Laws*, are more apparently programmatic. Yet commentators still divide as to their meanings.

There is thus small wonder that, in the generations after Plato's death, rival legatees of the master duly emerged. On the one hand, beginning with the first scholarchs after Plato, some Platonists developed elaborate metaphysical and theological systems, at the farthest removes from all scepticism.[2] On the other hand, after Arcesilaus (315–240 BCE) forms of 'academic' scepticism developed, which questioned the very possibility of knowledge, physical or metaphysical.

There is little extant evidence concerning life and pedagogy within the Academy. Debates will almost certainly continue as long as Western philosophy does concerning Plato's programmatic intentions.[3] It is proverbial that Plato placed over the gate of the Academy the challenge that anyone not educated in mathematics need not enter. We know also that the medieval curriculum of the seven liberal arts [**5.3**] evolved out of Plato's recommendations for the ideal philosophical education in *Republic* VII, including what would become the 'quadrivium' of arithmetic, geometry, astronomy and music (I. Hadot, 2005). Whatever the precise teaching programme of the Old Academy, the definitions of philosophy and its intentions that survive from its votaries confirm philosophy's eudaimonistic conception. Speusippus defined happiness as 'the state of perfection in natural things', and appears to have identified this as involving *aochlēsia*, 'freedom of disturbance', although Diogenes Laertius tells us he was himself a slave to pleasure (DL IV, 1; Dillon, 1996: 18). Xenocrates defined philosophy as aiming at 'the elimination of all sources of disturbance in life' (at Dillon, 1996: 33), and happiness as involving 'life according to nature', echoing Stoic definitions (Dillon, 1996; 33; Thorsrud, 2009: 38). Polemo, who famously converted to philosophy after a night of debauch, likewise stressed philosophy's ethicist calling:

> Polemo used to say that a man ought to exercise himself in action, and not in dialectic speculations, as if one had drunk in and dwelt upon a harmonious kind of system of art, so as to be admired for one's shrewdness in putting questions; but to be inconsistent with one's self in character. (DL, IV, 18; cf. Dillon, 1996: 40–1)

As we shall see, this eudemonistic conception of the *telos* of philosophy (7), if little else, continued to unite the sceptical legatees of Arcesilaus and the more metaphysical forms of Platonism until the closure of the Academy.

4.2 From Arcesilaus to Pyrrhonism: scepticism as a way life

'At first', we are told, the sceptical Academicians 'defended the position adopted by the School from Plato and Speusippus up to Polemo' (*Index Academica*, col. 18, at Thorsrud, 2009: 39). Nevertheless, Arcesilaus questioned the epistemological credentials of Plato's metaphysical claims. He came to maintain that in Plato's dialogues 'nothing is affirmed, there are many arguments on either side, everything is under investigation, and nothing is claimed to be certain' (Cicero, *Ac.* I, 46). According to Cicero's account in *De Academia*, Arcesilaus followed Socrates in arriving at a sceptical confession of ignorance. He did so by reflecting upon the limitations of our minds and senses, and the shortness of life:

> For these reasons, [Arcesilaus] thought that we shouldn't assert or affirm anything or approve it with assent: we should always curb our rashness and restrain ourselves from any slip. But he considered it

particularly rash to approve something false or unknown, because nothing was more shameful than for one's assent or approval to outrun knowledge or apprehension. (*Ac.* I, 45; cf. DL IV, 28, 32)

Instead, Arcesilaus proposed what would come to be called in Pyrrhonism the *epochē* or suspension of judgement as the key to wisdom: a refusal to assent to anything definitively about the way the world is.[4] We have already met, in Stoicism, the refusal to give one's assent to doubtful beliefs, for instance about others' behaviour, as a means to temper a passion like anger. In Arcesilaus's scepticism, the argument is that *all* our beliefs, even the most apparently indubitable, are finally uncertain, and as such demand the withholding of our assent (IV, 32; Thorsrud, 2009: 44–5). Arcesilaus accordingly set to work to justify his position by directing arguments against the other philosophies, 'to show that there is no impression from something true such that there could not be one just like it from something false' (Cicero, *Ac.* II, 77; cf. *De or.,* III, 67; Thorsrud, 2009: 45–7).

With the Pyrrhonian scepticism inaugurated by Aenesidemus in the first century BCE, Arcesilaus's sceptical orientation was radicalized. Only fragments are known of Pyrrho of Elis's own life (*c.* 365–270 BCE). Several of these fragments suggest that Pyrrho travelled to India with Alexander and conversed there with the 'gymnosophists' (naked wise men), bringing back Eastern, aporetic wisdom to Greece (Beckwith, 2015). However that may be, we know that Pyrrho originally conceived of philosophy as concerned, first of all, with how to live; and that only in this light did his radical scepticism emerge (**8**). 'The person who is to be happy', Pyrrho's disciple Timon tells us, must for Pyrrho 'look to these three points: first, what are things like by nature? Second, in what way ought we to be disposed towards them? And finally, what will be the result for those who are so disposed?' (Aristocles, at Thorsrud, 2009: 19) Pyrrho's responses however set apart his conception of the philosophical *bios* from those of the 'dogmatic' schools, as the Sceptics labelled their competitors:

> [Timon] says that [Pyrrho] reveals that things are equally indifferent and unstable and indeterminate (*adiaphora kai astathmêta kai anepikrita*); for this reason, neither our perceptions nor our beliefs tell the truth or lie. For this reason, … we should not trust them, but should be without opinions and without inclinations and without wavering, saying about each single thing that it no more is than is not, or both is and is not, or neither is nor is not (*ou mallon estin ê ouk*

estin ê kai esti kai ouk estin ê oute estin oute ouk estin). (Aristocles, at Thorsrud, 2009: 19)

The fullest extant account of Pyrrhonism is Sextus Empiricus's *Outlines of Scepticism*, a work whose rediscovery in the renaissance was, via Montaigne, to have a profound effect in shaping early modern philosophy [**6.3**]. 'Scepticism is an ability *(dynamis)* which opposes appearances to judgments in any way whatsoever', Sextus tells us, 'with the result that, owing to the equipollence (*isosthenia*) of the objects and reasons thus opposed, we are brought firstly to a state of mental suspense (*epôchê*) and next to a state of *ataraxia*' (Sextus, *Hyp.* I, 8).

Several things jump out from this definition. First, philosophy is a *dynamis*, not a *technê*, as for the Stoics [**3.1**]. A *technê* implies systematic bodies of knowledge, a *dynamis* need not do so. Secondly, the key notion of *isosthenia* differentiates the Pyrrhonists' 'critique of judgment' from those of the dogmatic Hellenistic schools which in some respects it resembles. At issue in this *isosthenia* is the conviction of the equal persuasiveness or 'probability' of the truth or falsity of any two beliefs (Sextus, *Hyp.*, I, 33).

Thirdly and above all, the Pyrrhonists adopt the same term, *ataraxia*, that the Epicureans used to describe the goal of philosophizing. Pyrrho, it seems, had first sought this inner tranquillity by trialling the different dogmatic philosophies of life. It was by a kind of happy failure that he was led to his 'Pyrrhonism':

> The Sceptic ... had the same experience which is said to have befallen the painter Apelles. Once, they say, when he was painting a horse and wished to represent ... the horse's foam, he was so unsuccessful that he gave up the attempt and flung at the picture the sponge on which he used to wipe the paints off his brush, and the mark of the sponge produced the effect of a horse's foam. So, too, the Sceptics were in hopes of gaining quietude by means of a decision regarding the disparity of the objects of sense and of thought, and being unable to effect this they suspended judgment; and they found that quietude, as if by chance (*hoion tuchikôs*), followed upon their *epôchê*, even as a shadow follows its substance. (Sextus, *Hyp.* I, 28–9)

Sextus's explanation for this happy accident again radicalizes a direction present in Stoicism and Epicureanism. This tied the *pathê* to forms of erroneous evaluative judgements, and conceived philosophy's therapeutic efficacy as involving the correction of these beliefs. It is just that, for Pyrrhonism, there are *no* certain evaluative judgements which survive sceptical examination. Indeed, it is the contrary supposition that underlies our mental sufferings, for

> the man who opines that anything is by nature good or bad is for ever being disquieted: when he is without the things which he deems good he believes himself to be tormented by things naturally bad and he pursues after the things which are, as he thinks, good; which when he has obtained he keeps falling into still more perturbations because of his irrational and immoderate elation, and in his dread of a change of fortune. (Sextus, *Hyp.* I, 27–28)

As again in the Stoics and Epicureans, Pyrrhonists are enjoined to have *procheiron* maxims like 'to every argument an equal argument is opposed' (Sextus, *Hyp.* I, 10, 209), to assist them on an ongoing basis in withholding assent to any positive assertions. Certain tell-tale qualifiers, amounting to a kind of permanent discipline of judgement (**3**), mark their discourses. The sceptic thus never categorically asserts that 'this is square' but say things like 'this is not more square than not square', or 'perhaps this is a square'; 'maybe', 'possibly', 'maybe not … this is a square'; 'I am unable to say that … ' (Sextus, *Hyp.* I, §§19–22).

Decisive for the lived practice of scepticism, indeed, are a series of argument-types known as 'Modes [*tropoi*]'. These the student should have at ready command, in order to live a Pyrrhonian life (**2, 3**). Like the rhetorical 'topics', memorized forms of plausible argumentation the orator could call upon to invent speeches, these sceptical modes can be used on nearly any occasion, when the sceptic is confronted with someone asserting a determinate, affirmative claim. Aenesidemus, as reported by Sextus, adduced ten such 'modes':

1. That different animals have different senses, and evidently perceive the world differently than we do, so we cannot be certain that what we perceive is (the most) accurate;
2. That like differences are evident between individual human beings, with like epistemic implications;
3. That for the same person, information perceived through the senses is sometimes self-contradictory, hence doubtful;

4. That what we perceive, even of the apparently same things, varies over time and depends for example on one's state of mind, whether we are dreaming or awake etc.;

5. That the data we receive through our senses is perspectival, differing according to local relations (the sun, for example, looks as big as a small ball to the naked eye, etc.);

6. That objects are experienced by us indirectly, and thus uncertainly, through the media of air, light, moisture etc.;

7. That objects seem to be in a condition of perpetual change in colour, temperature, size and motion, so our impressions of them must be uncertain;

8. That all our perceptions are relative to other perceptions, and interact one upon another, rendering each uncertain;

9. That our impressions tend to become less discerning through repetition, habit and custom;

10. Finally, that all men are brought up with different beliefs, under different laws and social conditions, rendering each perspective uncertain (i.e. cultural relativism). (Sextus, *Hyp.*, 1, 35–163, *Against Theoreticians* 7.345; see DL IX, 79–88; Philo, *On Drunkenness*, 35–162.)

To this sceptical arsenal, Agrippa (first century CE) developed five converging modes which again serve to motivate *epôchê* and produce its attendant *ataraxia*:

1. The argument from *diaphônia*: that in all matters, even the most learned disagree;

2. The argument *eis apeiron ekballonta* (or 'infinite *regress*'): that any reason brought forward to explain something needs something else in its turn to make *it* credible, and so on ad infinitum;

3. The argument *pros ti*, attesting to the *relativity of any perception* to the subject judging and to the things observed together with it (herein we find many of Aenisedums' ten modes);

4. The argument that *first principles are indemonstrable (anapodeiktôs)*: that all positions which demonstrate anything must rest on axioms or beliefs that *themselves* cannot be justified by the system they justify;

5. The argument *ton diallêlon*: that the proposition which ought to ground or confirm a given investigated matter itself very often requires confirmation (*pistis*) from that very matter, in a circular manner (Sextus, *Hyp.* I, 163–167).

Pyrrhonism has an ambivalent standing vis-a-vis the conception of PWL which we are examining. On the one hand, Pyrrhonism is itself advertised as one philosophical form of life, uniquely conducive to the *ataraxia* that the other schools had allegedly failed to achieve. On the other hand, it is a philosophical therapy for a few, struck by the riddles which present themselves to the senses and mind; as against a philosophy for the many, addressing the passions common to all (Sextus, *Hyp.* I, 12–13). Pyrrhonism seemingly leads one to be sceptical about the very possibility of any wisdom at all – let alone a wisdom which would have to rest on more or less *katalapetikê* impressions whose existence the Pyrrhonist doubts, on the basis of a decision to pursue *some particular* way of life which necessarily preceded the philosophical training to be undertaken (cf. Lucian, *Hermotimus*). Finally, Pyrrhonism's doubts about even the most everyday, functional beliefs seem so radical as to lead necessarily either to *apraxia*, the inability to navigate through practical life, or to a paradoxical conformism to whichever *nomoi* the Pyrrhonist finds in the society around him. The Pyrrhonist will not believe in these standards and conventions. Like the postmodernists of yesterday, he is equally unable to furnish constructive alternatives (Sextus, *Hyp.* I, 23–24).

4.3 Cicero: the philosopher as rhetorician and physician of the soul

Marcus Tullius Cicero (106–43 BCE), the author of two books (*De Academica* I & II) on the Academic scepticism that developed after Arcesilaus, repeats his own allegiance to a 'probabilistic' scepticism, as practised by Carneades, the Academic sceptic who came to Rome in 155 BCE and scandalized the Senatorial elite by showing himself equally adept at arguing for and against the cause of natural justice. For Cicero as for the Pyrrhonists, there is nothing 'rasher and more unworthy of the dignity and strength of character of a wise man than the holding of a false opinion, or the unhesitating defence of what has not been grasped and realised with proper thoroughness' (*De div.* I, 1) Yet, for Cicero – who was also, as we know, a leading Roman statesman, advocate and orator – Pyrrhonism leads to crippling *apraxia* and the inability to reason productively on normative questions. 'We Academicians are not men whose minds wander in uncertainty and never know what principles to adopt,' Cicero explains in *De Officiis* (II, 7–8):

> For what sort of mental habit, or rather what sort of life would that be which should dispense with all rules for reasoning or even for living? Not so with us; but, as other schools maintain that some things are certain, others uncertain, we, differing with them, say that some things are probable, others improbable. What, then, is to hinder me from accepting what seems to me to be probable, while rejecting what seems to be improbable, and from shunning the presumption of dogmatism, while keeping clear of that recklessness of assertion which is as far as possible removed from true wisdom?

Disputes surround Cicero's exact philosophical intentions. His *De Finibus* contains the longest continuous ancient presentation of Stoic philosophy (placed in the mouth of Cato the Younger). His *Stoic Paradoxes* presents these infamous propositions in attractive guise to Roman readers. *De Officiis*, addressed to his son, bears deep debts to the Stoicism of Panaetius. And much of *Tusculan Disputations*, including the account of the *pathê* in books III–IV can be read as thoroughly Stoic. Yet, at other times, Cicero expresses great admiration for Peripatetic philosophy, in particular for the aids it provides to the orator (Siegel, 1968: 24–5). William H. F. Altman (2016c) has recently put a case for Cicero's metaphysical Platonism, as in 'Scipio's Dream' from *De Republica* VI and the proofs for the soul's immortality in *Tusculan Disputations* I (11–31). Perhaps it is safest to say that Cicero was meaningfully eclectic, with the proviso that this eclecticism itself is justified by him in terms of his Academic allegiances:

> That liberty which no one has the privilege of using in philosophy but those of our school, whose discourses determine nothing, but take in everything, leaving them, unsupported by the authority of any particular person, to be judged of by others, according to their weight. (*TD* V, 29; cf. IV, 4)

Alongside two works of political philosophy, *De Republica* and *De Legibus* (both *c.* 53–52 BCE), Cicero wrote *twelve* philosophical dialogues in the last three years of his life, after Julius Caesar's *coup d'état*. The sweep of their subjects from metaphysics to practical ethics, alongside his several texts on rhetoric, reflects Cicero's conviction that philosophy involves inquiry concerning things human and divine [see **3.1**], if not a claim to certain knowledge thereof (*De off.* I, 43). Of particular note in our context are two lost dialogues, the first (*Hortensius*) a protreptic text defending philosophy against the charges of its uselessness for serious men (Ruch ed., 1958); the second, a *Consolatio ad se* Cicero penned to console himself after the devastating loss, in childbirth, of his daughter, Tullia, in 45 BCE (Baltussen, 2013).

The Prefaces of Cicero's surviving dialogues yield many of the most sustained, extant statements we have attesting to the predominant classical conception of philosophy as a way of life or therapy for the psyche (**6**) (see Ruch, 1958; Baraz, 2012). As the first Roman author, alongside Lucretius, to write philosophy in Latin and a renowned republican politician, Cicero acutely felt the need to protreptically justify his interest in philosophy, and to show why politically minded Romans should share this interest. Cicero tells us severally that his writing of philosophy, and the leisure it required, was forced upon him by the fall of the republic. Indeed, to write philosophy was a continuation of his *vita activa* by other means:

> After serious and long continued reflection as to how I might do good to as many people as possible and thereby prevent any interruption of my service to the State, no better plan occurred to me than to conduct my fellow-citizens in the ways of the noblest learning – and this, I believe, I have already accomplished through my numerous books. (*De div.* 2; cf. Seneca, *Do otio*, 3–4)

One signature of Cicero's philosophy is therefore his simultaneous attraction to the joys of contemplation and his continuing insistence that public duty is nevertheless the superior end of life (**8**):

> Again, that wisdom which I have given the foremost place is the knowledge of things human and divine, which is concerned also with the bonds of union between gods and men and the relations of man to man. If wisdom is the most important of the virtues ... [however,] ... service is better than mere theoretical knowledge, for the study and knowledge of the universe would somehow be lame and defective, were no practical results to follow ... And so, if that virtue [justice] which centres in the safeguarding of human interests, that is, in the maintenance of human society, were not to accompany the pursuit

of knowledge, that knowledge would seem isolated and barren of results. (*De off.* I, 43–44)

As for philosophy's justification in martial Rome, Cicero repeatedly stresses its 'practicist' aims to combat its detractors (**6**). Far from a source of moral dissipation, philosophy inculcates the virtues necessary for the good citizen.[5] Indeed, philosophy is capable of furnishing ethical and therapeutic counsel for nearly all the vicissitudes of life. In a single encomium to philosophy in the Preface to *Tusculan Disputations* V, philosophy is successively invoked as law-founding ('to you it is that we owe the origin of cities; you it was who called together the dispersed race of men into social life ... '), law-making ('you have been the inventress of laws; you have been our instructress in morals and discipline'), an asylum ('to you we fly for refuge; from you we implore assistance') as well as a 'guide for life' of the greatest service, which has 'bestowed on us tranquillity of life, and removed the fear of death' (TD V, 2).

It is in the Preface to *Tusculan Disputations* III, however, that we find one of the most influential depictions of philosophy as a *medicina animi* in the Western heritage (**6**):

> What reason shall I assign, O Brutus, why, as we consist of mind and body, the art of curing and preserving the body should be so much sought after, and the invention of it, as being so useful, should be ascribed to the immortal Gods; but the medicine of the mind should not have been so much the object of inquiry ... ? ... Philosophy is certainly the medicine of the soul (*medicina animi*), whose assistance we do not seek from abroad, as in bodily disorders, but we ourselves are bound to exert our utmost energy and power in order to effect our cure. (DL I, 1; I, 3)

Cicero's stress in this central Proemium in the *Tusculan Disputations* reflects the therapeutic practice of philosophy that we find within this text, in clear contrast to his political and rhetorical dialogues (**7**). The *Tusculan Disputations*, after Seneca's *Letters to Lucilius*, is perhaps the longest dedicated text of philosophical therapy in the Graeco-Roman tradition. Its five dialogues take as their objects the fear of death (book I), pain (II), the emotions (III) and grief (III), before a closing dialogue examines the virtues of the sage (V). Books III and IV feature an extended extant treatment of the Stoic theory of the four genii of *pathê* (grief, joy, fear and hope) – united by their founding, erroneous conviction that we need to possess or avoid some present or future external thing/s to be happy [**3.2**] (Graver, 2007: 10–12, 30–46).[6] 'The whole cause [of mental suffering] ... is in opinion', Cicero agrees with Socrates, the Stoics, Epicureans and Sceptics (**6**). For instance, grief arises 'from an opinion of some present evil, which includes this belief, that it is incumbent on us to grieve' (TD III, 31). It follows, for Cicero as for the Stoics, that philosophy's therapeutic efficacy rests upon its capacity to overturn such erroneous beliefs. The dialogues that make up the *Tusculan Disputations* each form, with this in view, spiritual exercises (**3**) that Cicero stages both for his readers and *ad se*, as he grieves the deaths of both Tullia and the Roman Republic (Baltussen, 2009; Altman, 2016c: chapters 4–5).

We focus here on Cicero's consolations for grief. *Tusculan Disputations* rehearses an eclectic regimen of different remedies for this *pathos*.[7] These go from the strict Stoic suggestion that the cure lies in convincing the bereaved that they have suffered no evil, and recalling *exempla* of others who have survived similar losses, to the argument we also find in Seneca, that it is folly to continue grieving when it does not help either the dead or the living (TD III, 32–3). Nevertheless, Cicero recommends a doctor's or *rhetorician's* sensitivity to the particularity of cases. Several of the proposed Stoic consolations, including the argument that what most prevents people from overcoming grief for a loved one is their own opinion that they *should* grieve, will in many cases be simply too demanding for sufferers, although they are theoretically valid (TD III, 33). For Cicero, the philosophical physician must tailor his medicinal arguments to his different patients, and to the specifics of each case. Cicero also shows himself aware of how deep-set peoples' 'pathological' opinions often are, and how recalcitrant they prove to simply argumentative cures. A regimen of daily practices (**3**) is necessary to prevent mourning from becoming melancholia. As Cicero writes, in a passage which we may suppose reflects his own difficulties:

> We have the greatest proof that the strength of it [the *pathos*] depends not merely on time, but on the daily consideration of it. For if the cause continues the same, and the man be the same, how can there be any alteration in the grief ... ? Therefore, it is from daily reflecting that there is no real evil in the circumstance for which you grieve ... that you procure a remedy for your grief. (TD III, 20)

Cicero's central place in our history of PWL does not however rest solely upon his protreptic defences of philosophy as *medicina animi*, nor even upon his illustrative, eclectic practice of this *medicina* in the *Tusculan Disputations*, *Cato Major* (on old age), and the lost *Consolatio ad se*. In the Renaissance [**6.1**, **6.2**], it would be Cicero's double-identity as both philosopher and *rhetorician* that would underlie his abiding influence. So, we need to add something on this side of Cicero's persona here.

The key Ciceronian text in this connection is the dialogue *De Oratore*. Herein, Cicero purports to show two things: first, that the complete philosopher will be a master rhetorician; and second, that the consummate orator must be a philosopher. Cicero undertakes this symmetrical task by crafting a kind of speculative history claiming that the original founders of human communities were extraordinary men, both wise *and* eloquent. In the beginning, Cicero claims: 'the ancients ... united all knowledge and science in all things, whether they appertained to morality, to the duties of life, to virtue, or to civil government, with the faculty of speaking ... '[8] The seven sages, excluding only Thales, were statesmen. Thales was successful in business (TD III, 34). The contemporary situation in which philosophy finds itself scorned by political men at the same time as philosophers scorn rhetoric is therefore neither desirable nor inevitable for either. For its part, philosophy has withdrawn from public life. Its modes of arguing have become increasingly esoteric and sectarian, then as now (*De or.* III, 66). Rhetoric, cut loose from its philosophical moorings, has become a by-word for amoral trickery, justifying the Platonic critique. In brief, philosophy without eloquence is 'is but of little advantage to states', while 'eloquence without wisdom is often most mischievous, and is never advantageous to them' (*De inv.* I, 1; cf. *De or.* III, 61).[9]

If philosophy is to resume its elevated calling as a force which can shape individuals' or communities' lives, it must be reunited with the arts of speaking: 'when I have given [philosophers] liberty to reason on all these subjects in corners to amuse their leisure, I shall give and assign to the orator his part, which is to set forth with full power and attraction the very same topics' (*De or.* I, 12). It is above all the power of oratory to move the *pathê* – the principal objects of philosophical therapy – that Cicero sees as so decisive, if philosophy is to follow Socrates back down into the streets and marketplaces. As he explains in *De oratore* (I, 12), 'The highest power of an orator consists in exciting the minds of men to anger, or to hatred, or to grief, or in recalling them from these more violent emotions to gentleness and compassion.'

Cicero's calls to reunite philosophy with rhetoric are tied to his lauding of republican politics, wherein the ability to move large audiences was at a premium. Our interest here is in how Cicero's ethical texts also see him deploying all of the rhetorical arts of invention and style – notably apostrophe, analogy, personification and *enargeia*, the vivid presentation of examples – to therapeutic and ethical ends (*De off.* I, 2). It is this 'Ciceronian' sense of the philosophical value of rhetoric as the means to move the passions which will re-emerge as central in the philosophising of the Italian *humanisti* [**6.1**].

4.4 Plotinus's philosophical mysticism

With the Neoplatonist Plotinus (204–70 CE), we move not simply centuries, but entire worlds away from Cicero. The latter is eclectic, civic-spirited and elusive. In Plotinus, we are presented, *sans ironie*, with a fully fledged, syncretic metaphysical System. According to this System, the entire material world is only derivatively real and alive, let alone the political realm dear to Cicero. Human souls are part of a larger order of 'Soul' which is supramaterial and immortal. Above and prior to this level of Soul is the level of the Intellect (*Nous*). Herein reside the Platonic Forms or Ideas: timeless, purely intelligible realities unsullied by change and matter. The order of our world is the imperfect, changing image or reflection of this greater eidetic order. All the intelligibility it has comes from how material things imperfectly 'participate' in these eternal Ideas. The highest principle, however, unifying and conditioning the Ideas themselves, is the One or Good: which Plotinus sometimes also calls (and calls upon) as God. This One is the metaphysical origin of all the lower levels of reality, reaching down to material beings. All reality is an emanation (*aporrhoia*) from it into the hypostases of Intellect, Soul and Matter.

Pierre Hadot has nevertheless argued that it is a mistake to conceive of Plotinus's metaphysical system, indebted to the Middle Platonism of his teacher, Ammonius Saccas (175–242 CE), as wholly 'abstracted' from all experience, or from all concerns with shaping a philosophical mode of life. Plotinus himself, his disciple Porphyry relates, lived in an extraordinary '*atopian*' manner (**9, 10**). Throughout his life, he would offer prayers and sacrifices on the birthdates of Plato and Socrates. Plotinus and his students refrained from eating meat. The philosopher is said to have slept little, and paid scant attention to his physical well-being, despite continuing commitments to teaching and to looking after children bequeathed to his care by wealthy Romans (remarkably enough) (Porphyry, *Life of*

Plotinus,.1–2, 7–10) 'Plotinus, the philosopher our contemporary, seemed ashamed of being in the body', Porphyry's *Life of Plotinus* opens by telling us:

> So deeply rooted was this feeling that he could never be induced to tell of his ancestry, his parentage, or his birthplace. He showed, too, an unconquerable reluctance to sit for a painter or a sculptor, and when Amelius persisted in urging him to allow of a portrait being made he asked him: 'Is it not enough to carry about this image in which nature has enclosed us? Do you really think I must also consent to leave, as a desired spectacle to posterity, an image of the image?' (Porphyry, *Life of Plotinus*, 1)

As Hadot has argued in *Plotinus, or the Simplicity of Vision* (1998), we accordingly need to be very careful before we take Neoplatonic metaphysics to have been a merely intellectual exercise.[10] At stake everywhere in Plotinus's work, as it is collated by Porphyry as the *Enneads*, are instead a very particular set of experiences, proceeding upwards from more mundane ethical concerns (the principal subjects of book I) towards mystical union with the One (the principal subject of book VI). The sole autobiographical passage we have from Plotinus is devoted exactly to the kind of 'unitive' or 'mystical' experience that he held to be the culminating point of the philosophical life. 'Many times it has happened', Plotinus begins:

> Lifted out of the body into myself; becoming external to all other things and self-encentered; beholding a marvellous beauty; then, more than ever, assured of community with the loftiest order; enacting the noblest life, acquiring identity with the divine; stationing within It by having attained that activity; poised above whatsoever within the Intellectual is less than the Supreme. (*Enn.* IV.8.1.1–11)

Each of the stages of Plotinus's Neoplatonic metaphysics, in this light, corresponds to different 'levels of inner life', in Hadot's formulation:

> within this framework, the experience Plotinus describes for us consists in a movement by which the soul lifts itself up to the level of divine intelligence, which creates all things and contains within itself, in the form of a spiritual world, all the eternal Ideas or immutable models of which the things of this world are nothing but images. Our text [the *Enneads*] even gives us to understand that the soul, passing

beyond all of this, can fix itself in the Principle of all things … All this traditional terminology is used to express an inner experience. (Hadot, 1998: 26–7; cf. Chase, 1998: 2–3)[11]

For most modern readers, it will be Plotinus's hostility to the body, and his acceptance of the Platonist understanding of philosophy as a dying to embodied experience (3, 7), which seems most foreign and incredible. The true sage, Plotinus writes – for his *Enneads*, also, contain a highly developed series of characterizations of such an ideal figure (10) – will 'work down or wear away the tyranny of the body by inattention to its claims; its rulership he will lay aside' (*Enn.* I, 4, 14). From such an other-worldly perspective, as Plotinus echoes Plato's *Laws*, the lives of non-philosophers (9) seem no more serious than the antics of stage-players: 'murders, death in all its guises, the reduction and sacking of cities, all must be … just such a spectacle as the changing scenes of a play; all is but the varied incident of a plot, costume on and off, acted grief and lament' (*Enn.* II, 2, 15).

Nevertheless, Plotinus remains struck, like his teacher Plato, by the sheer facts of beauty and order, even in the material world of the body and its passions. If Plotinus attacks the Gnostics for their teaching concerning matter as evil, as he notably does, it is firstly because they do not know how to 'look at the world' here below. Such blindness means that they are also 'far from being able to see the spiritual world' with clarity (*Enn.* II, 9, 16). What is needed, Plotinus argues, is to cultivate a philosophical manner of seeing which, like Homer's Lynceus, can discern in the least things the traces of an invisible, higher Order:

> Consider the marvellous art shown not merely in the mightiest works …, but even amid such tiny things as one would think Providence must disdain: the varied, wonderful workmanship in any and every animal form; in the world of plants, too; the grace of fruits and even of leaves, the lavishness, the delicacy, the diversity of exquisite bloom; and all this not issuing once, then to die out, but made ever and ever anew. (*Enn.* III, 2, 13)[12]

This experience of beauty is formative and profound, for Plotinus. It can shake our ordinary sense of reality, provoking 'awe-stuck terror and astonishment' and a pleasure 'mixed with pain' (*Enn.* IV, 5, 12, 33–35). But for Plotinus as for the Middle Platonists, the Order informing the material things which we glimpse in experiences of wonder cannot reside in these things' transient, changing materiality: 'material forms, containing light incorporated in them, need still a light apart from them that their own light may be manifest'(*Enn.* VI, 7, 21) And it is this higher, nonmaterial 'light' (one of Plotinus's recurring metaphors (7)) that the soul must discern: 'when the soul further sees that the beauties of the world flow away, she knows full well that the light which was shimmering above them comes from elsewhere' (*Enn.* V, 7, 31, 28).

Above all, as in Plato's *Symposium*, the experience of beauty for Plotinus provokes *Eros*. From the desire for sexual union, at the most basic level, up to the philosophical desire to know the causes of all things. The soul, sensing the order of the Ideas that underlies its experience, is moved by longing to unite itself with the source of this beauty (*Enn.* VI, 7, 22). There is always some part of the human soul which has remained transcendent, 'in us more than ourselves', Plotinus maintains. Philosophy's task is to reawaken this transcendent dimension:

> If it is desirable to venture the more definite statement of a personal conviction clashing with the general view – even our human soul has not sunk entire; something of it is continuously in the Intellectual Realm, though if that part, which is in this sphere of sense, holds the mastery, or rather [if it] be mastered here and troubled, it keeps us blind to what the upper phase holds in contemplation. (*Enn.* IV, 8, 8)

Above Soul stands the world of the unchanging Intellect and Platonic Ideas. Each Idea, Plotinus tells us, is at once perfectly well-defined, at the same time as it forms a part of the larger *taxis* of the totality of the Ideas: so the Idea of humanity includes animality within it, also rationality, materiality … This totality is structured according to rational relations discernible by philosophical dialectic (cf., e.g., *Enn.* VI, 7, 10 ff.; V, 8, 4, 36–37). With that said, Plotinus stresses the marvellous *beauty* of this interconnected Order, the metaphysical model which all the beauty we experience can only dimly intimate:

> Situated in pure light and pure radiance, it [*Nous*] includes within itself the natures of all beings. This beautiful world of ours is but a shadow and an image of its beauty …. It lives a blessed life, and whoever were to see it and – as is fitting – submerge himself within it and become one with it, would be seized by awe. (*Enn.* III, 8, 11, 26–33; cf. V, 8, 10, 26–30)

Yet even this awe does not mark the apex of the Neoplatonic ascent.[13] For the Order of the Ideas itself emanated from and reflects the prior, unifying principle of the One or Good. The final End of the soul's erotic itinerary, accordingly, involves a transcendence of the discursive, dialectical modes of reasoning which allow us to distinguish and define the Ideas. *Dianoia* and even *Nous* can take us only to the level of the Ideas. At stake in the highest unitive experience is something which Plotinus describes as belonging to the order of love:

> Once the soul receives an 'outflow' from the Good, it is stirred; seized with a Bacchic passion, goaded by these goads: thus love is born ... when there enters into it a glow from the divine, it gathers strength, awakens, spreads true wings, and however urged by its nearer surrounds, speeds its buoyant way elsewhere, to something greater to its memory: so long as there exists anything loftier than the near, its very nature bears it upwards, lifted by the giver of that love. Beyond *Nous* it passes, but beyond the Good it cannot go, for nothing stands above That. (*Enn.* VI, 7, 22)

Plotinus's texts on this unitive experience strain against the limits of language. Alongside a language of love and desire, we read metaphors of intoxication, inspiration, madness, flight, illumination and initiation into the mysteries (*epopteia*) (**6**). In unitive experience with the One, Plotinus explains, knower and known, seer and seen, consciousness and its object become fused. Such union cannot be achieved by our own efforts. It comes to the initiate by 'chance' or 'good fortune':

> Suddenly, a light bursts forth, pure and alone. We wonder whence it came, from the outside or the inside? It came from nowhere ... Here, we put aside all the learning; disciplined to this pitch, established in beauty, the seeker holds knowledge still of the ground he rests on but, suddenly, swept beyond it all by the very crest of the wave of Intellect surging beneath, he is lifted and sees, never knowing how; the vision floods the eyes with light, but it is not a light showing some other object, the light is itself the vision. (*Enn.* V, 5, 7, 33–36).

At this culminating apex of Plotinus's mystical itinerary, his *Enneads* stretches the PWL paradigm as far as it can go without becoming a distinctly religious vision.[14] Plato had distinguished *Dianoia*, discursive reasoning, from *Noesis*, which carries the sense of an intellectual 'seeing' of the Ideas. Aristotle, in *Nicomachean Ethics* X, famously depicted the life of *theoria*, a species of contemplation, as the highest form of human life. Again, the Platonic account of love given by Diotima in the *Symposium* involves a 'ladder' of loves and their objects, leading to a vision of Transcendent Beauty. Yet in this Platonic text, eros at each rung is depicted as an active force, productive of 'multiple thoughts and actions, producing science, education, and the organisation of the state' (Hadot, 1998: 56). Likewise, the philosophers who have seen the Good are compelled to 'go back down' into the cave in Plato's *Republic* VII. By contrast, Plotinian *Eros* for the One is an entirely sufficient End. The contemplative life is simply best: 'if [the seeker] feels that political activities are beneath him, let him remain up above, if he so desires, and this will be the conduct of one who has seen a great deal' (*Enn.* VI, 9, 7, 21–23, 26–27).

Nevertheless, Plotinus's discourses remain grounded in the Graeco-Roman philosophical tradition. Plotinus develops a discourse surrounding the idealized figure of the sage and his attributes (**9**), which forms the flipside of a critique of non-philosophers' ways of life (**8**). We have likewise remarked that dialectic remains at least one, enabling means to attain to the Ideas, although not to the One (**4**).[15] Above all, Plotinian philosophy remains a means of self-transformation conceived in light of a larger vision of the whole, as in the great Hellenistic schools, comparable to the work of a sculptor (**6**) who produces a beautiful human face not by adding to, but by artfully chipping unformed stone away.[16] In the works of his mature years, Hadot contends, Plotinus became increasingly attentive to ethical subjects, stressing the need for his philosopher to cultivate the virtues:

> For to say 'Look to God' is not helpful without some instruction as to what this looking imports: it might very well be said that one can 'look' and still sacrifice no pleasure, still be the slave of impulse, repeating the word 'God' but held in the grip of every passion and making no effort to master any ... God on the lips, without a good conduct of life, is only a word. (*Enn.* II, 9, 15, 24 ff.; cf. II, 9, 9, 45–60)

However, the meaning of the virtues is fundamentally reshaped by reference to the Transcendent Good Plotinus's philosophy extols. After individuals have attained the highest vision of the Truth, or even if they have momentarily glimpsed it, their souls 'necessarily become, as it were, amphibious, alternately living the life up above and the life down here below' (*Enn.* IV, 8, 4, 31–33). The task then becomes to keep the memory of the Good 'up above' alive. Needed then is a difficult inner discipline (3) or what Porphyry, describing his master, terms an attentiveness (*prosochê*),[17] vigilance, or 'wakefulness' (*Enn.* VI, 9, 11, 46–51).

The civic virtues as we usually understand them are accordingly refigured by Plotinus as 'purificatory', by contrast to 'contemplative', excellences (Hadot, 1998: 69–73; cf. Plato, *Phaedo*, 82d-83c).[18] Their aim becomes to allow the soul to separate its attention from material things, which are not simply indifferent for the Neoplatonic philosopher, but meaningfully *unreal* (*Enn.* I, 2, 4, 16; I, 1, 10, 7–10). As well as purificatory, these lower Plotinian virtues are also *preparatory* spiritual rungs on the initiatory ladder (6) towards contemplative *ekstasis*:

Newly awakened, [the soul] is all too feeble to bear the ultimate splendour. Therefore the soul must be trained – to the habit of remarking, first, all noble pursuits, then the works of beauty produced not by the labour of the arts but by the virtue of men known for their goodness: lastly, you must search the souls of those that have shaped these beautiful forms. (*Enn.* I, 6, 9)

As well as exercises cultivating our sense of the beauty in external things (3), many of these exercises involve injunctions to turn one's attention inwards, away from all material things, on the model of Plato's *Phaedo.* Thus:

If there is to be perception of what is thus present, we must turn the perceptive faculty inward and hold it to attention there. Hoping to hear a desired voice, we let all others pass and are alert for the coming at last of that most welcome of sounds: so here, we must let the hearings of sense go by, save for sheer necessity, and keep the soul's perception bright and quick to the sounds from above. (*Enn.* V 1, 12, 12–21)[19]

But we close this section with the following passage, in which we can see exacting directions for what is clearly a staged meditative process involving a Neoplatonic adumbration of the view from above exercise:

Let us, then, make a mental picture of our universe: each member shall remain what it is, distinctly apart; yet all is to form, as far as possible, a complete unity ... bringing immediately with it the vision, on the one plane, of the sun and of all the stars with earth and sea and all living things as if exhibited upon a transparent globe. [Next] bring this vision actually before your sight, so that there shall be in your mind the gleaming representation of a sphere, a picture holding all things of the universe, moving or in repose ... [Then] keep this sphere before you, and from it imagine another, a sphere stripped of magnitude and of spatial differences; cast out your inborn sense of Matter, taking care not merely to attenuate it. Then call on God, maker of the sphere whose image you now hold, and pray Him to enter ... He who is the one God and all the gods, where each is all, blending into a unity, distinct in powers but all one God in virtue of that one divine power of many facets. (*Enn.* V, 8, 9)

4.5 Boethius and the end of ancient philosophy

With Plotinus's conception of philosophy as a transcendent initiation, we also see how close the pagan thought of the later Imperium had drawn to the Christian religion which would soon supplant it. The Athenian and Syrian Neoplatonists who succeeded Plotinus would in fact 'place beyond philosophy what they call "hieratics": that is to say, sacred operations, the strict observance of rites and sacraments desired by the gods' (Hadot, 2020: 253, 255). For these figures, led by Iamblichus, human nature is too debased due to its union with the body for the kind of contemplative union with the One which Plotinus had envisaged. Hence:

The only way which is open towards the divine world is ... that which the gods themselves have fixed. It can appear repugnant to our reason, which understands neither the sense of rites, nor even the names that the gods want us to pronounce in the ceremonies. But ... we must carry out the rites without understanding them, because their effects surpass our intelligence. (Hadot, 2020: 254)

Nevertheless, Plotinus's *Enneads* cannot be accounted the last work bearing witness to the ancient pagan sense of PWL. This laurel goes to *The Consolation of Philosophy* (*De consolatione philosophiae*), the final work of Anicius Manlius Severinus Boethius (480–524 CE), written in the very decade in which Justinian would finally close the Athenian schools. Boethius was famously called by the great renaissance humanist Lorenzo Valla 'the last of the Romans, and the first of the Scholastics' (cited by Chadwick, 1981: xi).

Alongside the *Consolation*, Boethius wrote several works on mathematics, dialectic and logic. He translated Aristotle's works *Of Interpretation*, the *Topics* and *Sophistical Refutations*, together with the *Prior Analytics*: translations which would play a vital role in shaping Scholasticism [5.3]. Boethius, finally, authored several works of Christian theology including a book on the Trinity, and is recognized within Catholicism as a Holy martyr.

It has nevertheless puzzled commentators that, in the consolatory book Boethius penned in the final year of his life (523–4 CE) as he languished in prison facing execution on false charges of treason against Theodoric the Great, we find exactly *no* citations of Christian texts, nor any references to the life and passion of Christ (see Marebon, 2003: 146–63). Instead, *Consolation of Philosophy* opens with the lamenting Boethius receiving a distinctly pagan divinity, Lady Philosophy. On her gown is imprinted the form of a ladder (**6**), leading upwards from a Greek Pi (for praxis) to a Theta (for theory) (*Cons.* I, 1). The title announces the book's genre (**5**). Like Seneca's four *Consolations*, Cicero's lost *Consolatio ad se* and the *Tusculan Disputations*, philosophy is called upon in this remarkable work to provide solace to a man against whom fortune has turned her harshest blows: a man who had fallen from political favour and public fame to present disgrace and imminent death (Lerer, 1985; Zim, 2017). Fittingly for this last work of ancient philosophy, moreover, the opening three books of the *Consolation* bring together, as in a concise compendium, almost all of the features of PWL which we have been examining (Haldane, 1992; Glasscock, 2009).

Firstly, the text mixes dialectic, dialogue and rhetorical speeches with poems or 'songs' which Lady Philosophy sings to Boethius (**4, 5**), despite having initially expelled the muses of poetry and the other liberal arts (*Cons.* I, 1). Secondly, the action of the dialogue is structured around the medicinal metaphor which we have seen in this chapter so prominent in Cicero (**7**).[20] Like a skilled physician, Lady Philosophy will first deliver to the embittered prisoner her less demanding cures, before ascending in the face of Boethius's recurring protests to the delivery of her 'sharper' medicines after III 10:

> But since a throng of tumultuous passions hath assailed thy soul, since thou art distraught with anger, pain, and grief, strong remedies are not proper for thee in this thy present mood. And so for a time I will use milder methods, that the tumours which have grown hard through the influx of disturbing passion may be softened by gentle treatment, till they can bear the force of sharper remedies. (*Cons.* I, 6; cf. II, 3; II, 4; III, 1)

Thirdly, Lady Philosophy's milder cures, directed at overcoming Boethius's passions, all rest upon the fundamental Socratic claim that it is not fortune that oppresses the prisoner, but his 'mistaken' opinions about fortune and the nature of happiness: 'error and ignorance bewilder you' (6) (*Cons.* II, 4). Fourthly, reflecting the eclecticism characteristic of later Platonisms, Lady Philosophy's remedies bring together into a concentrated regimen different Stoic, Epicurean and Platonic arguments or exercises to help cure Boethius of his erroneous beliefs (3). The Goddess Fortuna has always been fickle. This is Her most constant feature (*Cons.* II, 1). The goods that She commands – money and property, power, fame, glory and pleasure – were by nature never Boethius's to possess or to lose. Nor did they have intrinsic worth (II, 5–7; III, 1–8). Everything and every*one* that climbs upwards on Fortune's wheel must eventually come down (II, 1). Boethius's ailment therefore hails specifically from his false beliefs which his own philosophical training should have inoculated him against.

Boethius has hence degraded his own rational nature by taking these externals to be essential to his happiness (II, 5). Money cannot provide the security, power the respect, nor glory the happiness that people seek in pursuing these externals (III, 3–6). Indeed, when it comes to curing the desire for glory – positioned by the text as particularly tempting for a man 'of noble quality' like Boethius (III, 7) – Lady Philosophy proffers her charge one of the purer extant prescriptions of the view from above exercise we could cite (3):

> Yet consider with me how poor and unsubstantial a thing this glory is! The whole of this earth's globe, as you have learnt from the demonstration of astronomy, compared with the expanse of heaven, is found no bigger than a point ... Now, of this so insignificant portion of the universe, it is about a fourth part ... which is inhabited by living creatures known to us. If from this fourth part you take away in thought all that is usurped by seas and marshes, or lies a vast waste of waterless desert, barely is an exceeding narrow area left for human habitation. You, then, who are shut in and prisoned in this merest fraction of a point's space, do you take thought for the blazoning of your fame, for the spreading abroad of your renown? Why, what amplitude or magnificence has glory when confined to such narrow and petty limits? (III, 7)[21]

When Boethius arrives at III, 10, however, the dialogue turns away from ethical concerns towards a philosophical theology which also directly ushers in the Christian problematics that would soon dethrone philosophy as 'queen of the sciences' for a millennium (4). If happiness is the highest and by definition self-sufficient good – that unto which nothing better could be added – Lady Philosophy argues that this happiness can only be identified with God Himself (III, 10). This God, who by definition can want for nothing, must accordingly be all-powerful, all-governing and all-knowing (III, 11; V, 1–6). As for the evil Boethius laments, and the seeming power that wicked men enjoy here below, these are rightly speaking nothing positive. For evil men will the good through their evil actions, but do *not* have the power to attain it through their vices (IV, 2). As Plato's Socrates had taught in the *Gorgias*, it is better for such men to be punished, since punishment participates in justice (IV, 4), than for them to be able to wrong innocents like Boethius with impunity: a fate which leaves these wrongdoers, like beasts, prey to their untethered passions (IV, 3). When Boethius protests one last time that, with this all being granted, he would still rather be a free man, 'in his own country, powerful, wealthy, and high in honour' (IV, 5), Lady Philosophy purports to show him that, despite appearances, all is for the best in the Providential ordering of the Divine Mind. It is just that humans cannot understand this 'appointed limit which guides all things to good' (IV, 6). Indeed, 'absolutely every fortune is good fortune', even that which will soon see Boethius wrongfully executed (IV, 7). The last book of the *Consolation* is given over to Boethius's famous purported demonstration of the consistency of human free will with the postulate of Divine prescience (V, 1–6).

Scholars dispute whether the *Consolation of Philosophy* can be taken to have succeeded in consoling Boethius, whatever the comforts figures like Alfred the Great and Dante report having taken in it [5.5]. Some have argued that the apparent irrelevance of the last theological arguments to speak to Boethius's specific fate must represent an intentional failure, an esoteric means to demonstrate the limits of philosophy and the crowning need for faith (Marebon, 2003: 154–9, 161). However that may be, it is poetically appropriate that, after having begun by arraigning in sequence almost all of the therapeutic arguments of the Hellenistic and Roman philosophical schools, this last text of ancient philosophy closes its second half with a call to hope and prayer (V, 6).

PART II
MEDIEVALS AND EARLY MODERNS

CHAPTER 5
PHILOSOPHY AS A WAY OF LIFE IN THE MIDDLE AGES

5.1 On Christianity as 'philosophy'

Given philosophy's uneasy alliance with the sciences against 'religion' since the nineteenth century, it is surprising that leading thinkers called Christianity itself *a*, or even *the*, true *philosophia* in the first centuries CE. On the one hand, the ancient schools we have examined hitherto offered variants of two kinds of critiques of the traditional religions of the ancient world. Firstly, as in Epicureanism, we find open criticisms of the religions' claims to speak knowledgably about supernatural, anthropomorphic deities, placatable by ritual, sacrifice and prayers. Secondly, as in Stoicism and some Platonisms, we find forms of the philosophical 'rationalization' of the claims of revealed religions. These lead to allegorical ways of reading the texts of the poets or indeed of biblical texts, in Philo Judaeus and others. The goal here was to render the religions' apparently suprarational claims about God or the gods consistent with the philosophers' discourses – whether with the physics of the Stoics or the metaphysics of Plato.

For its part, on the other hand, Christianity began as an eschatological religion convinced of the imminence of the end-times. Its first adepts were simple men and women. Porphyry, Celsus and other educated pagans lambasted them for their lack of learning and culture. Paul and other Church Fathers sometimes reciprocated, decrying the 'wisdom of the world' and celebrating the 'folly of the cross'. As Pierre Hadot comments, 'nothing, it seems, could have predicted that a century after the death of Christ some Christians would present Christianity not solely as a philosophy – that is, a Greek cultural phenomenon – but even as the sole and eternal philosophy' (Hadot, 2002: 237).

Nevertheless, this is exactly what did occur, beginning from Christian apologists like Justin the martyr (*c.* 100–165 CE), also called 'the philosopher'. The Fathers of the Church challenged, *qua* Christians, the ancient philosophies' theoretical claims. They believed that their Christian worldview, with its interventionist, God more truly described the natural world and human condition than the philosophical discourses of the pagans.

Yet what the apologists and Fathers disputed in the pagan philosophies, above all, was whether the pagan philosophies could furnish human beings with the true or sufficient way to lasting wisdom or perfection. In the second century CE, as the Christian movements began to grow, the early apologists thus began to carry over onto Christian soil much of the vocabulary of the pagan philosophies to describe their own ways of life. Several explicitly describe their work, in apologetics, as propounding a 'Christian philosophy', 'our philosophy', in contrast to the 'Barbarian philosophy' of the pagans (Hadot, 1995: 126). In doing this, they would look to illustrious Jewish precedents like Philo (*c.* 20 BCE–50 CE), who had brought the thought of the Greeks, led by Plato, to the understanding of the Sacred Jewish texts. Decisively, however, their criticisms shared the ancient meta-philosophical assumption that what *philosophia* pre-eminently involves is a manner of living in light of one's philosophical convictions.

Polish scholar Juliusz Domański points to three additional reasons explaining why the Church 3 adopted this rubric of 'Christian philosophy'. Firstly, Christianity lays claim to revealed truths concerning the highest things which form part of the ancient definitions of philosophy: namely God, the world and human fate, and nature. At this level, as Hadot rejoins, the appeal of the evangelist to the *Logos* that was God or was with God at the opening of the fourth gospel was read as describing the same *Logos* which, within Neoplatonism, operated as mediator between God and the World (Hadot, 2002: 237). Secondly, Christianity enshrines moral precepts in the light of these higher truths, like *ta ethika* as one part of the ancient philosophies. But thirdly, Christian texts present exemplars *of lives* lived according to Christian wisdom, led by the examples of Christ and the Saints. These exemplars were appealed to as models, more truly 'philosophical' than the lives of the ancient philosophers and statesmen (Domański, 1996: 25).

Indeed, the apologists soon claimed that their Christian philosophy superseded, and in different ways perfected, the pagan philosophers' pursuits of wisdom. Already in Justin, we read the claim that the teachings of Plato and other philosophers could only have been inspired by the biblical prophets (Justin, *1 Apol.*, chapter 20). Justin considers all men who lived according to the *Logos*, including those philosophers who squared their actions with their discourses, as 'Christians' *avant la Verbe* – he names 'Socrates, Heraclitus, and those like them' in this connection (Domański, 1996: 23; Hadot, 2002: 241). For Clement of Alexandria (*c.* 150–*c.* 215), divine Providence had given the Greeks and Romans philosophy so that they might become good men (Domański, 1996: 26). Yet not all of the

Logos, incarnated in Jesus, had been afforded them (Hadot, 1995: 128). According to Basil the Great (*c.* 329–79), wisdom involves realizing in life the virtues of which the philosophers had only spoken (Hadot, 1995: 27). The Fathers typically argue that the philosophers, for all of the theoretical achievements, could not fully actualize their noble theoretical teachings (Domański, 1996: 28).

John Chrysostom (*c.* 349–407 CE) thus instructively appropriates elements of the ideal of Stoic sage in his vision of the Christian life. Christian philosophy, for him, implicates a discipline touching the whole of life in order to realize virtue and wisdom. Pagan philosophers' conceptions of the virtues can even be used to critique and inspire Christians in their ethical efforts [see **5.4, 6.1**]. Yet, Chrysostom argues, human beings alone cannot realize the highest form of life. Indeed, pride accrues to the very acquisition of greatness of soul, a sin which Chrysostom sees writ large in Diogenes the Cynic's antics. The *atopia* of the post-Socratic philosophers came to seem a mere 'affectation' or a 'pose': a theatrical protesting too much concealing profound existential impotence (Domański, 1996: 29). Christ and the Saints have 'come to teach us the life proper to philosophers' (Domański, 1996: 29), which the philosophers themselves only glimpsed. Christianity alone 'teaches us to conduct ourselves so that we might resemble God, and to accept the divine plan [*oikonomia*] as the guiding principle of all our education' (at Hadot, 1995: 128).

Nevertheless, the supersession of pagan philosophy by Christianity did not prevent the successor from being shaped by the succeeded cultural form. Ancient philosophical pedagogy in the Hellenistic diaspora, after Sulla's sack of Athens (87–86 BCE) had become increasingly reliant on the exegesis of the texts of the founders of the schools (Hadot, 1981: 4): a conception of philosophical activity conducive to adaptation by religions of the Book. The Neoplatonists prescribed a reading order of Aristotle's, then Plato's texts, as means to a pedagogical and spiritual ascent: upwards from ethics, through physics, to metaphysics or 'epoptics'.[1] Just so, the Church Father Origen (*c.* 185–254 CE) had the pupils of his school – which is described in some sources as modelled on the pagan philosophical schools – read the *Book of Proverbs,* then *Ecclesiastes,* then the *Song of Songs* as the means (respectively) to ethical purification, physical knowledge (turning the mind towards non-sensible things), then theology, leading to union with God (**4**) (Hadot, 2002: 239–40).

Many of the Church Fathers' conceptions of 'our philosophy' did not remain untouched by their exposure to the pagan philosophers' *discourses.*[2]

Just how far this phenomenon of 'contamination' went can be seen clearly in the work of the remarkable early monastic author, Evagrius Ponticus (c. 345–99 CE) (see Hadot, 2020: 260–4). First, in his *Praktikos*, Evagrius describes the 'doctrine of Christ our Saviour' in philosophical terms, as 'composed of praxis, physics, and theology': the three parts of philosophy of the Platonic school since the first century CE [4]. He explains that *physics* is what is intended in the *New Testament*'s talk of the 'kingdom of heaven' and *theology* what is at stake in the Gospels' 'Kingdom of God'. Hadot is engaging in understatement when he comments that this is to give the biblical words a 'completely unexpected' meaning (Hadot, 2002: 250).

This identification of Christianity as 'philosophy according to Christ' (Leclerq, 1952: 221; Hadot, 1995: 129) was the widespread in late antiquity. We find versions of it in the Cappadocian Fathers in the fourth century (Basil of Caesaria, Gregory Nazianzus, John Chrysostom and Gregory of Nyssa), as well as in early monastic writers led by Evagrius (Hadot, 1995: 129). Jean Leclercq (1952: 221–6) and Juliusz Domański have documented how lasting this designation of Christianity as *philosophia* remained within the monastic lineages, until at least the thirteenth century. With that said, to understand what was at stake when, within this tradition, Odo of Canterbury (tenth century) could evoke 'the true philosophy of Christ' to describe the monastic calling; or when Peter the Venerable of Cluny (c. 1092–1156) could speak in the twelfth century about his assumption of the monastic frock as a taking up of the 'true philosophy of Christ'; or again, when the *Exordium magnum cisterciense* (late twelfth-thirteenth century CE), speaks of Bernard of Clairvaux instructing monks in 'the disciplines of celestial philosophy' (Hadot, 1995: 129; Leclerq, 1952: 221–4), we need always to underscore that what was at issue here was monasticism as *a rival way of life*, as against a set of discourses (Domański, 1996: 63–5). As Hadot reflects:

> This fact is highly significant: it shows that if Christianity was able to be assimilated to a philosophy, the reason was that philosophy itself was already above all else a way of being and a style of life. As Jean Leclercq points out: 'In the monastic Middle Ages, just as much as in Antiquity, *philosophia* did not designate a theory or a means of knowledge, but a lived, experienced wisdom, and a way of living according to reason.' (Leclerq, 1952: 221; Hadot, 2002: 130)

It is to this monastic Christianization of *philosophia* that we turn now.

5.2 Monastic *philosophia*, and the Christianization of spiritual exercises

It is again Pierre Hadot who has done most to examine this remarkable fact of the debts owed by the different early Christian monasticisms to classical PWL. The earliest Syrian and Egyptian monks, the Desert Fathers, were not erudite men. They based their understandings of the new form of life they had chosen on their readings of the Old and New Testaments. Almost certainly, they drew also on examples from Manichean and Eastern forms of asceticism, or the inspiration of groups like the Essenes and *Therapeutai* (called 'philosophers' by Philo in *On the Contemplative Life*) which dated back to the time of Christ (Merton, 1970; Hadot, 2002b: 242; MacCulloch, 2014: 69–79). Nevertheless, in the third-fourth centuries CE, influenced by Justin, Clement and Origen, new forms of 'learned monasticism' emerged (Hadot, 2002: 242). For these figures, the monastic life was a 'philosophy', precisely insofar as it aimed at the perfection of the Christian life, answering to Christ's evangelical injunction: 'If thou wilt be perfect, go and sell that thou hast, and give to the poor, and thou shalt have treasure in heaven: and come and follow me' (*Matt.* 19: 21).

Following Hadot's analyses, we can distinguish two levels in these monks' debts to the classical philosophical legacy. The first is at the level of the understanding of the goal of monastic philosophy (7):

> We must admit ... that under the influence of ancient philosophy, certain values which had been only secondary (not to say non-existent) within Christianity rose to the first rank of importance. The Gospel idea of the coming of the reign of God was replaced by the philosophical idea of union with God, as achieved by asceticism and contemplation. (Hadot, 2002b: 252)

The second is the monastics' assimilating and reshaping what Hadot calls the pagan 'spiritual exercises' (3).

i. The goals of monastic life

'The Kingdom of Heaven is *apatheia* of the soul along with the true knowledge of existing things,' writes Evagrius Ponticus in his *Praktikos*, a text whose Neoplatonic debts we have seen (at Hadot, 1995: 137). We can also recognize here [**3.1**], the close parallel between Evagrius's definition and the two parts of the Stoic definition of *sophia*: namely knowledge of things human and divine, and the *technai* of the virtues or the best human life. Evagrius's Greek term, *apatheia*, describing the state of the psyche in this 'kingdom of heaven', likewise, cannot but evoke the Stoics' usage of the same term. As we know, at stake in the philosophers' *apatheia* was the optative extirpation of disturbing passions [**3.2**]. This ideal would, in other Christian authors like Augustine, become the object of stern critique, since Christ suffered, was moved by compassion, and fear of God is the beginning of wisdom (Brooke, 2012: 1–11).[3]

However, Evagrius was not alone amongst the monastics in adopting such pagan terminology to describe the goal of monastic practice. Clement of Alexandria had claimed that the divine law must inspire fear, 'so that the philosopher [Christian] may acquire and conserve peace of mind (*amerimnia*), thanks to good deliberation (*eulabeia*) and attention (*prosochê*) to himself'. As Hadot rejoins (2002b: 241), 'This passage implies the whole thought world of ancient philosophy.' Four centuries later, Dorothea of Gaza (*c.* 505–65 CE) elevated *apatheia* as the goal of monastic philosophy, passing by way of *aprospatheia*, a detachment from worldly things (Hadot, 1995: 136). Dorothea goes so far as to claim that *apatheia* is of such value that one should desist from whatever else one is doing, should the activity endanger this spiritual state (Hadot, 1995: 138). At stake in such *apatheia*, in turn – and again, just as in the Stoic legacy, integrated into the Neoplatonism of late antiquity – was the aim to live according to nature or fate. In a passage whose culminating antimetabole echoes Epictetus's *Encheiridion* 7, as commentators have noted, Dorothea writes:

> He who has no will of his own always does what he wishes. For since he has no will of his own, everything that happens satisfies him. He finds himself doing as he wills all the time, *for he does not want things to be as he wills, but he wills that they be just as they are.* (at Hadot, 1995: 136; Hadot, 2002b: 243)

Such cutting off of the will merged into stricter forms of asceticism. These aimed at the complete denial of the body and were rooted far more deeply in Neoplatonic *philosophia* than in the monistic thought of the Stoa. Gregory of Nazianzus (*c.* 329–90 CE) directly quotes Plato's authority for the task of 'making of this life … a training for death, while … separating the soul from the body as far as possible' (at Hadot, 1995: 138). This 'is the practice of philosophy', he teaches (Hadot, 1995: 138). Evagrius, likewise, insists on the monks' capacity to separate the soul from the body and its passions, echoing the Platonic phrase from the *Phaedo*: 'for our fathers gave to the training for death and to the flight from the body a special name, *anachôresis* [i.e. monastic withdrawal]' (at Hadot, 1995: 138). The same Platonic echo resonates in Maximus the Confessor, in the seventh century, who enjoins his readers 'in conformity with the philosophy of Christ, ... [to] make of our life a meditation (*meletên*) upon death' (at Hadot, 1995: 138).

ii. The Christianisation of philosophical exercises

Given Ignatius Loyola's use of the term in the sixteenth century, the historical value of 'spiritual exercises' as a term to describe earlier Christian monastic practice, let alone ancient philosophical activities, has not gone unchallenged (Leclerq, 1935). Nevertheless, Jean Leclercq has documented the continuing usage, throughout the monastic Middle Ages, of variants of the Latin *exercitium* to designate 'the effort required by spiritual life in the two fields of action (in the old sense of the term: the practice of virtues) and contemplation, in other words: asceticism and mysticism': indeed, to 'designate the ensemble of practices into which the [monastic] day should be divided' (Leclerq, 1935).[4] Such practices, together with the daily regimens of different orders, are abundantly attested in the monastic tradition.[5]

Practices of the mortification of the body are only the most manifest of these exercises. These include the sometimes-spectacular ascetic feats of the hermitic monks (or the stylites); and the assiduous, hour-by-hour scheduling in coenobitic monasteries of prayer, song, liturgy and meditation, but also manual labour, fasts and vigils. Nevertheless, even at this level Hadot observes continuities with the philosophers. We thus can read exacting monastic diagnoses of the passions as the principal causes of the 'disruption, dispersion and dissipation of the soul' (at Hadot, 1995: 133). Such diagnoses, the flipside of the elevation of *apatheia* or *amerimnia*, speak to exercises in habituation, as when Dorothea of Gaza, like Epictetus [3.4], advises her charges to train themselves by first giving up small things, in order to inculcate the inner strength to then redress more deep-set attachments (at Hadot, 1995: 133; 2002b, 145). Evagrius echoes Cicero's *Tusculan Disputations* when he advises his charges to combat troublesome passions by means of other affections, like lust by the appeal to shame [4.3] (Hadot, 1995: 133). Nevertheless, in line with the Platonic heritage, these forms of bodily *askêsis* are often distinguished as merely 'practical' and subordinate in dignity to the more elevated mental or 'divine' practices. Cassian in his *Institutes* will thus insist that a would-be novice should not be allowed entrance to the order 'before he gives, by lying outside the doors for ten days or even longer, an evidence of his perseverance and desire, as well as of humility and patience' (Cassian, *Inst*. IV, chapter 3). To use a later medieval ordering, the higher exercises of *lectio, meditatio, oratio* (spoken prayer), and *contemplatio* must come later (Leclerq, 1935).

The call to ongoing, exacting forms of attention (*prosochĕ*) to self, world and God is also constant across different monastic orders.[6] Athanasius's *Life of Antony* describes Antony's conversion to the monastic life by simply saying that 'he began to *pay attention to himself*' (Hadot, 1995: 131). On his deathbed, Antony is depicted as enjoining his followers to 'live as though you were dying every day, paying *attention to yourselves* [*proschontes heautois*] and remembering what you heard from my preaching' (Hadot, 1995: 131). This link between the imminence of death, the fugacity of time and the call to attention is echoed in Dorothea, in almost Horatian terms: 'Let us pay heed to ourselves, brethren, and be vigilant while we still have time ... Look! Since the time we sat down at this conference we have used up two or three hours of our time and got that much nearer to death' (at Hadot, 1995: 131).

Basil of Caesaria (*c*. 330–78 CE) devotes a sermon to *prosochĕ*, based upon the text from *Deuteronomy*: 'give heed to yourself, lest there be a hidden word in your heart' (*In Illud 'Attende tibi ipsi'*, 31, col. 197 ff.)[7] Basil asks his readers to awaken the rational principle in their souls. As per the first *Alcibiades*, they must pay attention to what they are, rather than what is merely their own (the body). As in Stoic texts, Basil enjoins them to constantly observe and correct their inner judgements, recalling the materiality of riches, the splendid spectacles the cosmos affords even the lowly, and the intrinsic beauty of the soul (Hadot, 1995: 130–1). Thoughts, which arise spontaneously and constantly – like the water that drives the mill, in one of Cassian's metaphors (*Inst*. I, chapter 18) – require a much more exacting effort to direct than external actions. As Basil echoes Socrates and Epictetus, we should therefore 'let the eye of the soul never rest from the watch over yourself' (Vernay, 1935).

Associated with such vigilance, as in the Pythagorean, Epicurean and Stoic schools, come monastic prescriptions for the examination of conscience. In his commentary on the *Song of Songs*, a text closely associated with contemplative wisdom in the monastic heritage (von Severus & Solignac, 1935), Origen reads the scriptural 'unless you know yourself, O fair among women' allegorically. He sees within it a biblical injunction to the soul to assess whether it has made progress in its mastery of the passions and pursuit of the spiritual life (Hadot, 1995: 134). In Athanasius, Basil and John Chrysostom, monks are enjoined to undertake accounts of themselves every morning or, as we saw in Seneca [**3.3**], every night before sleep (Vernay, 1935). For John Climacus (579–649 CE), it is a matter of a spiritual account keeping, like that of a banker (Vernay, 1935). Dorothea recommends self-examinations daily, weekly, monthly, seasonally, even every six hours, paying particular heed to one's progress in overcoming the passions (Hadot, 1995: 134–5). Athanasius's Antony advises consigning such examinations to writing, as a means of exposing one's action to the scrutiny of a virtual other: 'let this record replace the eyes of our fellow ascetics' (Hadot, 1995: 133). Often enough, in practices of *exomologesis* and confession, a real other or confessor was mandated.

To these practices of attention and self-examination correspond practices of meditation. In the Christian monastic legacy, as in the ancient philosophies, meditation does not involve any emptying of the mind, or the transcendence of discourse – as against the practices of *contemplatio* in several of the mystical authors, influenced by Neoplatonism. At stake are instead practices of remembrance, whose objects are 'God and his commandments'. This means the biblical texts, but also those of the Fathers. Since the fall, Diadochus of Photice comments, 'it is only with difficulty that the human intellect can remember God and His commandments' (at Hadot, 1995: 132). Nevertheless, as for the Stoics or Epicureans, the monk must have these principles constantly at hand. Meditation on these precepts must then be as ongoing as possible, as the necessary means 'to possess these sayings at the opportune moment' (Dorothea, at Hadot, 1995: 134). One must constantly be able to interpret and *live* one's experiences through the monastic principles. Hadot notes in this connection the importance in monastic writings of several literary genres we noted in the Greek and Roman philosophers (**5**). Here too, we find numerous collections of the sayings or *Apothegmata* of the Desert Fathers, responding to particular queries, which read like the witty sayings of the philosophers in Diogenes Laertius (Merton, 1970). There are longer 'conferences' of questions and answers with authoritative figures comparable to the *Diatribai* Arrian recorded from Epictetus's classes. Finally, there are exemplary *Lives* of the Saints and Fathers, hearkening back to the gospel accounts of *the* life, that of Christ. As Hadot comments (1995: 133), 'These literary genres are responses to the requirements of meditation.' They answer to the need to condense bodies of thought into memorable sentences and inspiring stories to shape life and practice.

Perhaps the most revealing literary monastic productions for us are the monastic *florilegia*, which flourished throughout the medieval period into the renaissance (Moss, 1996). These usually anonymous texts – often entitled *Sententiae, Excerptiones, Excerpta* or *Scarapsus* – cannot be understood without considering the remarkable monastic practices of *lectio divina*: meditative reading intended to facilitate the deep internalization of sacred writings. The predominant biblical metaphor for this kind of reading (7), alongside that of digestion which we have met in the Stoics [**3.3**], is that of a rumination (von Severus & Solignac, 1935). *Lectio divina* was a holistic, embodied practice, involving first of all the reading out loud of the text, in a low voice, then chewing over it again and again in the mind and the mouth, until one wholly makes it one's own:

> For the ancients, to meditate is to read a text and to learn it 'by heart' in the fullest sense of this expression, that is, with one's whole being: with the body, since the mouth pronounced it, with the memory which fixes it, with the intelligence which understands its meaning, and with the will which desires to put it into practice … The *meditatio* consists in applying oneself with attention to this exercise in total memorization; it is, therefore, inseparable from the *lectio*. (Leclerq, 1996: 182)

The effect of such ruminative reading is to have made of the monks kinds of 'living libraries' whose inner discourses merged seamlessly into the tissues of quotations they would record for meditation in their florilegia:

> The monastic *florilegium* … grew out of spiritual reading. The monk would copy out texts he had enjoyed so as to savour them at leisure and use them anew as subjects for private meditation … He said himself: *Dicta mea, dicta Patrum.* … From this fervent reading … nurtured by desire for God, and savoured *in palato cordis*, these [Patristic and biblical] texts … emerged refined, polished, and enriched with new sweetness … [so] it is difficult to detect what is original and what comes from the Fathers. (Leclerq, 1996: 184)[8]

The continuities we have seen between pagan and monastic spiritual practices (attention, examination of conscience, reading, writing and meditation) in no way diminish the vast gulf between the two spiritual traditions. Hadot aims irenically to show how the monastics adapted and Christianized pagan philosophical ideas and practices we met in the opening four chapters. Yet the Christian emphasis on grace, not to say the doctrines of the incarnation, resurrection and eschatology, as well as the monastic emphases on humility and obedience, as in Cassian's *Institutes* (Foucault, 1997: 248), represent departures from the Hellenistic and Roman philosophers (Hadot, 2002b: 248–9).

At least two interconnected, further points in this connection need emphasis. Firstly, from the earliest monastic texts, there is an ontology and vocabulary of 'demons', inherited from *Deuteronomy* and other biblical texts, wholly foreign to the philosophical legacy before Iamblichus (Denielou, 1935; Brown, 1970; Smith, 1978; Brakke, 2001: 19–22, 46–8). These demons, called by Peter Brown 'the stars of the religious drama of late antiquity', tempt the monks, stand behind passions like lust or *accidia* (melancholy) and conspire to deceive the ascetic. In Athanasius's *Life of Antony*, various strategies to name, unmask and combat these demons are laid down. In Basil's homily on *prosochê*, one pays attention so that personified forces that can affect the soul are kept at bay, 'hidden nets are set for thee in all directions by the enemy' (Basil, *In Illud 'attende tibi ipsi'*).

This brings us to the second clarification. In Stoicism and Epicureanism, the premeditation of death and evils had been undertaken to show that these were *not* true evils. The examination of conscience was a means to assess how well one's actions had accorded with the impersonal principles of the philosophy. Cassian, by contrast, uses three telling metaphors to describe the Christian resignification of the examination of conscience (6): that of the miller, sorting the good from bad grains; the military officer, who divides between good and bad infantrymen; and that of the money changer, called to discern whether the visage that presents itself on the coins of our thoughts is that of the true monarch (God) or an imposter (demons or the devil himself). At issue in this last conception, as Foucault delineates, is a new, distinctly Christian hermeneutics of the self 'to decipher if, at the root of the movement that beings you the representations, there is or is not concupiscence or desire – if your innocent thought has evil origins, if you have something underlying which is the great Seducer, which is perhaps hidden' (Foucault, 1997: 241). Such a conception of self-examination is foreign to the pagan philosophical schools' versions of this exercise (Foucault, 1997: 240–1; 246–9).

5.3 Scholasticism, the theoreticization of *philosophia*, and the ascendancy of dialectic

Alongside the monastic appropriation of philosophical exercises, the Middle Ages saw a second tendency unfolding in medieval conceptions of *philosophia*. According to this tendency, a threefold devaluation of PWL takes place in the great medieval universities of the twelfth-fourteenth centuries in ways which Hadot in particular sees as presaging its end as the dominant Western meta-philosophy.

First, with the existential or 'practicist' dimension of ancient philosophical activity integrated into monasticism, the philosophy of the cathedral schools and then the universities increasingly became 'mere conceptual material' (Hadot, 2002b: 254). Christian thinkers took on those elements of Neoplatonic metaphysics and theology able to be rendered conversant with Christian theorizing about the Divine Nature. Alongside these metaphysical concepts were those parts of Aristotle's *Organon* concerning the rules of reasoning which could be put to work in explaining, clarifying and proselytizing Christian teachings. To these discourses were added, after the middle of the twelfth century, the newly recovered, translated Aristotelian writings on ethics, natural philosophy and metaphysics. The latter would dominate teaching curricula in the Arts Faculties of Europe North of the Alps after around 1250 CE (Ree, 1978; Leff, 1992). At this time, the identity of the professional philosopher as we still mostly know him as the interpreter of recondite texts was solidified. In Domański's words:

> The scholastic philosopher is a scholar who attempts to resolve the problems that reason poses itself *à propos* of the writings of Aristotle, and who explains to others the solutions to these problems, with all the arguments for and against. It is a solely intellectual work. In this situation, [the philosopher] is not himself obliged to give – by his comportment or by his personal merits – a testimony to the truth drawn from the text. (Domański, 1996: 50)

Secondly, this 'theoreticist' notion of philosophy tended over time to become equated with the 'liberal arts' in the post-Augustinian cycle of *De Divine* II, looking back to Platonic philosophy [**4.1**]: grammar, dialectic and rhetoric (the trivium), then arithmetic, geometry, music and astronomy (the quadrivium) (I. Hadot, 2005). Seneca and Aristotle before him had each differently positioned the liberal arts as propaedeutic to philosophy in its most elevated senses. The tendential scholastic devaluation of philosophy, wherein it is on the contrary identified with the liberal arts,[9] looks back to Philo of Alexandria. In his allegorical reading of *Genesis*, Philo identified geometry, music, rhetoric and grammar with Hagar, the Egyptian slave with whom Abraham had to couple to beget children, as against Sarah, Abraham's true spouse, identified with divine Mosaic wisdom. In the first centuries of the Christian epoch, both Clement and Origen accept Philo's allegoresis, replacing Mosaic wisdom with that of Christianity, and demoting philosophy to the liberal arts' propaedeutic level (Henrichs, 1968; de Mowbray, 2004; de Vries, 2009). Thus, in a letter to his student, Gregory the Thaumaturge, Origen explicates that as geometry, astronomy and the other liberal arts were to philosophy for the pagans, so pagan philosophy ought now to be to Christianity itself: 'I wish for you to borrow from Greek philosophy those branches which could serve at base for a general formation and constitute a preparation for Christianity' (Domański, 1996: 32).

Thirdly and emblematically, philosophy thus became in the medieval universities a mere 'handmaid to theology' (Henrichs, 1968). From a guide to life, *philosophia* had became an intellectual tradition/s whose riches could be plundered for theological ends, as the fleeing Hebrews had taken the treasures of the Egyptians (Evans, 1993: 13; Augustine, *De Doct. Chr.* II, 40, 60). The uneasy situation of philosophy within the lower Arts Faculties of Paris, Oxford, and the other great thirteenth-century universities in effect brought to institutional form these three, interconnected medieval devaluations of *philosophia*. The Arts Faculties after all furnished the *introductory* courses to university students. The aim was to provide them with the educational wherewithal to then specialize in the Higher Faculties: those of Theology, Law and Medicine. The emerging science of Theology would therefore now play the directive role of 'science of sciences' once assigned to philosophy. As Gregory IX put it to the Theology Faculty of Paris in 1228, drawing again on the *topos* of Hagar and Sarah:

> The young girl abducted to the enemy, whose hair was cut and nails trimmed, and who is united to the Israelite, should not dominate him; she must on the contrary obey him as a subject. Thus, theological intelligence, like a man, should command all faculties [of the university], and as the spirit should exercise its power over the flesh, indicate to them the path of uprightness so that they do not deviate. (at Imbach, 1996: 15)

There is much to support this Hadotian-Domańskian narrative of the fall of *philosophia* in the Middle Ages. A culture built around the Christian *epos* of creation, fall, incarnation, resurrection, atonement and judgement, with its Trinitarian God, can only have interpreted the competing philosophical visions of the ancient schools in the ways that it alternatively did. The pagan philosophies were either noble antecedents, from whom resources could be 'despoiled' in order to defend, demonstrate and proselytize the claims of faith. This is the position of Augustine, Aquinas, Anselm and others (Evans, 1993: 13). Or else, they were rivals and threats to orthodoxy. This was an attitude taken by Tertullian, Saint Jerome, Bonaventure (see Imbach, 1996: 33–7) or Giles of Rome, and reflected in the condemnations of heretical opinion like those at Paris in 1215 and then 1277 (Evans, 1993: 14). As G. R. Evans has observed, the world of a Hugh of Saint Victor, Robert Grosseteste, Anselm, Peter Abelard, John of Salisbury or Thomas Aquinas was simply:

> no longer ... a world where 'being a philosopher' was a practical alternative to being a Christian, and where one might meet and talk with men who had made that choice ... in the way that Augustine or Boethius could. There were no individuals in Western Europe after Bede's day (c.673–735) ... who were choosing a philosophical system as a basis for a way of life in preference to Christianity. (Evans, 1993: 3, 5)

Nevertheless, Domański is right to caution (1996: 38–9) that this narrative, without significant qualifications, runs the risk of oversimplifying the complex medieval, meta-philosophical landscape. The addition of the 'three philosophies' (physics, ethics, metaphysics) to the Arts curricula in the thirteenth century reflects a long and complex relationship between the parts of philosophy.[10]

On the one hand, when we look back to the ancient divisions of the parts of philosophy, we see that philosophy herself, and its transmission, was imbricated with the liberal arts from near to its inception. The latter were most often in fact included within philosophy's divisions, rather than subordinated *en bloc* to philosophy. Thus, as we commented in **Chapter 4**, in book VII of the *Republic*, Plato's Socrates already stipulates the necessary place of music, arithmetic, geometry and astronomy (the later quadrivium) in the education of the philosopher-guardians. Here, also, these mathematical disciplines are assigned a highly 'philosophical' intentionality. This is to 'compel the soul to reason about abstract number

... rebelling against the introduction of visible or tangible objects into the argument' (Plato, *Rep.* 525d), and accustoming it to reasoning about abstract Ideas, untethered by sensual images. When we ascend from mathematical to properly philosophical reasoning about these Ideas, we again find that it is none other than *dialectic*, another later 'liberal art', that Plato sees as the philosophical methodology of definition, division and demonstration par excellence (Hadot, 2020: 106–8, 135, 148, 152).

Certainly, dialectic is then demoted by Aristotle to an art of disputing using common notions, aiming at persuasion as against truth, and as such beneath the dignity of philosophy herself (Reeve, 2012; Hadot, 2020: 136–7). Yet dialectic remains a subpart of the division of logic within the Stoic philosophy. Here, it is found alongside *rhetoric*, another liberal art of the later medieval trivium. Then, as if to bring together the Platonic, Stoic and Aristotelian conceptions, the probabilistic Academy after Arcesilaus positioned dialectic as central to philosophy, whilst limiting it to seeking out and defending the most probable beliefs (Hadot, 2020: 150, 143–5). In all of the later ancient schools, in fact, as Pierre Hadot has documented, dialectical and rhetorical methods of teaching both sides of an issue (*in utramque partem*) were central to day-to-day pedagogy (Hadot, 2020: 141–8, 153–5). Even Plotinus taught by dialectical methods of question and answer, a practice which frustrated some of his students (Hadot, 1998: 84–7; Hadot, 2020 154). For these reasons, Aristotle's diminution of the status of all lesser sciences beneath that of first philosophy, Seneca's demotion of the liberal arts beneath philosophy as the teacher of the virtues, even Epicurus's famous attempt to dismiss *paideia* entirely from philosophers' concerns are exceptions to the lasting ancient imbrication of the liberal arts and philosophy. They do not represent an indisputable ancient standard.

On the other hand, we see the same inclusion of the liberal arts as parts of philosophy in medieval divisions of the sciences as we do in the ancients. Augustine, Martianus Capella, Ammonius and other later ancient commentators in fact inherited these divisions from the pagan schools.[11] In Ammonius and Boethius at the end of antiquity, for instance, the threefold division within speculative philosophy (as opposed to practical philosophy, following Aristotle) includes mathematics, which considers forms abstracted from matter. Mathematics is placed between physics, which considers material things, and *theologica*, which would contemplate the metaphysical realities completely separate from matter and motion (Figure 5.1) (Weisheipl, 1965: 59–61). Yet 'mathematics' here is itself divided (exactly) into the four disciplines of the quadrivium, 'the four lane road to wisdom', in

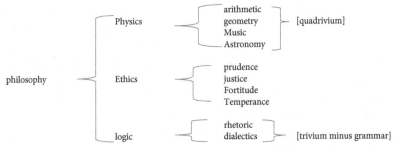

Figure 5.1 Classification of sciences in Saint Isidore. Adapted from Weisheipl, 1965: 64.

descending order of ontological purity and priority; from arithmetic, which considers number in complete abstraction from materiality; to music or harmony; then geometry which considers figures; and finally the science of astronomy, the most physical of the mathematical *scientia* (Weisheipl, 1965: 61–2; Caddan, 2013: 246).

Somewhat later, Saint Isidore (560–636 CE) of Seville's influential classification of the *scientia* in his *Etymologiae* unifies the Stoic tripartition of philosophy into logic, ethics and physics (or 'natural philosophy' [Caddan, 213: 246]) with the Neoplatonic heritage evident in Boethius.

This time, not mathematics but *physics* is identified with the quadrivium. 'Theology' or 'divine science' is not listed. Logic, meanwhile, is reinstated as a part of philosophy in contrast to Boethius. But it includes dialectic and rhetoric from what would become the trivium: so only grammar of all the later liberal arts are not named as parts of philosophy.

The twelfth-century *Didascalicon* of Hugh of Saint Victor, to take a later medieval example, divides philosophy into four parts (Wiesheipl, 1965: 65–6). It is a matter again here, as in Isidore, of uniting the Platonic, Aristotelian and Stoic schemata of the sciences. Logic, which now includes the entire trivium, is one part of philosophy. To logic is added the seven mechanical *artes*, then practical philosophy (in the threefold Aristotelian division of ethics, economics and politics), ascending up to speculative philosophy. As in Boethius, however, speculative philosophy embraces the mathematical quadrivium, set between natural philosophy and theology, and conceived as the science of forms separated from matter (Wiesheipl, 1965: 65–6).

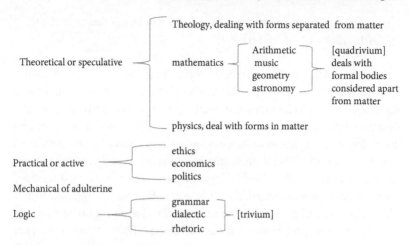

Figure 5.2 Classification of sciences in Hugh of Saint Victor. Adapted from Weisheipl (1965: 66).

In brief, philosophy is no more identified with the liberal arts, or reduced to them, in the leading classifications of the sciences in the medieval period as it was in the classical world. As in the ancient pagans, philosophy continues to encompass the liberal arts, which form its parts. As Peter Harrison has stressed in *The Territories of Sciences and Religion* (2015), we should moreover be careful before too quickly claiming, categorically, that the medievals understood the 'liberal arts', 'disciplines' or 'sciences' as we today do, identifying each with a body of 'conceptual material' or desubjectivized information. As late as the thirteenth century, Harrison (2015: 11–13) shows, Aquinas would still follow Aristotle's practice in *Nicomachean Ethics* VI by speaking of a *scientia* as an 'intellectual virtue': a 'habit' which transforms and perfects the intellectual powers of the inquirer, at the same time as it reveals truths external to him. 'Briefly', Harrison writes:

understanding was to do with grasping first principles, science with the derivation of truths from those first principles, and wisdom with the grasp of the highest causes, including the first cause, God [Aquinas, *Summa Theologica* 1a2ae, 57, 2]. To make progress in science, then, was not to add to a body of systematic knowledge about the world, but was *to become more adept* at drawing 'scientific' conclusions from general premises. 'Science' thus understood was *a mental habit that*

was gradually acquired through the rehearsal of logical demonstrations.
(2015: 12; cf. 120–1 [our italics])

When we look at the principles organizing the different medieval classifications of the sciences, likewise, we find that these are not unrelated to pedagogical considerations. Rather, the medieval classifications of *scientia* remain attentive to the demands of forming students, as well as informing them. Platonic-inspired classifications, as we have indicated, always retained the sense of the liberal mathematical disciplines (astronomy, music, geometry, arithmetic) as kinds of spiritual exercises (3). These disciplines were conceived as a training of the mind to be able to reason with pure forms, abstracted from all materiality and motion. The ascent towards 'abstraction' we see in these post-Platonic medieval classifications of the sciences is then in no way an escape from life into 'abstract' or 'empty' discourse. It is *intended* as a spiritual ascent, towards the true life and a contemplation of the highest objects. Hence, Aquinas can still describe the highest goal of theology as 'the enjoyment of the contact with God' (*Sum. Theol.* II q19 a7), as Hugh of Saint Victor had earlier argued that the study of the liberal arts aims to 'restore a divine likeness in the human mind – again, a likeness that had been lost as a consequence of the Fall' (Harrison, 2015: 66).[12]

Finally, let us note that Hadot himself closes his discussion of the scholastic transformation of philosophy in *What Is Ancient Philosophy?* with a revealing qualification of his depiction of the scholastic demotion of philosophy to *ancilla theologiae*. The characteristic teaching methods of the scholastics, reflected in their genres of writing (5) – namely, that of the *quaestio*, where both sides of an argument would be propounded by recourse to authorities, reason and experience – hearken back to the same dialectical teaching practices Hadot elsewhere identifies (2020: 140–8) as at the heart of ancient philosophical pedagogy. Abelard's *Sic et Non*, for instance, raises some 157 questions, before adducing contradictory authorities supporting either side of each question – all on the ostensibly pious grounds that 'the first key to wisdom is frequent and assiduous questioning … for by questioning we come to inquiry, and by inquiry, we come to truth' (at Durant & Durant, 1950: 939).

This scholastic technique of reasoning through raising questions and then considering the *sic et non* emerged in the twelfth to thirteenth century from out of masters' methods of expounding set texts, whether in the Arts or Theology (Marenbon, 1991: 18–19). Its other great manifestation, however, was the university disputations: again, teaching or intellectual exercises

(2) undertaken expressly to train students in the *ad utramque partem* inquiry that shapes scholastic texts. The *disputationes* involved mandated, highly codified games of questioning and answering. Students would be made to take up positions as either the objector (*opponens*) or respondent (*respondens*) to a given thesis. Then, they would try to win the dispute by recourse to authorities and to forms of syllogistic reasoning. Sometimes, as in the *quodlibet* disputes (in which the question about 'anything whatsoever' would be raised by an audience member), these discussions would be public spectacles (Marnebon, 1991: 19).[13]

The point here is that when we speak of the ascendancy of dialectic in scholastic philosophizing, we should be careful before we claim that this in itself is a sign of the 'theoreticist' insulation of philosophical activity from life. These disputes were instead highly developed forms of intellectual exercises (2) (cf. Hadot, 2020: 35, 58-9). Expressly, they looked back to Aristotle's *Topics* (Hadot, 1981: 1-2),[14] and aimed at forming students to be able to examine and argue in dialectical ways – albeit ultimately, as Peter Abelard and Siger of Brabant amongst others would discover, the better to defend and disambiguate established Christian doctrine, rather than to propound independent opinions.

5.4 Counter-strains: from Abelard to Dante's *il convito*

To be fair, Hadot himself has recognized the limits of his account of the fate of *philosophia* in the Middle Ages, acknowledging in this connection his debt to Juliusz Domański's *La Philosophie, Théorie ou manière de Vivre?* As we have indicated, Domański too sees the predominant tendency in the scholasticism of the twelfth and thirteenth centuries as reducing philosophy to a set of discursive or conceptual tools for Christian theology, elevating dialectic over the rest of philosophy, and rendering ancient philosophy's practicist dimension invisible. As Domański puts it (1996: 50), 'The names of ancient philosophers are only for [the scholastics] word-signs which serve to indicate doctrines and opinions.' This much remains mostly true for university philosophers today. Even ethics, conceived as the reading of Aristotle's *Nicomachean Ethics*, was in the universities now a theoretical or 'scientific' activity, on a par with the reading of 'the philosopher's' physics or metaphysics, suggesting no existential implications (1996).[15]

Nevertheless, Domański devotes a separate chapter of *La Philosophie* to qualifying this portrait of philosophy, and to examining competing meta-philosophical vision in the medieval period, even in philosophers working at the height of scholasticism. In the thirteenth century, at the very time that the great mediaeval universities were establishing their syllabi, Domański argues that a second lineage of thinking about philosophy and its roles emerged which was much more favourable to the ancient conception of *philosophia* than the scholastic conceptions of Thomas, Bonaventure and others. In the thought of Peter Abelard, Boethius of Dacia, Richard Kilwardy and Roger Bacon, Domański contends (1996: 65):

> One observes ... a high estimation of the attitudes and activities of the philosophers: their virtuous life can serve Christians, if not as an example, at least as a provocation, since this example make them feel ashamed, when they perceive that their life is worse than that of the pagan philosophers.

In Abelard's *Dialogue between a Philosopher, a Jew, and a Christian* (c. 1136–39 CE), to begin with, Abelard's outspoken philosopher proffers his opinions about, amongst other things, the ideal intellectual formation of the young. For the philosopher, such a *paideia* should begin with the theoretical arts and sciences, before arriving at ethics and with it, the ongoing attempt to live well. The Christian, in reply, accepts this 'practicist' ordering and gradation of the sciences. But he qualifies that what the pagan calls ethics 'we call divine wisdom' (1996: 66). Moreover, Christians consider the true goal to be communion with God, whereas philosophers only consider the means to arrive at this goal: namely the virtues. The philosopher then compliantly concedes that the Christian conception of the virtues, aimed at this *summum bonum*, is more elevated than his own. Yet what is at stake here, from beginning to end, Domański stresses, is the practicist post-Socratic sense of philosophizing as aiming to realize this Good in a life well lived (1996: 66).

In fact, in Abelard's *Epitome theologiae Christianae*, which raises the issue of whether or not non-Christians can be saved, Abelard presents the pagan philosophers very favourably: as in effect non-baptized Christians, as they had been for Justin Martyr and several other of the Fathers. Even Saint Paul admits that God had revealed to the pagan philosophers the Trinity, we are told. Many argued for an afterlife, in which punishment was assigned to wrongdoers, and rewards for the just. Some were surely proud, Abelard concedes. But then, so are many Christians. Nevertheless, the ancients' sophisticated descriptions of the virtues presuppose that they must have truly known these virtues. Indeed, Abelard proposes that divine Providence sent the Greek and Roman philosophers to instruct, incite and discipline Christians, by provoking remorse and serving as so many exemplary calls to righteous humility (1996: 68). Moving beyond the irenic position of a John Chrysostom, Abelard even proposes that some pagan philosophers *succeeded* in living admirable lives. Amazingly, he is bold enough to name in this connection Democritus the atomist, alongside Pythagoras and Socrates.

The second figure in this counter-*tendance* in the later mediaeval period whose meta-philosophical reflections Domański examines is a lesser-known thirteenth-century figure, Boethius of Dacia. Boethius was a Latin Averroist. In contrast to other scholastics, at least as Domański reads him, Boethius accorded philosophy complete autonomy from theology, treating it not as a propaedeutic to Christian teaching, but as an end in itself. In Boethius's *De summa bona sive de vita philosophi*, he thus proposes that the supreme good for human beings is 'what gives [human beings] the highest *virtus*', before claiming that 'the highest virtue of the human being is that of the intellect' (at 1996: 71). As for Aristotle, Boethius conceives the intellect as genus as having two species: the speculative (which aims at the true) and the practical (which aims at the good). It follows that, for him, 'the knowledge of the true and accomplishment of the good and their enjoyment is the highest good of man' (1996: 71–2). All human beings desire such knowledge and accomplishment. Yet only a few, the philosophers, consecrate themselves to '*studio sapientiae vaccant*'. So, skirting heresy, Boethius infers that *only philosophers live fully according to human nature*, an open reprisal of one of the ancient philosophers' paradoxes (1996: 72). Boethius's philosopher alone amongst peoples is conscious of 'the turpitude in action, which is vice; and knows nobility of action, which is virtue' (1996). So, he and he alone does not 'sin' against the order of nature. In the intellect and speculation, for Boethius, there is no sin. For, as Aristotle had upheld (*Nic. Eth.* X, 7), there can be no excess of this good.[16]

As Domański presents things, however, Roger Bacon (1214–94 CE) gives us the highest estimation of philosophers in the Christian era preceding the renaissance. Bacon is, for him, a figure who 'for many reasons, transcends the scholastic formation typical of his period', 'at the same time a scholastic and a mediaeval humanist' (1996: 74). For Bacon as for his contemporary, Richard Kilwardy (1215–79 CE),[17] ethics and not metaphysics or theology is the 'most precious' part of philosophy. For Bacon, it constitutes both the limit and the end of all other philosophical disciplines. In scholastic terms, Bacon describes this by saying that theoretical philosophy furnishes the conclusions which must become the principles of ethics.[18] With Bacon, though, we find also a singular interest in the biographies, apothegms and deeds of the philosophers, as well as their 'opinions and doctrines' (Domański, 1996: 76). For Bacon as for Abelard and later the humanists, the lives of the ancient philosophers can provide salutary ethical counter-models to humble Christians' pride.

We close this chapter, however, by recognizing the remarkable work of Ruedi Imbach concerning philosophy amongst the laity in the medieval period. All of the thinkers we have examined, even several of those whose propositions were condemned, like Boethius of Dacia, remain clerics, 'thinking as clerics and writing for clerics' (Imbach, 1996: 7). Laypeople, in whose ranks were included secular princes, were often *defined* in medieval literature by their alleged ignorance of the liberal arts and mysteries of the faith (Imbach, 1996: 8–13). Nevertheless, Imbach draws our attention to a series of philosophical works written by Saint Thomas, Giles of Rome, Jacques Legrand and others which were addressed to the laity, sometimes in response to epistolary inquiries made by the latter, sometimes involving translating philosophical texts from Latin into the vernacular. Such texts, on the one hand, attest to a demand for philosophical education amongst the laity located outside of the monasteries and universities (Imbach, 1996: 76–7). On the other hand, as Imbach is at pains to stress, the different addressees of these texts called forth different types of philosophical writing, a rhetorical consideration which is thematized in *De regimine principum* by Giles of Rome (1243–1316 CE) (Imbach, 1996: 52–5).

These texts also provided the venue for different meta-philosophical reflections, outside of clerical supervision and untethered to the university's educational curricula. The ambitious *Archiloge sophie* of Jacques Legrand (*c*.1360–1415 CE), after giving a vernacular epitome of the Aristotelian *Organon*, hence turns its attention directly to the question of the philosophical life. Legrand cites *Nicomachean Ethics* X, in conjunction with the opening of Aristotle's *Metaphysics*, to defend the ideas that all people desire happiness, and that this happiness lies in 'sapience' (Imbach, 1996: 57). He then proceeds, citing 'the ancients', to stipulate that what is in play in the pursuit of this wisdom is a way of life, 'the way of truth and mistress of good morals'; as well as a calling that demands a withdrawal from 'worldly occupations', whether to the mountain or to the desert (Imbach, 1996: 58).

Without doubt the most remarkable philosophical text Imbach examines which was written for laity in the medieval period is however Dante Alighieri's (1261–1321 CE) incomplete, *Il Convito* (*The Banquet*). This text is penned in the vernacular and in the first person by someone who, not being a cleric, has not feasted upon 'the bread of angels', yet has conceived the compassionate desire to make such a *convito* possible to the laity (Imbach, 1996: 135). *Il Convito* passes between autobiographical verse and Dante's own learned commentary upon the former. Upon the death of his beloved Beatrice, we are told in the second Treatise (II, 13), Dante took up Boethius's *Consolations of Philosophy* [**4.5**] and Cicero's *De Amicitia* [**4.3**] (Imbach, 1996: 135). At this time, the poem dramatizes, the poet was indeed himself visited by Boethius's Lady Philosophy (cf. Domański, 1996: 37), full of sorrow for Dante's widowed state. Philosophy implores Dante to replace his love of Beatrice with love for her. However, such a conversion of the eye of the soul is not easy:

> Because Love is not born suddenly, nor grows great nor comes to perfection in haste, but desires time and food for thought, especially there where there are antagonistic thoughts which impede it, there must needs be, before this new Love could be perfect, a great battle between the thought of its food and of that which was antagonistic to it, which still held the fortress of my mind for that glorious Beatrice. (II, 2)

Three features of the ensuing *psychomachia* are especially striking for us in this book. Firstly, there is Dante's opening insistence upon the demotic significance of Aristotle's quantifier in the famous declaration of the *Metaphysics* that 'all men by nature desire knowledge' (see Imbach, 1996: 136). For Dante, what this means is that 'those who, for familial or social reasons, remain in hunger, come to share the table with those who, for similar reasons, have also been selected' (at Imbach, 1996: 136). Laypeople can be philosophers, on the highest philosophical authority.

The second feature is the veritable eulogy to Philosophy that Dante's work unfolds as it proceeds. For Dante as for Boethius of Dacia (and likewise skirting condemnation), philosophy names the highest perfection at which humans can arrive:

> And of this Philosophy, in which Human Intelligence has part, there will now be the following encomiums to prove how great a part of her good gifts is bestowed on Human Nature … : *Her Maker saw that she was good, and poured,/Beyond our Nature, fulness of His Power/ On her pure Soul,/whence shone this holy dower/through all her frame.*

For the capacity of our Nature is subdued by [philosophy], which it makes beautiful and virtuous. Wherefore, although ... the first study, that whereby the habit [of Philosophy] is begotten, cannot perfectly acquire that philosophy ... here one sees her lowly praise; for, perfect or imperfect, she never loses the name of perfection. (III, 13)

Finally and most singularly, Imbach notes how Dante in *Il Convito* nevertheless – in this less like Boethius of Dacia than like Roger Bacon – oscillates between an orthodox Aristotelian meta-philosophy, for which metaphysics is the culminating goal of philosophizing, and a second meta-philosophical position which accords primacy to the practical efficacy of philosophy. Philosophy's aim, in pursuing wisdom, must ultimately be to cultivate the virtues, he argues, rather than to inculcate any disembodied theoretical Truth (see Palmer, 2016: 192). As he writes at III 15, 'For as the beauty of the body is the result of its members in proportion as they are fitly ordered, so the beauty of Wisdom, which is the body of Philosophy, ... results from the order of the Moral Virtues which visibly make that joy.'[19]

Philosophy should be ultimately a divinely sent 'guide' for living. That her solace and direction is in principle addressed to everyone (although few can pursue her 'habit' fully). And that 'the habit of philosophy' (II, 13), not faith or theology, allows us to attain to the perfection of our natures. All these positions in *Il Convito* justify situating Dante, in philosophy as well as in poetry, as the first sounding of what would become the Italian renaissance.

CHAPTER 6
THE RENAISSANCE OF PHILOSOPHY AS A WAY OF LIFE

6.1 Philosophy, the *humanisti* and the ascendancy of rhetoric

The curious student waits in vain to examine the philosophers of the European Renaissance in most philosophy syllabi today. The different courses s/he sits will almost always jump this extraordinary period, passing from Aquinas's or Scotus's theology to Bacon's or Descartes's texts on epistemology.[1] A striking clash exists between this state of affairs and the almost universally agreed significance of the Italian and Northern Renaissance in shaping modern culture. Our assessment that there was no real philosophy done in the renaissance, or that Aristotelianism alone continued in the universities, also butts up against the self-understandings of key renaissance figures. Francesco Petrarch insisted on being identified as a moral philosopher as well as a poet, as we will see. Coluccio Salutati, Leonardo Bruni, Erasmus of Rotterdam and other humanists also understood their own thought and activities as philosophical. Nor did their contemporaries question this 'philosophical' self-assessment (Siegel, 1968; Celenza, 2013).[2]

Indeed, even the most ardent sceptic cannot doubt that the fifteenth and sixteenth centuries saw the most remarkable opening up of Western European philosophical *culture* for many centuries. This was the period that saw the recovery of Lucretius, Xenophon, Epictetus, Sextus Empiricus, Stobaeus's and Diogenes Laertius's doxographies, Plotinus, all of Plato's dialogues, and later Marcus Aurelius (Hankins & Palmer, 2008). For the first time since Augustine or Boethius, Latinate scholars in the quattrocento could debate the great Hellenistic philosophies, as well as those of Plato, Porphyry and Aristotle, without relying on Cicero's, and the sometimes-hostile glosses of the Church Fathers. A host of commentaries on the recovered ancient texts followed, accompanying these new translations. To these commentaries were added works broaching the principal *topoi* of ancient moral philosophy: dialogues concerning the highest good (**8**), moral discipline, the virtues and expediency, true (versus apparent) nobility, the relation between the sciences, the power of fortune in human affairs, the ideal education, the ideal courtier, the active versus contemplative life and the immortality of the soul (Trinkhaus, 1965; Kristeller, 1980; Streuver, 1992). Petrarch in his later works advanced a form of Christianized Stoicism. Lorenzo Valla openly championed a Christian Epicureanism (Lorch, 2009). Marsilio Ficino propounded a Christianized form of Neoplatonism, heavily inflected by hermeticism. Within a century, Justus Lipsius [7.4] would be proposing a 'Neostoic' philosophy at the same time as Michel de Montaigne [7.3] conceived an eclectic form of philosophizing, drawing from Scepticism, Stoicism and Epicureanism.

When we assess the literary and philosophical outputs of the Italian Renaissance in light of our 'Tennead', in fact, renaissance philosophy includes each of the ten features we identified as characterizing PWL. Alongside a plurality of literary forms (5) and explicit concerns about the highest end (8), the period sees changing institutional forms of philosophical activity (1), with many of humanistic (and earlier scientific) thought's carriers located outside of the universities. There are heated disputes on the parts and ends of philosophy (4), and its relationships to law, medicine, dialectic and rhetoric. We see the prescription of intellectual (2) and spiritual exercises (3) aiming at forming new kinds of individual, as in Alberti's *Della Famiglia* or the description of their practice, as in Alberti's *Vita* (Zak, 2014). Most strikingly, as Juliusz Domański has documented, there is a rebirth for the first time since antiquity of interest in the lives and apothegms of the philosophers (5, 10).

This revival, as Domański presents it (1996: 97–100 [5.4]), looks as far back as the thirteenth century with Roger Bacon and John Wallis (Ionnes Guallensis) and his *Compendiloquium de vitis illust. philosophorum*, and his *Summa de regimine humanae vitae*.[3] Between 1425 and 1433, Ambrogi Traversari translated Diogenes Laertius into Latin with a commentary, dedicating the work to his patron, the elder Cosimo de Medici. Traversari stressed the superiority of the single conception Christianity affords of the good life, compared to the competing visions of the pagan schools (Domański, 1996: 100). Nevertheless, like Abelard and Roger Bacon [5.4], he appeals to these models to spur Christians to 'virtue and moderation' which these pagans pursued with 'zeal and probity' (Domański, 1996; 101). In Traversari, also, an appreciation of the *atopia* of the figure of the philosopher is renewed, after its medieval denigrations [5.1].[4]

There are the numerous biographies of the philosophers (8) written by renaissance figures themselves. In 1415, Leonardo Bruni wrote a life of

Cicero as a Preface to his translation of Plutarch's life. In 1429, Bruni wrote a life of Aristotle, whose *Ethics* he had translated. Bruni is also responsible for a translation of Plato's *Symposium*, featuring Alcibiades's biographical eulogy to Socrates, edited and edi*fied* for Christian readers (Domański, 1996: 103–4; Hankins, 2006: 187–8). Giannozzo Manetti wrote a life of Socrates (*c.* 1440), and another of Seneca. Ficino, a quarter of a century later, wrote biographies of Socrates and Plato (Hankins, 2006: 190–6).[5] All of the humanistic biographies evince a principal interest in the philosophers' lived moralities, as well as their proximity to Christian virtues. A *Vita Platonis* of uncertain attribution – either by Bruni or Guarino Guarini – halts its account of Platonic teachings to 'present ... what I know of his life, for it comprehends and teaches that the glory of virtue is contained in action' (at Domański, 1996: 106–7).

As James Hankins (2008: 204) has commented of Manetti's Socrates, these texts 'intended to make [the pagan philosophers] into authorities for and *exempla* of the humanist cultural project'. This is what is so remarkable for us, for the challenge it poses to the contemporary tendency to pass over the work of the humanists as not philosophical. Leading renaissance scholar Paul Otto Kristeller's main reason for denying the title 'philosopher' to Petrarch and his admirers is itself instructive.[6] Kristeller observes that the leading humanists hailed from the fields of grammatical and rhetorical studies, within the old trivium, as against those of logic, theology or the natural philosophy integrated into the quadrivium (4). Or else they were men of action, 'civic humanists', like Bruni and Salutati.[7] The humanists' pre-eminent achievement, as Kristeller asks us to see things, was to overturn the later medieval, scholastic prioritization of dialectic as the pedagogical method of methods (4), and to displace the mathematical quadrivium from Arts syllabi. In place of the seven liberal arts would come the five humanist disciplines of grammar, rhetoric, poetry, history and moral philosophy. These were to be studied not by recourse to Aristotle, the Arab commentators and the university textbooks.[8] Their instruction would proceed by reading the newly available works of ancient historians, poets, rhetoricians and philosophers. Thus, as Kristeller notes, even those humanistic texts with a direct concern with moral philosophy have an unmistakably rhetorical, exhortatory dimension.[9]

Yet there is nothing by itself about the humanists' desire to emulate classical, especially Ciceronian eloquence which speaks against their works also being philosophical. While Plato dismissed sophistic rhetoric in the *Gorgias,* in the *Phaedrus* he spoke eloquently in favour of philosophically directed rhetoric.[10] While Aristotle does not typically list rhetoric as a part of philosophy, he devoted an extensive work to its systematic examination.[11] And whilst the Epicureans dismissed rhetorical finery, the Stoics maintained rhetoric as one part of logic.[12] We recall from **4.3**, moreover, that Cicero had argued that while wisdom was superior to eloquence, and while eloquence uninformed by wisdom must become empty or amoral, wisdom without eloquence was incapable of moving human beings to action.[13] It hence behoves the philosopher who would also be an effective teacher to cultivate the rhetorical and pedagogical arts. The dialectic of the schoolmen, the humanists saw, calls only upon the logical dimension of discourse: that of definition, division and demonstration.[14] Their criticisms of scholastic dialectic, and their refusal to carry forwards the literary forms derived from the *yes and no* of the *disputationes* echo Cicero's criticisms of the syllogizing of the Hellenistic Stoics.[15] On the one hand, the language promoted by the *disputatio* was 'barbarous' and foreign alike to eloquence and everyday usage.[16] On the other hand, this remoteness from everyday discourse rendered dialectical philosophy completely lost upon the wider run of men. As Petrarch writes, flashing his teeth, in his *Familiar Letters*:

> They [the dialecticians] belong to the class of whom Quintilian speaks in his *Institutes of Oratory*, whom one finds wonderfully warm in disputation, but once get them away from their cavilling, they are as helpless, in a serious juncture, as certain small animals which are active enough in a narrow space, but easily captured in a field.[17]

By contrast, rhetoric's proper subjects are the concerns of citizens and laity, rather than clerics and specialists (see **Chapter 5.4**). One of rhetoric's cardinal rules is that the rhetor uses language accessible to different audiences. Evoking Aristotle's famous tripartition in the *Rhetoric*, the speech or writing of the orator also encompasses the dimensions of *ethos*, the self-presentation of the speaker to his audience, and that of *pathos,* the abilities to please and to move the audience. As we commented in **4.3**, it is above all this last dimension, the power of rhetorical language to move as well as teach, that Petrarch and his followers saw as an invaluable component of moral philosophy.[18] Reflecting their Christian inheritance as much as their admiration of the ancient pagans, the humanists were acutely aware of what Aristotle called *akrasia*: the insufficiency of knowing the good for actively pursuing it. In an iconic passage that would be echoed throughout the renaissance, Petrarch claimed in his 1367 *Of My Own Ignorance and That of Many Others* that Aristotle's ethical writings may increase our knowledge of the virtues and vices. However, 'by no facts was the promise fulfilled which the philosopher makes ... that "we learn this part of philosophy not with the purpose of gaining knowledge but of becoming better"' (Petrarch, *De Ign.*, 82). At issue in Petrarch's critique of 'the philosopher' here is a set of paired distinctions. On the one hand, there is knowledge and the understanding. On the other hand, there is love and the will:

> It is one thing to know, another to love; one thing to understand, another to will. He [Aristotle] teaches what virtue is, I do not deny that; but his lesson lacks the words that sting and set afire and urge toward love of virtue and hatred of vice or, at any rate, does not have enough of such power. (*De Ign.*, 102)

As Brian Vickers (2008) contends, it is above all the epideictic use of rhetoric that Petrarch and his followers saw as an essential addition to theoretical analyses of ethics. Herein, the censure of actions and exemplars can 'sting' the audience to shame, as Socrates had done with Alcibiades. Their praise and examples can 'set afire' our desire for emulation (Vickers, 2008: 734–7). We see what is at issue here if we compare the literary form of the *Nicomachean Ethics* with that of Epictetus's *Encheiridion*. As Nicolas Perotti wrote to Nicolas V, 'The fact [is] that because of others' writings, we know what justice is, and what valour and moderation, whereas through the exhortations of Epictetus *we become* valiant, just and moderate' (at Domański, 1996: 108 [italics added]). Manetti in his *Vita Socratis,* following Petrarch, likewise valorises Cicero's and Seneca's moral writings over those of Aristotle, on grounds of their greater power to affect and inspire readers, 'even those who sleep or who are occupied with other things, to a nearly unbelievable love of the virtues and hatred of the vices' (at Domański, 1996: 108–9).

With this much said, we turn to three leading renaissance *humanisti,* each of whom set about reanimating the ancient conception of PWL.

6.2 Petrarch's Christian-Stoic medicines of the mind

Francesco Petrarch's life (1304–74 CE) was as shiftless as his identity was complex (Trinkhaus, 1971; Celenza, 2017). The young Petrarch made his name by writing love poetry in the vernacular, inspired by his muse, Laura, and full of the 'fluctuation, fragmentation, and exile' that characterized his existence (Zak, 2010: 82). Nevertheless, it was as a moral philosopher as well as a poet that Petrarch would describe himself in the 'Letter to Posterity' (1898) that closes his *Letters of Old Age*. This opposition between the old Platonic rivals, philosophy and poetry, is just one of many oppositions that Petrarch's life and literary production span. There is also that between Christianity and the classical pagan culture Petrarch revered; the opposition between monastic withdrawal and the pursuit of worldly fame; as well as those between the medieval culture in which Petrarch was raised and the burgeoning modern world.

Petrarch's *oeuvre* ranges across a wide variety of literary genres (5) (Kirham & Maggi, 2012). Alongside vernacular poetry, there are *Familiar Letters* and the *Letters of Old Age* prepared by Petrarch for publication. There are historical biographies of *Illustrious Men*; the epic poem *Africa*; collections of sayings and anecdotes from the ancients and Church Fathers; a *Secret Book of the Conflict of My Desires* in dialogue; and a massive collection of *Remedies for Both Kinds of Fortune* which today languishes unread, but was amongst Petrarch's most popular works in the decades after his death (Petrarch, 1991).

The resemblance between Petrarch's literary profile and those of several ancient philosophers we have examined, led by Cicero and Seneca, is not coincidental. In Petrarch's work, as Gur Zak, Juliusz Domański, Étienne Anheim and Ruedi Imbach have examined (Domański, 1996: 91–7; Anheim, 2008; Zak, 2010; Imbach, 2015), we see a particularly pure rebirth of the Hellenistic and Roman sense of PWL. His philosophical *oeuvre* is founded on a stern critique both of scholastic dialectic and pedantry (4) and the lives of non-philosophers (8). It incorporates intellectual and spiritual practices (3), and furnishes consolation (and self-consolation), counsels and other 'remedies' for human miseries (6). Everywhere, as in his poetry, Petrarch's philosophical meditations are oriented by the search for wisdom and his own lasting, elusive happiness (7, 9). Let us consider each of these features in turn.

i. Philosophy, a way of life, not of 'prattling'

It is in the light of the ancient conception of PWL that Petrarch's frequently-resumed, acerbic critique of scholastic dialectic has to be seen (4). Petrarch sees the scholastic prioritization of dialectic in pedagogy as a recipe to prioritize words over things, and intellectual sophistication over more substantial epistemic and practical virtues. As Petrarch's alter, 'Augustinus' expresses it in book I of the *Secretum* (*Secret Book*):

> This prattling of the Dialecticians will never come to an end; it throws up summaries and definitions like bubbles, matter indeed for endless controversies, but for the most part they know nothing of the real truth of the things they talk about ... The best way of dealing with this brood, with their studied air of carelessness and empty curiosity, is to launch at their head some such invective as this: 'You wretched creatures, why this everlasting labour for nothing; this expense of wit on silly subtleties? ... Heaven grant that your foolishness hurts no one but yourselves and does as little harm as possible to the excellent minds and capacities of the young'. (Petrarch, 1989: 54)

What the dialecticians miss, even as they parse minute definitions of 'man', is that philosophy's true work is 'the formation of the soul', Petrarch contends (at Anheim, 2008: 601). The university protocols and ceremonials by which 'today's sages' are elevated are hence absurd, Petrarch ironizes, 'the true sages are elsewhere' (at Anheim, 2008: 603). As Petrarch explains:

> I do not give the name 'philosopher' to those who are called, to speak justly, 'men of the chair' (*cathedrarios*). For they philosophise in the chair, while in their actions they are unconscious [of their principles]; they give precepts to others and they are the first to be opposed to their own recommendations, to violate their own laws ... It is thus not of these men that I speak, but of true philosophers who, always less numerous, confirm by their actions what they preach: who love and care for wisdom. (*De vita solitaria,* at Domański, 1996: 94)

Philosophy is thus for Petrarch, as it was for the ancients, 'a school of life' (*De vita solitaria,* at Siegel, 1968: 44). Its task is to cultivate a 'good disposition of mind' in its votaries (*Fam.* 1, 9, 3). On the basis of this practicist sense of philosophy's calling, Petrarch also reanimates two of the other post-Socratic, ancient characterizations of PWL. Philosophy's business is the medicining or curing of the soul. The classical medical analogy defended in Epicurus and Cicero (7) is extensively developed in Petrarch's *oeuvre*. 'The care of the soul calls for a philosopher, while the proper use of language requires an orator,' he writes: 'We must neglect neither one, if, as they say, we are to return to the earth and be led about on the mouths of men' (*Remedies*, at McClure,

1991: 62–3).[19] Like the ancient Platonists and Stoics, Petrarch identifies the passions as the sources of our mental disorders, and understands these passions as involving corrigible species of false beliefs:

> Neither am I ignorant that, as in the bodies of man, so also in their minds that are affected with sundry passions, the medicines of words (*medicamenta verborum*) will seem to many to be without effect. But it does not escape me that as the diseases of the mind (*animorum morbi*) are invisible, so are their remedies. For even those who are assailed by false opinions must be liberated by true maxims, so that those who fell by hearing may be raised up by hearing. ('Preface' of *Remedies* I, at McClure, 1991: 54)

As Montaigne will, Petrarch propounds (with some vehemence) the Platonic-Ciceronian designation of philosophy as a preparation for death. 'What have you to say, O man of little strength? ... Remember you not that you are mortal?', thunders Augustinus at the start of the *Secretum*, addressing 'Francesco', the author's avatar (*Secr.*, 41). The *Invective against Medicine* likewise instructs its readers to 'reflect upon your death, arm yourself against her, train yourself to scorn her', a practice of meditation to which Petrarch's *Familiar Letters* attest (Zak, 2010: 144–5). *Meditatio mori* constitutes for Petrarch 'the true philosophy' (Petrarch, *Invectiva contra medicum*, II, 9, at Anheim, 2008: 600).

For Petrarch, the ideal philosophical life (7) is one of contemplative withdrawal, a mode of living closer to the monasticism of his brother Gherardo, than to the civic humanism of Bruni, Salutati and other of his humanistic admirers (see Blanchard, 2001: 401–2). The longing for such *otium* shadowed Petrarch throughout his life. It forms the flipside of acerbic criticisms of the life of non-philosophers (8) which echo the monastic genre of the *contemptus mundi*, as Blanchard has shown (2001; McClure, 1991: 55–8). Petrarch can barely maintain his equanimity when he comes to describe his 'disgust for this place where I live, in the most melancholy and disorderly of towns' in *Secretum* II (91):

> The motley crew of people, swarms of vile beggars side by side with the flaunting luxury of the wealthy, the one crushed down in sordid misery, the others debauched with pleasure and riot; and then ... the endless clamour of ... confused voices, as the passers-by jostle one another in the streets

Petrarch's *De Vita Solitaria* raises a secular hymn to the life of leisured withdrawal, 'so full of peace and so like to the life of the sky' (at Anheim, 2008: 595). The *vita ativa* is conducive to haste, unease, confusion and distraction. By contrast, the *vita contemplativa* enables the 'return to himself' (*Fam.* 2, 5, 6; cf. 1, 88; Zak, 2010: 87) at the heart of Petrarch's understanding of *philosophia* (**6**):

> O life, which reforms the soul, corrects morals, renews affections, erases blemishes, purges faults, reconciles God and man ... which scorns bodies, cultivates spirits, moderates the excessive, awakens the drowsy, engenders noble appetites, nourishes and sustains the virtues, tames and destroys the passions; palaestra for the fight, arena for the course, field for the combat, arch for the triumph, library for reading, cell for meditation, sanctuary for prayer, mountain for contemplation ... all [these things] at once. (at Anheim, 2008: 595–6)[20]

ii. Philosophy as medicina animi

True to his meta-philosophy, Petrarch in his letters as well as his *Remedies for Fortune, Fair and Foul* presents himself as a *medicus animorum* (**6**) capable of delivering cures in words for a compendious range of ailments.[21] *De Remediis* alone presents some *two hundred and fifty four* species of prosperity and adversity that could profit from the philosophical doctor's prescriptions.[22] These *malaises* are headed by grief and bereavement, sadness or *aegritudo* (McClure, 1991: 69–70; 25, 29), exile, ambition, the fickleness of love and fortune, and mortality. In Stoic vein, Petrarch's cures are placed in the mouth of '*Ratio*' (Reason) itself, who addresses personified versions of each of the four species of passion, as reported by Cicero in *Tusculan Disputations* III–IV: *Spes* (hope), *Gaudium* (joy), *Metus* (fear) and *Dolor* (sadness) (McClure, 1991: 46–72).

In Petrarch's 'psychotherapeutic' texts (Panizza, 2009), as in both the pagan and Christian literature we have examined in previous chapters, Petrarch's orienting move is to direct his own and his addressees' attention inwards (**5**). They should turn away from the external occasions for the philosophical or spiritual therapy, towards how they have responded to these events. 'What is exile?', Petrarch, for example, asks Severo rhetorically in the *Familiar Letters* (2, 3, 5): 'Is it the very nature of the situation, the absence of a dear one, or rather the indignation and impatient desire of a languishing mind that is irritating?' For Petrarch as for Epictetus (Panizza, 2009), it is not external things that trouble people. It is their opinions about these things:

But if you choose to consult yourself (*te ipsum consulere*) and to speak with yourself rather than with others, I would never stop expecting great things from you and would call you most happy since you serve as your own judge, and I would consider you worthy of envy rather than of pity.

Petrarch's diagnoses of the nature and causes of human malaises pass almost seamlessly between Christian and pagan, philosophical vocabularies. Ten years before the Stoicizing *De Remediis*, in book II of the *Secretum*, Petrarch's Augustinus – transparently modelled on the historical Saint Augustine – gets his charge to confess, despite himself, to his own forms of the seven deadly sins: Lust, Avarice, Sloth, Wrath, Pride, Envy and Gluttony. Contra Gur Zak, there seems clear continuity between this process and the Christian practices of writing as a means to excavate guilt in Augustine, Guigo I and Thomas à Kempis (cf. Zak, 2010: 114–16). Petrarch's Augustinus also suggests a distinctly Christian hermeneutic of the self [see **5.2**]. He thus tries to force the resisting Francesco to confront the manifold forms of self-deceit that prevent him from overcoming his ailments:

No man can become or can be unhappy unless he so chooses; but as I said at the beginning, there is in men a certain perverse and dangerous inclination to deceive themselves, which is the most deadly thing in life. For if it is true that we rightly fear being taken in by those with whom we live, … how much rather ought you to fear the deceptions you practise on yourself, where love, influence, familiarity play so large a part, … where Deceiver and Deceived are one and the same person? (*Secr.*, 46)

With that said, at other places within the *Secretum*, Petrarch's aetiology of human malaise is more clearly Platonic in inspiration. The root of our difficulties is said to come from how human beings are 'overwhelmed with too many impressions' that 'plague' the bodily senses (Zak, 2010: 60), preventing us from raising our eyes towards eternal things:

A law was imposed on me together with my body when I was born, that from its association with me I must suffer many things which I would not suffer otherwise. The poet [Virgil], aware of the secrets of nature, when he ascribed to human souls a certain burning force which he called of heavenly origin, added the following by way of exception: 'Insofar as mortal bodies don't slow them down and earthly organs and mortal members do not weaken them. This is why they fear and desire and suffer and rejoice but cannot recognize the heavens since they are enclosed in the darkness of a blind prison.' (*Fam.* 2, 5, 4; Zak, 2010: 88–9)

Zak is certainly right that Petrarch's Augustinus elsewhere gives voice to what in the Christian perspective is a Stoicizing 'Pelagianism' about the prospects of people effecting their own spiritual correction. More like Seneca than his historical namesake, 'Augustinus' insists from near the start of *Secretum* I that s/he who wills their own salvation, honestly and humbly, *will be able by that willing* to effect that salvation.[23] What then emerges is a heavily Stoicizing model of *medicina animi* that pictures spiritual amelioration as involving not an opening to grace, but an internalization of the rule of virtue:

You will know that you have finally cut off this yoke when, having scorned human passions, you have submitted wholly to the rule of virtue. From then on you will be free, needing nothing, subject to no human being – at last a king both truly powerful and completely happy. (*Secr.*, 78)[24]

iii. Reading and writing as spiritual exercises (3)

What above all marks out Petrarch's practice of PWL, however, concerns his practices of reading and writing (Anheim, 2008; Zak, 2010: 81–6). Here again, we observe Petrarch's deep indebtedness to both the Christian-monastic and pagan-philosophical lineages that we have examined in our earlier chapters. Reading for Petrarch is in one of its modalities, as in Seneca's *Consolation to Polybius*, a solace and distraction from the cares of life, as his consolatory letter to Severo (like his 1372 letter to Bocaccio [*Sen.* 1, 5, 51; *Letters of Old Age*, 1, 23; Zak, 2010: 146–7]) shows.[25] Petrarch is as acutely aware as the monastic authors of the limits of reading, without actively meditating upon what one reads, if what is aimed at is ethical transformation [see **4.2**]. 'This way of reading is become common now; there is such a mob of *litterati*, a detestable herd, who have spread themselves everywhere and make long discussions in the schools on the art of life, which they put in practice little enough,' Augustinus complains to Francesco early in *Secretum* II (92). Francesco should learn to read differently, so as to 'derive fruit from your reading' (Zak, 2010). Francesco should actively make *hypomnêmata* as he reads: writing down striking maxims and exempla that emerge, with the aim of committing them to memory. In this way, recurring to the medical analogy for philosophizing, such thoughts may furnish models, guides and remedies in situations of need:

> Whenever you read a book and meet with any wholesome maxims by which you feel your spirit stirred or enthralled, do not trust merely to the resources of your wits, but make a point of learning them by heart and making them quite familiar by meditating on them, as the doctors do with their experiments, so that no matter when or where some urgent case of illness arises, you have the remedy written, so to speak, in your own mind. (*Secr.*, 92–3)

As in monastic *lectio*,[26] but here with the secular writings of the pagan poets, orators and philosophers also in mind (Zak, 2010: 144–8), the Petrarchan philosopher should therefore read aloud, with the mouth as well as the mind. The aim is to effect the complete internalization of edifying external discourses: 'I cannot tell you of what worth to me in solitude are certain familiar and famous words not only grasped in the mind but actually spoken orally ... [and] how much delight I get from repeating the written words either of others or sometimes even my own!' (*Fam.* 1, 9, 11–12; cf. 1, 49; Zak, 2010: 80–1).

Finally, the act of writing is conceived and undertaken by Petrarch as its own spiritual practice(s) (**3**). Firstly, there is the 'common-placing' of others' maxims and exempla, for recollection and edification: a practice underlying the emergence of the early modern essay, and in Petrarch's *oeuvre*, directly productive of *Rerum memorandarum libre* (Moss, 1996; Chechi, 2012). Secondly, Petrarch's writing is often undertaken as its own means of self-consolation, self-examination and self-cultivation, as well as a medium to proffer others counsel and advice. It was 'to the best of my abilities to mollify or, if possible, to extirpate *my own passions* and those of my readers' that Petrarch relates that he attempted the monumental *De Remediis* (*Sen.* 16, 9; McClure, 1991: 56). We clearly see the same therapeutic intention underlying many of his letters. Vital here again is the function of exposing oneself to the examination of another that writing involves, as a means to reframe, examine and evaluate one's own conduct.[27] The dialogue of the *Secretum*, in which Augustinus is a kind of elevated ego-ideal and spiritual director, fictively dramatizes the same work of self-examination. Unpublished in

Petrarch's own lifetime, its Preface explains its aim as an 'intimate and deep' example of self-writing, close in intent to Marcus Aurelius's *Ta Eis Heauton*:

> That this discourse ... might not be lost, I have set it down in writing and made this book: not that I wish to class it with my other works, or desire from it any credit. My thoughts aim higher. What I desire is that I may be able by reading it to renew as often as I wish the pleasure I felt from the discourse itself ... and when I would think upon deep matters, all that [this book] preserves in remembrance, that was spoken in secret, will be told to me in secret over again. (*Secr.*, 39)

There is however a third, more novel signification at play in Petrarch's forms of writing and self-writing, as Gur Zak (2010: 100–4; 2012: 501) has noted. The careful preparation of Petrarch's *Familiar Letters* for publication, in part on the model of Cicero's correspondence which Petrarch had discovered, in part on a Senecan model, attest to Petrarch's ambition to present his own life as an *exemplum*. Through these epistles, we are made privy to Petrarch's mundane activities and travels, and his vacillating responses to the vicissitudes of a fortune which, on the one hand, saw the poet-philosopher rise early to worldly fame and, on the other hand, suffer grievous losses and ongoing inner turmoils. Petrarch's autobiographical self-writing, which weaves a sometimes-disarming self-disclosure into a digressive inner discourse laced with a profusion of deeply-internalized classical *sententiae* heralds the genre of the essay we find in Michel de Montaigne (5).

6.3 Montaigne: the essayist as philosopher

The renaissance of classical thought and the arts that began in Italy migrated North after the passing of the generation of Ficino, Pico della Mirandola and the 'Platonic Academy' (Kristeller, 1980: 69–88). The ravages of the French invasion and the fall of the Florentine republic, the rounding of the Cape of Good Hope and the consolidation of Islamic control over the Eastern Mediterranean, the discovery of the New World and the shift of Europe's economic centre of gravity towards the Atlantic seaboard – all contributed to what scholars have called the waning of the Italian Renaissance (Bousma, 2002). Nevertheless, alongside the new art and architecture, the ancient and humanistic conception of PWL migrated North with the humanist teachers, and in the new editions in Latin and the vernaculars they produced of recovered Stoic, Epicurean and Sceptical texts. Erasmus, for example, prepared an edition of Cicero's *De Officiis*, and his *Encheiridion Militis Christiani* of 1503 clearly reflects Erasmus's moral-philosophic ambition of forging 'a Christianity which, by taking account of the solutions to ethical problems provided by the classics, should place the stress upon the feasibility of leading a moral life largely through the exercise of reason and will' (Ettinghausen, 1972: 5–6; Dealy, 2017). Juan Louis Vives, following Petrarch's lead in *De Remediis Utriusque Fortunae* set out to achieve his own synthesis of Stoic and Christian moral thought in the 1524 *Introductio ad Sapientium* (Curtis, 2011). Perhaps the most influential (and the most lovable) philosopher to emerge from the Northern Renaissance is Michel de Montaigne (1533–92), author of the *Essais* of 1580, expanded in 1588.

Montaigne was every bit as immersed in classical pagan history, poetry and philosophy as Petrarch and the Italian humanists. The *Essais* include dedicated considerations of 'Cato the Younger', 'Upon Cicero', 'Of Democritus and Heraclitus', 'A Defence of Seneca and Plutarch' (Montaigne's favourite ancient authors),[28] and an abundance of references to Socrates (Limbrick, 1973; Gontier & Mayer eds., 2010). Every essay, even the most personal, is dotted with citations of the Romans and Greeks, Pliny, Horace, Cicero, Virgil, Lucretius, Herodotus, Thucydides, Plato and more. As we will see, whether or not Pierre Hadot (2002a: 374) is right to claim that the *Essais* are nothing other than spiritual exercises (3), Montaigne was certainly intimately familiar with the ancients' ideas of PWL. 'My trade and my art is living,' he professes (7) (II, 6, 274).

Montaigne's *Essais* were penned after Montaigne had retired in his late thirties from life as a magistrate. To their author's professed surprise, they were an immediate popular success. The *Essais* have never since gone out of print. Nor have they ceased to attract a host of admirers including Shakespeare, Voltaire, Diderot, Nietzsche, Virginia Woolf and Stefan Zweig. The literary form (5) of Montaigne's book was distinct and innovative. In its final form, Montaigne's *Essais* comprise 107 chapters, divided into three books, plus a curt Preface. The essays vary from a few pages to 'The Apology of Raymond Sebond', almost a monograph on its own. Yet the whole seems to have no clear plan. It proceeds paratactically, from subject to subject, each examined by way of a litany of stories and examples from ancient, modern, pagan and Christian sources, rather than through linear, syllogistic argumentation. Montaigne is unfazed by this apparent lack of order. He boasts of the *Essais*' 'wild and desultory plan' (II, 8, 278), and of his own 'play[ing] the fool' (II, 3, 251)[29] There is a real opening up in the *Essais* to the miniscule and contingent which takes us far beyond even Petrarch's disarming personal frankness in his *Letters*. 'There is no subject so frivolous that does not merit a place in this rhapsody,' Montaigne muses (I, 13, 32). He feels it worth writing essays 'Of Smells', 'Of Cannibals', 'Of the Custom of Wearing Clothes', 'Of Names', 'How We Cry and Laugh for the Same Thing', 'Of Thumbs' or 'Of Sleep'. Montaigne's humanistic commonplaces and learned Latin citations trade places with anecdotes from his own life and curios from different places, peoples, climates and times.

What then can we say of the genre (5) of this remarkable work? The French *essayer* means to test, to exercise, to attempt, to experiment or examine (II.11, II.13, III.12), to experience or learn by experience (I, 20; II, 6; III, 13; Edelman, 2010). In Montaigne's defence, many ancient writings share with his *Essais* the apparent lack of order, and the frequent circling around and play of digressions. The proximity of ancient writing to spoken dialogue speaks in favour of such meandering modes of discourse (Hadot, 2020: 81–90). Montaigne himself cites Seneca and Plutarch as his favourite authors, since 'the knowledge I seek there is discoursed in loose pieces that do not require of me any trouble of reading long ... for they have no sequence or dependence upon one another' (see II, 10, 300).

In one register, the *Essais* seem to embody a new form of philosophical *hypomnêmata*, like Marcus Aurelius's *Meditations* (for, improbably, Montaigne complains that he has a poor memory) (see I, 9, 21–2). The frequency with which Montaigne adduces *exempla*, quotations and stories to illustrate or qualify subjects attests to the origins of the essays (in this at least, like Bacon's later *Essayes* [Zeitlin, 1928; Hovey, 1991])[30] in Montaigne's commonplace books, as Pierre Villey in particular has suggested (Villey, 1908; cf. I, 25, 100). The earlier, shorter pieces, like Bacon's brief 'essayes', often seem to be woven almost wholly out of this kind of self-writing, with Montaigne taking quotes and *exempla* from different sources on the titular subject, and adding connectives to make the sequence into its own discrete article (Mack, 1993). In another register, like Petrarch's letters, the *Essais* are autobiographical. Indeed, Montaigne's Preface (2) warns us, with some hyperbole, that the *Essais* are about Montaigne himself, almost entirely:

> In contriving [the *Essais*], I have proposed to myself no other than a domestic and private end: I have had no consideration at all either to thy service or to my glory ... I desire therein to be viewed as I appear in mine own genuine, simple, and ordinary manner, without study

and artifice: for it is myself I paint. ... Thus, reader, my self is the matter of my book: there's no reason thou shouldst employ thy leisure about so frivolous and vain a subject. *Therefore farewell*. Michel de Montaigne, 12 June 1580.[31]

Yet, here as in Marcus or Petrarch, it is as much the activity or performance of writing, as its thematic objects, that bespeaks the man himself. His book and his self 'go hand in hand', Montaigne tells us in 'Of Repentance' (III, 2, 611). Indeed, by writing down these dispersed meditations, Montaigne tells us that he has actively transformed who he is:

And though nobody should read me, have I wasted time in entertaining myself so many idle hours in so pleasing and useful thoughts? In moulding this figure upon myself, I have been so often constrained to temper and compose myself in a right posture, that the copy is truly taken, and has in some sort formed itself ... I have no more made my book than my book has made me: 'tis a book consubstantial with the author. (II, 18, 304)

While the *Essais* can be read in different registers (cf. Schaeffer, 1990),[32] what concerns us here is, firstly, Montaigne's indebtedness to the ancient idea of PWL and, secondly, the transformations Montaigne's *Essais* introduce into this tradition.

i. Montaigne's Neohellenistic meta-philosophy

Montaigne does not argue for, but takes for granted the practicist, ethical intentionality of philosophizing which this book is examining (5). 'Philosophy is that which instructs us to live'; it is 'the formatrix of judgment and *moeurs*' (I, 25, 120), 'a science that regulates the manners of men' (I, 25, 117) 'Either our reason mocks us or it ought to have no other aim but our contentment,' he can proclaim, 'nor to endeavour anything but, in sum, to make us live well' (I, 20, 122).[33] Montaigne is effortlessly conversant with Stoic, Epicurean, Platonic and Sceptical philosophies, and their eudaimonistic profession (7). In 'Of Virtue', Pyrrho is praised, like 'all the rest who were really philosophers', for making 'his life correspond with his doctrine' (II, 30). In 'Of Books', Seneca's and Plutarch's teachings on how to live are named the 'cream of philosophy' (II, 10, 300).

The question of how to live, Montaigne echoes Socrates, is the most difficult and important thing, despite the pretentions of serious thinkers. 'We are great fools,' Montaigne complains:

> 'He has passed over his life in idleness,' say we: 'I have done nothing to-day.' What? have you not lived? that is not only the fundamental, but the most illustrious of all your occupations. 'Had I been put to the management of great affairs, I should have made it seen what I could do.' Have you known how to meditate and manage your life, you have performed the greatest work of all ... Have you known how to regulate your conduct, you have done a great deal more than he who has composed books. (III, 13, 850)

Montaigne at the same time recognizes and qualifies the ancient philosophical ideal of the sage (9), with his ideal tranquillity and greatness of soul (II, 11, 387). Like the Stoics, Montaigne takes Socrates and Cato the Younger as such exemplary figures, whose virtue has become a second nature, 'the very essence of their soul, its natural and ordinary habit; they have *rendered it such by a long practice of philosophical precepts* having lit upon a rich and fine nature' (II, 11, 310 [italics ours]).

As in Petrarch and the ancients, the elevation of this practicist sense of philosophy also forms one side of a normative coin whose other side reveals a fierce critique of unworldly 'pedantry' (8) which 'stuffs the memory and leaves the conscience and the understanding unfurnished and void', like birds who bring grain 'home in their beaks without tasting it themselves to feed their young' (I, 24, 100). Far from models, for Montaigne university scholars are 'as incapable of public employment as leading a life and conforming themselves to the mean and vile manners of the vulgar' (I, 24, 99). 'Of Cripples' is acerbic concerning 'those who profess knowledge and their immeasurable self-conceit' (III, 11, 792). As Bacon will soon do, Montaigne bridles against all ways of conceiving the *vita mentis* for which 'there is more ado to interpret interpretations than to interpret things' (III, 13, 818) The goal of philosophy, Montaigne agrees with the Hellenistic schools, is not learning per se but the cultivation of the virtues, and with them the *eupatheiai*. 'Of all the benefits virtue confers upon us, the contempt of death is one of the greatest as the means to a soft and easy tranquillity,' Montaigne writes (I, 19, 37). Montaigne echoes Marcus Aurelius in describing the efficacy of philosophical practice as involving clearing out a kind of psychological back-room into which one can readily retreat, if not an 'inner citadel' (5):

> We should have wives, children, property and, above all, good health ... if we can: but we should not become so attached to them that our happiness depends on them. We should set aside a room, just for ourselves, at the back of the shop, keeping it entirely free and establishing there our true liberty, our principal solitude and asylum. (I, 38, 177)

At the heart of Montaigne's *Essais* is the assessment of the potency of our faculty of judgement in shaping the character. *Judgment, conscience* and *entendment* are key terms in Montaigne's moral psychology (6), 'judgment is a tool to use on all subjects, and comes in everywhere' (I, 50, 219; de la Charité, 1968). *Essais* I, chapter 14 is a direct reflection on the Stoic Epictetus's maxim that it is not things which affect us, but our judgements of them. Montaigne agrees that 'opinion is a powerful party, bold, and without measure' (I, 14, 41). Fortune does not govern how people respond to events; to show this, the essay multiplies *exempla* of humble people who have submitted to death with great dignity, and of soldiers dying rather than deserting their posts. "Tis the sharpness of our mind that gives the edge to our pains and pleasures,' Montaigne maintains (I, 14, 38). Echoing Epicurean maxims, he claims that even how we respond to severe pain falls within the mind's power: 'still it is in us, not to annihilate [such pain] but to lessen it by patience ... and to maintain the soul in good condition' (I, 14, 37).

For Montaigne as for the Hellenistics, the decisive cause of a great deal of suffering is the human imagination, 'the rambling liberty of our own fancies' (I, 14, 39). 'How many has mere force of imagination made ill?', 'The Apology of Raymond Sebond' asks rhetorically: 'When real infirmities fail us, knowledge lends us hers' (I, 12, 358). As in Marcus, imagination and rhetoric are not problematic in themselves for Montaigne, provided they are used philosophically, tested against experience and exempla. As to the rest, 'we attribute to ourselves imaginary and fantastic goods, future and absent goods, for which human capacity cannot, of herself, be responsible; or goods that we falsely attribute to ourselves by the license of opinion' (I, 12, 357; cf. III, 11, 787–8).

To philosophize is then for Montaigne 'to learn how to die' (I, 19) (5), both literally, and in terms of letting go of our imaginary illusions. Montaigne's famous essay on this ancient subject collects a full regime of Sceptical, Stoic and Epicurean therapeutic exercises upon the subject of mortality (3).[34] 'It is impossible [that the soul] will ever be at rest, whilst she stands in fear of [death],' Montaigne claims (I, 19, 63). But it is this fear, not death itself, as natural as birth, which is to be redressed (I, 18, 53). 'The premeditation of death is the premeditation of liberty,' Montaigne follows Seneca, *because it shows such fear to be groundless* (I, 19, 60). It is not morbidity or life-denial that is at work here. Instead, 'He who would teach men to die, would teach them to live' (I, 19, 62).

ii. From ancients towards the moderns

If so much of Montaigne reprises ancient conceptions of philosophizing, what exactly is new in the *Essais*, transforming or carrying forwards the meta-philosophical traditions we have been tracking here? Firstly, there is Montaigne's deep indebtedness to forms of ancient scepticism, rediscovered with the texts of Sextus Empiricus in the sixteenth century, and now available to the educated for the first time in over a millennium (Hankins & Palmer, 2008; **4.2**).[35] Montaigne hoped to introduce sceptical philosophical remedies as an irenic cultural force into a Europe riven by sectarian Christian violence. 'The Apology of Raymond Sebond' is as close to a 'discourse on method' as Montaigne comes (cf. I, 4. I, 26; 1, 31; 1, 47). It centrally praises Pyrrhonian scepticism for its cultivation of the suspension of judgement, which Montaigne reads as a means to greater sociability through teaching toleration of opposing perspectives:

> It leads them to their *ataraxia*, which is a peaceable condition of life, temperate, and exempt from the agitations we receive by the impression of opinion and knowledge that we think we have of things; whence spring fear, avarice, envy, immoderate desires, ambition, pride, superstition, love of novelty, rebellion, disobedience, obstinacy ... ; nay, and by that they are exempt from the jealousy of their discipline; for they debate after a very gentle manner; they fear no requital in their disputes ... to engender doubt and suspense of judgment, which is their end. (II, 12, 372)

Montaigne elsewhere criticizes the extremism of Pyrrhonism and can be read as closer to an academic probabilist (Force, 2009).[36] He assesses truth claims grounded in experience (III, 13) to be far more probable than claims to metaphysical truths. The 'Apology' deploys almost all of the ancient sceptical tropes, led by *diaphonia* (the disagreement of the wise) to justify the claim that human beings can know nothing concerning God or the gods, the nature of the soul and what happens after death (II, 12, 370–457).[37] As Montaigne frames things, this is a matter of epistemic moderation: 'Tis a moderate and gentle opinion, that our own understanding may conduct us to knowledge of some things, and that it has a certain measure of power, beyond which it is temerity to employ it ... but it is hard to limit the mind' (II, 12, 421) At times, Montaigne's theological scepticism seems to pull against his own Catholic fideism: 'It is Socrates' opinion and mine too, that it is best judged of heaven not to judge of it at all,' and 'man is stark raving mad: he cannot make a flea, yet he will make gods by the dozens!' (II, 12, 395) For Montaigne, indeed, 'the true field and subject of imposture are things unknown, in as much as in the first place, their very strangeness lends them credit, and moreover, by not being subjected to our ordinary reasons, they deprive us of the means to question and dispute them' (I, 31, 159).

Secondly, Montaigne's metaphysical scepticism increasingly translates into an ethical scepticism concerning the achievability or desirability of the pagan ideal of the sage (**9**). Montaigne's essays 'Of Moderation' (I, 30), 'Of Drunkenness' (II, 2), 'Of Virtue' (II, 29) and 'Of Cruelty' (II, 11) all challenge the ancient paradigm by suggesting that an excessive sense of one's own righteousness, rather than the untethered passions, is a principal cause of vice and conflict. 'How imperceptibly near to madness is the effects of a supreme and extraordinary virtue?', Montaigne can ask (II, 12, 362). With one eye on the troubles of his times, Montaigne indeed assesses that the most abominable cruelties are linked not to immoderate appetites, but to rival forms of 'presumption': the unshakable sense of knowing what one does not know (II, 17). In this light, Montaigne both admires Cato the Younger, as we saw, and calls into question the stern temper of his virtue (I, 36; II, 11; II, 37). As for Socrates's ability 'to meet death with an ordinary countenance, to grow acquainted with it, and to sport with it', Montaigne finds this 'too high and too difficult' for the ordinary run of people (II, 11, 309).[38] While constant practice was most certainly one factor, Montaigne suggests that Socrates and Cato must also have been moved to it by an innate but idiosyncratic 'exaltation of soul', enabling them to take 'extraordinary pleasure and manly voluptuousness' in their actions (II, 11, 309). His own virtue, such that it is, Montaigne confides to owe as much to his naturally stodgy disposition as to the philosophical exercises he nevertheless certainly had undertaken (II, 11, 311; cf. I, 19).

Thirdly, then, we find in Montaigne a new valorization of the ordinary. This is the demotic, and in this sense modern, flipside to his Neostoic or Neo-Epicurean criticisms of glory (II, 16) and his sceptical unmaskings of presumption. 'I propose a life ordinary and without lustre,' Montaigne reflects in his final essays: 'It is all one; all moral philosophy may as well be applied to a common and private life, as to one of richer composition: every man carries the entire form of human condition' (III, 2, 611, 614). At issue for Montaigne in this kind of joyful humility is a Socratic claim concerning self-knowledge as the knowledge of one's limits whose influence on the French enlightenment would be profound [8.1–3]:

> The pretty inscription wherewith the Athenians honoured the entry of Pompey into their city is conformable to my sense: 'By so much thou art a god, as thou confessest thee a man.' … We seek other conditions, by reason we do not understand the use of our own; and go out of ourselves, because we know not how there to reside. (III, 13, 857)

It is in this ironic, Socratic frame that we need also to understand Montaigne's 'gay and civil wisdom' (III, 5, 642), which only in some ways anticipates Nietzsche [9.2]. 'The most manifest sign of wisdom is a continual cheerfulness, her state is like that of things in the regions above the moon, always clear and serene,' Montaigne rhapsodizes (I, 25, 119). As for himself:

> Were I to live my life over again, I should live it just as I have lived it; I neither complain of the past, nor do I fear the future; and if I am not much deceived, I am the same within that I am without. 'Tis one main obligation I have to my fortune, that the succession of my bodily estate has been carried on according to the natural seasons; I have seen the grass, the blossom, and the fruit, and now see the withering; happily, however, because naturally. I bear the infirmities I have the better, because they came not till I had reason to expect them, and because also they make me with greater pleasure remember that long felicity of my past life. (II, 2, 620)

The *atopic* methodology of the *Essais*, finally, takes on rationality once we understand the Montaignian conception of philosophy. Montaigne's 'piling up' of memorable *sententia* and examples is its own Sceptical spiritual exercise (3). The aim is to inculcate epistemic humility, as a counter to the sectarian dogmatisms and cruelties Montaigne saw surrounding him. 'The perplexity of so many worldly forms has gained this over me,' Montaigne thus reflects, 'that manners and opinions contrary to mine do not so much displease as instruct me; nor so much make me proud as they humble me, in comparing them' (II, 12, 383). This is one intention of the famous essay 'Of Cannibals' (I, 31) which was to profoundly influence Voltaire, Rousseau and others: 'That we may strengthen and enlighten our judgment by reflecting upon this continuous variation of human things' (I, 48). On the one hand, this exercise in *essayer* shakes the somnolence of habit and awakens the mind to the transience, complexity and nuances of our experience. Literally the last words of the second book of the *Essais* are that 'the most universal quality is diversity' (II, 37, 598). On the other hand, the essays rail against the presumptuous ways 'that seeing so clearly into [others'] faults, we should be so blind to our own' (II, 30, 155). It remains above all the figure of Socrates (**10**), albeit Socrates the husband of Xanthippe and not the man-God of Ficino and many others (Magnard, 2010) that remains Montaigne's principal inspiration.

6.4 Justus Lipsius's Neostoicism

What later modern scholars have come uncertainly to call the 'Neostoicism' of the later European Renaissance (Papy, 2010) is identified above all with the Belgian philosopher, Justus Lipsius (1547–1606 CE). Lipsius flourished in the last decades of the sixteenth century, a near-contemporary of Montaigne. His fame and influence in early modern Europe, based principally upon the 1584 dialogue *De Constantia Libri Duo* and the *Politicorum sive Civilis Doctrinae Libri Sex* of 1589, rivalled that of his French admirer (Montaigne, *Ess.*, II, 12, 436). Lipsius's work licenses the title 'Neostoicism' because, as Papy comments, in his work Stoicism becomes 'the unique foundation of a new secular ethics that could be regarded as a true complement to Christian, biblical morality' (Papy, 2010: 51). Whereas Montaigne looked to an eclectic scepticism to promote civic peace in a Europe riven by Protestant-Catholic conflict, that is to say, Lipsius looked to a kind of Stoicism, rendered consistent where possible with Christianity, to secure the same irenic ends.

This ethico-political hope is writ large in Lipsius's most popular work, and the work of greatest interest to us here, *De Constantia* (*On Constancy*). In terms of the genre (**5**) of this text, John Sellars has contended that 'although the dialogue [*On Constancy*] shares a superficial similarity with philosophical works of consolation (such as Boethius's well-known dialogue)', we should also read it as a therapeutic dialogue with himself,[39] not unlike Petrarch's *Secretum* [**6.2**]. In the Preface 'To the Reader', Lipsius attacks people who use philosophy as a 'divertissement, not a remedy' (2006: 28–9) Philosophy's only aim, he tells us, is to produce 'a peaceable and quiet mind' (**8**) (Sellars, 2017: 351–2). As for other readers of the book, 'one is enough, none is enough' (*Const.* 'To the Reader', 29). With that said, Lipsius explains in a letter to Alexander Ratho that the text was intended 'for the use of my "Belgians" and as a consolation for my afflicted homeland' (Papy, 2010: 53).

Let us turn examine *On Constancy* in some detail, attentive to its renovation of the ancient model of philosophy as *medicina animi* (**7**).

i. Diagnosis: the inner cause of private, and public evils

On Constancy arose out of Lipsius's private experience of the Belgian affliction. In 1572 and 1579, his property in Leuven was destroyed by pillaging troops in civil war. The text is a dialogue spanning two days and two books. Lipsius himself is present as a character in the text. But he is the younger man, looking to his revered friend Langius for moral advice. The latter is depicted as the kind of sage-councillor we saw Petrarch creating with the Augustinus of the *Secretum*, and which Seneca presented to Lucilius.[40] From near the text's beginning, the ancient, therapeutic or medical conception of philosophy (**6**) is explicit in *On Constancy*. 'Lead me and learn me as you list; direct and correct me; I am your patient prepared to admit any kind of curing, be it by razor or fire, to cut or sear,' Lipsius enjoins his mentor (*Const.*, 1, 7, 41).[41] Langius, in a response which accepts the medical analogy in full, promises 'lancing tools, *wormwood*, and sharp vinegar' in the form of arguments to his young friend (*Const.* I.10, 47).

As in Seneca's *Consolation to Helvia* and many of Petrarch's letters, the problem occasioning this spiritual exercise is the philosopher's exile. The dialogue is set in 1572, when Lipsius stops in at Liege to visit Langius on his way to Vienna, fleeing from troubles at home (*Const.* I, 1, 31; Sellars, 2017: 343). What should Lipsius do, as a man of good will, faced with 'the blood of innocents spilt, the loss of laws and liberty' (*Const.* I, 8, 45)? Following the Socratic precedent (**5**), Langius begins by redefining Lipsius's real problem as internal. It lies in the 'smoke of opinions' (*fumo Opinionum*) within him, not the chaos without (*Const.*, I, 2, 33). Langius's solution, accordingly, is to be found not in travel, but in philosophy. There is no wholly peaceful place in the world, outside of the soul of the wise man (cf. *Const.*, I, 9,

45–6). What Lipsius must do is cultivate the Stoic virtue of constancy of mind *(constantia)*: 'a right and immovable strength of mind, neither lifted up nor pressed down with external or causal accidents' (**8**) (*Const.*, I, 4, 37; Sellars, 2017: 345).[42] To acquire such an elevated frame of mind, however, will require a difficult ethical training, 'a voluntary sufferance, without grudging, of all things whatsoever can happen to or in a man' (**3**) (*Const.*, I, 4, 37). Echoing Marcus Aurelius [see **3.5**], Lipsius must erect a kind of inner 'castle' above and against 'the waves of doubtfulness, without any certain resolution, murmuring, troublesome, injurious to God and men' of his pre-philosophical opinions (*Const.*, I, 5, 440).

What is at issue is Lipsius's attachment to externals, 'false goods', as well as his irrational wish to avoid 'false evils': 'I define them both to be, such things as are not in us, but about us' (*Const.*, I, 7, 42; Sellars, 2017: 343–4). Such things cannot rightly be termed 'good' or 'evil', and their pursuit or avoidance 'puffs up the mind' with needless passions (*Const.*, I, 7, 42; cf. I, 11, 49).[43] Such false evils can be either 'private' (like Petrarch's longing for Laura) or 'public', when they affect many people.[44] Given that Lipsius's main affliction lies in such public occasions, in the second half of *De Constantia* book I, Langius changes the predominant meta-philosophical metaphor, from being a doctor for Lipsius's afflictions to 'a good Captain', who will oppose his public woes. The ensuing combat with what he terms three specific 'enemies' to Lipsius's constancy (*Const.*, I, 8, 44–5; Sellars, 2017: 346) occupies the remainder of the two days' dialogue.

The first of these enemies is 'dissimulation'. When people bewail the public evils of their nations, Langius diagnoses, we should beware that they do not speak more from 'the tongue' or 'the teeth' than from 'the heart' (*Const.*, I, 8, 44). Often, he warns, 'those words: "My country's calamity afflicts me", carry with them more vainglory than verity'. While bewailing 'Public evils', the teacher means, people often only bewail their own private share in the larger affliction, or 'for fashion's sake', so as to be seen to be mourning in the marketplace (I, 8, 44).[45]

The second cause of perceived public evils is provocatively labelled 'Piety'. For whatever reason, Langius equates it with what we would call patriotism: Christian piety itself is expressly, and perhaps prudently, excluded. If Lipsius loves and laments his own nation, he loves and laments a thing that is the product of custom and opinion, not nature and reason, Langius reasons. 'The whole world is our country', Langius corrects his pupil, 'wheresoever is the race of mankind sprung of that celestial seed. Socrates being asked of what country he was, answered: "of the world"' (*Const.*, I, 9, 46).

The third cause of Lipsius's *inconstantia* is 'pity' towards the suffering of his fellow citizens (*Const.*, I, 12, 52). This affection of pity, Langius claims, bespeaks 'the fault of an abject and base mind' or a 'softness and abjection' (*Const.*, I, 12, 53), pushing against the Christian morality of *charitas*, as Sellars comments (2017: 347). Mercy is merited by others' sufferings, not pity. We should assist others, not bemoan their fates. Our compassion should be ruled by our reason. In this way, we will 'be not infected by other men's contagion; and … (as Fencers say) … bear not others' blows upon [our] own ribs' (*Const.*, I, 12, 53).

i. The main (prognostic) battle: The four troops of constancy

Following book I, chapter 13, the philosophical cure passes from such diagnoses to prognoses, and from skirmishes to 'the main battle', using the martial metaphor that runs through *On Constancy* (*Const.*, I, 13, 54). Captain Langius now deploys four 'troops' to establish Lipsius's constancy of mind against its three enemies. Interestingly, reflecting once more how PWL does not exclude but reframes metaphysical considerations, these four troops are what we might otherwise call theological arguments. Here as in the latter books of Boethius's *Consolations* which they often echo,[46] these arguments are also positioned as cognitive remedies.

a. The first 'troop': That public evils are willed by God
If Lipsius accepts God's providence, as all Christians do, then he must also accept public evils, Langius contends. To complain of such putative 'evils' is therefore to complain against God. This is impious. No other animals complain of their fate, only humans do. More than this, like grief for Seneca,[47] complaint does no good. What is fated must be endured. Like soldiers called to the march, Lipsius must accede to what is necessary.[48]

b. The second troop: That public evils are necessary
In the remainder of book I (chapters 15–22) of *De Constantia*, Langius martials two classically Stoic observations into his ranks. First, mortality and constant change is generic to all things. Lipsius would do well, like Marcus Aurelius, to meditate upon this simple, profound truth. Arguing from the larger to the smaller, if change and mortality befall even such great things as the earth or stars, we should not be surprised that they befall beings as tiny as ourselves.[49] Arguing from smaller to larger, Langius advises that Lipsius should not lament the fact that States like Belgium must pass away, just as the human body matures, ages and passes away in time.[50]

c. The third troop: That public evils serve a purpose

Thirdly, public evils serve as material for *exercising*: they are challenges and occasions to develop and steel one's virtue. As Seneca had written in *De Providentia* (3, 3): 'I count nothing more unfortunate than that man who has never had the feeling of adversity' (Sellars, 2017: 353). Such evils serve as a punitive instrument of God's justice, chastizing people who deserve chastisement. Moreover, public evils form a necessary, perhaps even a beautiful, component of God's grand plan (*Const.* II, 11, 94–7).[51]

Faced with this third troop, Lipsius raises the kind of Job-ean protest that Voltaire would raise against forms of theodicy after the 1755 Lisbon earthquake, and which we have seen motivates the metaphysical turn within Boethius's *Consolations* [**4.5**]: *but what of innocents who suffer? What of the guilty who go free? And why should the sons pay for the sins of their fathers?* Langius, in reply, gives five responses, before sagely underlining that 'they be very deep mysteries' (*Const.* I, 17, 110; cf. I, 16, 107). The wicked all are eventually punished (*Const.* II, 13, 99–101). Some punishments which the wicked suffer are internal and unobservable. Some will take place only in the next life, and no one after all is perfectly innocent (II, 16, 105–7), given original sin. Finally, as people have no problem with sons inheriting property from their fathers, why does Langius protest the justice of sons inheriting the wages of sin from their parents and their parents' parents (II, 17, 108–11)?

d. The fourth troop: That public evils are neither grievous nor unforeseeable

In *On Constancy*, II 19 (112–14), Langius asks Lipsius in Epictetan style to think of lost goods as goods returned to nature or God. Property is not theft, but it is a conventional thing whose inevitable loss it is folly to lament. "Twas mine, 'tis his', as Iago put it. Langius then brings in the heavy rhetorical artillery, reminding his charge of the truly dismal litany of sufferings, wars, slaughters, plagues and famines related in the Bible, and the Greek and Roman histories (II, 23, 120–2; Sellars, 2017: 354–5). This list is followed in the succeeding chapter by a like inventory of *exempla* of human cruelty and tyranny (*Const.* II, 24, 122–4). These lists are intended to make vividly present to Lipsius how foolish it is to be amazed at the evils of our own time. It is a matter again of evoking something like the view from above, or of what we could term history as therapy (Sellars, 2017: 354, 355), aimed at relativizing the individual's sense of present, exceptional hardship.

Underlining the status of the preceding arguments as spiritual exercises (**3**), *On Constancy* ends with Langius enjoining Lipsius, like Augustinus in Petrarch's *Secretum*, to repeatedly reflect on their discussion (Sellars, 2017: 355–9).

> God grant it be not only pleasing but profitable unto thee; and that it do not so much delight as benefit or help thee. As certainly it will do if it sink not into thy ears alone but also into thy mind; and if, having once heard the same, thou suffer it not to lie still and wither away as feed scattered upon the face of the earth. Finally, if you repeat the same often, and take due consideration thereof (*Const.* I, 24, 129).[52]

In Sellars's words: '*De Constantia* is in effect Lipsius's attempt to train himself; it is a dialogue with himself in which he tries to "digest" the philosophical theories that he already knows' (Sellars, 2017: 357). As such, its Neostoic continuity not simply with Seneca, Lipsius's most frequent source, but Petrarch's *Secretum* and Marcus Aurelius's *Meditations*, is especially telling.

CHAPTER 7
CULTURA ANIMI IN EARLY MODERN PHILOSOPHY

7.1 The end of PWL (again)?

As we saw in **Chapter 5**, Pierre Hadot claimed that PWL decisively ended with the advent of scholastic theology. This form of university learning, focusing upon dialectic and commentary, consolidated a tendency to treat philosophy as theory-construction looking back to later antiquity, following the dispersal of the Athenian schools [**5.3**]. In **Chapter 6**, we examined the evidence from the renaissance which suggests the real need to qualify Hadot's contention. The philosophy of the seventeenth century, that 'century of genius' associated with those transformation(s) of the 'scientific revolution' is the second period that leading scholars of PWL have identified as seeing the decisive end of philosophy as self-cultivation, an art of living or way of life.

Two predominant versions of this position exist. The first is represented by eminent intellectual historians Stephen Gaukroger (2001) and (with some variations) Peter Harrison (2015). Here, it is Francis Bacon's reconception of natural philosophy which reshaped philosophical activity, so that it was no longer understood pre-eminently as a work of transforming the selves of philosophers. Convergent claims inform the argument. Firstly, there is Bacon's interest, as a natural philosopher, in changing the external world through truly understanding and skilfully acting upon it to 'effect all things possible', as Bacon writes of the guardians of his utopia in *New Atlantis*. Secondly, there is Bacon's claim in the Preface to the *Novum Organum* that the new 'organon' he has discovered to understand natural forms does not require great acuity or genius, being more like a machine operable by anyone. Thirdly, due to the sheer scale of the endeavour of re-understanding the natural world in the ways Bacon recommends, there are in *Novum Organum* and elsewhere passages wherein the collectivization of inquiry is expressly recommended (cf. See AL II. Proem. 13; NO I 57; I 108; I 113; Sargent, 1996). When a true philosophy needs to rest upon detailed experimental inquiries, no individual can do it alone. New cultures and institutions of experimental inquiry with many members are requisite, like that which would emerge in Bacon's wake in the Royal Society. Finally, the knowledges acquired at earlier stages of any cumulative understandings of natural forms and processes need to be carefully written down (Ong, 2007; see Bacon, 1863). This is a development favouring what Harrison (2015) suggestively calls the 'reification' of *philosophia* and *scientia* as self-standing discourses, rather than processes inculcating virtues in different inquirers.

The second position is championed by Michel Foucault in the lectures comprising *The Hermeneutics of the Subject* (2005). It looks not to Bacon, usually considered the founder of 'empiricism' but to the founder of 'rationalism', René Descartes. Ancient philosophical pursuits, Foucault argues (2006: 17), were characterized by what he terms 'spirituality': meaning here the ancient sense that higher forms of knowledge both depend upon and engender ethical or spiritual transformation in philosophers. By contrast, Foucault claims, 'we can say that ... the history of truth enters its modern period ... when it is assumed that what gives access to the truth, the condition for the subject's access to the truth, is knowledge (*connaissance*) and knowledge alone' (2006). It is Descartes's new method for the conduct of philosophy, outlined in *The Discourse on Method* and enacted in *Meditations on First Philosophy* that decisively inaugurated this new epistemic regime. As Foucault continues, echoing Bacon's claims concerning his new *organon*, from now on 'the philosopher (or the scientist, or simply someone who seeks the truth) can recognize the truth and have access to it in himself and solely through his activity of knowing, without anything else being demanded of him and without him having to change or alter his being as subject' (2006: 18). On top of merely 'formal' or 'internal conditions of the act of knowledge and of the rules it must obey to have access to the truth', only 'cultural' conditions need to be met: 'to have access to the truth we must have studied, have an education, and operate within a certain scientific consensus' (2006: 18). Such conditions 'only concern the individual in his concrete existence, and not the structure of the subject' at stake in ancient philosophical technologies of self-cultivation (2006:18).

In this chapter, drawing notably on Sorana Corneanu's groundbreaking *Regimens of the Mind: Boyle, Locke, and the Early Modern Cultura Animi Tradition*, we will challenge these claims. According to Corneanu (2011: 6–7), 'the philosophy-as-a-way-of-life framework' remains 'applicable to the experimental philosophical programs of early modern England' at the least. Corneanu claims that Bacon's thought [7.2] and early modern experimental philosophy [7.4] – reaching across to Descartes [7.3] via figures like Charleton and Glanvill (Corneanu, 2011: 84–7, 107–12) – needs to be understood in relation to a larger early modern literary tradition of *cultura animi* (cultivation of the soul). This tradition brought together an eclectic array of Christian, rhetorical and philosophical texts on 'the passions of the soul, anatomies of the mind, rhetorics, tracts of wisdom and of consolation' (Corneanu, 2011: 4). What united these texts, despite their doctrinal and other differences, is that in each of them we find proposed what Corneanu terms 'convergent models of *medicina animi*' (Corneanu, 2011: 88), the medicine or therapy of the mind. On the one hand, as in the ancient therapeutic philosophies, we find diagnoses of what are explicitly dubbed 'diseases', 'distempers' or 'vices' of the mind, drawing in different measures on the Augustinian conception of the human mind as corrupted by the fall (Harrison, 2006; 2007) and on the ancient Stoic-Ciceronian diagnoses of the *pathê* as shaped by erroneous factual and evaluative judgements. On the other hand, we find prescriptive 'regimens of the mind' recommending spiritual and cognitive exercises (2, 3) to counter-act the deleterious effects of our fallen nature and passions upon our beliefs.

The later modern category of 'epistemology', Corneanu contends, needs to be used cautiously to describe the texts of Bacon, Boyle, Hooke, Sprat, Charleton, Glanvill and Locke. In the programmatic prescriptions for new 'logics' of experimental inquiry, we should be sensitive to 'the late scholastic and early modern shifts in the conception of logic, towards a novel concentration on the operations of the cognitive faculties apart from the issue of formal validity, coupled with the redefinition of logic as a method of conducting the intellect's reasoning' (Corneanu, 2011: 88). In this context, likewise, 'physics' or 'natural philosophy' was conceived as pursuing a double purpose (Corneanu, 2011: 99). On the one hand, the new philosophies aimed at discovering new, potentially fruitful truths concerning the natural world, as both Bacon and Descartes famously extol (Bacon, *Adv.* I XI, 5; Descartes, *Disc.* VI, 61). On the other hand, *contra* the Harrison-Gaukroger and Foucaultian theses, they continued the classical project of cultivating new *kinds* of philosophical inquirers, including through advocating for the cooperative organization of research (Corneanu, 2011: 8, 53–8).

With this much said, we turn first to perhaps the most enigmatic figure whom we examine in this book, Sir Francis Bacon (1561–1626 CE).

7.2 Francis Bacon: the Idols and the Georgics of the mind

Celebrated and reviled as a founder of the scientific age, Bacon was in his own time an admired rhetorician and orator, a statesman who rose and fell from the Lord Chancellorship of Britain, and the author of essays, apothegms, a work of great beauty on ancient mythologies, and the utopian *New Atlantis* (Vickers, 2000).[1] Born January 1561, the second son of the Lord Keeper of the Privy Seal, Francis was educated for a career in the law, with an early command of Greek, Latin and several European languages. Nevertheless, as a famous letter to Lord Burley reports, Bacon was from a young age torn between his expected, active responsibilities, and a definitively 'philosophical' love of learning: 'I confess that I have as vast contemplative ends, as I have moderate civil ends: for I have taken all knowledge to be my province ... This, whether it be curiosity, or vain glory, or nature, or (if one take it favourably) *philanthropia*, is so fixed in my mind as it cannot be removed' (Bacon, 1591 [1753]).

While Bacon joins Petrarch and Descartes as one of many early modern critics of Aristotelianism, that is, he shares with Aristotle the sense of philosophy as involving encyclopaedic learning (4). Philosophy is for Bacon also the science of sciences. The second book of the 1605 *Advancement of Learning* undertakes what Bacon calls 'a general and faithful perambulation of learning' in all of its branches, divided by reference to the different human cognitive faculties: forms of history, grounded in memory; forms of poetry, products of the imagination; and forms of philosophy, pertaining to human understanding (*Adv.*, I, VII, 15). There is a practical end to this survey, which Bacon compares to that which a monarch might make of his realm: to learn 'what parts thereof lie fresh and waste, and not improved and converted by the industry of man' (*Adv.* II, Proem, 15). With imperious self-certainty, Bacon finds many areas of human inquiry unsatisfactorily or 'deficiently' treated. He is disappointed that there have since the Roman Imperium been so few advances in the medical and mechanical arts that minister to 'the relief of man's estate' (*Adv.* I, V, 11). His 'Great Instauration', the lifelong project which we are told that Bacon conceived as a youth at Cambridge, would involve teaching others new practices of inquiry in different fields, led by natural philosophy. 'I have taken upon me to ring a bell to call other wits together,' Bacon advised Dr Playfer at Cambridge (Bacon, 1841). At the end of *Advancement*, again, the propaedeutic dimension of his work is pictured in one of Bacon's astonishing array of analogies:

And being now at some pause, looking back into that I have passed through, this writing seemeth to me, as far as a man can judge of his own work, not much better than that noise or sound which musicians make while they are tuning their instruments, which is nothing pleasant to hear, but yet is a cause why the music is sweeter afterwards. So have I been content to tune the instruments of the Muses, that they may play that have better hands. (*Adv.* II, XXIV, 1)

How then does Bacon's conception of philosophy relate to the different ancient and renaissance conceptions of PWL? In at least two ways. First (i), Bacon's great instauration is grounded in one of the most discerning accounts of epistemic psychology in the Western tradition (**8**). As Corneanu (2011), Gaukroger (2001) and several recent commentators have examined, Bacon's new philosophy is, in at least one of its dimensions, a further chapter in the long history of philosophy as a therapeutic activity (**5**), as well as the pursuit of 'bodies of knowledge' (Harrison, 2015). Second, both in championing new forms of inquiry in natural philosophy (ii, a) and in his specific contributions to moral philosophy (ii, b), Bacon is animated by a sense, shared by earlier PWL practitioners, of the need to wed theory and practice more closely, including prescribing new regimes of intellectual and ethical exercises.

i. The idolatry of the mind

Bacon's definitive mature account of the forms of epistemic pathology which he sees writ large in the deficiencies of extant forms of early modern learning comes in *Novum Organum* I. It is the account of the four idols (*idola*) of the mind. First amongst these are the idols of the human 'tribe' (*genus*) (NO, I, XLI-LII).[2] All human beings have the tendency to assume more order in the world than we can presently attest or verify. We pre-emptively 'anticipate' or leap to generalizations based on too few observations, or on our present unexamined presumptions (NO, I, XVIII-XXXVII, LXV). Furthermore, we are wont to be persuaded by powerful impressions; isolated experiences or claims which 'strike and enter the mind suddenly, and by which the imagination is immediately filled and inflated', as Montaigne could have agreed (NO, I, XLVII; cf. I, XXVII). Then there is confirmation bias. Once the human mind has formed some belief, we 'almost imperceptibly' fall to comparing and reducing all new instances 'to the few similar objects which have taken possession of the mind' (NO, I, XLVII). We tend to then ignore, define away or dismiss 'negative' or 'contrary instances' which challenge our beliefs, often enough with 'injurious prejudice' towards their messengers (NO, I, XLVI).

To these idols of the tribe Bacon adds, secondly, idols of the cave (NO, I, LXII-LXVIII). Different individuals have different cognitive abilities. But everyone has a tendency to think that the forms of craft or inquiry at which they excel are the most important, and to scorn or undervalue others: like the analytic philosopher who thinks all philosophy should be done that way; the classicist who professes vehemence against 'modernity' etc. The idols of the theatre, thirdly, bespeak the powerful roles inherited philosophical and theological theories play in shaping, and blinkering, people's thoughts – as if we did not see the real world, but the stage-setting laid up by our favourite theorists, a 'Deleuzian world' or 'Heideggerian world' etc. (NO, I, LXI-LXII) Fourthly, the idols of the marketplace speak to the distorting effects of language on learning, since the language of the street has not been developed to enable more exacting, supra-practical inquiries (NO, I, XLIII, LIX-LX).[3]

If new forms of knowledge are to be produced, Bacon argues, we must remain aware of these *idola*, and devise therapeutic epistemic measures to cast them down.

ii. Reuniting Saturn and Jupiter

Bacon's call to renewed forms of inquiry based upon a more systematic experimental examination of the natural world, as against the exegesis of authoritative texts (*Adv.*, I, IV, 12; NO, I, LXXXIV), is coupled with a call to unite contemplation and action, theory and practice, in new ways (6). Yet, for Bacon, the human mind's impatience with contrary instances, and its wont to jump to preemptive generalizations, express a deep distaste we have for getting our cognitive hands dirty by examining particulars, 'especially since such matters generally require labour in investigation, are mean subjects for meditation, harsh in discourse, unproductive in practice, infinite in number, and delicate in their subtlety' (NO, LXXXIII).

Bacon's proposal to reunite Saturn, planet of limitation, rule and discipline, and Jupiter, planet of contemplation (*Adv.* I, V, 11) – or more humble, empirically grounded modes of inquiry with philosophical speculation – plays out firstly in his stipulations concerning the *novum organum scientiarum*; and secondly, in Bacon's contribution to the particular field of 'moral philosophy'.

The novum organum as epistemic cultura animi

Our seeing Bacon as the founder of the empirical sciences overlooks that one stake of *Novum Organum* II's prescriptions for a new kind of natural philosophizing is the training of a new kind of inquirer, with new epistemic habits – of observing and tabulating instances, then of singling out different 'prerogative instances' for their specific epistemic value, and of cautiously ascending thereby from particulars to hypothetical, testable generalizations. As one of the authors has recently argued (Sharpe, 2018a), these prescriptions for the new organon are evidently expressly designed to counter the idols of the mind. Indeed, some six of the twenty-seven 'prerogative instances', like the observation of 'proportionate instances' (wherein a common quality surprisingly appears in different species of phenomena which have nothing else in common), or 'deviating instances' (which show prodigies within species) or 'frontier instances' (which involve species which apparently bring together features of two or more separate species, like the platypus), are introduced expressly because of their *therapeutic* function (5). Training oneself to observe them is an intellectual exercises (2) for 'taking the intellect away from humdrum experience', as in a 'purging' (NO, II, XXXII), 'levelling its glass, polishing it to let in the dry and pure light of true notions' (Sharpe, 2018a), 'restoring an intellect corrupted by custom and the general run of things' (NO, II, XXVII), 'eliminating the phantoms and mere appearances of things' (NO, I, XXXV), or even 'attracting the intellect's gaze to the wonderful and exquisite subtlety of nature, so as to arouse and waken it to due attention, observation and investigation' (NO, II, XLII).

Figure 7.1 The twenty-seven Baconian prerogative instances. From Francis Bacon, *Novum Organum*, 1869.

Genus: 1 Informative instances
Subgenus 1.1: Aids to understanding:

1.	**Solitary instances:** which have nothing in common except a form (colour in reflected light, and on paint, skin…) Hastens exclusion of forms
2.	**Migratory instances:** which show things coming into being and passing away.

3.   **Indicative/shining/liberated and predominant instances:** which show a form in highest, unhindered manifestation (e.g. heat in calendar glass)

4.   **Clandestine/twilight instances:** which show genera at lowest level of manifestation (e.g. attraction of water to surfaces in droplets)

5.   **Constitutive/collective instances:** which show genera with subspecies (e.g. of lists like this)

Therapeutic/preparatory instances

---

6.   **Instances of correspondence/proportionate instances/parallels/ physical resemblances:** which show common configurations and forms in apparently wholly different, unrelated classes of phenomena

7.   **Monadic/irregular/heteroclite instances:** which show apparently unthinkable species in nature (e.g. some deep sea fishes)

8.   **Deviating instances:** prodigies within species

9.   **Frontier instances/participles:** which show species which apparently bring together features of two or more seprate species (e.g. platypus, we might say)

10.   **Instances of power/fasces:** artful things human power has made.

11.   **Instances of companionship and hostility:** forms usually, perhaps universally conjoined (e.g. snow and coldness)

12.   **Subjunctive instances/instances of an ultimate state or limit:** nature at her greatest degree or efficacity (whales amongst mammals)

13.   **Instances of alliance or union:** instances that show species/genii are allied that are taken to be unallied

14.   **Crucial, decisive and judicial instances/of the oracle and instruction:** instances deciding between two hypotheses (e.g. cannonball and lighter object off Pisa tower)

15.   **Instances of divorce:** divide forms usually manifested together (e.g. heat and light, by moonlight, which is cool)

Subgenus 1.2: Aids to senses: "instances of the lamp"

---

16.   **Instances of access or gateway instances:** microscopes and other aids to senses, given natural limitations

17.   **Summonsing/evoking Instances:** allow us to envisage things/processes invisible to unassisted senses (e.g. due to intervening bodies)

18.   **Instances of the pathway/en route or step-by-step instances:** observe motions of nature over long periods time

19.	**Supplementary instances or instances if substances:** supplement senses by analogy or approximation, when we cannot using other instances make invisible visible.
20.	**Dissecting or prompting instances:** wherein one force or body can act on surprising varieties of bodies.

Genus 2: Operative instances

21	**Instances of the measuring rod or ruler:** measuring spaces
22	**Instances of the race-track/instances run by water:** measuring times
23	**Instances of quantity/doses of nature:** measuring weights
24	**Instances of wrestling/ascendancy:** observation of different kinds of motion, and relations between them
25	**Intimating instances:** 'which intimate or point out what is useful to man' in natural events/processes.
26	**Multi-purpose Instances:** the seven ways that humans can act on or 'into' nature
27	**Magical instances:** instances where great effects issue from apparently small causes in nature.

The double nature of the Good and the Georgics of the mind

Turning to moral philosophy, Bacon here also is animated by his global aim to bring Jupiter to Saturn, and practical considerations to the purely theoretical (Sharpe, 2014b). Strikingly, he divides moral philosophy into two components. 'The platform of the Good' consists in theoretical analyses of the nature of the Good, the number, degrees and relations of the virtues, and like considerations (*Adv.* II, XX, 4). This 'metaethical' part of moral philosophy, Bacon tells us, has been well treated by the ancients, with the single, decisive hesitation (see below) that those ancient pagans who elect contemplation as the *summum bonum* mistake the highest human good (7) (*Adv.* II, XX, 4; cf. *Adv.* II, XIV, 9; I, VII, 1; II, 8). There is a 'double nature' to the Good, Bacon contents (II, XX, 7). On the one hand, there is the Good concerning the individual and his flourishing, conceived in abstraction from wider social duties. This forms the focus of much ancient ethics. On the other hand, there is the Good concerning human beings as members of political communities, and the wider human species. This second component of the Good, says Bacon, 'is greater and the worthier, because it tendeth to the conservation of the more general form' (*Adv.* II, XX, 7). Accordingly, the contemplative life of 'private repose and contentment' dear to Epicureans or Peripatetics, and to earlier renaissance figures like Petrarch and Montaigne, is deficient.[4] Likewise, Bacon sees his larger conception of the Good as speaking against the Stoics' notion that we are fully in control of everything requisite for the best life (*Adv.* II, XX, 11). According to Bacon as for the other philosopher-statesman, Cicero [**4.3**], that is, it is 'a thing much more happy to fail in good and virtuous ends for the public, than to obtain all that we can wish to ourselves in our [own] proper fortune ' (*Adv.* II, XX, 10).

Bacon's sense of the double nature of the Good also affects the second, and from our perspective more intriguing part of Baconian moral philosophy. This part of moral philosophy involves what he calls 'the regiment and culture of the mind' or 'the husbandry and tillage thereof' (*Adv.* II, XX, 3). Such 'Georgics of the mind' – Bacon borrows the agricultural title from Virgil – aims to shape 'the will of man to become true and conformable' to the pursuit of the Good, even 'in ordinary and common matters' (*Adv.* II, XX, 2). As Petrarch and his followers had done, so Bacon attacks Aristotle for 'passing [it] over altogether' or treating it 'slightly and unprofitably' (*Adv.* II, XII, 1). Without such a Georgics, Bacon contends, all talk of the good or virtues is empty, 'no better than a fair image or statue, which is beautiful to contemplate, but … without life and motion' (*Adv.* II, XXII, 1). The moral philosopher who would move his audience to a love of virtue, and reshape their passions and desires, must for Bacon as for Petrarch be a master of epideictic and exhortatory rhetoric (**5**). 'To show [virtue] to reason only in subtlety of argument' has 'no sympathy with the will of man', Bacon echoes the *humanisti*. 'If the affections in themselves were pliant and obedient to reason, it were true there should be no great use of persuasions and insinuations to the will, more than of naked proposition and proofs', Bacon continues. But, as things stand, 'reason would become captive and servile, if eloquence of persuasions did not practice and win the imagination from the affections' part, and contract a confederacy between the reason and imagination' (*Adv.* II, XVII, 1).

Such a rhetorically adept moral philosopher will, in the ancient metaphor, be a 'physician' of the soul (**7**). His objects are the disturbances occasioned by the passions:

> for as in medicining of the body, it is in order first to know the divers complexions and constitutions; secondly, the diseases; and lastly, the cures: so in medicining of the mind, after knowledge of the divers

characters of men's natures, it followeth in order to know the diseases and infirmities of the mind, which are no other than the perturbations and distempers of the affections. (*Adv.* II, XXI, 5)[5]

Such a *medicina animi*, Bacon believes, will also need a far more systematic observation of the different characters and tempers (*Adv.* II, XXII, 4), as well as the effects of age, upbringing, and political and social fortune upon people than has hitherto been attempted (*Adv.* II, XXII, 5). Bacon credits Aristotle for having stressed the role of habit or custom, a 'second nature' (*Adv.* II, XXI, 8),[6] in shaping how people behave. But again echoing Petrarch, he impugns 'the philosopher' for neglecting to then teach how to inculcate such habits (*Adv.* II, XXI, 8). Bacon accordingly sets out some sixteen headers describing what we have been calling spiritual exercises (3) that he believes need more adequate attention in any effective, future *medicina animi*: 'custom, exercise, habit, education, example, imitation, emulation, company, friends, praise, reproof, exhortation, fame, laws, books, studies' (*Adv.* II, XXII, 7).

To illustrate what this Georgics will involve, Bacon in *Advancement* adduces several precepts for the 'exercise of the mind', stressing also the vital need for 'vows and constant resolutions' (*Adv.* II, XX, 14). The aim of such 'exercise' is constancy of mind, as for Lipsius and the Stoics: to 'fix and cherish the good hours of the mind, and obliterate and take forth the evil' (*Adv.* II, XXII, 14). Bacon's exemplary precepts with this aim in view are:

i. Not to aim too high, lest disappointment be courted;

ii. To practise all things both at your best and worst times, so you strengthen the mind in the boon, and 'make great strides' in the lean times;

iii. To balance a known vice by going too far the other way (an Aristotelian point repeated in 'Of Nature' in Bacon's *Essays*);

iv. To bring the mind to hard things indirectly, by apparently aiming at something else (*Adv.* II, XXII, 9–12).

The first letter of advice to Rutland, and the highest good

It was Ronald Crane who first noted how many of Bacon's recommendations for the Georgics, and the field of 'civil knowledge', in *Advancement of Learning* speak to subjects in Bacon's *Essays* of 1597, 1612 and 1625 (Crane,

1968). Bacon's most *systematic* single set of prescriptions for *cultura animi*, 'the tilling and manuring of your own mind', are however contained in his remarkable first 'Letter of Advice to the Earl of Rutland' (Bacon, 2008: 69, 69–76). In this epistle, Bacon (writing pseudonymously as the Earl of Essex) plays Seneca to Rutland's Lucilius, providing prescriptions for his aristocratic charge who is about to travel about how to cultivate beauty, health and strength of character (Bacon, 2008: 69).

To attain *beauty* of mind and carriage, Rutland should carefully observe different customs and manners, and collect and imitate admirable exempla (3) (Bacon, 2008: 69–70). For mental or spiritual health, he should learn to dispassionately observe his own passions and predilections (5), and take particular notice of how great the force of resolution is, which can overcome even the fear of death, let alone lesser troubles (Bacon, 2008: 70–1). As for *strength or greatness* of mind, Rutland should habituate himself to virtuous forms and actions and cultivate a kind of para-Stoic discernment: 'to esteem of the goods of fortune not for themselves, for so [people] are but jailors to them, but for their use, for so they are lords over them' (Bacon, 2008: 71). Rutland should also come to 'know that it is *beatius dare quam accipere* [better to give than to receive], the one being a badge of sovereignty, the other of subjection' (Bacon, 2008: 71). Here as in *Advancement* II, moreover, studies are recommended – particularly, for Rutland, histories which 'make men wise' in civic affairs ('Of Studies') – as a necessary support for each of the cardinal virtues, and in addition to these, for 'true religion', liberality and 'constancy or patience' (Bacon, 2008: 72). Of especial value here, for Bacon as again for Petrarch, is the prescribed art of note-taking and common-placing (5) (Bacon, 2008: 74). This is an art which Bacon treats in 'A Letter and Discourse to Sir Henry Savill, Touching Helps for the Intellectual Powers', and which underlies the gem-like epigrams of the *Essays* (Bacon, 2008b; Sharpe, 2019). Finally, and of especial importance, is the seeking out of wise counsellors. Rutland should 'rather go a hundred miles out of the way to speak with a wise man, than five to see a fair town' (Bacon, 2008b: 74).

We see then how far we are with Bacon from the end of the PWL tradition, and how closely he conceived his own *persona*, in more than one register, on classical models. Harrison is right (2015: 106–7, 122–4) that there is in Bacon the beginning of a new conception of the *scientia* as collective ventures, which will effect changes to the external world (Sargent, 1996). It is not for nothing that he will emerge as the hero of the *Encylopaedists* in the enlightenment [8.3]. This separation of the utility and nobility of the pursuit of natural philosophy from the person of the inquirer, even in principle, sounds the first note of what will later become the incremental, intergenerational 'sciences' which would after 1700 increasingly usurp the older object domains of philosophy. But, to ape the style of Bacon to the measure of our meagre abilities, the first note is far from yet a symphony, and Descartes too will tune the instruments.

7.3 On Descartes, method and meditations

i. The Discourse on Method, or Portrait of the Philosopher as a Young Man

Like Bacon, René Descartes tends to be looked at through epistemological lenses, or else, following the post-structuralists, as the founder of a new subjectivist 'conception of Being' (Heidegger, 2008). Here as in the case of readings of other thinkers we are examining, such approaches are tone deaf to the literary and philosophical genres in which Descartes conveyed his 'first philosophy' (5). In turn, they blind us to the distance between these writings, the practice and conception of philosophy within them, and our own.

We will return in due course (iii) to the genre of the *Meditations on First Philosophy*, and what meta-philosophical position they bespeak. It is first of all remarkable that the text known as *The Discourse on Method*, unlike the almost Euclidean presentation which its title might suggest, proceeds by way of an intellectual biography. The *Discourse* is a kind of portrait of the philosopher as a young man (5). This intellectual biography is presented as having an exemplary value, very much in line with a long-standing humanistic literary genre looking back to Plutarch or Diogenes Laertius:

> My design here is not to teach the method which everyone should follow in order to reason well, but merely to reveal the way in which I have tried to conduct my own reasoning … since I intend this text only as a history, or, if you prefer, a fable, in which, among some examples which you can imitate, you will, in addition, perhaps find several others which you will have reason not to follow. (*Disc.* I, 42)

Descartes was born in La Haye en Touraine in 1596. At eight, he entered the Jesuit Collège Royal Henry-Le-Grand at La Flèche, graduating in December 1616 and becoming licenced in the law by 1618. Yet, like Bacon with Cambridge, Descartes reports in the *Discourse* that his studies left him deeply perplexed and unsatisfied. Famously, he commented that 'I learned from my college days on that one cannot imagine anything so strange and so incredible that it has not been said by some philosopher' (*Disc.*, II, 46). Hence, just as Montaigne or Bacon recommends to young men who would become wise, he travelled, 'resolving not to look any more in any other science except one which could be found inside myself or in the great book of the world' (*DM* I, 44). 'The greatest profit which I derived from this', he tells us, in almost-Montaignean mode:

> was that, by seeing several things which, although they seem really extravagant and ridiculous to us, were commonly accepted and approved by other great people, I learned not to believe too firmly in anything which I had been persuaded to believe merely by example and by custom. (*Disc.* I, 44)

As with Montaigne and the sceptics, this confrontation with *diaphonia* did nothing to stabilize Descartes's sense of what could be knowably true or false. Instead of taking this insight into the uncertainty of human knowledge as itself the Socratic portal to wisdom, though, Descartes took it as the stimulus to seek out new, surer foundations for knowledge. As an architect might lay new foundations or a statesman undertake the complete reform of existing laws:

> So far as all the opinions which I had received up to that point and which I believed credible were concerned, I convinced myself that the best possible thing for me to do was to undertake to remove them once and for all, so that afterwards I could replace them either by other better ones or perhaps by the same ones, once I had adjusted them to a reasonable standard. (*Disc.* II, 45)

Given the post-Heideggerian association of Cartesianism with humanism (Heidegger, 2008b), we need to underscore the vast gulf between Descartes's radical project of re-founding knowledge *de novo*, and the humanistic 'renaissance' of classical philosophy [6.1–4]. Descartes's search for new foundations takes its light from logic, algebra and geometry, in which latter disciplines he was especially adept. He expressly puts aside the wisdom of the ancient poets, historians and philosophers. Such humanistic authorities, Descartes tells us, 'contain many really true and excellent precepts, [but] mixed in with them ... always so many injurious or superfluous ones that it is almost as difficult to separate them as to draw a Diana or a Minerva out of a block of marble which has not yet been carved' (*Disc.* II, 46). We are a long way from Petrarch, Montaigne, Lipsius, even Bacon.

Having resolved to pursue a life of the mind (see ii.), Descartes tells us, he instead devised four precepts which would enable his new re-founding of philosophy. (In fact, despite their claim to novelty, their Euclidean and Platonist resonances are clear). Thus, the first rule was, like Cicero, to 'not accept anything as true which I did not clearly know to be true ... carefully avoid[ing] being over-hasty or prejudiced' (*Disc.* II, 47). It is here that Descartes resolves to only give assent to evidence that 'presented itself so clearly and distinctly to my mind that I had no occasion to doubt it'. The second is to divide complex problems into soluble parts; the third, 'to conduct my thoughts in an orderly way, beginning with the simplest objects, ... so that little by little I could gradually climb right up to the knowledge of the most complex' (*Disc.*, II: 46). The final rule is 'to make my calculations throughout so complete and my review so general that I would be confident of not omitting anything' (*Disc.*, II: 46).

Descartes's continuing, ambiguous relationship with the ancient conception of PWL is most clearly on display in what he calls his 'provisional morality', outlined in *Discourse on Method* III (48–51). This morality he sets out to hold constant whilst undertaking his philosophical project of applying his new method in metaphysics and physics. Its first two maxims see Descartes resolving not let his radical theoretical pursuits upset his conformism with conventional morality, or his recondite uncertainties stymy his practical resolve. The third maxim looks very like a paraphrase of Epictetus's *Encheiridion*, despite Descartes's anti-humanism:

> My third maxim was to try always to overcome myself rather than fortune and to change my desires rather than the order of the world, and generally to get in the habit of believing that there is nothing which is entirely within our power except our thoughts, so that after we have done our best concerning those things which lie outside of us, everything which our attempt fails to deal with is, so far as we are concerned, absolutely impossible. That alone seemed to me to be sufficient to prevent me from desiring anything in future which I might not achieve and thus to make me happy. (Disc., II: 49)

It is with this 'method' in place that Descartes sets out in *Discourse on Method* IV to outline the content of the first three of those '*meditationes*' which he made 'just eight years ago' (*Disc.* II: 51), and which are detailed in the *Meditations on First Philosophy* of 1636.

ii. Philosophy as bios and discipline of judgement

Before we turn to the *Meditations*, let us consider further what Descartes tells us in the *Discourse* concerning his motivations for his radical philosophical project (**8**). On the one hand, most certainly, Descartes was convinced that all previous philosophies were fundamentally – that is, at their foundations – uncertainly established. If a new philosophy could be established, Descartes famously confides in *Discourse* VI (61), he was moved to a hope that:

> it is very possible to attain knowledge which is very useful in life, and that, instead of the speculative philosophy which is taught in the schools we may find a practical philosophy by means of which, knowing the force and the action of fire, water, air, the stars, heaven, and all the other bodies that environ us, as distinctly as we know the different crafts of our artisans, we can in the same way employ them in all those uses to which they are adapted, and thus render ourselves as the masters and possessors of nature.

On the other hand, in *Discourse* III (49–50), at the conclusion of his para-Stoic morality (i), Descartes confides a different series of motivations for his project. He drew up at one time a list of all possible vocations, to try to decide which way of life was best, Descartes tells us. His conclusion was that 'I could not do better than to continue in the very occupation I was engaged in, that is, using all my life to cultivate my reason and to progress as far as I could in a knowledge of the truth, following the method which I had prescribed for myself' (*Disc.*, III: 49–50). Like Aristotle, of whom (like Bacon) he is otherwise highly critical, Descartes here tells us that the activity of pursuing philosophy gave him 'such extreme contentment once I started using this method that I did not think that one could find anything more sweet and innocent in this life' (*Disc.*, III: 50) (**8**) (The echo of Boethius of Dacia's heresy will be clear here [**5.4**]).[7]

Descartes next adds a comment which justifies in full Foucault's recognition (*malgré lui*) of what he terms after all certain 'moral conditions' for practising the Cartesian philosophy in *Hermeneutics of the Subject*.[8] '*I would not have known how to limit my desires nor how to rest content*', Descartes tells us (italics ours), 'if I had not followed a road by which I believed I could be confident of acquiring all the knowledge ... [and] the true benefits I was capable of obtaining' (*Disc.*, III 50). Pursuing a philosophical discipline of judgement, here as in the Stoics, is here positioned as necessary in order to flourish. Descartes's reasoning speaks to a specific variant of the kinds of 'cognitivist' understanding of motivation which we have seen underlies the ancient claim to a therapeutic value for philosophical activities (**6**):

> Since our will tends to follow or to fly away from only those things which our understanding has represented to it as good or bad ... in order to act well it is sufficient to judge well, ... that is, to acquire all the virtues, along with all the other benefits which one can get. (*Disc.*, III: 50)

Descartes's theory of error in *Meditations on First Philosophy* IV hence serves the same function in his thought as Bacon's unveiling of the idols of the mind [**7.2, i**]. By this point in the text (see **iii**), Descartes has established clearly and distinctly, as he supposes, that an Infinite God must Exist (since Descartes has His Idea in mind, yet his mind is finite and could not itself conceive anything Infinite); that such a perfect being could never deceive, since deception implies weakness, nor create any human faculty subject to imperfection. How then to explain humans' propensity to errors which we witness everywhere?

Descartes's very Catholic contention is that error comes from an 'excessive' power, that of infinite free will, which God in his bounty has bestowed upon us. As Corneanu notes (2011: 84–6), this postulate of a *separate faculty* of the will operative in the (degrees of) assent we give to different beliefs is foreign alike to the classical philosophers, as to almost all of the British, post-Baconian experimentalists. The idea of degrees of assent, and of the very need for individuals to actively assent (or not) even to wholly theoretical truth-claims, however, is directly continuous with the latter lineage. In making erroneous judgements, Descartes contends, our will runs ahead of what the intellect has established, like some runaway epistemic train. Philosophy hence becomes exactly *a discipline which restrains, if not the passions (although these too), then the will within the bounds of what the intellect can, through methodical inquiries, certify*, 'for as often as I so restrain my will within the limits of my knowledge, that it forms no judgment except regarding objects which are clearly and distinctly represented to it by the understanding, I can never be deceived' (*Med.* IV, 92).

iii. Cartesian, meditations

It is notable that when Pierre Hadot reflected upon the differences between his own, and Michel Foucault's understandings of the history of philosophy, he stressed his critical distance from Foucault's claims concerning Descartes (Hadot, 2020: 131–2). Hadot disputes whether we can say that, in Descartes, the ancient principle was decisively overthrown: 'Truth always has a price; no access to truth without ascesis' (at Dreyfus & Rabinow, 1983: 251–2). Above all, Hadot points in these moments to the literary genre announced by Descartes's title of the *Meditations of First Philosophy*. The Latin *Meditationes*, he ventures, could indeed be translated as 'exercises': '*meditatio* in Latin signifies originally "exercise", "preparation", "apprenticeship", and corresponds to the Greek *meletê*' (Hadot, 2019: 197). As Hadot comments, it is nevertheless striking that this title of 'meditations' does not appear to have been previously used in any philosophical text, remembering that Marcus Aurelius left his manuscript untitled [**3.4**]:

> Descartes has written, precisely, *Meditations*, and this word is very important. Concerning these *Meditations*, Descartes advises his readers to dedicate a number of months, or at least a number of weeks, to 'meditate' the first and second meditations, in which he speaks of universal doubt, then of the nature of the mind. This clearly shows that for Descartes also, 'evidence' can only be recognized on the basis of a spiritual exercise. (Hadot, 2002: 299; 2019: 194–5; 2020: 232)

Intriguingly, in Foucault's 1972 criticism of Derrida's reading of Descartes's *Meditations*, 'This Body, This Paper, This Fire', Foucault himself criticized what he took to be Derrida's 'reduction of discursive practices to textual traces … this "textualisation" of discursive practices' (Foucault, 1998: 416). Foucault charges that Derrida attends exclusively, albeit critically, to the demonstrative dimension of Descartes's *Meditations*. In doing so, he overlooks precisely the literary status of the text as 'meditations' which Hadot stresses:

> Any discourse, whatever it may be, which are produced each in its space and time, as so many discursive events. Even if it is a question of pure demonstration, these utterances can be read as a series of events linked one to another according to a certain number of formal rules … On the other hand, a 'meditations' produces, as so many discursive

events, new utterances that carry within them a series of modifications of the speaking subject: through what is said in a meditation, the subject passes from darkness to light, from impurity to purity, from the constraint of passions to detachment, from uncertainty and disordered movements to the serenity of wisdom. (Foucault, 1998: 405–6)

Hadot's and this *earlier* Foucaultian reading of Descartes point to a larger literature including groundbreaking pieces by Amelie Rorty (1983), Gary Hatfield (1986) and Zeno Vendler (1989). In this book, we have encountered practices of meditation in the Stoics [**3.4**] and in monastic meditative exercises upon scripture and sacred texts, so as 'to possess these sayings at the opportune moment' [**4.2**] (Dorothea of Gaza, at Hadot, 1995: 134). In both traditions, this practice was moreover tied to specific forms of writing. Yet both in Marcus Aurelius and in the monastic *apothegmata*, *sententiae* and *florilegia*, the sayings for meditation were recorded in aleatory form, according to the needs of the moment (in Marcus), or else gathered under alphabetized headings (in the *florilegia* and common-place books [see **6.2**, **7.2**]). By contrast, these authors situate Descartes's *Meditations on First Philosophy* within a Christian genre of written meditations in which 'the author attempts to transform himself by following a *staged reflection*, a self-reform through self-examination' (Rorty, 1983: 540 [our italics]). Rorty distinguishes between two types of this meditational literature, presaging Descartes's inauguration in *The Meditations on First Philosophy* of a novel, third, 'analytic' (Rorty) or 'cognitive' (Hatfield) species (Rorty, 1983: 550–3).

The first, 'ascensional' species of meditation stages the author-reader's ascent towards a new way of being through exhortation, admonition, celebration or prayer, as in Saint Bonaventure's *Itinerarium Mentis Deum* and Saint Robert Bellarmine's *The Ascent of the Mind to God by a Ladder of Things Created* (Rorty, 1983: 550). The second species of Christian meditational literature, exemplified by Saint Ignatius Loyola's *Spiritual Exercises*, is penitential (Rorty, 1983: 551–3). Here, the author-reader is positioned as so fallen or corrupt as to be in need of radical *kenósis* or self-emptying through ritual exercises, sensory deprivations and trials. In the Augustinian lineage, whose Neoplatonic debts are evident [**4.4**], penitential meditations aimed at assisting the exercitant to rediscover the image of God within their own soul, as 'an invisible, immaterial, yet mutable power' (Hatfield, 1985: 14). Descartes's 'rationalist' claim that the bases of the sciences lies not in the data afforded us by the senses, but in the 'clear and distinct' ideas of the natural light (*lumen naturale*) of the intellect granted by God, mark out his debts to this Augustinian meditative lineage.

However, Vendler shows convincingly to what extent the literary staging of Descartes's *Meditations* also reflect his close debts to the founding Jesuit, Ignatius Loyola's, Thomistic conception of penitential meditations. According to this conception, since our sinful attachments and errors hail from our senses, so the process of 'preparing and disposing the soul to rid itself of all inordinate attachments, and, after their removal, of seeking and finding the will of God in the disposition of our life for the salvation of our soul' (Ignatius, at Vendler, 1989: 196) requires the inquirer to consciously practice a regimen of rhetorical and other exercises addressed pre-eminently to the passions and imagination, as well as the mind. Like Descartes's *Meditations,* staged over six days, so Ignatius's *Spiritual Exercises* proposes a programme of spiritual exercises to be undertaken over a precisely defined period of time (eight weeks) beginning with a week of penitences and culminating in the 'decision for Christ' (Vendler, 1989: 197). Comparably, Descartes's *Meditations* begins with the day of kenotic, sceptical doubt, then proceeds (via the discovery of the cogito) to knowledge of God on the third day, which enables Descartes to diagnose the source of his errors (as above, on day 4), then reconstruct the basis for the new sciences (on days 5 and 6). As Foucault's stress on the definite articles in his title 'This Body, This Paper, This Fire' registers, Descartes also goes to pains to specifically locate his *Meditations* in space and time. He writes in the first person, and in the present tense, throughout. The opening of Meditation I announces that 'today I ... rid my mind of all worries (*hodie mentem curis ... exsolvi*)'; Meditation II refers us back to 'yesterday's meditation (*esterna meditatione*)'; Meditation IV looks back upon what he has achieved 'these past few days (*his diebus*)', and then on what 'today I have learned (*hodie ... didici*)'; just as Meditation V and VI speak of 'doubts into which I fell a few days ago (*dubiis, in quae superioribus diebus incidi*)' (Vendler, 1989: 201). As Hadot stresses, Descartes underlines that he expects his readers to follow this dated itinerary, so in effect the 'I' of the *Meditations* is also identified with the 'you' of Descartes's intended audience (Hadot, 2019: 195–6). 'I would advise none to read this work, unless such as are able and willing *to meditate with me in earnest,* to detach their minds from commerce with the senses, and likewise to deliver themselves from all prejudice' (*Meds.* 'Preface', 73 [italics ours]). As for readers unwilling to read the text in this manner, 'without caring to comprehend the order and connection of the reasonings, … I may say that such persons will not profit greatly by the reading of this treatise'.

There is more. In written meditations, Ignatius recommends a 'first prelude', in which the author engages in a vivid imagining of the place where s/he is to undertake the exercise(s); then a 'second preface', stating the aim of the ensuing exercise; followed by several 'Points', in which the exercitant is exhorted to apply sequentially his memory, understanding and, decisively, his will (Vendler, 1989: 197). Vendler's 'Descartes' Exercises' (198–211) shows just how closely Descartes's structuring of his six Meditations follows these Ignatian directives, adapting their content to his philosophical subjects and ends. Thus, echoing Ignatius's advice that 'the progress made in the Exercises will be greater, the more the exercitant withdraws from all friends and acquaintances, and from worldly cares' (at Vendler, 1989: 202), Descartes opens by referring us to the place and isolation of his first Meditation: 'today, then, I have expressly rid my mind of all worries and arranged for myself a clear stretch of free time. I am here quite alone' (*Meds.*, I, 74). The aim, a second Ignatian Preface, follows: 'I will devote myself sincerely, and without reservation to the general demolition of my opinions' (Vendler, 1989: 77). The main work of Meditation 1 is the cognitive *ascesis* (**3**) in which Descartes adduces 'points' speaking to the unreliability of the senses, the possibility that what we experience as real may be dreamed up, and the possibility that there exists a deceiving God. Again per Ignatius, he appeals to the memory at the beginning of each of these points: 'Whatever I have up till now accepted … but from time to time I have found … '; 'How often, asleep at night … as if I did not remember other occasions … '; 'and yet, firmly rooted in my mind is the opinion that there is an omnipotent God' (Vendler, 1989: 75–7).

The key meta-philosophical point here is that if the *Meditations* were solely a demonstrative, and not also a wider spiritual exercise (**3**), at the point in each Meditation, including Meditation 1, when the key argumentative claims have been established, the text should end. But Meditation 1 continues. After the unreliability of all previous knowledges has been demonstrated, per Ignatius, we instead get a firm resolution of the will: 'so in the future *I must withhold my assent* from these former beliefs just as carefully as I would from obvious falsehoods, if I want to discover any certainty' (*Meds.* I, 77). But why does the will need to be exhorted in this text of 'system-building rationalism'? Because, as we saw (**ii**), for Descartes as for the ancients, our judgments are shaped by passions and habits which cannot be lastingly moved by argument alone. As he tells us, no matter what his intellect has ascertained, 'my habitual opinions keep coming back, and, despite my wishes, they capture my belief, which is as it were bound over to them as a result of long occupation and the law of custom' (Vendler, 1989: 77).

So, how can Descartes break the force of his inveterate cognitive and other habits? Like Bacon [**7.2, ii, b**], Ignatius recommends to his exercitants that, to engender ethical change, they self-consciously go to the opposite extreme of what their habitual ways suggest. Just so, Descartes now bids up the first Meditation by self-consciously introducing the famous 'evil demon', precisely as a means 'to turn my will in completely the opposite direction (*voluntate plane in contrarium versa*) and deceive myself, by pretending that these former opinions are utterly false and imaginary' (Vendler, 1989: 77). As he explains: 'I shall do this until the weight of preconceived opinion is counter-balanced and the distorting influence of habit no longer prevents my judgment from perceiving things correctly.'

Meditation II likewise opens with a first Prelude situating the exercise: 'It feels as if I have fallen unexpectedly into a deep whirlpool which tumbles me around so that I can neither stand on the bottom nor swim up to the top' (Vendler, 1989: 77). The aim follows, in Ignatian style: 'I will proceed ... until I recognize something certain ... to find just one thing, however slight, that is certain and unshakeable' (Vendler, 1989: 77). The 'points' of the Meditation follow: Descartes recalls yesterday's results (with an explicit mention of lying memory [*mendax memoria*]) (*Meds.* II, 78); then, famously, he demonstrates the performative indubitability of the *cogito* (*if he doubts, he thinks; but if he thinks, he exists*). Once more, however, after the argumentative work has been done, Descartes's recalcitrant habits recur: 'but it still appears–and I cannot stop thinking this–that the corporeal things of which images are formed in my thought, and which the senses investigate, are known with much more distinctness than this puzzling "I" which cannot be pictured in the imagination' (*Meds.* II, 79). To 'restrain' his wandering mind 'within the bounds of truth', Descartes hence introduces the famous 'wax example' (Vendler, 1989: 80). Interestingly, here it is the senses that are called upon, as Descartes vividly describes this object ('it has not yet lost the taste of honey; it retains some of the scent of flowers ... its colour shape and size are plain to see; it is hard, cold ... if you rap it with your knuckle it makes a sound ... ' [Vendler, 1989: 80]), albeit on the way to conceiving clearly how the object's only invariant quality, extension, is invisible except to the eye of the mind. As the closing colloquy of the Meditation puts it, this exercise has added nothing to what the previous demonstration had established, so much consolidated his own resolve: 'I have now finally got back to where I wanted' (Vendler, 1989: 81).

The same post-Ignatian structuring of Meditation III as a 'spiritual exercise' applies. The prelude gives us the place: 'I will now shut my eyes, stop my ears, and withdraw all my senses' (*Meds.* III, 81). Descartes's aim is to 'converse with myself and scrutinize myself more deeply; and in this way … attempt to achieve, little by little, a more intimate knowledge of myself' (Vendler, 1989: 81–2). The key points of the Meditation involve an examination of his own ideas, with a view to ascertaining where they could have hailed from. The Meditation culminates in the claim that the Idea *of* an Infinite Being can only have come *from* such a Being, who must also exist – since (so Descartes contends) his finite mind could not have generated this Infinite Idea. Instead of an exercise to consolidate his will, calling upon the imagination or the senses, however, what follows in Meditation III are a series of anticipated objections and replies to consolidate the previously established claims. The closing colloquy, however, to which Hadot also draws our attention (Hadot, 2019: 199), sees Descartes in momentarily 'ascensional' mode, turning away from all of this to contemplate His Creator (3): 'I should like to pause here and spend some time in the contemplation of God; to reflect on his attributes, and to gaze with wonder and adoration on the beauty of this immense light' (*Meds.* III, 89).

In fact, and in a way that continually confounds readings of Descartes as a wholly secular thinker, it is upon the basis of the putative 'proof' of the existence of this Infinite and perfect, thus non-deceiving God, that Descartes's new philosophy is constructed in the final three Meditations. 'And now, from this contemplation of the true God, in whom all the treasures of wisdom and the sciences lie hidden, I think I can see a way forward to the knowledge of other things,' Meditation IV (89) confides. As the Preface to this Meditation underscores, this achievement itself has nevertheless only become possible through the staged, post-Ignatian meditative exercises that we have seen. In ways that recall Platonic and medieval formulations [5.4], Descartes specifies that his mind has decisively been strengthened in its capacity for abstraction from the senses:

> I have been habituated these bygone days to detach my mind from the senses, and I have accurately observed that there is exceedingly little which is known with certainty respecting corporeal objects, that we know much more of the human mind, and still more of God himself. I am thus able now without difficulty to abstract my mind from the

contemplation of sensible or] imaginable objects, and apply it to those which, as disengaged from all matter, are purely intelligible. (Hadot, 2019)

Such are the existential foundations of the new rationalism, as a PWL approach allows us to recall.

7.4 Conclusion: from experimental philosophy to the enlightenment

If PWL lies at the basis of the founding texts of what would become scientific culture, what can we say about its evolution after the deaths of Bacon and Descartes, and the complete eclipse this meta-philosophy seems to have suffered by the first decades of the twentieth century? In Britain, in the wake of Francis Bacon's work, two directions for PWL can be discerned. On the one hand, a transformed form of Stoicism was adapted by leading thinkers of the British and Scottish enlightenments, who, influenced by the Cambridge Platonists, nevertheless looked to qualify the Stoic evaluation of *apatheia* in a valorisation of the moral sentiments, led by forms of sympathy (Brooke, 2012: 111–20, 159–80; John Sellars, 2019). Work by John Sellars on Shaftesbury's *Askêmata* (2016) has hence shown how directly this text, the author's *hypomnêmata*, is indebted in form and content to Marcus Aurelius's Stoic *Meditations* and the Stoic practice of self-writing. As the seventeenth and eighteenth centuries progressed, however, the uneasy *rapprochements* of Stoicism and Christianity we find in Petrarch and Lipsius (as well as figures like Du Vair and Thomas Gataker [Brooke, 2012: 134–5]) was challenged by figures like Jacob Thomasias, in the 1676 *Exercitatio de stoica mundi exustione* (Brooke, 2012: 137), Ralph Cudworth, in his 1678 *True Intellectual System of the World* (Sellars, 2011), Johann Franz Buddaeus's *Theses theologicæ de atheismo et superstitione* of 1716, and we should not neglect to mention here David Hume (Brooke, 2012: 139–42). Stoicism, impugned by the atheistic Hume for its excessively 'monkish' profile (Davie, 1999), was increasingly impugned by other early moderns as 'atheistic', notably following disputes surrounding Spinoza's pantheism in Germany and elsewhere. The porch thence entered into a lasting decline in the anglosphere which growing secularization in the eighteenth-nineteenth centuries did not arrest (Brooke, 2011: 136–48).

The second tendency, flagged above and documented by Corneanu's *Regimens of the Mind*, involves the texts and initiatives of the 'experimental philosophers' associated with the founding of the Royal Society: figures like Boyle, Hooke, Sprat, Charleton, Glanvill and, most famously, John Locke. In their texts advocating for new forms of experimental, empirical inquiry directly inspired by Bacon, we see the same interweaving of therapeutic and aretaic (as well as theological) motifs we have seen now in both Bacon and Descartes (7). There is firstly an acute sense, presaged in Bacon and Montaigne, of the limits of human understanding, compared with the complexity of 'the book of God's works', the natural world (Corneanu, 2011: 8, 97; 55–6). Responding to this sense, these texts proffer convergent post-Baconian diagnoses of the 'distempers', 'diseases' or 'vices' to which the human mind is typically prey. For the *virtuosi* as for Aristotle, human beings have a desire to know, even a 'greed' or 'insatiable Appetance of knowledge', in Charleton's suggestive formulations (at Corneanu, 2011: 91). Yet, as Bacon had diagnosed, they also wish profoundly that the knowable world should conform to their own passionate wishes, inveterate prejudices and unmeasured vanity.

Nevertheless, secondly, the 'distempers', 'diseases' or 'vices' of the inquiring mind are not for these thinkers irredeemable. It is just that, if they are to be 'mitigated' and countervailing epistemic virtues inculcated (Corneanu, 2011: 105, 208), new regimens of philosophical exercises will be required. As Locke clarifies in his unpublished work of *medicina animi*, *The Conduct of the Understanding*:

> Would you have a man write or paint, dance or fence well, or perform any other manual operation dexterously and with ease, let him have never so much vigor and activity, suppleness and address naturally, yet nobody expects this from him unless he has been used to it and has employed time and pains in fashioning and forming his hand or outward parts to these motions. Just so it is in the mind; would you have a man reason well, you must use him to it betimes, exercise his mind in observing the connection of ideas and following them in train. (Locke, *Conduct*, §6)

The meta-philosophical kinship we are claiming between Bacon, the *virtuosi* and Descartes lies in their shared sense of philosophical activity as a *cultura animi*, as well as (not despite) being the means to develop novel understandings of physics and metaphysics. This meta-philosophical parallel in no way minimizes their profound substantive differences. Locke's criticism of the 'innate ideas' with which Descartes's *lumen naturale* is furnished is well known, and Glanvill will charge that Descartes's method leaves him prey to 'the naked *Ideas* of his own mind' (at Corneanu, 2011: 107), when it is far wiser 'to measure or strengthen [one's thoughts] by the assistance of others'. Indeed, the kind of experimentalist sage (**10**) that we glimpse in the texts of the *virtuosi* has a very different profile than Descartes's philosopher: combining the 'Socratic modesty' (Corneanu, 2011: 105) to recognize his own limitations and moderate the degrees of his assent to the degrees of probability of each proposal, with the patience to systematically collect and tabulate particular instances of phenomena, and the forbearance to remain open to the possibility that any standing conclusion might be refuted by one's own or others' subsequent researches. Above all, if such a figure is to be trained, it can only be on the basis of their participation in new intersubjective practices of inquiry – not withdrawing, like Descartes, into one's study, but conducting experiments and submitting their results to the scrutiny of peers in new academies and societies.

Experimental inquiry, with this in view, did not in the early modern period form a project of wholly objectifying and depersonalizing knowledge and philosophy. It was also conceived as a therapeutic and aretaic pursuit producing newly chastened inquirers and forms of intellectual sociability. As Stephen Shapin and others have contended, the cultivation of 'experimental philosophy' was indeed tied on the British Isles to a wider irenic programme, with political valences, hoping to put an end to ongoing religious and civil strifes (Shapin, 1994; Corneanu, 2011: 96). As we shall see in **Chapter 8**, it is this link that emerges in the British empiricists' work between experimental inquiry and a call for tolerance towards others' views that will be decisive, on the European continent, in shaping the re-conception of *philosophia* in the leading French *lumières*.

CHAPTER 8
FIGURES OF THE *PHILOSOPHE* IN THE FRENCH ENLIGHTENMENT

8.1 'The *philosophe*'

'Nothing is easier to acquire today than the name philosopher,' begins a small essay penned by César Chesneau Du Marsais (2002), entitled 'Le Philosophe'. The name 'philosophe', the article continues, is presently assigned to anyone who leads 'an obscure and retired life, [gives] a few outward signs of wisdom, with a bit of reading'. Others assume the mantle for themselves, and 'regard themselves as the only true philosophers because they have dared to overturn the sacred boundaries established by religion and have broken the shackles by which faith bound their reason'. From these presumptive heights, they 'regard others with disdain, as weak souls'. Nevertheless, the article continues, 'one ought to have a more just idea of the philosopher'. It is this just idea that Du Marsais's little essay proposes to communicate.

Valuable researches over the last decades have recovered a sense of the complexity of the French enlightenment, and studies such as those of Wade (1977a; 1977b), Gay (1995a; 1995b), Jonathan Israel (2013), Pagden (2013) and Rasmussen (2013) warn us against adducing any given text as wholly representative of the period. Yet Du Marsais's 'Philosophe', which appeared anonymously in 1743 under the title *Apology for Philosophy* circulated widely in eighteenth-century Paris, eventually forming the entry on the subject in Diderot and D'Alembert's *Encyclopedia*. It was then republished by Voltaire. As such, it furnishes as sound a basis as any to understand the figure of the eighteenth-century 'philosophe'.

What then does Du Marsais's little text elucidate about his 'philosophe'? And how does its portrait stand in relation to our history of PWL? 'Reason is to the philosopher what grace is to the Christian,' the text announces. We are prompted to imagine that a Rationalist vision of philosophy, influenced by Descartes above all [7.3], is imminent. What ensues is a classical, practicist claim concerning reason as master of the passions, not builder of systems or guarantor of certitudes: 'other men are carried away by their passions, without their actions being preceded by reflection: these are men who walk in the shadows; whereas the philosopher, even in his passions, acts only after reflection; he walks in the night, but he is preceded by a torch'.

In fact, epistemologically, this philosophe is no Rationalist. When he seeks out the principles and causes of things, his principal means are the senses, as per the British experimentalists [7.4], not any *lumen natural*. To this empiricism is moreover tied a form of distinctly post-sceptical self-awareness. 'The philosopher ... brings causes to light *to the degree that he is able*', Du Marsais qualifies (our italics). Here as in the Royal Society *virtuosi*, that is to say, at issue is a modern form of the qualified scepticism associated in the ancient world with the probabilistic academy of Cicero and others [4.3, 7.2]. Du Marsais's philosophe, echoing Montaigne or Bacon:

> certainly does not confuse [truth] with probability; he takes as true that which is true, as false that which is false, as doubtful that which is doubtful, and as probable that which is only probable. He goes further – *and here is a great perfection of the philosopher* – when he has no proper motive for judging, he remains undecided.[1]

Wisdom, on this model, does not consist in wit or fertility in conjecture, a telling denial in the age of Voltaire. *Sagesse* consists in a learned sobriety or 'discernment'; not judging boldly but judging well. This discernment principally includes the sceptical art of *epôchê*, reserving one's assent until adequate grounds for this assent present themselves:

> He is more satisfied with himself when he has suspended the faculty of making a decision than he would be to have come to a decision before having a sense of the proper reason for a decision. Thus, he judges and speaks less, but he judges more surely and speaks better.

Above all, despite the postmodern scarecrows that have proliferated since the 1960s, the enlightenment philosophe is an *enemy to Rationalist system building*. The pretension to have explained everything presents itself to him as a species of epistemic immoderation, comparable to the imaginative excesses of the superstitious. To the extent that the philosophe accepts any one vision of phenomena, he does so with reservation, to use a Stoic term: 'The philosopher is not so attached to a system that he is unable to feel all the force of objections.'[2]

From epistemology, therefore, Du Marsais's 'philosophe' turns seamlessly to the *ethos* of this *philosophe*. Unlike Petrarch or even Montaigne, Du Marsais's philosophe is a man of this world, almost Epicurean, who 'wants to enjoy like a wise housekeeper the goods that nature offers him' and 'to find pleasure with others'. Too much meditation, or meditation of the wrong kind, Du Marsais muses, make certain nameless philosophers 'ferocious towards everyone; they flee men, and men avoid them'.[3] By contrast, our philosophe is civic-mindedness itself, in this attribute more like a Stoic, or a Cicero, than an Epicurean: 'For him, civil society is, as it were, a divinity on earth; he flatters it, he honours it by his ... exact attention to his duties, and by a sincere desire not to be a useless or embarrassing member of it.'[4]

So is he then a Stoic, this singular 'philosophe'? No. For his humane sentiments oppose him to the idea of *apatheia*, at the same time as his urbane scepticism counsels him against its impossibility. Moderation and *metriopatheia* are his ethical watchwords: 'he works at not being dominated by [his passions], ... and at making reasonable use of them, because that is possible, and because reason directs him to do so'. All in all, the article does not stop short of recommending its subject, now in a Platonic strain, as not simply a sage (**10**), but in principle as the most eligible figure to govern:

> The philosopher is thus an honourable man who acts in everything according to reason, and who joins to a spirit of reflection and precision, morals and sociable qualities. Graft a sovereign onto a philosopher of whatever stripe and you will have a perfect sovereign.

Nearly every line of this brief *Encyclopaedia* entry would reward further commentary. Let us adduce here just six observations. Firstly, it is vital for us here that Du Marsais's subject is the philosophe as a figure or *persona*, in contrast either to philosoph*y* as an activity, or to 'philosophies' embodied in systems or written discourses (**10**). In taking this figure as its subject matter, 'Le Philosophe' was far from untimely. All told, Ira Wade tells us, there were some 225 plays in enlightenment France featuring a philosopher as a character:

> Some playwrights satirized [the philosopher] bitingly as a dangerous member of society. Palissot, for instance, whose *Les Philosophes* was patterned after Moliere's *Femmes savantes*, actually put upon the stage recognizable philosophes of the time, such as Mme. Geoffrin,

Diderot, Helvétius, and Rousseau. Other playwrights endeavoured to stress that despite his pretence of being stoically above the human passions, the philosophe was, as everybody else, subject to those passions, particularly that of love. ... Still others, such as Sedaine ... [in] *Philosophe sans le savoir* ... tried to show that the philosophe was in reality a character endowed with common-sense and bourgeois virtues, a good citizen free from prejudices. (Wade, 1977a: 14)

Despite its near-complete disappearance from philosophy syllabi, we see, the French enlightenment stands alongside the Italian Renaissance as one of those periods of Western intellectual history wherein reflection on the personae and vocations of the philosopher was most intense (**10**). This was a period in which a group of philosophers, notably in France, rose to the forefront of social, cultural, religious and political debates in ways seldom seen before or since. As such, despite what Caroline Wilson (2008: 417) has called their academic 'delisting', the *philosophes* of the French enlightenment justly command our attention here.

Secondly, we have already observed that Du Marsais's 'philosophe' looks at once like but unlike the other figures we have encountered in this history. In the guise of a general characterization, Du Marsais presents us with a very particular ideal type; indeed, an apology for a particular model of 'true', versus merely 'ordinary' philosophers. At stake in this little apology, in our terms, is a distinct figure in the history of PWL, the *philosophe* as against the philosopher. This new type was instantiated above all by Voltaire and Diderot. But it was anticipated by Montesquieu and Fontanelle (Gaukroger, 2008), and before them, by the 'free thinkers', new Pyrrhonians or *libertins érudits* of the seventeenth century (figures like Gabriel Naudé, Jean de La Bruyère, Le Mothe du Vayer and Cyrano de Bergerac) (Keohane, 1980: 144–50; Popkins, 2003: 80–98; Moreau, 2007; Cavaille, 2012). As Margaret Jacob has argued (2001), the persona of the philosophe, despite Du Marsais's genteel apology, 'took shape in the shadowy world of hidden printing presses, coteries of bold talkers, and aspirants to living by the fruits of one's pen' (Jacob, 2001).

Thirdly, for all of their debts to the systematic philosophers of the seventeenth century led by Descartes, Spinoza, Malebranche and Leibniz, it is vital to differentiate the enlightenment *philosophes* from these earlier figures' conceptions of philosophy. As Ernst Cassirer commented in *The Philosophy of the Enlightenment*:

The eighteenth century takes reason in a different and more modest sense [than the seventeenth-century Rationalists]. It is no longer the sum total of 'innate ideas' given prior to all experience, which reveal the absolute essence of things. Reason is now looked upon ... as ... the original intellectual force which guides the discovery and presupposition of truth ... a kind of energy, a force which is fully comprehensible only in its agency and effects. (Cassirer, 1955: 13)

In post-reformation Germany, as Ian Hunter has shown, 'it was anti-metaphysical civil philosophy – rather than Cartesian physics or Galilean mechanics – that did most to undermine Aristotelian university metaphysics' (Hunter, 2007: 582). Thinkers led by Samuel von Pufendorf (1632–94 CE) then Christian Thomasius (1655–1728 CE) set out to challenge the authority of theology and metaphysical philosophy, and establish a separation of civic from religious authority. But they did so by drawing on 'Christian doctrines of the damage done to man's faculties at the Fall, together with Epicurean doctrines of the helplessness of human reason in the face of the corporeal passions' (Hunter, 2007: 581). By contrast, the French philosophes took inspiration in their convergent critiques of the *esprit de système* primarily from British philosophy, and the approach to what would become scientific inquiry that we saw in **Chapter 7** modelled in Bacon's *Novum Organum* and the texts of the Royal Society *virtuosi* [**7.2, 7.4**]. Five of the most crucial of Voltaire's *Philosophical Letters* of 1734, a work often credited as inaugurating the French enlightenment, concern Bacon, Locke and Newton (Voltaire, 1733 [2007]: 37–58). As per Du Marsais's 'Philosophe', what Voltaire admires most in Locke is the learned ignorance that admits the limits of reason, at the same time as it proposes careful inquiry into what lies within the bounds of possible experience (Voltaire, 1733: 41–6). Voltaire's letter on Locke famously singles out the British philosopher's saying, 'we shall, perhaps, never be capable of knowing whether a being, purely material, thinks or not', for especial praise (Voltaire, 1733: 43). Against those pious critics who had decried in this Socratic profession an opening to irreligion, Voltaire replies:

But why may not God, if He pleases, communicate to our more delicate organs, that faculty of feeling, perceiving, and thinking, which we call human reason? To whatever side you turn, you are forced to acknowledge your own ignorance, and the boundless power of the Creator. (Voltaire, 1733: 44)

Likewise, if Voltaire was moved by his exile in England (1726–30) to adulation for Sir Isaac Newton, it is in large measure due to Newton's acknowledgement of his inability to do more than mathematically chart the effects of the force of gravity, without presuming to hypothesize concerning its essence: '*Procedes huc, et non amplius*' (Voltaire, 1733: 58). Newton's acknowledgement of the limits of human understanding is favourably contrasted by Voltaire, exactly, to the metaphysical 'romances' of Descartes (Voltaire, 1733: 42; Voltaire, 2004: 374). Descartes for Voltaire was 'mistaken in the nature of the soul, in the proofs of the existence of a God, on matter, on the laws of motion, and on the nature of light' (Voltaire, 2004: 51). And he made these mistakes *because of his failure* to rein in his prodigious 'humour of forming hypotheses' to the bounds of experience and experiment (Voltaire, 2004: 51; 42). This kind of systematic philosophizing would be memorably satirized by Voltaire's Pangloss in *Candide*, the professor of 'métaphysico-théologo-*cosmolonigologie*' who champions the Leibnizian claims that everything is for the best, and this the best of all possible worlds (Voltaire, 1977). But the entry 'System' in the *Encyclopedia* is also a touchstone here, if we are to understand the enlightenment:

Now, such systems, far from dispelling the chaos of metaphysics, are only fit to dazzle the imagination by their bold consequences, to seduce the mind by the false lights of evidence, to nourish obstinacy in believing the most monstrous errors, to eternalize disputes as well as the bitterness and the anger with which they are maintained ... there are systems that deserve the praise people give them, and even some works that compel our admiration, they resemble those palaces in which taste, comfort, splendour, and magnificence compete to produce an artistic masterpiece, but their foundations are so weak that they appear supported only by a magic spell. (Diderot, 1765 [2009])

Fourthly, we note in this connection one other precursor to the eighteenth-century philosophes, the extraordinary figure of Pierre Bayle (1646–1707 CE). Little read today except by specialists, Bayle's *Historical and Critical Dictionary* was one of the most widely read books in the eighteenth century. In form and content, this veritable 'arsenal of the enlightenment' (Smith, 2013) anticipated firstly the *Encyclopaedia* of Diderot and D'Alembert, in which he is eulogized (Diderot, 2003), and the alphabetized entries of Voltaire's *Philosophical Dictionary* and *Questions on the Encyclopedia*. The 'critical' in the title of Bayle's *Dictionnaire* is meaningful. Bayle's intention in his *Dictionary*, he tells us, is first of all to correct the errors of other dictionaries. His method is borrowed from the ancient sceptics, and his admiration for Pyrrho, Arcesilaus and Carneades is explicit [**4.2**]. Above all, Bayle argues for, and obeys, the necessity of critically considering all available perspectives on an issue, in the meanwhile 'suspending one's judgment' (Bayle, 2006: 'Project' III, 228b). For Bayle as for Bacon [**7.2**], each of us tends to be blind to our own defects and can 'see but one part of the defects of the adversary' (Bayle, 2006: 'Project' III, 229a). To proceed scrupulously, 'one must not allow one's preconceived opinion to give more weight to the arguments that favour it, nor to diminish reasons opposed to it' (Bayle, 2006: 'Maldonat L', 169a). The Stoic Chrysippus is thus praised by Bayle both for compiling a list of all the objections to his *own* system and for his *inability* to present cogent rebuttals for them all (Smith, 2013: 23).[5] By contrast, only the 'academicians proposed with equal force the arguments of both sides', as in Carneades' famous orations for and against justice in 155 BCE in Rome (Bayle, 2006: 'Carneades, G' and 'Pyrrho, B'; Smith, 2013: 25–6). When we underscore that Bayle applied this method of antinomy, in long discursive footnotes, not only to the consideration of historical figures, but also to biblical subjects like King David and theological issues like the problem of evil,[6] we approach an understanding of how vital Bayle's philosophizing was in shaping the enlightenment persona of the *philosophe* (Mason, 1963).

Fifthly, what marks out the *philosophes* from other, earlier and more recent philosophical personae is their principal engagement with social, political and religious subjects (Wilson, 2008). The censored, burnt or confiscated philosophical works of the eighteenth century, Catherine Wilson notes, included treatises 'on monarchy, despotism and colonialism, also works concerned with comparative morals' (Wilson, 2008: 416) led by Montesquieu's *Lettres Persans* (Wade, 2015: 361–91).[7] The targets of the *philosophes* would no longer exclusively be desires and passions that fall within agents' own control, as per the Stoics or Epicureans. Nor would the *philosophes* preach serene acceptance of what we cannot control, like the Stoics or Sceptics, when this class of 'externals' includes forms of avoidable human evils: 'the targets of the philosophes included colonialism, luxury, austerity, hypocrisy, antifeminism (but also some forms of feminism), monarchy, aristocracy, clergy, religion, physicians, and the arts and letters' (Wilson, 2008: 416).

Sixthly and finally, then, the *philosophes*' intended audiences, in line with Du Marsais's emphasis on their amiable sociability, were not academics or clerics, but laypeople in civic society who might be capable of changing the secular world. The flourishing network of learned academies, salons presided over by illustrious women like Madame de Pompadour and Julie de L'Espinasse, the Baron D'Holbach and others, as well as bourgeois coffee houses, were the philosophes' characteristic environs (Goodman, 1989; Habermas, 1989; Pekacz, 1999) – when they were not forced into exile. '*J'écris pour agir*', Voltaire famously wrote, but his thought, here as elsewhere, became representative:

> The philosophes … expressed a conception of the philosopher's role as that of a historical actor, who, rather than focusing on the management of his 'thoughts', attempted to change the world to fit with his desires, and who applied himself to external matters that he at the same time recognized as largely outside his control. (Wilson, 2008: 417)

For this reason, as with the humanists and the *libertins erudits*, the enlightenment philosophers wrote in a farrago of different literary media which today would be considered off-limits for serious scholars (**5**). But the systematic treatise gave place in this period less to the meditations, consolations, letters, manuals, memory aids, collections of apothegms or exhortations that we have seen [**3.4**, **4.3**, **5.2**, **6.2**, **7.2**] than to more experimental literary forms, designed at once to reach and please the denizens of the burgeoning bourgeois public sphere, as well as to elude theologico-political censorship:

> French authors of foreign-published volumes rarely put their names on the title page, and when they were accused of authorship they lied with a stout conscience; this was part of the game, sanctioned by the laws of war. Voltaire not only denied the authorship of several of his books, he sometimes foisted them upon dead people, and he confused the scent by issuing criticisms or denunciations of his own works. The game included devices of form or tricks of expression that helped to form the subtlety of French prose: double meanings, dialogues, allegories, stories, irony, transparent exaggeration, and, all in all, such delicate wit as no other literature has ever matched. The Abbé Galiani defined eloquence as the art of saying something without being sent to the Bastille. (Durant & Durant, 1965: 497–8)

With this much said on the figure of the philosophe in general, let us turn to two particular exemplars, 'the patriarch' Voltaire, and the thinker known to friends simply as 'the philosophe', Denis Diderot.

8.2 Voltaire and the view from Sirius

There were two fundamental intentions underlying Voltaire's extraordinary career, according to Ira Wade. The first, conceived in the early 1730s and echoing the Aristotelian conception of the *Sophos*, was to make himself 'an encyclopaedic man' (8) (Wade, 1977b: 26). We see the fruits of this extraordinary ambition when we survey Voltaire's profuse *oeuvre*, in which he combines the apparently unrelated personae of 'poet, Newtonian scientist, political and economic thinker, literary critic, historian, critical deist, moralist, encyclopaedist' (Wade, 1977b: 28); as well as the literary genres (5) of poetry, romance, novella (or *conte*), dictionary entries, encyclopaedia entries, histories, tragedies, satires, comedies, essays, pamphlets, and treatises on metaphysics and toleration (Wade, 1977b; Wade, 2015b, 367–450; 755–67).[8] Voltaire's second, unifying intention was 'of preparing himself through the intellectual processes of the encyclopaedic man for the making of a new organic way of life' (Wade, 2015b: 28). Voltaire, adds Wade, 'accepted the responsibility for structuring all these preoccupations into a new conception of life, he literally had to forge a philosophy, a philosophy which was at the same time an art – the art of living' (Wade, 2015b: 28). What then are the relationships between this Voltairean art of living, and those of the Hellenistic, Roman and Christian sources we have examined in this book?

It is Peter Gay above all who highlights the importance of the reception of pagan poetics, historiography and ethical philosophy in shaping the French enlightenment (Gay, 1995a: 46–56; 105–9; Montesquieu, 2002). Voltaire is aware of the ancient sense of PWL as the therapy of beliefs and desires. 'The sage is a physician of souls,' his entry 'Philosophe' thus tells us in the *Philosophical Dictionary* (1901). The entry had opened in these terms:

> Philosopher, 'lover of wisdom', that is, 'of truth'. All philosophers have possessed this two-fold character; there is not one amongst the philosophers of antiquity who did not give examples of virtue to mankind, and lessons of moral truth. (Voltaire, 2004: 334)

Voltaire immediately qualifies that, in the post-Newtonian world, we can know that the ancient philosophers were largely mistaken in natural philosophy. However, 'that is of comparatively so little importance to the conduct of life, that philosophers had then no need of it' (Voltaire, 2004). As the entry continues, Voltaire's classical sense of philosophy's calling is further underlined.[9] If the Greek philosophers are still to be respected, 'it is because they were just, and because they taught mankind to be so', not on account of their competing theoretical systems (Voltaire, 2004: 335). Plato is singled out for praise on the grounds of certain passages which, echoing Petrarch, Voltaire says move us to 'ardent love of generous actions'. Then there is Cicero [**4.3**], 'who alone is perhaps more valuable than all the philosophers of Greece', an evaluation he shares with Montesquieu and others in this period (Sharpe, 2015). After Cicero come 'Epictetus in slavery, and the Antonines and Julian upon a throne' (Voltaire, 2004: 335). All of these men are admirable because of the exemplars of philosophical lives they proffer. Voltaire never mentions Epictetus or Marcus Aurelius except to praise their humility and *moeurs*, and to number them – alongside Confucius, Solon, Socrates, Charron and several others – as 'great men who, having taught and practised the virtues that God requires, seem to be the only persons possessing the right of pronouncing his decrees' (Voltaire, 2004: 180). Just so, Voltaire asks us:

> Where is the citizen to be found among us who would deprive himself, like Julian, Antoninus, and Marcus Aurelius, of all the refined accommodations of our delicate and luxurious modes of living? Who would, like them, sleep on the bare ground? ... Who would, like them, keep perfect mastery of all his passions? We have among us devotees. But where are the sages? Where are the just and tolerant, serene and undaunted souls? (Voltaire, 2004: 335–6)

With this much said, Voltaire's adherence to the ancient PWL paradigm needs to be qualified in at least two ways. Firstly, Voltaire never prescribes spiritual exercises (**3**) in anything like the sense with which we are now familiar in Plato or Socrates, Epicurus, Epictetus, Philodemus, Marcus Aurelius, Petrarch, Montaigne or Bacon.[10] Voltaire goes beyond Montaigne's scepticism in his ironic assessment of the feasibility of the ambition to make oneself a perfected sage (**10**). The brief story of 'Memnon', with subtitle 'the Philosopher, or Human Wisdom' stages a day in the life of the eponymous hero, after he has decided to become 'a great philosopher, and of course to be perfectly happy' (Voltaire, 1807: 181). For Memnon as for the Stoics, what this firstly involves is removing all the passions, including sexual desire, using philosophical exercises:

When I see a beautiful woman, I will say to myself: 'These cheeks will one day grow wrinkled, these eyes be encircled with vermilion, that bosom become flabby and pendant, that head bald and palsied.' I have only to consider her at present in imagination, as she will afterwards appear; and certainly a fair face will never turn my head. (1807: 181–2)

Needless to say, Memnon proceeds to fall in love with the first girl who walks by his window, who ruthlessly conspires with her uncle to extort him. Then, he gets drunk with friends and loses more money gambling, and one eye in the dispute that ensues. At last, the hapless Cyclops is forced to go begging at court, cup in hand, only to return home to find men repossessing his furniture. As Memnon goes to sleep on his philosopher's bed of straw, an angelic being from the planet Sirius (on which more shortly) appears to him, and the broken philosopher begs his aid:

'Your fate will soon change,' said the animal of the star. 'It is true, you will never recover your eye, but, except that, you may be sufficiently happy if you never again take it into your head to be a perfect philosopher.' 'Is it then impossible?', asked Memnon. 'As impossible as to be perfectly wise, perfectly strong, perfectly powerful, perfectly happy … There is a world indeed where all this is possible; but, in the hundred thousand millions of worlds dispersed over the regions of space, everything goes on by degrees'. (1807: 188)[11]

Secondly, Voltaire's conception of the *philosophe* is conceived almost constantly in contradistinction to a distinctly socio-political foe, 'fanaticism'.[12] Fanaticism for Voltaire, like presumption for Montaigne, involves two components. First, there is the 'internal' claim to know with a certainty fuelled by passionate identification that which is beyond the limits of human understanding. Fanaticism is firstly 'the effect of a false conscience, which makes religion subservient to the caprices of the imagination, and the excesses of the passions'.[13] So far, so classical. Yet secondly, it involves the sense of being entitled to 'compel others to come in', and to reprove, censor, exile or kill those who do not adhere to your metaphysical beliefs or practice your rites. 'Fanaticism is to superstition, what delirium is to fever, or rage to anger,' Voltaire thus qualifies: 'He who is involved in ecstasies and visions, who takes dreams for realities, and his imaginings for visions, is an enthusiast. The man who backs his madness with murder is a fanatic' (2004: 200–1).

The only remedy for this evil, Voltaire argues, is philosophy. In his work, as we might say, the therapist of desire hence becomes the social critic proselytizing 'that spirit of philosophy, which ... at length civilizes and softens the manners of men and prevents the access of the disease [of fanaticism]' (7) (Voltaire, 2004: 203).[14] The philosophical work of criticizing untenable beliefs strikes fanaticism at its cognitive roots. Hence, 'the different sects of ancient philosophers were not merely exempt from this pest of human society, but they were antidotes to it: for the effect of philosophy is to render the soul tranquil, and fanaticism and tranquillity are totally incompatible' (Voltaire, 2004: 203).

But how, exactly, can philosophy conduct this irenic philosophical–social therapy? On the one hand, the answer is by writing philosophy in a multitude of genres accessible to the reading public at large, not restricted to scholars and universities. Here is a first rationale for the profusion of *contes*, fables, dramas, dialogues, poems and pamphlets that Voltaire continued to pour out, in particular after 1761 and the Calas affair, when his famous campaign to *écrasez l'infâme* began (Durant & Durant, 1965: 727–44). As Voltaire told D'Alembert, 'Never have 12 volumes in folio made a revolution [*viz.* the *Encyclopedia*]; it is the little portable books for 30 sous a piece which are to be feared. If the gospel costs 1200 sisterces, the Christian religion would never have been established' (at Durant & Durant, 1965: 740).

On the other hand, Voltaire was acutely aware that, in order to promote the causes of a scientific culture and political toleration, he would need not simply to show the intellectual weaknesses of opponents' beliefs. He would also have to show readers, almost viscerally, that sectarians' actions were ridiculous or absurd. Herein we approach the heart of Voltaire's philosophizing, his infamous, more-than-Socratic irony (5). Voltaire not only professes his ignorance again and again. He wears masks, multiplies personae, stages dramas, concocts fables, adduces a thousand exempla from ancient, modern, Near and Far Eastern history, devises dialogues, and paints heroes and villains. Voltaire's own definition of 'Esprit' in the *Philosophical Dictionary* is perhaps the best description of his own creative *élan*:

What we call 'wit' (*esprit*) is either a fresh analogy, or a delicate allusion: sometimes it is the use of a word which is presented as having one meaning, but which the reader is invited to understand in another; sometimes it is the subtle linking of two ideas which have little in common; ... wit is the art of bringing together two separate things, or of dividing them where they appear linked, or of setting one against the other; it is a way of revealing only half of one's thinking in order to let the reader guess the rest.[15]

We have seen that several of the ancient spiritual exercises (3) involved practices of reframing the familiar, like the exercise of the view from above or the Stoic exercise of physical definition [3.4]. As his 'Esprit' entry underscores, many of Voltaire's literary conceits exercise kindred effects of cognitive estrangement. To highlight the distance between the earliest, simple forms of Christianity and eighteenth-century Catholicism, the *conte, Ingenu* borrows a motif from Montesquieu's 1723 *Lettres Persans*. Voltaire has a naïve and virtuous American Indian visit contemporary France, knowing only the *New Testament*. The comedy ensues when he tries to live Christ's ideals, amidst the pomp and power of the Catholicism of eighteenth-century France. To highlight the distance between the morality of neighbourly love and the spirit of theological sectarianism, Voltaire imagines 'the licentiate Zapata, ... appointed Professor of Theology at the University of Salamanca'.[16] Zapata presents a series of questions to a committee of doctors in 1629 expressive of the supposition that a man of God would do the greatest service to his fellows by preaching a simple, humane morality, rather than proselytizing an esoteric, dogmatic theology. Voltaire's conclusion is devastating:

> Zapata, receiving no answer, took to preaching God in all simplicity. He announced to men the common father, the rewarder, punisher, and pardoner. He extricated the truth from the lies, and separated religion from fanaticism; he taught and practised virtue. He was gentle, kindly, and modest; and he was burned at Valladolid in the year of our Grace 1631. Pray God for the soul of Brother Zapata.[17]

It is exaggerating to say that Voltaire's *contes philosophiques* are disenchanting spiritual exercises (3), in the service of engendering in readers a more irenic, philosophical spirit. We have underscored his scepticism about the efficacy of such exercises. Several of these tales, and of Voltaire's other conceits, nevertheless centrally stage such exercises, as the means to engender change in readers. Arguably one of Voltaire's finest philosophical *contes* has the telling title *Micromégas* ('small-big') (1807: 118–45). Seen in a PWL lens, it is in fact one extended playing out of the view from above exercise shared by the different ancient schools [see **3.3**, **3.5**]. *Micromégas* is in the first instance a 'comedy of scale', both in space and in time:

On one of the planets that orbits the star named Sirius there lived a spirited young man, who I had the honour of meeting on the last voyage he made to our little ant hill. He was called Micromégas, a fitting name for anyone so great. He was eight leagues tall, or 24,000 geometric paces of five feet each. He knows many things. He invented some of them. He was not even 250 years old when he studied, as is customary, at the most celebrated colleges of his planet, where he managed to figure out by pure willpower more than 50 of Euclid's propositions. That makes eighteen more than Blaise Pascal. (Voltaire, 1807: 118–19)

All untrained perceptions and self-perceptions are relative to the capacities of the perceiver, Voltaire's fable echoes the ancient sceptics [4.2]. So, when Micromégas meets an 'academic' from Saturn, who is only about 6,000 feet tall, the academic complains that on his planet, people have 'only' seventy-two senses. Micromégas, more sage, understands and replies that 'on our planet we have almost 1,000 senses; and yet we still have a kind of vague feeling, a sort of worry, that warns us that there are even more perfect beings' (Voltaire, 1807: 123). As for longevity, the Saturnian academic waxes mordant that on his planet, people live for only about 500 revolutions of the sun (about 15,000 earth years): 'So you can see yourself that this is to die almost at the moment one is born; our existence is a point, our lifespan an instant, our planet an atom. Hardly do we begin to learn a little when death arrives, before we get any experience' (Voltaire, 1807: 124).

When the interstellar giants arrive on earth, they espy a human ship, as miniscule for them as an ant is for us. Micromégas picks the minute artefact up and, struck with wonder, offers its tiny denizens his protection. At this, Voltaire writes, the humans each tried to understand this new and terrifying phenomenon according to what Bacon [7.2] calls the idols of the den: 'The chaplain of the vessel recited the exorcism prayers, the sailors swore, and the philosophers of the vessel constructed systems; but no matter what systems they came up with, they could not figure out who was talking' (Voltaire, 1807: 137–8). Unfortunately, a scholastic was on board [5.3], and this is what ensued:

He looked the two celestial inhabitants up and down. He argued that their people, their worlds, their suns, their stars, had all been made uniquely for mankind. At this speech, our two voyagers nearly fell over with that inextinguishable laughter which, according to Homer, is shared with the gods. (Voltaire, 1807: 145)

Micromégas, we see, is a fictional, personified conceit for Voltaire to undertake the view from above. The same intentionality as we find in Marcus Aurelius's or Seneca's practice of the exercise also operates here. When we are told that Micromégas could not help feeling 'a little angry that the infinitely small [humans] had an almost infinitely great pride' (Voltaire, 1807: 145), it is of course Voltaire who is vexed. Through the thought experiment of the *conte*, he is prompting his readers to share in his vexation. Above all, it is the art of Voltaire's little fable to have *enabled* us to relook at our condition as if from above, and to see it through Micromégas's eyes as infinitely minute in the cosmic scale. At the same time as the *esprit philosophique*, on Voltaire's view, asks us always to test our theories against the particular realities of our experiences ('*micro*'), it also asks us to frame our theories and experiences in the enlarged perspective opened to modern Europeans after Copernicus and Newton, the discoveries of the new world and of the deep antiquity of Indian and Chinese civilizations ('*mégas*'). The 'sage of Ferney''s own search for encyclopaedic knowledge in the natural and human sciences, as well as the literary arts, is explicable only when we see it as the basis of his own pursuit of such an enlarged yet ultimately humbling philosophical perspective.

8.3 Diderot and his Seneca

Since history sometimes works in improbabilities, Denis Diderot (1713–84), a younger contemporary of Voltaire, was almost as mercurial an intellectual force as the patriarch. Like Voltaire, whose works and deeds he admired, Diderot worked across a humbling range of literary and philosophical media (5): novels (philosophical and erotic), letters (real and fictive), criticism, dialogues, dramas, encyclopaedia entries, essays, anonymous interpolations and 'supplements' to others' writings, and texts circulated during his lifetime only amongst his friends, led by *D'Alembert's Dream* and *Rameau's Nephew*. Critics as eminent as Ira Wade (1977b) have nearly despaired of finding any 'organic unity' in this extraordinary *oeuvre*. It is in the *Encyclopedia*'s famous entry on 'Eclecticism' that we probably get Diderot's most concise statement of his vision of the persona of the *philosophe*, and of his own modus operandi. Blending scepticism, empiricism and a defiant independence of spirit that steals the march from Kant's more famous Horatian declaration, it also captures the extraordinary ambition and complexity of his philosophical identity:

> The eclectic is a philosopher who, riding roughshod over prejudice, tradition, antiquity, universal consent, authority, in a word, everything that subjugates the mass of minds, dares to think for himself, goes back to the most clear and general principles, examines them, discusses them, allowing only that which can be demonstrated from his experience and reason; and having analyzed all philosophical systems without any deference or partiality, he constructs a personal and domestic one that belongs to him ... He is not a man who plants and sows; he is a man who reaps and sifts. (Diderot, 1967: 86)

Fortunately, we do not need to fathom all of the dimensions of Diderot's output here. Our focus is solely on Diderot's conception of philosophical activity. The greatest project which Diderot undertook, spanning two decades after 1750, was his co-editing and co-writing of what became the fifteen volumes of the *Encyclopédie ou Dictionnaire raisonné des sciences, des arts et des métiers*. In this project, we see one side of Diderot's conception of the role of the philosophe: the thinker who reaps and sifts and wants to share the epistemic harvest. S/he is someone of universal or as we might say 'trans-disciplinary', knowledge. But s/he is also someone devoted not to secretively hoarding, but to spreading the lights of the sciences with the intelligent public. The philosophe-as-encyclopaedist is nevertheless acutely aware of his own limitations, in line with Voltaire and Du Marsais, and before them Locke and others. The encyclopaedic endeavour, as the 'Preliminary Discourse' by D'Alembert underscores, is necessarily collective, bringing together experts across the diverse sciences and professions, exactly insofar as no one man can command all knowledges:

> What man, then, could be so brash and so ignorant in understanding as to undertake single-handedly to treat all the sciences and all the arts? It thus became clear to us that to support such a great load as the one we would have to carry, it would be necessary to share it; and forthwith we cast our eyes upon a sufficient number of artisans who were competent and well-known for their talents, and scholars well-versed in the particular discipline which was to be their share of the work. To each one we distributed the part that was suited to him. (D'Alembert, 1751 [2009])

The 'Discours Préliminaire' sings a paean to the Italian Renaissance [**6.1, 6.2**]: 'It is from her that we have received the sciences which later produced such abundant fruit in all Europe; it is to her above all that we owe the *beaux-arts* and good taste of which she has furnished us with so great examples' (D'Alembert, 1751 [2009]). Above all, however, it is Francis Bacon who is named as the spiritual forefather of the project [**7.2**], and who furnishes Diderot and D'Alembert the bases for their division of the sciences. Bacon's scope and vigorous style, combining imaginative power with analytic rigor, prompts the encyclopaedists 'to regard [him] as the greatest, the most universal, and the most eloquent of philosophers'. Nevertheless, there is no whiggish sense of the inevitable march of knowledge in human history in this text, despite the poorly informed postmodernist clichés that at present go without saying in too many disciplines. If it seemed necessary for the philosophes to collect in one place all extant knowledge, the 'Discours Preliminaire' specifies, it is precisely out of an awareness that 'barbarism lasts for centuries and seems to be our natural element, while reason and good taste are but passing phenomena' (D'Alembert, 1751 [2009]: II). An *Enyclopedia,* albeit in seventeen huge volumes, will have some chance of surviving the deluge, and bequeathing to forgetful posterity, as in a time capsule, the bases of the sciences (Rosenberg, 1999).

Yet, Diderot as philosophe was more than the principal encyclopaedist. One further side to his philosophical persona, notably in his aesthetic criticism and in political texts like the interpolations into Raynal's *Histoire,* is that of the *moraliste.* More so than Voltaire, in fact – although not perhaps Montesquieu – Diderot, who was also known to his friends as Monsieur Topla (i.e. Plato in anagram), continually hearkened back to the ancient philosophical schools' models of life, in his ongoing attempts to orient himself. 'For many years I read a canto of Homer before bedtime as religiously as a good priest says his prayers', Diderot reports of his *paideia,* which was abetted (like Voltaire's) by his schooling with the Jesuits: 'I was suckled from a young age on the milk of Homer, Virgil, Horace, Terence, Anacreon, Plato and Euripides, diluted with that of Moses and the prophets' (Diderot, cited by Goulbourne, 2011: 14). In 1749, imprisoned for impiety in 'The Letter on the Blind for the Purposes of Those who See', Diderot began to translate Plato's *Apology* as a consolatory exercise (**3**). Voltaire's letters to him from this time often address him as 'our Socrates' (Goulbourne, 2011: 21–2). Both philosophes saw the parallel between Socrates's condemnation by the Athenians and their own persecution by the censors (Goulbourne, 2007; Bourgault, 2010).[18] Diogenes's blend of acerbic wit and idealistic ethical criticism spoke powerfully to Diderot (Goulbourne, 2007: 22–3). The figure of the Cynic, as a mode of life, is present at both beginning and end of

Rameau's Nephew, wherein the derisory 'Lui' mocks the philosophe's 'Moi' throughout as a hopelessly impractical 'Cato' (Shea, 2010: 45–73).

Diderot stages a kind of internal dialogue in the *Salon de 1767* between Socrates, the principled defender of *parrhesia*, come what may, and Aristippus, who accommodates his philosophical speech to *le monde, comme il va* (Goulbourne, 2011: 22–3). 1769's comic *Regrets for my Old Dressing Gown* pits the philosophe as Aristippus, now decked out in elegant new attire, against his former Diogenic self which had landed him in Vincennes: 'O Diogenes, if only you could see your disciple wearing the fine coat of Aristippus, how you would laugh!', Diderot writes, in one of his characteristic vocatives: 'I have left the barrel wherein you reigned in order to serve under a tyrant' (Diderot, 1875).

This ongoing playing out of Diderot's self-understandings by putting into dialogue the *dramatis personae* of the different ancient philosophers culminates in Diderot's book-length *Essay[s] on the Life and Works of Seneca the Philosopher, and the Reigns of Claudius and Nero* of 1778 (1828) then 1782 (1792). As the title underscores, Diderot's last book/s treat 'Seneca' not only as the proper name for a body of texts, but as an historical figure, as he is described by Tacitus, Suetonius, Dio Cassius, and others. An extensive biographical treatment of the philosopher's life, historical context and political career forms the first half of Diderot's *Essay*, culminating in an edifying comparison of the philosophe's noble suicide with the ignominious demises of the two despots under whom Seneca served (3) (Diderot, 1828: 186–96; 234–9). The second half of the books move, one-by-one, through *The Letters to Lucilius*, Seneca's three *Consolations*, and the Roman Stoic's eleven other philosophical works [**3.3**]. Diderot's Seneca books are in their own ways documents of the highest interest for us here.

Critics like Edward Andrew (2016) and Elena Russo (2009) have not failed to criticize the close identification between author and subject that characterizes these extraordinary texts. Diderot takes Seneca as an alter, they argue, as a way of dignifying Diderot's attempts to vindicate himself in the eyes of posterity for his inglorious five months at the court of Catherine II, and the acrimonious end of his friendship with Jean-Jacques Rousseau (**10**) (Russo, 2009).[19] For all of its merits, this kind of reading leaves us flatfooted when it comes to assessing Diderot's reading of Seneca's philosophical *oeuvre*, how it sits with other historical receptions of the Roman Stoic, and what the works tell us about Diderot's larger sense of the means and *moeurs* of the philosophe.

Diderot's Preface reveals the deeper stakes of the document. As Diderot presents things, the study is intended to serve as the basis of a spiritual or intellectual exercise by mature readers (**2, 3**):

> An experiment that I will voluntarily propose to a man of sixty-five or sixty-six years, who will [perhaps] judge my reflections as either too long, too frequent, or too distant from the subject, would be to bring with him, in retreat, Tacitus, Suetonius and Seneca; to jot down on paper the things which interest him, the ideas that they awaken in his mind, ... the sentiments that he feels, without having any other project than that of instructing himself ... I am nearly certain that, by stopping at the places [in the texts] where I have stopped, comparing his own century to centuries past, and considering the same circumstances and characters, he will come to the same conjectures as he finds in this Work, such that it is, about what the present announces to us and what one can hope or fear for the future. (Diderot, 1828: 3–4)

The proximity of Diderot's depiction of Seneca to his own self-conception, and of the persona of the *philosophe*, can hardly be questioned. He tells us that 'it is as much my own soul that I am painting as that of the different characters who figure in my account' (Diderot, 1792: 8). His aim is to write an 'apology for Seneca' against those envious Anytus', ancient and modern, who have blackened Seneca's name (Diderot, 1828: 7). Above all, if we want to read the philosopher as he intended to be read, it will be a question of 'profiting from his counsels', Diderot observes: Seneca's philosophy aimed to guide lives, not beautify intellects (**8**). Diderot himself regrets not having reaped the Senecan harvest earlier in his life:

> O Seneca, it is you (*toi*) whose breath dispels the vain phantoms of life; it is you who knows how to inspire men to dignity, firmness, indulgence towards friend and enemy alike; to contempt for fortune, sniping, slander, dignities, glory, life, death; it is you who know how to speak of virtue, and to inspire enthusiasm for her. You would have done more for me than my father, my mother, and my teachers. (Diderot, 1828: 431–2)

This is not to say, as some critics imply, that Diderot slavishly idolized Seneca, never contesting his actions, thoughts or authority. Instead, as the *philosophe* explains in the Preface of the second half of the work: 'I will talk about the works of Seneca without prejudice or partiality: exercising with his thought a privilege which he himself exercises with no other philosopher, I will sometimes venture to contradict him' (Diderot, 1828: 317). Far from a simple encomium to a sage (**10**), Diderot signals to his reader that an elaborate art of mask-wearing characterizes the text: 'Here, presenting the censor with the philosopher behind whom I am hidden; there, performing the opposite role, and offering myself up to the arrows that will only hurt Seneca, hidden behind me' (Diderot, 1828: 317–18). As Lojkine comments, what starts as a eulogy therefore looks increasingly like a 'contradictory dialogue' as we proceed from history to philosophy, and from the first to the second halves of the *Essai* (lojkine, 2001: 109). In this light, let us consider here four distinct features of the Diderotian profile of the philosophe, as he presents it in the mirror of Seneca's life and works.

Firstly, Diderot reads Seneca as an eclectic, *not* a dogmatic Stoic. He celebrates the liberality that sees Seneca in his early letters to Lucilius happily citing precepts from Epicurus, when he sees truth in them. As Diderot writes:

> Seneca ... was a mitigated Stoic, or perhaps even an eclectic, reasoning with Socrates, doubting with Carneades, struggling against nature with Zeno, and striving to elevate himself with Diogenes. Of the principles of the [Stoic] sect, he embraced only those which detach one from life, from fortune, from glory, from all these goods at the centre of what can make us unhappy; which inspire scorn for death, and which give to a man the resignation which accepts adversity, and the strength which supports him. This is a doctrine which suits and follows from instinct under the reign of tyrants, as the soldier takes the shield at the moment of action. (Diderot, 1828: 42)

Secondly, like Voltaire, who we have seen dismisses the physics and metaphysics of the ancient schools, so as Diderot passes through Seneca's philosophical *oeuvre*, he emerges as a staunch critic of Stoic logic and theology. It is clear that, whilst Diderot shares the Stoics' sense of the interconnectedness of all things, Diderot sees in Stoic theology an avatar of its equally indemonstrable Christian successors. This position is especially evident in Diderot's cold response to *Of Providence*. 'And what side does a wise man take between these disputants?', Diderot asks rhetorically, and does not answer (1828: 371).[20]

Thirdly, Diderot registers consistent doubts about several of the sterner tenets at the heart of the Stoics' ethical system. From the start, Diderot contests the Stoic teaching that virtue is more natural than vice, arguing that the claim stands contrary to all observation (1828: 273–4). Above all, he questions whether the Stoic life without affects is *kata physin* or rather engaged, despite itself, in a struggle *against* nature (1828: 371). Diderot likewise repeatedly challenges the Stoic teaching that one should expunge all the passions, including anger and compassion (Duflo, 2003: 495–8). His staged dialogue with Seneca in his commentary on *De Ira* is worth citing at some length in this connection:

> *Anger is a short madness, a passing delirium … Animals are thus devoid of anger …* – Why anger instead of love, hatred, jealousy and other passions? … *Because anger arises only in beings capable of reason …* – Say this also of memory and feeling! But why should animals be devoid of anger? … *Anger is not consistent with the nature of man …* – I do not know any passion that is more consistent with the nature of man. Anger is the result of injury; and the wisdom of nature has placed resentment in the heart of man, to supply the want of the law … Without anger and resentment, the weak would be abandoned, bereft of resources, to the tyranny of the strong, and nature would gather about her most violent children innumerable multitudes of slaves. *But surely our virtue is to be pitied, if our reason needs the help of the vices [like anger] …* (*De Ira*, Book I, chapter x) – No: our passions are not vices: according to the use we make of them, they are either vices or virtues. The great passions annihilate the imaginings which are born of frivolity and *ennui*. I cannot conceive how any sentient being can act without passion. The magistrate should judge without passion, it is true. But it is his taste or passion that has made him a magistrate. (Diderot, 1798: 448–9 [our italics]).

Diderot rages against Seneca's presentation of the Stoic teaching that the sage could suffer even the loss of a friend without grief. Our passions in response to such losses are a testament to our natural sociability, he contends – here approaching Shaftesbury, whom he had translated, and the moral sentiment thinkers. So, silencing them altogether is less enlightened than inhumane:

> What, Seneca? ([*De Ira*] Book I, chap. XII.) You say that '[t]he sage is not angered, if someone should kill his father or take away his wife; or

if a man violates his daughter before his very eyes?' ... Then you ask the impossible; indeed, maybe the harmful. It is not a matter here of behaving just as a man, someone more of less indifferent to the case at hand; but as a father for a child, or as a husband. Socrates himself became angry when he cried out to his servant: 'I would strike you, if I was not so angry!' (Diderot, 1828: 375)[21]

Fourthly, in line with this critique of *apatheia*, Diderot charges Stoic fatalism with rationalizing complete passivity before despotic injustice. Diderot is particularly scathing about this seeming implication of the Stoic *amor fati*. 'This morality, is it inspired in a Seneca by a Caligula?', he asks, despite the continuing proximity of the author of the *Lettre à Landres* and *Jacques La Fataliste* to just such a determinism (Diderot, 1828: 521; Duflo, 2003: 498 ff; Andrew, 2004: 295–6). Once more, it is above all Diderot's defence of the sociable passions, and of the public responsibilities of the *philosophe* as an actor in the arena, that grounds his opposition to the *vita contemplativa*, against Seneca's qualified argument in its favour in *De Otio*, as well as against the view of 'M. R. de G', the 'solitary walker', that time spent with others is time lost (Diderot, 1828: 153–4, 158–60). When Seneca tells Lucilius, in *Letter 36* to 'abandon the squares and retreat to the darkness from the new honours that awaited', Diderot replies:

Most advantageous for him, perhaps; but for society? There is in Stoicism a monastic spirit that I dislike. This is a philosophy to bring to the court, close to great men, in the exercise of public functions, or it is a lost voice crying in the wilderness. I like the sage in the limelight, like the athlete in the arena: the strong man will only be recognized on occasions when there is strength to show. (Diderot, 1828: 267–8)[22]

We only grasp the full radicality of Diderot's portrayal of Seneca when we see how the four features we have now highlighted in Diderot's reading of Seneca's texts – namely Seneca's eclecticism, Diderot's metaphysical scepticism, critique of *apatheia* and defence of the engaged *philosophe* – lead Diderot to an impassioned rebuttal of the ancient and modern charges that Seneca's life gave the lie to his noble precepts. Diderot accepts the inconsistency between Seneca's theory and practice that these criticisms allege. Yet, he does so exactly in order to raise up Seneca the man as an ethical exemplar, in favourable contrast to Seneca the Stoic (**10**). Seneca spoke as boldly as anyone could against Nero's whims, and did everything a tutor could to tame them, claims Diderot (1828: 148–50, 160–1). Seneca's staying on at court was testimony to Seneca's altruism, not his lusts for riches or power (1828: 174–7, 206–22). It would have been suicidal for Seneca to have withdrawn from the bloody stage earlier, as if this were possible when a tyrant commanded *imperium*. Decisively, Diderot's Seneca realized acutely, as a father, a brother, a friend and a husband, that he would not have been the only one to perish from such an action: 'Seneca would have been the murderer of all those he had abandoned to the ferocity of Nero ... His wife perhaps, his brothers, his friends, a host of honest and brave citizens' (1828: 440). So, Diderot's Seneca is altruistic, despite his doctrines. He is the model of an engaged sage, not because but *despite* his Stoic commitment to *apatheia* and occasional arguments in favour of the contemplative life:

> O good Seneca! ... [p]ersonally, I do not believe that there was ever a man less inclined by his own nature as you to the Stoic philosophy: gentle, humane, benevolent, tender, compassionate. You were a Stoic 'from the head', yet at every moment your heart pointed you beyond the school of Zeno. (1828: 338)

At this point, the extent to which Seneca has become an avatar of Diderot's own ideal of the benevolent philosophe in the political arena, and the distance between this enlightenment figure and the ancient original, is clear.

Concluding remarks: The end of PWL, again?

As late as the French enlightenment, we have now shown, the notion of the philosopher remained alive as a distinct, atopic figure critical of established norms (**9**), not located in a university Faculty, self-consciously identifying with ancient therapeutic models (**7**), characterized by his training in specific intellectual exercises (**2**), his use of different literary genres so as not simply to make arguments but change minds and lives (**5**), with a eudaimonistic conviction that philosophy should help people to live better lives (**8**). With that said, in the French *philosophes* we do not read prescriptions concerning spiritual exercises (**3**). Both Voltaire and Diderot are sceptical about the possibility or desirability of *apatheia* as an ethico-philosophical ideal, and Diderot can only eulogize Seneca despite this Stoic teaching (**8**). Moreover, whilst the *philosophes* revered Bayle and Locke, they do not write texts dedicated to, as against drawing upon, the forms of experimental *medicina animi* of the British philosophers [**7.2**, **7.4**]. A PWL perspective enables us to highlight, therefore, the vital extent to which 'enlightenment' should be identified less with any one systematic doctrine or 'project' than with an *esprit philosophique* which adapts elements of Cynical, Sceptical, Stoic and Epicurean elements to the work of social and theological criticism.

It is Immanuel Kant who can be identified as perhaps the first modern academic or university-based philosopher, at least amongst the thinkers presently widely enshrined in syllabi as 'great philosophers' bringing a totalistic system (Hunter, 2001). (This chapter has shown the gulf between this persona and that of the French *philosophes*.) With the turn of the nineteenth century, and the advent of the Napoleonic and Humboldtian University organizations, we arrive finally at what seems to be the definitive end of PWL as the predominant Western meta-philosophy. The reassertion of PWL in figures we now turn to, Schopenhauer, Nietzsche and Foucault, will by contrast in each case be pushing against the wider 'universitized' current, as we will now explore.

PART III
THE MODERNS

INTERLUDE: THE NINETEENTH-CENTURY CONFLICT BETWEEN PWL AND UNIVERSITY PHILOSOPHY

Nineteenth-century German philosophy was the scene of conflict over ancient Hellenistic and Roman traditions of PWL. Late eighteenth-century German culture saw the rise of what E. M. Butler described as a powerful and influential philhellenic tradition, which privileged Greek culture over Latin Rome (1934/2012). German philhellenism undoubtedly shaped the dominant modern German reception of the ancient philosophical schools. Its depreciation of Latin Rome's philosophical and cultural traditions and sources partly explains why many nineteenth- and twentieth-century German philosophers were hostile to, or deeply sceptical about the philosophical value of the Hellenistic and Roman schools. As we observed in our Introduction, the Hellenistic and Roman periods were the victim of a 'classical' prejudice hailing from late eighteenth- and early-nineteenth-century German scholarship, which depreciated Cynicism, Stoicism, Epicureanism and Scepticism as expressions of philosophical decline.

Yet, as we shall see, this dominant view was by no means without its critics. In fact, Schopenhauer and Nietzsche, who prided themselves on their institutional and intellectual independence, revisited the idea of PWL. Contemporary scholars have begun to recognize how Schopenhauer and Nietzsche reignited debate about philosophy's aims, methods and styles (see, e.g., Ure, 2008: 4–6; Ure, 2019: 1–22; Loeb & Meyer, 2019: 1–6). Defenders of PWL like Hadot, for example, gave new traction to Schopenhauer's bitter fulminations against so-called 'university philosophy' (Hadot, 2004: 260).

Nietzsche's challenge to philosophers' traditional conception of their practice, a challenge that drew heavily on Schopenhauer's example, is now at the heart of debates about his philosophical legacy (Loeb & Meyer, 2019: 1).

In the following two chapters (**9 & 10**), we argue that in some respects, albeit from opposing normative perspectives, Schopenhauer and Nietzsche reclaimed elements of the ancient idea that philosophy is a transformation of our way of inhabiting and perceiving the world. As we shall see, they addressed the meta-philosophical question through their polemic against the nineteenth-century institutionalization and professionalization of philosophy, explicit accounts of philosophy's therapeutic ends, and, particularly in Nietzsche's case, experiments with a range of ancient genres, styles and spiritual exercises. If there is one point Schopenhauer and Nietzsche might have agreed on, it was that in their time 'the dignity of philosophy is trampled into the dust' (*SE* 8). It is worthwhile then briefly examining the stakes and shape of this nineteenth-century debate about philosophy's 'dignity' before turning directly to Schopenhauer and Nietzsche's complex and critical engagement with ancient PWL.

In many ways, Hegel and the young Hegelians established the parameters of this conflict. Far from reviving PWL, in many ways the Hegelians sought to ring its death knell (Shea, 2010: ix). Let us briefly consider how Hegel located the Cynics and Stoics in his teleological or progressive philosophy of history, which conceived history as the dialectical development of reason or spirit. Whether ancient Cynicism constituted a philosophy or only a way of life was occasionally questioned in antiquity, though in the main it was generally considered a philosophy (Hadot, 2002: 109). Hegel emphatically sides with the former view, deploring ancient Cynicism as a philosophically irrelevant mode of life. 'There is nothing particular to say of the Cynics', he asserted 'for they possess but little philosophy, and they did not bring what they had into a scientific system ... Antisthenes' principles are simple, because the content of his teaching remains general; it is hence superfluous to say anything further about him.' If their lack of a philosophical system made them unworthy of comment, then their style of life warranted banishing them from philosophy altogether. Hegel depicts the Cynic mode of life as notable only for its crudity and vulgarity (Hegel, 2006: 172, 174). In this context, he maligns the famous Cynic couple, Crates and Hipparchia, as 'nothing more than swinish beggars, who found their satisfaction in the insolence which they showed to others. They are worthy of no further consideration in Philosophy' (Hegel, 2006: 171, fn. 122).[1] 'Philosophy' with a capital P, Hegel assumes, need not concern itself with how philosophers live, let alone with Crates and Hipparchia's flouting of all social, sexual and religious proprieties. Hegel's judgement echoes a popular post-Renaissance refusal to credit Cynicism as a philosophy. 'It cannot be helped that dogs bark and vomit their foul stomachs', wrote William Harvey in the seventeenth century, 'and that Cynics should be numbered among philosophers' (quoted in Hard, 2012: ix).[2] Hegel contributed to the demise of Cynicism, as Louisa Shea remarks, 'by expunging the biographical and anecdotal material from the pages of his history of philosophy' (Shea, 2010: 133).

If Cynicism has a place in the grand history of reason's unfolding, Hegel suggests, it belongs among the minor Socratics insofar as the Cynics continued Socrates's subjective turn or moral individualism. Yet, because Cynicism 'lacked' a systematic theoretical discourse, as Desmond explains, Hegel conceived it as 'more a way of life than a true philosophy, and so the spirit could not rest content with it. The Cynics' vaunted freedom was in fact merely the negative freedom of renunciation, and was thus secretly dependent on what they renounced (e.g. the city); they did not attain the rational freedom of recognizing oneself in all forms of otherness' (Desmond, 2010: 573–4). 'In Hegel's view', Desmond observes, 'this Socratic attitude anticipates Christianity and Kantian *Moralität*, but the Cynics themselves barely progressed beyond superficial maxims like "The wise man is self-sufficient" and "the good is virtue"' (Desmond, 2010: 573–4).

Important here is that Hegel's criticism of ancient philosophy relies not only on his metaphysical teleology that construes it as a primitive stage in reason's unfolding, but also on his implicit assumption that philosophy is the construction of theoretical discourse rather than a practice of a way of life that entails the use of a whole range of spiritual exercises to realize an ideal of the good life. Heinrich Niehues-Pröbsting's history of Cynicism's modern reception shows that Hegel's dismissal of Cynicism succeeded in nearly eradicating the Cynics from the philosophical canon throughout the nineteenth century and well into the twentieth century (Niehues-Pröbsting, 1996). But in Hegel's narrative, Stoicism scores only a slightly higher grade than its Cynic progenitor.[3] According to Hegel, Stoic philosophy developed the Cynic's crude notion of freedom into a higher, more systematic, but still fundamentally limited form. In *The Phenomenology of Spirit* (1807/1977), he maintains that Stoicism's recognition of the freedom of self-consciousness is an important and necessary stage in the Spirit's progress. But it only expresses the wish rather than the reality of freedom. Hegel criticizes Stoicism for proposing a merely abstract or 'internal' concept of freedom (see Ure, 2016). 'Freedom in thought', he explains apropos Stoicism:

has only pure thought as its truth, a truth lacking the fullness of life. Hence freedom in thought too is only the Notion of freedom, not the living reality of freedom itself. For the essence of that freedom is at first only thinking in general, the form as such [of thought], which has turned away from the independence of things and returned into itself. (1977: 200, 122)

Hegel identifies its indifference to external goods, its constant 'withdrawal out of the movement of existence, out of affects and out of passions, into the simple essentiality of thought', as a betrayal of freedom (1977: 200, 122). In Charles Taylor's pithy summation, for Hegel a 'purely inner freedom is only a wish, a shadow. It is an important stage of human development when man comes to have this wish, this idea, but it must not be confused with the real thing' (Taylor, 1979: 51).

In his *Lectures on the Philosophy of History*, Hegel explains Stoicism, Epicureanism and Scepticism as self-defeating rationalizations of an enforced disengagement from public affairs that followed the collapse of Greek city states and the later demise of the Roman Republic. He diagnoses the appeal and success of the major Hellenistic philosophies as symptomatic of the political pathologies of the late Roman Empire. The Hellenistic schools' notion of inner freedom or self-sufficiency, he suggests, was a vain attempt to make a virtue out of necessity, or what we are now more like to describe as a mere 'rationalization'. They became popular under the Roman Empire, he argues, because its atomizing despotism made the mind in isolation the only impregnable spiritual fortress. In a political world in which the emperor ruled without limits, as he explains, private 'individuals were perfectly equal (slavery made only a trifling distinction) and without any political rights' (Hegel, 1900: 328). Under these conditions, Hegel claims, 'the whole state of things urged them to yield themselves to fate, and to strive for a perfect indifference to life – an indifference which [one] sought … in freedom of thought'. Stoicism, as well as Epicureanism and Skepticism, served this goal by 'rendering the soul absolutely indifferent to everything the real world had to offer' (Hegel, 1900: 329). Or, in the maverick young Hegelian Max Stirner's gloss, the 'Stoics want to realize the *wise man* … they find him in contempt for the world, in a life without development, without spreading out, without friendly relations with the world, thus in the *isolated life* … not in life with others; only the Stoic *lives*, all else is dead for him' (Stirner, 1995: 25). According to the Hegelian view, the Hellenistic schools' ideal of sovereign, rational self-mastery offers nothing more than an illusory substitute for civic freedom.

Hegel's deflationary critique shaped the modern German philosophical reception of the Hellenistic schools. On this score, Hannah Arendt's mid-twentieth-century critique of the Hellenistic philosophies, for example, reveals the extent to which Hegel's view became a philosophical stock in trade. 'Just as Epicureanism rests on the illusion of happiness when one is roasted alive in the Phaleric Bull', she argued, 'Stoicism rests on the illusion of freedom when one is enslaved' (Arendt, 1958: 235). 'Both illusions', she suggested, 'testify to the psychological power of imagination, but this power can exert itself only as long as the reality of the world and the living ... are eliminated to such an extent that they are not even admitted as spectators to the spectacle of self-delusion' (Arendt, 1958: 235).

Yet the Hegelian critique of ancient philosophy was not uncontested in German philosophy.[4] Against the Hegelian tide, Schopenhauer and Nietzsche, albeit in very different ways, both attempted to address, challenge and reconstitute some key aspects of the ancient ideal of PWL. How so? In the first place, they fired a broadside at the meta-philosophical presuppositions of contemporary German philosophy. They saw themselves as writing the epitaph of academic philosophy. In effect, Schopenhauer and Nietzsche sought to turn the tables on PWLs Hegelian critics. If, as we have seen, the Hegelians argued that ancient Cynicism and Stoicism rested on a flawed, outdated notion of freedom, which, they claimed, arose as a pathological symptom of political alienation, Schopenhauer and Nietzsche argued that the Hegelian rejection of PWL was itself symptomatic of the pathologies of the modern state and its levelling communitarianism. Modern philosophy, as they saw it, had become a pedagogic instrument that the modern state uses to cultivate and discipline selfless communal creatures. 'For the state was for Hegelry', as Schopenhauer mocked

'the absolutely perfected ethical organism'; for it, the whole purpose of human existence was realized in the state. Could there be a better preparation for future barristers and soon-to-be civil servants than this, as a result of which their whole essence and being, with body and soul, was completely forfeited to the state, like that of the bee in the beehive, and they had to work towards nothing, neither in this world or the next, but to become efficient wheels by contributing to keeping the great machine of the state running, this ultimate end of everything good? The barrister and the human being were thus one and the same. It was a true apotheosis of philistinism. (*PP* 1: 132–3)

Both Schopenhauer and Nietzsche lamented that the modern state's drive to professionalize philosophy spelt the end of philosophy as a lived practice. In this context, they claimed, philosophy was transformed into a purely theoretical discipline, focused on narrowly epistemological and historical questions, with no concern at all with the central questions of ancient philosophy: how can philosophy help us cultivate beatitude or the 'true *enjoyment of life*'? (Stirner, 1995: 25). If this new university philosophy had any concern with self-cultivation at all, they suggested, it was focused on training efficient civil servants. Yet educating specialized professors and public servants, they argued, is fundamentally incompatible with the ancient philosophical goal of curing and transforming souls. University philosophy trained students for public careers rather than guided them towards philosophical conversions. It demanded that they acquire theoretical knowledge rather than practise spiritual exercises. It cultivated civil servants rather than sages. On their view, as Hadot explains Schopenhauer's polemic, university philosophy's 'goal [was] no longer, as it was in antiquity, to train people for careers as human beings, but to train them for careers as clerks or professors – that is to say, specialists ... Such knowledge, however, no longer involves the whole of life, as ancient philosophy demanded' (Hadot, 1995: 260).

Schopenhauer himself expressed his criticisms far more trenchantly. With the Hegelians firmly in his sights, Schopenhauer claimed that the professional philosopher

now concerns himself with deifying the state, making it the pinnacle of all human striving and all things, and thereby not only transforms the philosophical lecture-hall into a school of the most shallow philistinism, but in the end, as for example Hegel, arrives at the scandalous doctrine that the destiny of human beings merges with the state – like, for instance, that of the bee with the beehive; whereby the lofty end of our existence is completely removed from view. (*PP* 1: 138)

Following Schopenhauer, Nietzsche maintained that modern universities do not give students an 'education in philosophy' but 'a training in passing philosophical examinations, the usual outcome of which is ... that the youth to be tested ... admits to himself with a sigh of relief: "Thank God I am no philosopher, but a Christian and a citizen of my country!'" (*SE*: 187). Both agreed that university philosophy had betrayed the spirit of ancient philosophy. Both sought to write its death notice. What is their epitaph for university philosophy? Fittingly, Nietzsche drew on Diogenes the Cynic for its inscription: 'Diogenes said when someone praised a philosopher in his presence: "How can he be considered great, since he has been a philosopher for so long and has never yet *disturbed* anybody?" That, indeed, ought to be the epitaph of university philosophy: "it disturbed nobody"' (*SE*: 194).

Ancient PWL gave Schopenhauer and Nietzsche a window onto an alternative, independent conception of philosophy's task. As we shall see, each of them radically reworked the ancient ideal of philosophy as a transformation of our way of inhabiting and perceiving the world. Both revived the ideal of the philosopher as physician and formulated therapeutic programmes. 'In offering respectively the safety of total denial and the greatness of total affirmation', as Christopher Janaway remarked, 'both Schopenhauer and Nietzsche produce a therapeutic vision which attempts to show human beings that what they are is far from desirable, and that they can become in some sense better' (Janaway, 1998: 350). In the following two chapters, we will examine their efforts to counter the Hegelian-inspired demotion of the ancient tradition of PWL and forge new philosophical therapies.

CHAPTER 9
SCHOPENHAUER: PHILOSOPHY AS THE WAY OUT OF LIFE

9.1 Introduction

Pierre Hadot identifies Schopenhauer's philosophy as one of several modern reinventions of PWL. Schopenhauer's philosophy, he claims, is an invitation 'to radically transform our way of life' (Hadot, 1995: 272). In this chapter, we examine the lines of continuity and discontinuity between the ancient philosophical paradigm and Schopenhauer's metaphysical philosophy. We begin by showing that Schopenhauer draws on the ancient conception of philosophy as the gold standard against which he judges and condemns contemporary university philosophy. Schopenhauer reignites the ancient quarrel between philosophy and sophistry. He defends the Socratic notion of philosophy as a practice exclusively concerned with the care or salvation of the self. He argues that the modern professionalization of philosophy as a university discipline has turned it into a sophistic discourse that answers to the needs of the marketplace rather than the soul. Philosophy, as he conceives it, seeks to explain and overcome the suffering we experience as willing, passionate creatures. In this respect, Schopenhauer reclaims and revises the ancient philosophical schools' ideal of philosophy as a spiritual and therapeutic exercise that converts or cures the soul.

Yet Schopenhauer also radically contests ancient philosophy's optimistic rationalism, taking Stoicism as his central case.[5] Put simply, he argues that the ancient philosophies necessarily fail as therapies: they wrongly assume that we can exercise rational self-control over our passions. Against the ancient schools, Schopenhauer maintains that we cannot free ourselves from suffering through the exercise of reason. It is true, he acknowledges, that Stoicism, for example, might temporarily temper our passions, but it cannot definitively or permanently liberate us from suffering. Ultimately, he argues, the ancient ideal of the rational sage is an empty fiction.

In this chapter, we first consider Schopenhauer's defence of the ancient philosophical concern with the care of the self in his magnum opus *The*

World as Will and Representation, vols. 1 & 2.[6] As we shall see, Schopenhauer ties philosophy to the project of the salvation of the soul. Section 2 examines his criticisms of what he sees as ancient philosophy's unjustified rationalist optimism. He argues that the Socratic and Stoic assumption that reason is sufficient for happiness is false. According to Schopenhauer, as long as we remain creatures of the will, or practical agents, we are bound to suffer. Schopenhauer therefore argues that a happy life is a contradiction in terms. This is the essence of Schopenhauer's philosophical pessimism. If we grasp the metaphysical truth of the world as will to life, he maintains, we will see that our salvation cannot lie in rational self-mastery; ultimately, he claims we cannot subject the will to life to reason. Rather, our salvation, he argues, lies in systematic 'self-denial or self-renunciation, *abnegatio sui ipsius*; for the real self is the will to life' (*WWR* 2: 606). For Schopenhauer, the real self is identical with the eternally suffering will to life. 'We are', as he puts it, 'nothing more than the will to live ' (*WWR* 2: 634).

In Section 3, we show that according to Schopenhauer's metaphysical philosophy true salvation requires finding a way *out* of life, rather than establishing a rational way *of* life. 'The pure, true and profound cognition of the essence of the world', as he expresses it, 'is … the way out of life' (*WWR* 1: 295). Schopenhauer replaces the sage who seeks happiness through the exercise of reason with the saint who rejects the very notion of a happy life and aims to liberate himself from himself, or from the willing or striving that constitutes the essence of all life. However, Schopenhauer suggests that if we still wish to give the phrase '*summum bonum*', or absolute good, an 'emeritus status', then figuratively speaking it is 'the complete self-abolition and negation of the will, the true absence of will, the only thing that can staunch and appease the impulses of the will forever, the only thing that can give everlasting contentment, the only thing that can redeem the world' (*WWR* 1: 362). For Schopenhauer, as we shall see in the final section, our salvation consists in the saint's complete elimination of agency. All that remains after the abolition of the will, he claims, is a purely passive mirroring of the world. 'Only cognition remains; the will has vanished' (*WWR* 1: 439).

9.2 Philosophy against sophistry (again)

Schopenhauer draws on the ancient meta-philosophical paradigm in his polemic against modern 'university' philosophy.[7] In 'On University Philosophy', published in the first volume of *Parerga and Paralipomena*

(1851), he argues that contemporary university philosophers corrupt the ancient model of philosophy. The professionalization of philosophy, he claims, necessarily degrades it. As the epigraph of his polemic, Schopenhauer quotes a line from Plato's attack on sophistry in the name of true philosophy: 'Philosophy has fallen into disgrace, because people do not engage in it in accordance with its own worth; not spurious, but genuine philosophers should undertake it' (*Rep.* VII, 535c). In doing so, Schopenhauer explicitly reignites the ancient quarrel between philosophy and sophistry, firmly siding with Socrates's defence of philosophy. University philosophers, Schopenhauer claims, are mere sophists. 'Those representatives of philosophy in civil life', he suggests, 'represent it mostly in the same way that an actor represents the king. For instance, were the Sophists, whom Socrates fought so tirelessly and Plato made the subject of his ridicule, anything but professors of philosophy and rhetoric? Is it not really that ancient feud, never extinguished since then, that is still carried on by me in the present?' (*PP* 1: 141)

University professors, he opines, are mere sophists who only produce 'comic philosophy' or 'state philosophy'. Schopenhauer ridicules comic philosophers for creating meaningless, pseudo-technical discourse that conceals their lack of philosophical insight. Comic philosophy is vacuous. 'In order to hide the lack of real thought', he scoffs, these so-called philosophers 'devise an imposing apparatus of long, composite terms, intricate phrases, immeasurable periods, new and unheard-of expressions, which all together then make for a jargon as difficult and scholarly sounding as possible. However, with all of this they say – nothing' (*PP* 1: 143). These comic philosophers write unintelligibly, he implies, in order to dupe their readers. 'Almost every pathetic scribbler' Schopenhauer suggests 'has sought to write with affected obscurity, so that it looks as if no words could express his lofty, or deep, thoughts' (*PP* 1: 146).

Schopenhauer maligns state philosophers for betraying the philosophical commitment to truth. Hegel, Schopenhauer's *bête noire*, is the target of his scorn. According to Hegel, philosophy is no longer 'practised as a private art, as it was by the Greeks, but now has an official existence, which therefore concerns the public; and it is principally or exclusively in the service of the State' (quoted in Hadot, 2002: 260). Where contemporary philosophers are not producing meaningless pseudo-technical jargon that aims to enhance their charisma and sales, Schopenhauer suggests, they are the paid functionaries who enter into an unwritten agreement to serve as propagandists. Rather than unconditionally pursuing the truth, these state philosophers, he claims, transform philosophical discourse into an ideological justification of church and state authority. 'It never occurs to a philosophy professor', Schopenhauer writes 'to study an emerging new system in regard to its truth; on the contrary, he immediately checks only whether it can be reconciled with the doctrines of established religion, the interests of the government, and the dominant views of the time. Afterwards he decides its fate' (*PP* 1: 134). The modern state and church, he claims, have thoroughly domesticated university philosophers. 'A philosophy, bound to established religion as the chained dog is to the wall', he mocks, 'is only the exasperating caricature of the highest and noblest endeavour of humankind' (*PP* 1: 129). University philosophy domesticates its Cynics.

Against contemporary 'sophists', both comedians and propagandists, Schopenhauer reprises the Socratic claim that true philosophy can only derive from those who live *for* philosophy rather than those who live *off it* (*WWR* 2: 163). Schopenhauer cites Stobaeus's report of the Stoics drawing the same distinction:

> A difference must be drawn between those who declare that they act as sophists and impart the doctrines of philosophy for money, and those who think that to embrace teaching as a sophist is worthless, as if hawking ideas, and who believe that it is wrong to earn money for the education of those who seek it, since this kind of money-making devalues the dignity of philosophy. (*PP* 1: 139)

Schopenhauer himself only briefly worked as an unsalaried lecturer (*Privatdozent*) at the University of Berlin (1819–20) before abandoning his academic career and living off a private income. Schopenhauer deliberately scheduled the single lecture course he delivered to coincide with Hegel's, at that time Europe's most famous philosopher at the height of his powers. Only five pupils attended (Cartwright, 2010: 365).

Against his Hegelian contemporaries, he cast himself as waging the 'ancient battle' between philosophers who make their lives a mere means to pursuing truth, and sophists who make their ideas the means to secure their lives. 'Two masters as different as the world and truth', Schopenhauer asserts, 'cannot be served at the same time' (*PP* 1: 138). Schopenhauer takes the ancient philosophers as the measure against which we can judge and condemn university philosophers. Rather than fearlessly seeking the truth, he argues, professional philosophers cater to the marketplace. They are no longer critical Socratic gadflies or scandalous Cynics. Profit excludes parrhesia.

We might easily dismiss Schopenhauer's attack on university philosophy on *ad hominem* grounds. It is no doubt true that partly as result of his own failed academic career, he harboured a deep resentment towards Hegel and contemporaries Hegelians like his teacher Fichte. Yet, on balance, as Janaway astutely observes, Schopenhauer's polemic is a blend of vindictiveness and high-minded principles, an envious attack on his successful contemporaries and 'a powerful and poignant defence of intellectual freedom against craven, time-serving conformism, a plea for the pursuit of truth over that of livelihood and self-interest, and a devastating attack on the perversion of thought by the influence of regimes and religions' (Janaway, 2014: xxvii). If we focus on the principles of Schopenhauer's defence of ancient philosophy rather than its envious motivations, we can see how it resonated powerfully with modern philosophers like Nietzsche and with more recent anxieties about the routinization of philosophy. Schopenhauer's polemic foreshadows contemporary criticisms of professional philosophy for betraying the ancient philosophic commitment to truth or 'parrhesia' and its practical goal of achieving the good life (Frodeman & Briggle, 2016; Sharpe & Turner, 2018).

Schopenhauer develops a clear conception of philosophy's true purpose against which he believes we should measure and condemn university philosophy. He defines proper philosophy as an 'uncompromising search for the truth' regarding the 'problem of existence' (*PP* 1: 140). 'If anything in the world is desirable', he writes, 'it is that a ray of light should fall on the obscurity of our existence, and that we should obtain some information about this enigmatic existence of ours, in which nothing is clear except its misery and vanity' (*WWR* 2: 164). This is the desire that philosophy aims to satisfy. Philosophy, he asserts, concerns the 'question of the worth or worthlessness of existence, of salvation or damnation' (*WWR* 1: 271). More specifically, he suggests that what distinguishes philosophy is that it addresses our metaphysical need to make sense of the suffering of existence. As a species, he argues, we are distinctive insofar we have the capacity for reason, or reflection upon ourselves and our existence. We are, as he puts it, an *'animal metaphysicum'* (*WWR* 2: 160). We are the only natural creatures in whom nature can become conscious of itself; nature, he claims, sees itself in the mirror of our consciousness (*WWR* 1: 275). In the mirror of human intellect, Schopenhauer suggests, the will comes to self-knowledge and in doing so recoils against itself.[8] Schopenhauer identified his own philosophy as the will arriving at complete self-knowledge. 'With me', as he explains in *WWR* 2, 'will arrives at self-knowledge through its objectification ... whereby its abolition, conversion, and salvation became possible' (*WWR* 2: 141).

Qua *animal metaphysicum*, Schopenhauer claims, we are unpleasantly surprised by our natural existence. We might say that Schopenhauer's analogue for the Cartesian cogito is 'I suffer, therefore I think'. Philosophy does not derive from wonder at the beauty or perfection of existence, but anguish at its ugliness or imperfection. It is not delight, but distress that motivates philosophy. 'Philosophy, like the overture to Don Juan', as he succinctly states, 'starts with a minor chord' (*WWR* 2: 171). It is, 'the suffering and misery of life', as he puts it 'that give the strongest impulses to philosophical reflection and metaphysical explanation of the world. If our lives were without end and free from pain, it would possibly not occur to anyone to ask why the world exists, and why it does so in precisely this way, but everything would be taken as a matter of course' (*WWR* 2: 161). Schopenhauer illustrates the reasons for our distress in a trademark tableau, which vividly depicts the extraordinary suffering through which nature reproduces itself: 'we see only momentary gratification, fleeting pleasure conditioned by wants, much and long suffering, constant struggle, *bellum omnium*, everything a hunter and everything hunted, pressure, want, need, and anxiety, shrieking and howling; and this goes on *saecula saeculorum*' (*WWR* 2: 354).

Schopenhauer claims then that philosophy springs from a metaphysical need, peculiar to human beings, to understand the misery of existence. 'For what offence', Schopenhauer asks, 'must they suffer this agony? What is the point of this horror?' (*WWR* 2: 354). He conceives his own philosophy as a response to the tormenting problem that motivates true philosophy, namely, 'not merely that the world exists, but still more that it is such a miserable and melancholy world' (*WWR* 2: 172). According to Schopenhauer, therefore, the fundamental philosophical question is 'Why do we exist as suffering creatures?' We pursue this philosophical question, he suggests, in order to find 'consolation for the deep sorrows of life' (*WWR* 2: 167).

Whilst his vision of the world is deeply, almost definitively unGreek, we can see how Schopenhauer's conception of the origins of philosophy motivates him to develop a philosophy that in several key respects is continuous with the ancient paradigm we have surveyed in previous chapters. First, and most obviously, Schopenhauer conceives philosophy as a deeply practical project that aims to transform our way of life rather than merely the produce abstract, theoretical truths. Schopenhauer's philosophy, as Nietzsche suggests, transforms rather than merely teaches (8). By holding up a mirror reflecting the world's sublime grandeur, the young Nietzsche felt compelled by Schopenhauer's philosophy to undergo an ontological transformation.

'Every line', as he put it, 'screamed renunciation, denial, resignation' (quoted in Janaway, 1998: 16). For Schopenhauer, to know the truth is to undergo an ontological transformation. Schopenhauer maintains that the necessary effect of acquiring metaphysical truth is a radical conversion of our being. 'Cognition' in his words 'opens the way to redemption' (*PP* 2: 166). Schopenhauer, as Julian Young argues, 'denies the possibility of separating a person's moral will from their metaphysical knowledge' (cf. Nietzsche, 1985: 152; Young, 1997: 105).[9] Or, in Nietzsche's words:

> The Schopenhauerian man voluntarily takes upon himself the suffering involved in being truthful and this suffering serves to destroy his own wilfulness and to prepare that complete overturning and conversion of his being, which is the real meaning of life to lead up to. (*SE*: 152)

Acquiring intuitive knowledge of the world as will to life, Schopenhauer repeatedly insists, entails not just a modification of our character, but its complete suppression, or borrowing from Asmus, what he called a 'transcendental alteration' (*WWR* 1: 431; see *WWR* 1: 421, 425). This knowledge, as he explains 'reverses the whole essence of a person so that he no longer wills what he used to will so violently and a new human being truly takes the place of the old' (*WWR* 1: 432; see also *WWR* 2: 604). Through our metaphysical enlightenment, we discover that we must, as he puts it, 'become something quite different from, indeed the very opposite of, what we are' (*WWR* 2: 604).

Second, and relatedly, he conceptualizes philosophy in terms of the ancient analogy between medicine and philosophy that we have discussed in the earlier chapters (6). As we have observed, Schopenhauer's conceives philosophy as a therapy that addresses the problem of suffering, offering 'a transformative knowledge' or 'radical remedy' (Janaway, 1998: 161, 178). Schopenhauer aims to show how we can be '*cured of the passion for enjoying and indeed for living*, and may be turned away from the world' (*WWR* 2: 635; emphasis added). Our lust for life, he argues, is the disease that we must cure. Our treatment, he suggests, must take the form of a certain type of asceticism that successfully extirpates this passion for life. Schopenhauer identifies this therapy with the asceticism he sees as common to Hindu sannyâsis, Buddhist monks and Christian saints. Schopenhauer's philosophy finds its consummation in their ascetic practices, which, he argues, offer the *only* viable path to salvation. For Schopenhauer, these ascetics realize the pessimistic truth that non-existence is preferable to existence.

Thirdly, like the ancient schools, Schopenhauer argues that we must transcend our ordinary egoism to escape our emotional turmoil. Yet it is not just ordinary egoism, which seeks happiness in satisfying our desire for external goods, that Schopenhauer diagnoses as an illness, but also what we might call the extraordinary egoism, or sage-like wisdom, that, so he claims, the ancient philosophers mistakenly identified as the cure for troubles of ordinary existence. Schopenhauer philosophical therapy aims to treat not just the ordinary human condition as a malady, but also the new disorders he believes the ancient philosophies create in trying to overcome it. On Schopenhauer's view, ancient philosophy's faith that reason alone is sufficient for happiness and can elevate us above all of our ordinary passions is itself a disorder. We will consider the latter claim more closely in our next section.

Against the ancient philosophers' optimistic belief that we can attain beatitude through the exercise of reason, Schopenhauer aims to demonstrate that we are bound to suffer because of the very nature of existence as will to life. 'The world and life', as he puts it, 'are certainly not arranged for the purpose of containing a happy existence' (*WWR* 2: 634). Schopenhauer argues, then, that we suffer not simply because we fail to reason correctly, as the ancient philosophers maintained, but because of the very nature of existence.

He is deeply antipathetic to the ancient philosophers' optimistic rationalism. For this reason, he argues that the emotional turmoil that derives from ordinary egoism requires a far more radical cure than the Stoic (or Spinozist) philosophical conversion. Rather than follow the course of ordinary egoism and seek to satisfy our desires, or the ancient philosophical 'delusion' that we can identify ourselves with universal reason or logos and rise above our desires and passions, Schopenhauer's radical cure demands that we strive to abolish our will to life altogether. Our salvation lies in mortifying rather than rationalizing the will. It is a matter of completely abolishing the practical subject of willing rather than merely attempting to rationalize its will. The goal of ascetic ethics, as he puts it, is to 'deaden [the will] completely' (*WWR* 1: 416). In other words, Schopenhauer defines and defends 'the complete self-effacement and denial of the will, true will-lessness' as the 'only radical cure for the disease against which all other goods, such as all fulfilled wishes and achieved happiness, are only palliatives, anodynes' (*WWR* 1: 389). Salvation, as he defines it, necessarily requires that we find a way *out* of life.

In some respects, therefore, Hadot is clearly right that Schopenhauer's philosophy reanimates PWL. Yet Foucault is right to qualify this claim.

On Foucault's interpretation (2005: 251), if Schopenhauer belongs to this meta-philosophical paradigm insofar as he invites us to radically transform our manner of living, he does so only in a disconcerting and controversial fashion. Unlike the ancient philosophies, Schopenhauer's philosophical pessimism maintains that we must deny rather than cultivate the self. We can illuminate Schopenhauer's relationship to the paradigm of PWL by considering his criticisms of the ancient ethics of self-cultivation in more detail. Why does he hold that pursuing the ancient ethical ideal of rational sovereignty necessarily fails to deliver happiness or beatitude?

9.3 Two cheers for Stoicism

Ancient philosophers, Schopenhauer complains, lack knowledge of the depths of life. It is this lack of insight into the metaphysical ground of existence, he suggests, that led them to endorse an irrational faith in reason. Schopenhauer identifies their unfounded rationalist optimism with the classical formula, which we sketched in Chapter 1, that reason or virtue is sufficient for happiness. 'The ancients, particularly the Stoics', he suggests, 'laboured in vain to prove that virtue is enough to make life happy; experience cried loudly against this ... Man's greatest offence is that he was born ... as the poet Calderon, inspired by Christianity, has expressed it from a knowledge far profounder than was possessed by those wise men' (*WWR* 2: 603; see also Cartwright, 2010: 116). Despite their noble intentions to alleviate human misery, Schopenhauer suggests that pagan philosophies fundamentally misdiagnose our suffering and its cure. The ancient schools argue that we suffer because we wrongly value external goods and in doing so make ourselves vulnerable to emotional disturbance. On this ancient view, we can eliminate our suffering through the correct use of practical reason combined with 'spiritual exercises' that strengthen our capacity for rational self-control.

In this respect, Schopenhauer specifically targets Stoic ethics, which he describes as an 'ethics of pure reason' (*WWR* 1: 117). He questions Stoicism's claim that it formulates a valid and successful philosophical therapy. Like all moral systems of antiquity, Schopenhauer argues, Stoicism is a eudaimonistic philosophy: it is a guide to the blissful life (*WWR* 2: 150), aiming to make its votaries 'invulnerable' to the 'intense anxiety and suffering' that ordinarily characterize human desire (*WWR* 1: 114). The touchstone of these ethical systems, he suggests, is whether 'the practice of it would inevitably and necessarily produce happiness immediately and unconditionally. Unless it can do this, it does not achieve what it ought, and is to be rejected' (*WWR* 2: 151). But does the Stoic exercise of practical reason lift the sage above all pain and sorrow? Can practical reason, as Stoics insist, make us invulnerable? Is it possible for the sage to live in harmony with nature, completely free, autonomous, emotionless, and – notoriously – happy even when being tortured on the rack? (see, e.g., DL X, 118; Aristotle E. N. 1153B19-21). Schopenhauer answers these questions in the negative. Stoicism, he asserts, is an unsuccessful 'guide for a blessed life' (*WWR* 1: 117). Indeed, he claims that the ideal of the Stoic sage is a myth that 'contradict[s] the essence of humanity' (*WWR* 1: 118).

Stoic philosophy fails, Schopenhauer argues, because it wrongly assumes that practical reason enables us to realize the highest good. The Stoics 'purely rational ethic', he suggests, is insufficient to deliver on this promise (*WWR* 1: 117), although he acknowledges its merit in trying to alleviate suffering.[10] Through the correct use of reason, he asserts, Stoics 'are still very far … from being actually removed from all the burdens of life, and led to a blissful state' (*WWR* 1: 90). Against the Stoics, he indeed argues that *ataraxia* is impossible in this world. Why then is Stoic *ataraxia* impossible? Schopenhauer's critique of Stoicism follows from his metaphysics of the will. Schopenhauer argues that there is no highest good or absolute good for creatures who are phenomena of the will to life. For Schopenhauer, the 'highest good' or '*summum bonum*' signifies 'an ultimate satisfaction of the will, following which there will be no new willing' (*WWR* 1: 389). Yet, the essence of life, as he defines it, is *ceaseless* willing. It follows from this definition that it

> is no more possible for some satisfaction to stop the will from willing new things than it is for time to begin or end. The will can have no lasting fulfilment that gives perfect and permanent satisfaction to its strivings. It is the vessel of the Danaids: there is no highest good, no absolute good for the will, but rather only ever a temporary good. (*WWR* 1: 389)

We might satisfy one particular will, Schopenhauer reasons, but it will merely be replaced by another and so on ad infinitum. 'Every satisfied desire gives birth to a new one' – and so no particular achieved happiness, can remove all our wants, and none can endure for long (*WWR* 2: 573). Schopenhauer draws an analogy between satisfying the will and giving alms to a beggar, in both cases we relieve a present misery only to prolong it until tomorrow. If to will is to suffer, and we constantly will, then existence is suffering, not enjoyment.

Moreover, Schopenhauer claims that all so-called 'happiness' is negative or chimerical: it is simply the momentary elimination of one painful desire, which serves to prepare the way for the emergence of another distressing desire. Schopenhauer argues that even when we satisfy a particular desire, we do not have a positive experience of joy, we merely experience the absence of one desire, which is then immediately replaced by another. 'All satisfaction or what is generally called happiness', he claims, 'is actually and essentially only ever *negative* and absolutely never positive ... Thus satisfaction or happiness can never be anything more than the liberation from a pain or need: we never gain anything more than liberation from some suffering or desire, and so we find ourselves just the way we were before we had the desire' (*WWR* 1: 345–6). Strictly speaking, Schopenhauer's metaphysics implies that we can get no satisfaction. What we value most highly, permanent or eternal satisfaction, is fundamentally at odds with who we are at the 'deepest' level: creatures of the will to life. According to Schopenhauer, therefore a 'blessed life', which is what Stoicism promises, is a contradiction in terms: to live is to suffer from the incessant striving that he calls the will to life (*WWR* 1: 117).

It is a Stoic illusion, he maintains, that we can consistently and freely exercise rational control over our impulses, desires and aversions, or (in his language) our will to life: 'a capable mastery of reason over the immediate feelings of suffering is seldom, if ever, to be found' (*WWR* 1: 342). Schopenhauer argues that Stoics might correctly reason that what does not depend on us, all the so-called external goods, are valueless or indifferent (preferred or dispreferred), but making this judgement does not necessarily mean that in practice we will respond to them as matters of indifference, or of no concern. Our rational judgement, he argues, simply does not consistently dictate the motives of our will. The Stoic fails to account for how 'the will cannot be trifled with, and cannot enjoy pleasures without becoming fond of them; that a dog does not remain indifferent when we draw through his mouth a piece of roast meat, or a sage when he is hungry; that between desiring and renouncing there is no mean' (*WWR* 2: 156). According to Schopenhauer, that is, we necessarily suffer from a lack of rational self-control, which the ancient Greek philosophers called *akrasia* and that he expresses with the Latin phrase '*ratio regendae voluntatis impotens*' (*WWR* 2: 149).[11] By nature, we are primed to act against our better judgement. To borrow from the gospels, the spirit is willing, but the flesh is weak (*Matt.* 26:41).

Schopenhauer depicts our incorrigible *akrasia* in the opening of his chapter 'On the Practical Uses of Reason and on Stoicism'. Here he asserts that even the most powerful intellect can be disconcerted and perturbed by trivial events and persons, if these trivialities 'affect it very closely' (*WWR* 2: 149). Schopenhauer conceptualizes reason's impotence in terms of a law regulating our motives. According to this paradoxical law, our most insignificant, thoughtless motives trump our most significant, reasoned motives as long as the former are much 'closer' to us than the latter (*WWR* 2: 149).[12] If this law applies, then the Stoics' attempt to use practical reason to regulate their lives must end in failure.

The Stoics' defence of suicide, Schopenhauer suggests, demonstrates that they remain so troubled by the incessant demands of the will that under some circumstances they seek to escape from life through suicide. If Stoics could achieve happiness through the proper application of reason and rise above the 'tempestuous strain of desiring and shunning', they would wish for eternal life.[13] Yet, he argues, the basic contradiction between happiness and life:

> is … revealed in the ethics of pure reason itself, since the Stoics are forced to include in their guide for a blessed life … a recommendation for suicide in the case of excessive and incurable bodily suffering incapable of being philosophized away with principles and inferences … In this case, bliss, the only purpose of life, has been thwarted and suffering can now only be evaded through death, which should itself be undertaken with indifference, like any course of medication. (*WWR* 1: 117–18)

Like Augustine, ultimately Schopenhauer condemns ancient eudaimonism as an expression of the vice of pride. In their pride and conceit, he claims, the Stoics failed to recognize that passions always shipwreck the frail barque of reason. Schopenhauer therefore ends by dismissing the sage, the highest Stoic ideal, as an empty, lifeless fiction. The Stoics, he concludes:

> were never able to present their ideal, the Stoic sage, as a living being with inner poetic truth; he remains stiff and wooden, a mannequin that no one can engage with and who does not himself know what to do with his own wisdom. His perfect composure, peace and bliss

really contradict the essence of humanity, so that we are unable to form any intuitive representation of him. (*WWR* 1: 118)

With this said, Schopenhauer's appraisal of Stoic ethics is not simply a blanket dismissal. He gives two cheers for Stoicism. Indeed, he acknowledges that Stoic ethics as 'is in fact a very valuable and estimable attempt to adapt that great privilege of humanity, reason, to an important and salutary end, namely that of raising us above the suffering and pain that every life encounters' (*WWR* 1: 117). For Schopenhauer, Stoicism utilizes our species' distinguishing feature: namely practical reason or abstract cognition. Through practical reason, 'we grasp not only what is narrowly and actually present, but also the whole of the past and the future and the whole wide realm of possibility: we can freely survey life on all sides, far beyond what is present and actual' (*WWR* 1: 111). By contrast, other animals are confined to intuitive cognition, i.e., only that which is immediately present to them in time, i.e., real objects. Armed with their abstract cognition, the human species has 'the same relation to the animals that a ship's pilot (who, thanks to nautical chart, compass and quadrant, always knows with precision his ship's heading and position on the sea) has to the unskilled crew who see only waves and sky' (*WWR* 1: 111–12).

Following Schopenhauer's analogy, we might say that even if the most skilled pilots are doomed to shipwreck, their skills must be of some use. In practice, Schopenhauer concedes, Stoic philosophers are the happiest insofar as they occasionally, as he puts it, 'carry concepts over into life' (*WWR* 1: 117). Indeed, Schopenhauer admits that the Stoics' exercise of reason might in some ways sooth or temper our suffering and pain. Schopenhauer suggests that a popular type of stoic fatalism can and, in many cases, does succeed in significantly mitigating or even eliminating *some* forms of suffering peculiar to rational, self-conscious animals by cultivating a degree of insensibility towards suffering.[14]

Let us then clarify Schopenhauer's evaluation of the limited therapeutic prospects of the Stoic guide for rational living. In brief, while Schopenhauer argues that suffering is our metaphysical fate, he also argues that to some extent it falls within our power to regulate the scope and intensity of our suffering. That is to say, he implies that the intensity and duration of our suffering is variable, and this variation turns on how well we exercise our practical reason so that we do not always fall victim to erroneous beliefs. Schopenhauer identifies one error that greatly intensifies our sorrow which philosophy can address: 'There is only one inborn error, and that is the notion that we exist in order to be happy' (*WWR* 2: 634). Schopenhauer suggests that this error expresses the basic orientation of our body as a phenomenon of the will to life (*WWR* 2: 634). Yet Schopenhauer suggests that we intensify and temporally extend our basic ontological suffering by endorsing this 'inborn error'. In other words, we suffer not just because we constantly will or desire, but also because we wish that our lives could and should be free from all suffering. Our 'optimistic dogma' that we exist in order to be happy, and indeed *should* be happy, hence paradoxically intensifies the suffering it seeks our release from (*WWR* 2: 634). While individuals who thoughtlessly pursue their desires are repeatedly vexed because the world is not arranged for the purpose of realizing their happiness, those who consciously endorse the view that we exist in order to be happy, or for the sake of realizing the highest good, also suffer a 'theoretical perplexity' as 'to why a world and life that exist so that [they] may be happy in them, answer their purpose so badly' (*WWR* 2: 634).

The limited good news is that Schopenhauer implies that we can liberate ourselves from the intense suffering that derives from this second-order attitude, and confronting the contradiction between our judgement that life ought to satisfy our ideal of happiness and the fact that it repeatedly fails to do so. We can eliminate our erroneous second-order desires, he suggests, through Stoic practices that cognitively reframe our experience of willing or desiring. Stoic fatalism, as he puts it metaphorically, can heal our 'wounds' and turn them into scars (*WWR* I: 333). It is especially through Stoic fatalism, he suggests – the attitude that we cannot avoid what is inevitable – that we are better able to endure and feel less keenly the pain of first-order desires (or willing), by accepting our suffering as a necessity rather than as a contingency that might and ought to be otherwise. If instead we correctly recognize that suffering is inevitable and essential to life, and that nothing but its 'mere' form depends on chance, we might achieve 'a significant measure of Stoical equanimity' (*WWR* 1: 342). 'We take the greatest comfort', as puts it 'in the full certainty of irrevocable necessity' (*WWR* 1: 333). From Schopenhauer's perspective, Stoic fatalism can effectively draw the sting from our suffering. Schopenhauer acknowledges the merit of this position relative to the ordinary life of egoistic desire, granting it a degree of nobility:

> Magnanimity and intrinsic merit are to be found in our silently and patiently bearing what is inevitable, in melancholy calm, remaining the same while others pass from jubilation to despair and from despair to jubilation. Thus we can also conceive of Stoicism as a spiritual

dietetics, and in accordance with this, just as we harden our body to the influences of wind and weather, privation and exertion, we also harden our mind to misfortune, danger, loss, injustice, malice spite, treachery, arrogance and men's folly. (*WWR* 2: 159)

Yet, Schopenhauer argues, we should not confuse this stoical endurance of the will to life, for true salvation from suffering.[15] 'If we consider closely the goal of Stoicism, this *ataraxia*', as Schopenhauer explains, 'we find in it merely a hardening and insensibility to the blows of fate … this however is not a happy state or condition, but only the calm endurance of sufferings which we foresee as inevitable' (*WWR* 2: 159). Stoicism is a simulacrum of salvation. We are still in need of a more radical therapy to achieve its reality. Schopenhauer identifies salvation with the figure of the saint, who stands in sharp opposition to the sage. Compared with the Stoic sage (**10**), Schopenhauer writes

how completely different they seem … those who the wisdom of India sets before us and has actually brought forth, those voluntary penitents who overcome the world; or even the Christian saviour, that splendid figure, full of the depths of life, of the greatest poetical truth and highest significance, but who, with perfect virtue, holiness and sublimity, nevertheless stands before us in a state of the utmost suffering. (*WWR* 1: 118)

We turn to this figure now.

9.4 The saint versus the sage

Against the Stoics, then, Schopenhauer argues that *ataraxia* is not possible in this world because suffering is intrinsic to our existence as phenomena of the will to live. In developing his case against Stoic optimism, Schopenhauer draws from Buddhism, Brahmanism and Christian pessimism about the value and purpose of existence. 'The power by virtue of which Christianity was able to overcome … paganism of Greece and Rome', he writes, 'is to be found solely in its pessimism, in the confession that our condition is both exceedingly sorrowful and sinful … whereas … paganism [was] optimistic. That truth, profoundly and painful felt by everyone, took effect, and entailed the need for redemption' (*WWR* 2: 170). This pessimism judges that the world as it is ought not to be. 'The true spirit and kernel of Christianity, as of Brahmanism and Buddhism also, is the knowledge of the vanity of all earthly happiness, complete contempt for it, and the turning away to an existence of quite a different, indeed, opposite, kind' (*WWR* 2: 444). In the history of philosophy, Schopenhauer claims, his philosophy is the very first to translate into abstract concepts the truth that religious ascetics know intuitively and express in their conduct (*WWR* 1: 410).

However, while Schopenhauer endorses the Christian contempt for this world, he also denies the Christian belief and hope for salvation in another world of eternal perfection.[16] Schopenhauer argues that the world as it ought to be – a blissful, happy world of complete gratification of the will – does not exist:

> It is true that all men wish to be delivered from the state of suffering and death; they would like, as we say, to attain to eternal bliss, to enter the kingdom of heaven, but not on their own feet; they would like to be carried there by the course of nature. But this is impossible; for nature is only the copy, the shadow, of our will. Therefore … she cannot bring us anywhere except always into nature again. Yet everyone experiences in his own life and death how precarious it is to exist as a part of nature. Accordingly, existence is certainly to be regarded as an error or mistake, to return from which is salvation. (*WWR* 2: 605)

If against Stoicism he maintains that reason cannot grant us happiness in this world, against Christianity he maintains that there is no other world beyond it. If like Augustine he rejects Stoicism's faith in reason, at the same time he also resolutely denies Christianity's faith in another world beyond the vale of tears or the world as will to life. In Nietzsche's sense of the term, Schopenhauer is a nihilist. 'A nihilist', as Nietzsche explains, 'is a man who judges of the world as it is that it ought not to be, and the world as it ought to be that it does not exist' (*WP* 585). Schopenhauer therefore aims to formulate a radical cure of human suffering that avoids what he sees as the errors of both classical immanence and Christian transcendence. Neither God, nor reason can save us. Schopenhauer develops his soteriology on the basis of his metaphysical philosophy.

What then can be the ontological bases for Schopenhauer's 'positive' account of the Saint? Controversially, he argues that the world as it is in-itself is a single, indivisible, purposeless and eternal will to life. Since all individuals are merely temporary phenomenal expressions of the single, eternal will to life, they participate in all suffering. Schopenhauer therefore conceives egoists who pursue their own interest to the point of causing others to suffer as analogous to the mythical Thyestes: they devour their own flesh (*WWR* 1: 400). Schopenhauer identifies two distinct paths to metaphysical knowledge, both of which abolish the ego, the conventional experience of ourselves as an 'I', or an individual will to life separate and distinct from the rest of the world. The 'first route' is the revelation of one's identity with the world, a transformative knowledge which quietens one's individual will, but is attained only rarely by saints. The more common 'second' way is through pain and sorrow, on which Schopenhauer quotes the words of Meister Eckhart: 'Suffering is the fleetest animal that bears you to perfection' (*WWR* 2: 633). The first path, he claims, 'is the narrow path of the elect, the saints, and consequently is to be regarded as a rare exception'; the second path is the only hope of salvation for the majority (*WWR* 2: 638). 'Our eyes are opened to a better knowledge', as Schopenhauer explains the first route, through uncanny experiences that suspend our ordinary representation of the world. Through experiences that disrupt our ordinary cognition, he suggests, we see through the conventional illusion that the world is made up of separate entities and discern instead that *all* phenomena express one eternal will to life. Seeing through our conventional representations of the world to the world as will, he suggests, entails a dramatic conversion:

> From the perspective of the true nature of things, everyone must regard all the sufferings of the world as his own ... For cognition that sees through the *principium individuationis*, a happy life in time, as a gift of chance or effect of prudence, in the midst of the sufferings of countless others, – all this is just a beggar dreaming he is king, a dream from which he must awake to discover that it was only a fleeting illusion that had separated him from the suffering of his life. (*WWR* 1: 380)

Regardless of which of these two paths we take to arrive at this metaphysical knowledge, Schopenhauer claims that it necessarily marks the beginning of the denial of the will to life that expresses itself through our own drives and passions. Why does our salvation turn on denying this will to life? It does so, Schopenhauer argues, because to will is to suffer. All willing, he maintains, springs from want or lack, and hence from suffering. 'All striving', he maintains, 'comes from lack, from dissatisfaction with one's condition, and is thus suffering as long as it is not satisfied' (*WWR* 1: 336). Given that the will to life constitutes our essential nature, if we actually satisfy one of our particular passions, which, in any case, he considers the exception that proves the rule, it is immediately placed by another passion directed towards a new object or by an objectless desire he calls boredom. 'Hence', Schopenhauer writes, 'life swings like a pendulum back and forth between pain and boredom; in fact, these are the ingredients out of which it is ultimately composed' (*WWR* 1: 338).[17]

If this metaphysical insight is true, he reasons, it demonstrates that we cannot escape suffering as long as we continue to affirm the will to life. We cannot realize happiness in this life; a 'blessed life', one of perfect contentment, untroubled by desire or will, is simply a contradiction in terms. If the essence of humanity is willing and to will is to suffer, our salvation necessarily entails a *transcendental* conversion: we must undergo a radical change from willing creature to will-less saint:

> That great fundamental truth contained in Christianity, as well as in Brahmanism and Buddhism is the need for salvation from an existence given up to suffering and death, and its attainability through the denial of the will, hence by a most decided opposition to nature is beyond all comparison *the most important truth* there can be. (*WWR* 2: 628, emphasis added)

As we have seen, Schopenhauer rejects all forms of pantheism and theism, yet he discovers a kernel of truth in the ascetic practices (3) common to Buddhism, Brahmanism and Christianity; they have, as he puts it, the 'greatest poetical truth and highest significance' (*WWR* 1: 118). The truth of these religions lies not in their metaphysical doctrines, he maintains, but in their ascetic practices, which turn the will to life against itself (*WWR* 1: 406–7). By deliberately maximizing our own suffering through extreme asceticism, he suggests, we can extinguish ourselves as expressions of the will to life that causes our suffering (*WWR* 1: 432–3). Through asceticism or self-mortification, Saints cultivate an aversion to willing and in the process come to deny rather than affirm the will to life. At the same time, these ascetic practices, including repaying everything evil with goodness, voluntary chastity, renunciation of all pleasure, throwing away all possessions, poverty and fasting (*WWR* 1: 415) reinforce their metaphysical knowledge of the will as suffering by constantly associating their own willing with the direct experience of pain. Schopenhauer identifies 'asceticism' as the way of life that gives visible, practical shape to this metaphysical truth. Asceticism, as he defines it, is the '*deliberate* breaking of the will by forgoing what is pleasant and seeking out what is unpleasant, choosing a lifestyle of penitence and self-castigation for the constant mortification of the will' (*WWR* 1: 419). Asceticism teaches saints to turn from the will to life as a source of suffering rather than gratify it in the delusory hope that they might yield happiness. Saints deliberately intensify the pain that they know must always accompany willing, and do so by inflicting on themselves constant suffering and welcoming every chance misfortune and deliberate evil perpetrated against themselves. They do so 'in order to keep breaking and deadening the will through constant deprivation and suffering, since he [sic] recognizes and abhors the will as the source of his own suffering existence and that of the world' (*WWR* 1: 409).

If ancient sages attempt to rationally temper their will so that they calmly and uncomplainingly endure suffering as their fate, Schopenhauer's ascetic saints eliminate the will that is the very source of our suffering. Ascetic practices transform a willing creature into a will-less saint and in doing so realize 'the complete self-abolition and negation of the will, the true absence of will, the only thing that can staunch and appease the impulses of the will forever, the only thing that can give everlasting contentment, the only thing that can redeem the world' (*WWR* 1: 389). Schopenhauerian saints do not attempt to tranquilly accept suffering as a universal fate, they free themselves entirely from suffering. The saint's salvation requires, as Schopenhauer puts it, 'self-denial or self-renunciation, *abnegatio sui ipsius*; for the real self is the will to life' (*WWR* 2: 606).[18] As Schopenhauer's borrowing from the late medieval Christian spiritualist Thomas à Kempis suggests, salvation requires the imitation of Christ (see *WWR* 2: 636). Schopenhauer sees this as a *radical* cure insofar it entails fundamentally turning against our real self, which is the embodiment of the will to life. It is also radical in another sense: salvation requires that our heart is 'cured of the passion for enjoying and indeed for living' (*WWR* 2: 635, 638). The Schopenhauerian saint denies the value not just of his own particular life, but of the essence of all life: the will to life itself. 'Complete cognition of the essence of the world', as Schopenhauer puts it, 'acts as a *tranquillizer* [L. *Quietiv*] of the will and leads to resignation, the abandonment not only of life, but of the whole will to life' (*WWR* I: 253).

Schopenhauer's position is made clear in the distinction he draws between the asceticism of ancient Cynics and that of religious saints, penitents, Samanas and sannyâsis. Superficially, he observes, Cynics appear similar to the monks and sannyâsis: both practise similar forms of asceticism. Yet ancient Cynics and religious saints adopt an ascetic way of life to achieve radically different ends. Christian and Hindu ascetics practise renunciation and mortification for the sake of 'transcending life', whereas the Cynics aim at attaining happiness within life (*WWR* 2: 155; see *DL* vi. 9). In this respect, Schopenhauer argues, Cynicism and Stoicism do not correct the inborn error (or *proton pseudos*) which, he claims, is 'inherent in us', but perpetuates this error in its belief that happiness is possible within this life (*WWR* 2: 635).

Schopenhauer elaborates this distinction between the saint and sage in terms of the opposition between virtue of humility and the vice of pride. 'The fundamental difference between the spirit of cynicism and that of asceticism', he explains, 'comes out very clearly in the humility essential to asceticism, but so foreign to cynicism that the latter, on the contrary, has in view pride and disdain for all other men' (*WWR* 2: 155; see also Foucault, 2011: 262). Schopenhauer suggests that rather than undertaking ascetic exercises to train themselves to deny the will to life, Cynics and Stoics did so in order to attain and take pride in their own invulnerability [see **5.2** above]. The ancient Cynics, for example, tried to appropriate glory for themselves by claiming to be true Olympic victors (Desmond, 2006: 107; see, e.g., *DL* 6.33, 6.43).

In their self-mortifying lives, self-denying religious ascetics, Schopenhauer suggests, express their 'intuitively grasped, direct cognition of the world and of its essence' (*WWR* 1: 410). They embody the truth in their way of life. Intuitive knowledge of the world as it is in-itself, he claims, finds its 'complete expression' not in abstract concepts, but '*only*' in 'his deeds' (*WWR* 1: 410). If we are to properly understand the metaphysical truth these ascetics fathom, he suggests, we must go beyond their abstract philosophical concepts and study their lives (**10**), not their dogmas and superstitions. For the philosopher, Schopenhauer maintains, the biographies of Christian, Buddhist and Hindu ascetics, which reveal to us saints who 'overcome' the world are 'incomparably more instructive and important' than Plutarch's *Parallel Lives*, which show us Greek and Roman heroes who 'conquer the world', including famous Stoics like Cato the Younger (*WWR* 1: 412).

9.5 Schopenhauerian salvation

What is the Schopenhauerian ascetic's way of life? How do ascetics live after they have silenced the siren song of the will to life? Curiously, in answering this question Schopenhauer blurs the lines between the aesthetic and the ascetic way of life, between the saint and the artist. Or more precisely, he conceives the ascetic's serenity as the fullest and purest realization of the artist's pleasure. In one sense, then, asceticism is the pinnacle of aestheticism. Schopenhauer's account of ascetic salvation turns on his particular conception of aesthetic pleasure, which he derives from his synthesis of Platonic and Kantian idealism. We need to briefly examine his aesthetic theory in order to grasp in what sense asceticism completes aestheticism.

Schopenhauer clarifies this notion of aesthetic pleasure by drawing an invidious contrast between artistic and ordinary cognition. Both ordinary and scientific knowledge, he claims, are objectifications and instruments of the will to life that expresses itself in the ego's motives and actions. Through ordinary cognition, he suggests, the ego sees the world through the lens of its motives as an embodiment of the will to life. As such, the ego strives to preserve itself and propagate new life. Science, Schopenhauer claims, is simply a much more effective practical instrument through which the ego co-ordinates its ceaseless, yet vain practical efforts to satisfy the will to life. He conceives science as calculative or instrumental reason.[19] As a rule, then, cognition is 'entirely in the service of the will' (*WWR* 1: 199). Cognition is enslaved to the will to life. In one of his most famous passages, Schopenhauer draws on a series of Greek myths of eternal punishment to characterize the terrible consequences of cognition's enslavement:

> As long as our consciousness is filled by our will, as long as we are given over to the pressure of desires with their constant hopes and fears, as long as we are the subject of willing, we will never have lasting happiness or peace. .... So the subject of willing remains on the revolving wheel of Ixion, keeps drawing water from the sieve of the Danaids, is the eternally yearning Tantalus. (*WWR* 1: 220)

Yet Schopenhauer maintains there is one exception that proves the rule of cognition's enslavement to the will. Aesthetic cognition is this exception: it is consciousness unchained from the will to life. Aesthetic contemplation, he maintains, liberates us from the wheel of Ixion by lifting:

> us out of the endless stream of willing, tearing cognition from its slavery to the will, our attention is no longer directed to the motives of willing but instead grasps things freed from their relation to the will, and hence considers them without interests, without subjectivity, purely objectively; .... It is the painless state that Epicurus prized as the

highest good and the state of the gods: for that moment we are freed from the terrible pressure of the will, we celebrate the Sabbath of the penal servitude of willing, the wheel of Ixion stands still. (*WWR* 1: 220)

We can see in Schopenhauer's analysis of aesthetic cognition both the continuities and discontinuities between ancient PWL and Schopenhauer's pessimistic way out of life. Schopenhauer claims that artistic geniuses can momentarily realize the highest goal of the ancient philosophical schools: namely *ataraxia*. Aesthetic contemplation, as puts it, is a 'peaceful, quiet, will-less state of mind' (*WWR* 1: 221). For Schopenhauer, we can discern this in the Dutch masters' genre of 'still life', such as Ruysdael's landscapes, which both reflects their inner tranquillity and produces it in the spectator:

Figure 9.1 Jackob van Ruysdael, Landscape with Windmills near Haarlem (1651). Public domain. Source Wikimedia Commons: https://commons.wikimedia.org/wiki/File:Van_Ruisdael,_Jacob_-_Landscape_with_Windmills_near_Haarlem_-_Google_Art_Project.jpg

In pure contemplation of the beautiful, Schopenhauer claims, the subject is transformed into a pure subject of cognition, whose object is the Platonic Idea (see *WWR* I: 191ff.). However, artistic geniuses realize godlike serenity through the complete elimination of the will rather than through the exercise of practical reason, as the Stoic or Epicurean sage sought to do. Aesthetic cognition requires a fundamental conversion of the self from a willing creature to a pure subject of knowledge; or, as he puts it 'the elevation of consciousness to the pure, will-less, timeless subject of cognition, independent of all relations' (*WWR* 1: 223). Schopenhauer suggests that ascetic salvation lies in the radicalization and purification of this aesthetic experience of will-less contemplation. After definitively silencing their will to life through self-mortification, ascetics become nothing other than pure subjects of knowing permanently free from the distress of willing. Schopenhauer conceives ascetic redemption as akin to *unwavering* aesthetic contemplation:

> We can gather from this how blissful life must be for someone whose will is not merely momentarily placated, as is in the pleasure of the beautiful, but calmed forever, indeed extinguished entirely except for the last glowing spark that sustains the body and is extinguished along with it. Such a person who, after many bitter struggles with his own nature, has ultimately prevailed completely, remains as only a pure, cognizing being, as an untarnished mirror of the world. Nothing can worry him anymore, nothing more can excite him, because he has cut all the thousands of threads of willing that keep us bound to the world and which, in the form of desires, fears, envy and anger, drag us back and forth amid constant pain. (*WWR* 1: 417)

Schopenhauer claims that ascetics who deny the will to life realize salvation: that is to say, they vanquish the evil of suffering and the fear of death that, as we have seen, he believes motivates true philosophy. If ascetics no longer will the will to life, then their own suffering and death is a matter of complete indifference. Schopenhauer's ascetic, as he puts it:

> gazes back calmly and smiles back at the phantasm of this world that was once able to move and torment his mind as well, but now stands before him as indifferently as chess pieces after the game is over ... Life and its forms merely glide before him, like a fleeting appearance, like a gentle morning dream that floats by someone who is half awake,

> where reality is already shining through and cannot deceive anymore. And just like this dream, life and its forms finally disappear without any violent transition. (*WWR* 1: 417)

Schopenhauer maintains, however, that even when cognition has become a 'tranquilliser of the will', ascetics do not attain 'peace and blissfulness' as a *permanent* possession. Rather, the negation of the will is something they have to constantly regain through practical struggle. The will to life always strives anew. The saint's tranquillity, Schopenhauer writes, 'is only a flower that emerges from the constant overcoming of the will, and we see the constant struggle with the will to life as the soil from which it arises; on earth nobody can have lasting peace' (*WWR* 1: 418). In other words, Schopenhauer acknowledges that in practice the ascetic way of life is a constant struggle to overcome the will to life. To this end, the ascetic must deliberately deploy a series ascetic practices of self-mortification to defeat the ever renewed will to life. Schopenhauerian ascetics, like the Socrates of the *Phaedo*, therefore gladly welcome death as the definitive end to their own will to life (*WWR* 1: 393). For those in whom the will is completely extinguished 'there can be nothing bitter in the death of the body … and this death is in fact very welcome' (*WWR* 1: 418) as 'the hour of redemption' (*PP* 2: 168).

Schopenhauer concludes his magnum opus by considering one 'objection' to his soteriological vision. 'The objection', he explains, 'is that once our investigation has finally succeeded in placing before our eyes, in the phenomenon of perfect holiness, the negation and abandonment of all willing, and in so doing, the redemption from a world whose entire being is presented to us as suffering, then this will seem like a transition into an empty *nothing*' (*WWR* 1: 436). What does Schopenhauer mean by 'being' and 'nothing' in this context? For Schopenhauer, what we accept as positive or being, and what ascetics negate for the sake of nothing, is precisely the world of representation, which is the mirror in which the will to life comes to know itself. In other words, Schopenhauer's ascetics do not represent or mirror phenomena. They know nothing of what the willing subject, or 'ordinary' ego which mirrors the world conceives as being, namely the 'constant urges and drives that have no goal or pause … the will's whole appearance and ultimately its universal forms as well, time and space, and also its final fundamental form, subject and object' (*WWR* 1: 438). 'The negation, abolition, and turning around of the will', he observes, 'is also an abolition and disappearance of the world, its mirror'. Put another way, Schopenhauer's point is that ascetics cannot mirror the world since they have abolished the will to life that ordinarily motivates us to represent it in terms of spatio-temporally distinct, causally connected phenomena. Schopenhauer puts this point telegraphically: 'no will: no representation, no world' (*WWR* 1: 438). 'With the abolition of the will, the world melts away, [o]nly nothing remains before us' (*WWR* 1: 438).

For Schopenhauer, therefore, the world without will, the ultimate goal of his soteriology, is beyond any positive knowledge. Reflecting on the close of *WWR* 1 Book 4, which he describes as the highest point of his teachings, Schopenhauer writes:

> It can speak ... only of what is denied or given up; but what is gained in place of this, what is laid hold of, it is forced ... to describe as nothing; and it can add only the consolation that it may be merely a relative, not an absolute, nothing. For, if something is no one of all the things that we know, then certainly it is for us in general nothing. Yet it still does not follow from this that it is nothing absolutely, namely that it must be nothing from every possible point of view and in every possible sense, but only that we are restricted to a wholly negative knowledge of it; and this may very well lie in the limitation of our point of view. (*WWR* 2: 612)

Schopenhauer therefore does not evade the claim that with the ascetic denial of the will 'only nothing remains before us'. However, if the denial of the will leads to a 'melting way into nothingness', as he admits, why should we idealize rather than fear it (*WWR* 1: 438)? Schopenhauer's closing argument for his soteriology turns on persuading us to shift our perspective, or to reverse signs so that we see 'that what is being for us is nothing, and what is nothing for us is being' (*WWR* 1: 437). Rather than follow our natural inclination to see the prospect of nothingness from the perspective of the will to life, Schopenhauer invites us to suspend our ordinary, 'petty concerns' and examine ascetics who have overcome the world and attained peace or tranquillity. In effect, he asks us to consider how being looks from the perspective of nothing. Or more concretely, he asks us to evaluate our ordinary egoism from the vantage point of the ascetic's state of nothingness. We can, he implies, banish our natural fear of nothingness when:

> instead of the restless impulses and drives, instead of the constant transition from desire to fear and from joy to suffering, instead of the never-satisfied and never-dying hope which are the elements

that make up the life-dream of the human being who wills – instead of all this, we are shown the peace that is higher than all reason, we are shown that completely calm sea of the mind, that profound tranquillity, imperturbable confidence and cheerfulness, whose mere glint in a countenance such as those portrayed by Raphael or Correggio is a complete and reliable gospel: only cognition remains, the will has vanished. (*WWR* 1: 438–9)

In such art, this inner experience, which, he claims, all Indian, Christian and Mohammedan mystics share, 'is vouchsafed by the mark of inner truth' (*WWR* 1: 439). Artistic depictions of saints like Raphael's St. Cecilia, he suggests, redeem nothingness as an ecstatic state.

Figure 9.2 Raphael, The Ecstasy of St. Cecilia (1516–17). Public domain. Source Wikimedia Commons: https://commons.wikimedia.org/wiki/File:Cecilia_Raphael.jpg

For Schopenhauer, such an artistic figuration of nothingness as ocean-like calmness is the only thing that can give us 'lasting comfort' when we recognize that the world as will binds us to incurable suffering, yet that the world without will melts away into empty nothingness. When we behold the 'imperturbable peace, a profound calm and inner serenity' in figures like Raphael's St Cecilia we cannot help feeling the greatest longing, since we acknowledge that this alone is in the right and infinitely superior to everything else, and our better spirit calls to us the great 'Dare to know' (*WWR* 1: 416–17). They reveal the denial of the will to life, the refusal of all earthly pleasures, or the silencing of the sirens' song, as the ultimate salvation. Such art banishes our childish fear of nothingness. We can then embrace nothingness as true redemption. Against paganism, and echoing certain Christian monastics [**4.2**], Schopenhauer claims that this radical denial of life delivers a 'peace that is higher than all reason' (*WWR* 1: 439).

CHAPTER 10
NIETZSCHE: PHILOSOPHY AS THE RETURN TO LIFE

10.1 Introduction

As we have seen, two central figures in our field of research, Hadot and Foucault, have suggested that historians of philosophy fail to recognize the extent to which the Graeco-Roman model of philosophy has shaped important strands of modern European philosophy. In this context, as we observed in the previous chapter, they both hypothesize that we might comprehend the scope, nature and significance of Nietzsche's philosophical project if we conceptualize it as an attempt to reconstitute the ancient model of philosophy. 'The philosophies of Schopenhauer and Nietzsche', as Hadot notes, 'are … invitations to radically transform our lives' (Hadot, 1995: 272). Similarly, Foucault locates Nietzsche as one among a disparate group of the nineteenth-century German philosophers whose implicit goal was to revive the Graeco-Roman model of philosophy as an art of living against long-standing efforts to expunge it from philosophy (Foucault, 2005: 251).

Hadot and Foucault claim then that Nietzsche adopted a specifically ancient conception of philosophy as an art or *techne* of living. In this model of philosophy, as we have observed throughout this book, systematic discourse only has a point and purpose insofar as it contributes to the formation of a certain ethos or character. To practise philosophy is to construct a certain kind of self and mode of conduct as a result of accepting a set of beliefs. On this account philosophers are more admired for their manner of living and dying than for the doctrines they construct. Jacques Louis David's famous neoclassical depictions of Socrates's philosophic poise or Seneca's stoic indifference in confronting death illustrate this Graeco-Roman belief that philosophy demonstrates itself through *argumentum ad oculos* (or visible proof). In the ancient context, in short, philosophy is a way of transforming one's life, and so the measure of the value of philosophy is how one lives and dies.

One of Nietzsche's principal aims is to re-organize philosophy so that it once again takes its lead from the medical analogy that structured the

Hellenistic philosophies, especially Epicureanism and Stoicism (see Cicero, 1927: 3.6; chapters 2–4). However, as we shall see, Nietzsche aims to show that earlier philosophical physicians, the ancient Cynics, Epicureans and Stoics, formulated 'cures' worse than the diseases they purported to treat, and to replace them with new philosophical physicians. In doing so, Nietzsche faces a particular challenge: whether it is possible to revive the ancient medical model of philosophy despite the emergence of Schopenhauerian or 'romantic' pessimism that he claims poisons modern culture. Nietzschean philosophy poses the following question: 'Is it possible to lead a flourishing life despite, or perhaps because of this very "pessimism"?' We can illuminate Nietzsche's attempt to remain true to the ambition of classical philosophical therapy in the context of the emergence of modern pessimism by briefly examining his intellectual formation.

10.2 Nietzsche's metaphilosophical meditations

As a high school student, Nietzsche attended Schulpforta gymnasium, renowned for its classical pedagogy and then began his academic career as a classicist (or philologist) at the University of Bonn (1864–5) and the University of Leipzig (1865–9). Under the tutelage of the renowned philologist Friedrich Ritschl, whom he followed from Bonn to Leipzig, he made his name with a series of precocious essays on the sources of the third-century doxographer Diogenes Laertius's *Lives of Famous Philosophers*.[1] It was on the basis of these essays, and Ritschl's glowing recommendation of Nietzsche as a 'phenomenon' of classical philology, that on 28 January 1869 the twenty-four-year-old Nietzsche was appointed to *Professor Ordinarius* at the University of Basel without a formal dissertation and then thirteen months later promoted to *Professor Extraordinarius*.

At the same time that the young Nietzsche forged his philological career, he was also being swept away by the German philosopher Schopenhauer's grand metaphysical pessimism and the charismatic personality and musical genius of the great German composer and Schopenhauerian, Richard Wagner.[2] 'The best and most elevated moments of my life', the young Nietzsche wrote to Wagner, 'are linked with your name, and I know only one other man, your great spiritual brother Arthur Schopenhauer, whom I regard with such admiration, even in a kind of religious manner (*religione quadam*)' (22 May 1869: *KSB* 3/8). Nietzsche identified with Schopenhauer's philosophical pessimism and as an aspiring composer and accomplished pianist, he treasured Schopenhauer's bold claim that of all the arts music alone leads to metaphysical insight into the will to life [**10.4**]. Nietzsche's discovery of Schopenhauer and his ardent enthusiasm for Wagner's music derailed his academic career and transformed his life.

Nietzsche reports that he accidentally discovered Schopenhauer's magnum opus, *The World as Will and Representation* in Rohn's Leipzig bookstore around October 1865. He immediately became an impassioned disciple. Two years later he dramatically recalled this serendipitous discovery:

> I do not know what daemon whispered to me: 'Take this book home with you' [...] At home I threw myself into the sofa corner with the treasure I had acquired, and started to allow that energetic, sombre genius to work upon me. Here every line screamed renunciation, denial, resignation, here I saw a mirror in which I caught sight of world, of life, and of my own mind in terrifying grandeur. Here the full, disinterested, sun-like eye of art looked upon me, here I saw sickness and healing, exile and sanctuary, hell and heaven. (quoted in Janaway, 1998: 16)

Nietzsche described Schopenhauer as 'the greatest philosophical demigod of the whole of the last millennium' (Janaway, 1998: 1). At the same time as Nietzsche was being swept away by Schopenhauer's metaphysically inspired vision of sickness and healing, he was also working with extreme ascetic discipline on tracing the sources of Diogenes's *Lives*. Schopenhauer's pessimism and Diogenes's biographical sketches of ancient philosophers became the key sources informing Nietzsche's model of philosophy.

In making the transition from a professional academic philologist at the University of Basel (1869–77) to an itinerant philosopher (1877–88), Nietzsche carried over and developed important strands of this classical legacy. Through his intensive philological study of Diogenes's *Lives* Nietzsche came to appreciate Greek philosophy. Of Diogenes, Nietzsche wrote that he is 'by accident the clumsy watchman guarding treasure whose value he does not know. He is the nightwatchman of the history of Greek philosophy; no one can enter into it without getting the key from him' (*BAW* 5: 126, 1868/1869).

Here close to the renaissance humanists, with their interest in philosophical biography [**6.1**], Diogenes's *Lives* became one of the foundations of Nietzsche's philosophical orientation.[3] He imbibed the idea widespread in antiquity that above all else philosophy is a way of life and the philosopher is a physician. In his inaugural Basel lecture (28 May 1869), 'Homer and Classical Philology', Nietzsche explicitly invoked Seneca's lament that the rise of sophistic teaching was transforming philosophy, the study of wisdom, into philology, the study of mere words: '*Itaque quae philosophia fuit facta philologia est*' [*Ep*. 108.23; see **10.1**]. In his own 'confession of faith', Nietzsche declares his intention of performing the reverse operation: turning philology back into a discipline that teaches us how to live: '*Philosophia facta est quae philologia fuit.*'

In the early 1870s, Nietzsche developed an unpublished study of ancient Greek philosophy, *Philosophy in the Tragic Age of the Greeks* (1873), and a contemporaneous series of unpublished notes for a book on the philosopher, his so-called *Das Philosopenbuch*. In both cases, he singles out the ancient ideal of the philosopher as a physician of culture and gives priority to philosophers' lives and personality over their written doctrines. One of his sketches for his book on the philosopher is entitled 'The Philosopher as Cultural Physician'. 'The philosopher's product', he claims here in the classical vein, 'is his *life* (which occupies the most important position, *before* his *works*). His life is his work of art' (Nietzsche, 1979: 48).

In *PTG* Nietzsche extends his commitment to a history of philosophy as a lived practice. Here he aims to emphasize only that aspect of a philosopher's doctrines that constitutes a mark of his personality: 'I am going to tell the story – simplified – of certain philosophers. I am going to emphasise only that point of each of their systems, which constitutes a slice of their *personality* and hence belongs to that incontrovertible, non-debatable evidence which it is the task of the historian to preserve' (*PTG*: 24). Nietzsche gives priority to the study of the pre-Platonic philosophers' characters over their systems: 'What we must ever *love and honour* and what no subsequent enlightenment can take away: the great human being' (*PTG* Preface). Indeed, Nietzsche rehabilitates Diogenes Laertius's unfashionable genre of anecdotes: 'The only thing of interest in a refuted system is the personal element. It alone is whatever is irrefutable. It is possible to present the image of a man in three anecdotes. I shall try to emphasise three anecdotes in each system and abandon the rest' (*PTG* Preface).

Nietzsche also uses this ancient model of philosophy to frame two of his so-called *Untimely Meditations*,[4] 'On the Uses and Disadvantages of History for Life' (February 1874) and 'Schopenhauer as Educator' (October 1874). As we shall see, Nietzsche's so-called meditations are shaped by the ancient ideal of PWL, its conception of the philosophical or cultural physician and its emphasis on what, following Hadot, we have called 'spiritual exercises'.

Nietzsche resurrects the ancient model by assuming the role of a latter-day philosophical physician. Let us very briefly consider these two meditations to see how they are informed by the meta-philosophical presuppositions of ancient philosophy.

Nietzsche's conception of untimeliness (*Unzeitgemasse*) is freighted with several connotations that are significant for our purposes. First, Nietzsche uses this term to identify himself as a critic of contemporary culture who looks upon what it considers one of its greatest achievements, namely the historical sense, and evaluates it from a specifically *classical* perspective:

> It is only to the extent that I am a pupil of earlier times, especially the Greek that though a child of the present time I was able to acquire such untimely experiences ... for I do not know what meaning classical studies could have for our time if they were not untimely – that is to say, acting counter to our time and thereby acting on our time and, let us hope, for the benefit of a time to come. (*HL* P)

In a Cynic vein, as we might say, Nietzsche defaces the currency of modern culture: he evaluates what it conceives as one of its highest virtues as in fact a corrupting vice or illness. As an untimely critic who observes the modern age through the lens of classical antiquity, Nietzsche sees that it is suffering from a particular malady, what he calls the 'consuming fever of history' (*HL* 1). This new historical malady prevents modern individuals from drawing on the past for the sake of stimulating and cultivating their own actions. Rather than incorporating the past into their own life and personality, they become merely 'objective' spectators of history. Nietzsche defines this modern historical malady as the loss of the capacity to incorporate and transform knowledge into action.

By contrast, Nietzsche conceives his own classical perspective as one that follows the principle that knowledge must serve to enhance life. It assumes an ideal of flourishing that prioritizes life over knowledge. We must, as he emphatically states, 'learn better how to employ history for the purpose of *life!*' (*HL* 1). For Nietzsche, modern culture's illness is precisely that it eliminates the incorporation of the truth into lived practice that is the hallmark of PWL. Modern philosophers, he laments, no longer conceive PWL, but as a theoretical discourse. They compile erudite and comprehensive histories of philosophical systems without putting these philosophies to the test as ways of life:

No one dares venture to fulfil the philosophical law in himself, *no one lives philosophically* with that simple loyalty that constrained a man of antiquity to bear himself as a Stoic wherever he was, whatever he did, once he had affirmed his loyalty to the Stoa. (*SE* 5)

Following Schopenhauer [**10.1**], Nietzsche implies that the demise of PWL is symptomatic not only of the modern historical malady, but the fact that philosophy has become a pedagogic instrument of the state:

All modern philosophizing is political and official, limited by governments, churches, academies, customs and the cowardice of men to the appearance of scholarship; it sighs 'if only' or knows 'there once was' and does nothing else. Within a historical culture philosophy possesses no rights if it wants to be more than a self-restrained knowing which leads to no action ... Are there still human beings, one then asks oneself, or perhaps only thinking-, writing- and speaking-machines? (*SE* 5)

Second, Nietzsche shows that to look at the modern age through this ancient lens is to take the perspective of a cultural physician who diagnoses the present in terms of health and sickness and who aims to cure its maladies. Here if not in other respects, he approaches the enlightenment *philosophes* [**8.1**]. One of this work's leitmotifs is its repeated use of medical metaphors to conceive the problems Nietzsche believes flow from modern culture's overvaluation of historical sciences. Nietzsche aims to cure the modern age of what he calls its 'maladies', 'injuries', 'diseases'.

Third, as 'medical' or 'diagnostic' observations of the present, his untimely meditations also prescribe a range of exercises (**4**) as remedies for the maladies they diagnose. In the meditation on history, for example, Nietzsche identifies what we might call a quasi-Cynic treatment and a quasi-Stoic antidote to cure the 'stifling of life by the historical, by the malady of history' (*HL* 10). Nietzsche describes the former 'unhistorical' medicine as an exercise in '*forgetting*' and the latter 'suprahistorical' antidote as seeing things from the perspective of eternity, or of 'bestowing upon existence the character of eternity' (*HL* 1 & 10). Nietzsche identifies ancient Cynicism with the exercise in forgetting. Ancient Cynicism, as he conceives it, is a philosophical *askesis* aimed at reclaiming healthy animal understanding. Drawing on Schopenhauer's distinction between animal and human cognition [**9.2**], Nietzsche suggests that Cynics exercise the former's intuitive cognition in order to reclaim their happiness. Unlike humans, whose abstract cognition allows them to recall the past and imagine the future, and who are therefore burdened by regret and anticipatory fear, animals are entirely immersed in the present moment (*HL* 1). Memory, or the phrase 'it was', as he puts it, is 'the password which gives conflict, suffering and satiety [boredom] access to man so as to remind him what his existence fundamentally is – an imperfect tense that can never become a perfect one' (*HL* 1). However, unlike Schopenhauer, Nietzsche does not argue against Cynic philosophy and affirm the pessimistic conclusion that we are fated to suffer, but instead shows how the Cynic exercise in forgetting is necessary for overcoming the pessimistic desire to escape or turn against the will to life:

> If happiness, if reaching out for new happiness, is in any sense what fetters living creatures to life and makes them go on living, then perhaps no philosopher is more justified than the Cynic: for the happiness of the animal, as the perfect Cynic, is the living proof of the rightness of Cynicism … In the case of the smallest or of the greatest happiness, … it is always the same thing that makes happiness happiness: the ability to forget or … the capacity to feel unhistorically during its duration. He who cannot sink down on the threshold of the moment and forget all the past, who cannot stand balanced like a goddess of victory without growing dizzy and afraid, will never know what happiness is. (*HL* 1)

Nietzsche's third meditation, *Schopenhauer as Educator*, continues his resurrection of PWL. Significantly, he largely disregards Schopenhauer's metaphysical system to concentrate almost exclusively on his 'biography'. In this sense, Nietzsche's study of Schopenhauer is modelled on Diogenes Laertius's classical conception of the overriding importance of the philosopher's life (cf. Sellars, 2001). Nietzsche put this classical assumption into practice in his manner of eulogizing Schopenhauer as an educator. By 1874, Nietzsche had in fact rejected the central tenets of Schopenhauer's metaphysics and ethics, but he nevertheless held that Schopenhauer retained a philosophical significance as an exemplar of a philosophical way of life.[5] Nietzsche's 'biography' represents Schopenhauer as a heroic exemplar of the struggle great individuals must wage against their own epoch in order to liberate themselves from its limits and pathologies. For Nietzsche, Schopenhauer's philosophical life offers an education in how to overcome the main pathology of modern culture: namely its creation of weakened personalities who fail to cultivate themselves because they cannot integrate knowledge and action and who instead act in conformity with the herd. Once again, Nietzsche takes up the role of the philosophical physician in diagnosing what he calls our bad conscience:

> In his heart every man knows quite well that being unique, he will be in the world only once and that no imaginable chance will for a second time gather together into a unity so strangely variegated an assortment as he is: he knows it but hides it like a bad conscience – ... let him follow his conscience, which calls him: Be yourself! All you are now doing, thinking, desiring, is not you yourself. (*SE* 1)

Schopenhauer's life, as Nietzsche conceives it, is a proper philosophical education insofar as it exemplifies how to become who we are. Nietzsche describes himself seeking and finding in Schopenhauer 'a true philosopher as an educator who could raise me above my insufficiencies insofar as these originated in the age and teach me again to be simple and honest in thought and life, that is to say to be untimely' (*SE* 2). Nietzsche makes his reflections on Schopenhauer's life an occasion for charting the many stages 'in the liberation of the philosophical life' (*SE* 3). It should come as no surprise then that in *Schopenhauer as Educator* Nietzsche explicitly affirms the ancient ideal of PWL:

> I profit from a philosopher only insofar as he can be an example. [...] The philosopher must supply this example in his visible life, and not merely in his books; that is, it must be presented in the way the philosophers of Greece taught, through their bearing, what they wore and ate, their morals, rather than by what they said, let alone what they wrote. How completely this courageous visibility of the philosophical life is lacking in Germany! (*SE* 3)

Nietzsche here judges that the philosopher's 'visible life' is philosophically more important than what he/she says or writes. Alluding to Plutarch's anecdote about how Diogenes affirmed his 'ascetic' mode of life in the face of his own doubts Nietzsche reflects:

> I am thinking of the first night of Diogenes: all ancient philosophy was aimed at simplicity of life and taught a certain absence of needs, the most important remedy for all thoughts of social rebellion ... As

long as philosophers do not muster the courage *to advocate a lifestyle structured in an entirely different way and demonstrate it by their own example, they will come to nothing.* (*KSA* 7, 31[11] 752, emphasis added)

Philosophy, as Nietzsche conceives it, requires the advocacy of an exemplary mode of life that departs from convention, a 'strange mode of life' demonstrated through exemplary conduct (**10**). For Nietzsche, the purpose of philosophy is the practice of a mode of life, and it is 'demonstrated' by means of this practical realization. Of course, Nietzsche does not mean to suggest that theoretical doctrine is not integral to philosophical practice, but he does claim that doctrine only matters to the extent that it is put into practice in the way a philosopher conducts his/her life.

Following what he calls Schopenhauer's 'celebrated treatise on university philosophy' [**10.2**], Nietzsche's resurrection of the ancient model of PWL also fuels his complaint against modern university philosophy as erudition disconnected from life and action (**9**). Nietzsche draws an invidious contrast between Schopenhauer's commitment to living a heroic philosophical life and contemporary university philosophers who he conceives as beholden to the state as its paid employees. University philosophers, he argues, as state philosophers, conceive their discipline as largely a matter of systematization, historical erudition and 'criticism', not as a way of life. In a withering polemic, Nietzsche implies that contemporaneous historians of philosophy like Eduard Zeller do not practise, but forget philosophy:

Who will blow aside, for example, the Lethean vapour with which the history of Greek philosophy has been enveloped by the dull though not very scientific works of Ritter, Brandis and Zeller? I, at any rate, would rather read Diogenes Laertius than Zeller, because at least *the spirit of the old philosophers* lives in Diogenes, but neither that nor any other spirit in Zeller. (*SE* 8)[6]

Nietzsche overturns the Hegelian-inspired philosophical disdain for Diogenes Laertius's *Lives* and revalues precisely his fidelity to the spirit of those ancient philosophers who practised PWL. As he writes:

The only method of criticising a philosophy that is possible and proves anything at all – namely to see whether one can live by it – has never been taught at the universities; only the criticism of words, and again words, is taught there. (*SE* 8)

10.3 Nietzsche's philosophy *as* a spiritual exercise

In the works that followed his *Untimely Meditations*, the so-called free-spirit trilogy (1877–82), Nietzsche extends his application of the ancient model of PWL and its meta-philosophical assumptions. For the sake of clarity, we will distinguish three steps in Nietzsche's development of the ancient model of philosophy in the books that made up his free spirit trilogy: namely (1) *Human, All Too Human* (1877), *Assorted Opinions and Maxims* (1879), *The Wanderer and His Shadow* (1880), which he subsequently published together as *Human, All Too Human*, vol. 2; (2) *Daybreak* (1881); and (3) *The Gay Science* (*GS*) (1882/1887). Nietzsche himself flags these connections between his own meta-philosophy and the ancient schools in the 1886 *Prefaces* he added to each book in the trilogy. What are these connections and continuities?

First, in these middle period works, Nietzsche claims that not only is philosophy a way of life, as he had in *Schopenhauer as Educator*. He now also recognizes that philosophical *discourse* is one principal means of shaping and transforming one's life. Nietzsche gives this thesis a therapeutic edge: it is an exercise in curing oneself (**3**). It is just that not all philosophies realize the goal of health or flourishing. Nietzsche's so-called aphoristic style partly grew from his efforts to put into practice a philosophical therapy. Here as in the case of other philosophers we examine in this book, Nietzsche's rhetorical styles are an index of his commitment to PWL (**5**).

Second, in the 1886 Prefaces added to *Human, All Too Human* volumes 1 & 2 and *GS*, Nietzsche retrospectively identifies his own philosophical explorations in the free spirit trilogy as therapeutic exercises (**3**) that enabled him to overcome Schopenhauerian or romantic pessimism. Nietzsche reflects that, to do this, he drew on the ancient philosophical therapies, most clearly Cynic, Stoic and Epicurean therapies: the 'ointment boxes and medicines of *all* ancient philosophies'. In the middle works, Nietzsche follows his self-directed injunction: 'Become ancient!' (*KSA* 8: 28 [41]; *KSA* 8: 28 [40]).

Third, and finally, in the last book of the trilogy, *GS*, Nietzsche treats the ancient philosophical therapies as a scaffolding that he kicks away in order to ascend to what he calls '*the* great health' (*GS* 382). Restoring one's equanimity by means of Cynic forgetting of suffering, Epicurean remembrance of pleasures, Stoic fortitude in the face of adversity or sceptical indifference towards all values, is now positioned as only the first rung of an ascent to a much higher type of health. The ancient therapies, he claims, enable one to overcome the ascetic denial of life, but not to fully affirm life. Nietzsche now identifies 'Dionysian pessimism', a complete affirmation of life, as the antipodes of Schopenhauerian pessimism. Nietzsche's ideal, as Janaway recognizes, is the anti-thesis of Schopenhauer's:

'Only through the denial of the will to life can this pain-ridden existence be redeemed'; anti-Schopenhauer: 'Only through the affirmation of life with all its pain can strength and greatness be achieved'. Schopenhauer: 'It would be better if I had not existed, if there were no world'; anti-Schopenhauer: 'I love and will everything that has happened, and wish its recurrence endlessly'. (Janaway, 2003: 171)

In *GS*, Nietzsche's overarching project is to formulate a post-classical philosophical therapy (see Ure & Ryan, 2017). Nietzsche reformulates the ancient doctrine of the eternal recurrence as the spiritual exercise for cultivating and attaining this healthy Dionysian pessimism. Since Nietzsche's middle works embody his most significant contribution to PWL we will focus on these texts and claims.

Philosophical discourse as a therapeutic exercise

As we have seen, in the *Untimely Meditations* Nietzsche argues that philosophy consists in how philosophers live rather than what they say or write. In the free-spirit trilogy, Nietzsche considers the significance of philosophical writing or discourse in the lives of philosophers. In *Daybreak* Nietzsche focuses on showing that philosophical discourse is conceptual autobiography (*D* 481). Rather than developing a history of philosophy in terms of competing theoretical systems, Nietzsche compares and evaluates philosophies as biography. Nietzsche's claim is that philosophical thinking is an expression of one's life or personality. As he puts it, philosophical 'thinking' is an 'involuntary biography', a written expression of a soul or character, or at least this is what marks out great philosophy from ordinary, professionalized philosophy (*D* 481).[7] Great philosophy *is* biographical. Or more precisely, Nietzsche conceives these philosophies as unconscious self-confessions or '*mémoires*' expressing different aspects of this life or different types of personality: the vicissitudes of the passions (Plato, Spinoza, Pascal, Rousseau, Goethe); a stable character or temperament (Schopenhauer), a 'head' (*Kopfes*) or intellectual mechanism (Kant). In cases where philosophy is 'a passionate history of the soul', Nietzsche observes it could take shape as a *novel* [*Roman*] replete with crises, catastrophes or death scenes. Nietzsche unfavourably compares Kant with such philosophical 'novelists':

> When he does shine through his thoughts, Kant appears honest and honorable in the best sense, but insignificant: he lacks breadth and power; he has not experienced very much, and his manner of working deprives him of the *time* in which to experience.
>
> (*D* 481)

However, Nietzsche does not simply claim that philosophers *involuntarily express* their inner experiences and drives through philosophical discourse. He also claims that they can *voluntarily deploy* these discourses as exercises through which they shape themselves. In this optic, Nietzsche claims that his own free-spirit trilogy was a voluntary exercise of the self on itself, an exercise of his own 'spiritual cure', or a form of self-writing (*HH 2* P 2; (**4**)). He stresses that *Human, All Too Human* records an 'experience', namely his own 'history of his illness and recovery' (*HH 2* P 6).[8] *Human, All Too Human*, Nietzsche writes, was 'a continuation and redoubling of a *spiritual cure*, namely of the anti-romantic self-treatment that my still healthy instinct had itself discovered and prescribed against a temporary attack … they are *precepts of health* that may be recommended to more spiritual natures of the generation just coming up as a *disciplina voluntatis*' (*HH 2* P).

Ancient optimism as a therapy for modern pessimism

Nietzsche explicitly identifies his philosophical discourse as a war he waged 'against the pessimism of weariness with life' (*HH 2* P 5). In other words, Nietzsche recognizes that he employed his philosophy as a therapeutic exercise to treat himself for the illness of Schopenhauerian pessimism. 'Around 1876', Nietzsche observed in his notebooks, 'I grasped that my instinct went into the opposite direction from Schopenhauer's: toward a justification of life, even at its most terrible, ambiguous, and mendacious; for this I had the formula "Dionysian"' (*KSA* 12/354–5). In the 1886 Prefaces to *Human, All Too Human* volumes 1 & 2, Nietzsche acknowledges that he had applied the ancient philosophical therapies to himself – principally Cynicism, Stoicism and Epicureanism – in his battle to combat his own weariness with life:

Just as a physician places his patient in a wholly strange environment ... so I, as physician and patient in one, compelled myself to an opposite and unexplored *clime of the soul*, and especially to a curative journey into strange parts ... A *minimum* of life, in fact, an unchaining from all coarser desires, an independence in the midst of all kinds of unfavourable circumstances together with pride in being *able* to live surrounded by these unfavourable circumstances; a certain amount of cynicism, a certain amount of 'barrel'. (*HH* 2 P 2)

In the preface to *Human, All Too Human* vol. 2, he records how he drew on the ancient philosophies not as theoretical doctrines, but principally as means of 'spiritual strengthening', using the conventional ancient trope of philosophical training as analogous to athletic exercise, most closely associated with Cynicism and Stoicism (6) (*HH* 2 P 5). Nietzsche identifies this as a 'self-testing' through which he aimed to recover his 'equilibrium and composure in the face of life and even a sense of gratitude towards it' (*HH* 2 P 5). He describes the exercises he practised as a 'discipline designed to make it easy as possible for the spirit to run long distances, to fly to great heights, above all again and again to fly away' (*HH* 2 P 5). He recalls how through these exercises he turned his 'perspective *around*' from Schopenhauerian or romantic pessimism, which condemns the world on the basis of experiences of suffering, to 'optimism for the purpose of restoration so that at some future time I could gain have the *right* to be a pessimist' (*HH* 2 P5). Nietzsche's 'optimism' took the form of realizing the general Hellenistic goal of tranquil endurance of misfortune and suffering (7).

Nietzsche thereby reverses Schopenhauer's critical judgement: rather than rejecting Cynicism and Stoicism as premised on a lack of metaphysical insight, Nietzsche diagnoses Schopenhauer's metaphysical pessimism as a symptom of illness, and claims that these schools offer us exercises that can cure us of this malady. He dismisses Schopenhauer's metaphysical claims as 'mystical embarrassments and subterfuges', including 'the unprovable doctrine of the One Will', and instead diagnoses them as symptoms of declining life (*GS* 99).

At the same time, like Petrarch [**6.2**] or Montaigne [**6.3**],[9] Nietzsche conceives his philosophical writing as an art of self-doctoring that other 'free spirits' can then draw on as exemplary, to develop their own cure:

Shall my experience – the history of an illness and recovery, for a recovery was what eventuated – have been my personal experience alone? And only my 'human, all-too-human'? Today I would like to believe the reverse; again and again I feel sure that my travel books were not written solely for myself, as sometimes seems to be the case – May I now, after six years of growing confidence, venture to send them off again? May I venture to commend them especially to the hearts and ears of those burdened with any kind of 'past' and who have sufficient spirit left still to suffer from the spirit of their past too? (*HH* 2 P 6)[10]

Nietzsche's free-spirit trilogy is also replete with spiritual exercises that aim to restore equanimity (3), including, for example, versions of two of the four 'Epicurean formulae' or *tetrapharmakon* (*WS* 6) and the ancient view from above (*WS* 14). Rather than systematic theoretical disquisitions, Nietzsche composes innumerable pithy, memorable aphorisms and maxims that make it easy to recall, for example, Stoic and Cynic lessons (5). In *Human, All Too Human*, for example, Nietzsche applauds the conventional Stoic wisdom contained in its account of the sage. He pinpoints and affirms the general Stoic ideal of rational self-sufficiency through independence of all externals:

> *Movable goods and landed property.* – If life has treated a man like a brigand, and has taken from him all it could in the way of honours, friends, adherents, health possessions of all kinds, he may perhaps, after the first shock, discover that he is richer than before. For it is only now that he knows what is truly his, what no brigand is able to get his hands on; so that perhaps he emerges out of all this plundering and confusion wearing the noble aspect of a great landed proprietor. (*HH* 2 334)[11]

In this case, Nietzsche's great landed proprietor is a figuration of the ancient sage who achieves complete self-possession (**10**).

As we saw in **Chapter 3**, for the Stoics, what people think about the world and themselves is decisively important in understanding the causes of suffering (7). The Graeco-Roman philosophical therapist identified the source of patients' distress in their beliefs and judgements, not in the malevolence or sinfulness of their natural desires. Taking a similar view, Nietzsche emphasizes that he conceives patients' distress as deriving from intellectual errors. Nietzsche's doctor of the soul 'aids those whose head is confused by opinions', not by 'wicked' or 'sinful' personal desires (*D* 449). In *Daybreak*, indeed, Nietzsche explicitly recasts Epictetus's famous aphorism: 'It is not things, but opinions about things that have absolutely no existence, which have so disturbed mankind!' (*D* 563).[12] By eliminating metaphysics, or opinion about things that he claims have no existence, Nietzsche (here like Voltaire [**9.2**]) supposes that philosophers might also eliminate the emotional troubles deriving from such errors (*HH* 27). Nietzsche understands his own critique of metaphysics, including Schopenhauerian metaphysics, in this vein: i.e. as a therapeutic exercise. Nietzsche then carries forwards the ancient therapeutic model of philosophy, though, as we shall see shortly, ultimately, he will reject the ancient ethical ideal of equanimity on the grounds that it falls well short of what he calls '*the* great health'.

Nietzsche's post classical therapy

As we have seen, in the first two instalments of the free-spirit trilogy, *Human, All Too Human* and *Daybreak*, Nietzsche explores the merit of recalibrating philosophy so that it might once again take its lead from the medical analogy that structured the Hellenistic philosophies, especially Epicureanism and Stoicism. It is in this vein that Nietzsche asks in *Schopenhauer as Educator*: 'Where are the physicians for modern mankind who themselves stand so firmly and soundly on their feet that they are able to support others and lead them by the hand?' (*SE* 2) In *Daybreak* he imploringly repeats this question: '*Where are the new physicians of the soul*'? (*D* 52) In the final instalment of the trilogy, *GS*, Nietzsche revives the ancient idea of philosophy as a medical art by attempting to put it into practice, acting as both the cultural physician to the modern age and physician to his own soul. It is the culmination of Nietzsche's decade-long attempt to reconceive philosophy as an art of living and therapeutic practice.

Yet *GS* does not simply recycle the ancient model of philosophy. In *GS* Nietzsche aims to develop a rival, post-classical philosophical therapy. As we have seen, Nietzsche in *HH* and *D* Nietzsche had applied the classical philosophical therapies to cure himself of his romantic or Schopenhauerian pessimism. Nietzsche had also drawn on enlightened scientific scepticism, especially the newly emerging methods of natural history, to liberate himself from the turmoil of irrational moral emotions and religious feelings. We can use 'science', as he puts it, 'to deprive man of his joys and make him colder, more statue-like, more stoic' (*GS* 12). This is what Nietzsche had sought to do in *HH* and *D*. In these first two instalments of his free-spirit trilogy, Nietzsche's 'anti-romantic, scientific regimen', as Paul Franco aptly called it (Franco, 2011: 206), was an integral part of his cure for how own 'pessimism of weariness with life' (*HH* 2 P 5). In the final instalment of the trilogy, *GS*,

Nietzsche steps forwards himself as the progenitor of a rival, post-classical philosophical therapy. *GS* in this light marks an important turning point in Nietzsche's philosophy, at which he begins to formulate an ethical project and ideal of happiness that radically breaks with the values motivating the classical philosophical therapies (**8**).[13]

In *GS*, to be specific, Nietzsche now targets as illnesses both 'romantic' pessimism *and* the Hellenistic 'petrification' of life that the free-spirit trilogy had drawn on as a counterweight to his own case of romantic pessimism. That is to say, in *GS* he comes to reconsider the ancient forms of 'optimism' not as remedies, but as continuations or refractions of the illness of weariness with life. We should not confuse tranquil endurance or fortitude, he warns, with human flourishing. *GS* criticizes rather than celebrates Cynic and Stoic pride as a sickness rather than cure, a form of self-tyranny rather than self-enhancement. Likewise, the Hellenistic ideal of *ataraxia* or *apatheia* becomes for him a symptom of the 'petrification' or 'fossilization' of life (*GS* 326). In a note from this period focusing specifically on Stoicism, he echoes Montaigne's suggestion concerning Cato [**6.3**], that Stoic philosophy is an *ex post facto* rationalization of a disposition that fears the passions, and it formulates exercises to fortify the self against its vulnerability to the passions:[14]

I believe one misjudges Stoicism. The essence of this disposition – for that's what it is, before the philosophy conquers it for itself – is its attitude against pain and disagreeable perceptions: a certain weightiness, pressure, and inertness are heightened to the extreme in order to feel but little pain: stiffness and coldness are its anaesthetic devices. The primary intention of Stoic education: *to annihilate easy excitability, to restrict more and more the number of objects that can affect at all,* belief in the contemptibility and low worth of most things that arouse the passions, hatred and hostility against excitement, *as if the passions themselves were a sickness* or something ignoble: scrutiny for all ugly and distressing revelations of suffering – in sum: petrification as a remedy against suffering, and henceforth all the high names of divine virtue are offered before a statue. (*KSA* 9:15[55])[15]

More generally, Nietzsche's new ethics rejects the central ethical *teloi* of the classical and Hellenistic philosophies: it does not aim at radical detachment vis-à-vis the world, perfect tranquillity or total insensitivity to the agitation of the passions. Rather Nietzsche's positive ethics entails a practice of the self open to the passions as possible instruments of self-affirmation and self-enhancement. In defining his own morality Nietzsche's declares that 'he abhors every morality that says: "Do not do this! Renounce! Overcome yourself!" But I am well disposed towards those moralities that impel me to do something again and again from morning to evening and to dream of it at night, and to think of nothing else than doing this *well*, as well as *I* alone can!' (*GS* 304) Nietzsche's ethics then entails both an openness to the many drives of the self and the affirmation of value judgements that cultivate an all-consuming passion to exercise and perfect those drives that lend themselves to realizing personal distinction. If negative virtues slander the natural drives, Nietzsche's positive morality endows them with value as means to our self-affirmation. Such a morality focuses on affirming an ideal goal, rather than on prohibiting certain drives or passions; they are exclusively *for* something, not *against* something. Nietzsche supports positive moralities that make what we do (the all-consuming pursuit of personal distinction) determine what we forgo, and opposes negative moralities that make what we must forgo determine what we can do. If some drives fall away from our lives in this case they do so because they are superfluous to our craving to repeat and relive the cherished ideal, not because they are hated or proscribed. 'When one lives that way', as Nietzsche explains, 'one thing after another drops off: without hate or reluctance one sees this take its leave today and that tomorrow, like the yellow leaves that every faint wisp of wind carries off a tree' (*GS* 304).

On the other hand, Nietzsche condemns morality as a proscriptive code as a symptom and cause of disease: 'I do not want to strive for my own impoverishment with open eyes; I do not like negative virtues – virtues whose very essence is … self-denial' (*GS* 304). According to Nietzsche, if we suffer from our natural drives this is by no means a consequence of exercising them, but of the judgement that they are 'evil' (*GS* 294). It is this moral judgement, he argues, that is the 'cause our great injustice towards our nature, towards *all* nature!' (*GS* 294) If we become sick from exercising natural drives, this sickness stems from moral judgements that compel us to interpret and experience them as contemptible or shameful. As Nietzsche sees it, the drives themselves are 'innocent' and cause no suffering or illness unless they are morally slandered. Nietzsche diagnoses moral codes or negative moralities as afflicting us with the disease of self-denial, 'a constant irritability at all natural stirrings and inclinations and as it were a kind of itch' (*GS* 305).[16]

It is the ancient Stoics who are best known for conceiving the inner fortress or citadel as the analogue of philosophical freedom (**4.3–5**; Marcus

Aurelius, *Meds.* IV, 3; Seneca, *Ep.* 82.5). Through Stoic self-control, Nietzsche claims, we risk becoming 'impoverished and cut off from the most beautiful fortuities of the soul! And indeed from all further *instruction*! For one must be able to lose oneself if one wants to learn something from things that we ourselves are not' (*GS* 305). To borrow from Diogenes Laertius, we might say then that in *GS* Nietzsche laments that Stoicism requires taking 'on the colour of the dead', the famous reply Zeno is said to have received from the Delphic oracle when he asked how to live the best life (DL 7.1).

All this is to say that Nietzsche now treats Hellenistic therapies as *objects* of therapeutic treatment, rather than as its *mediums*. From the vantage point of a post-classical philosophical physician, we must develop a therapy to cure the diseases expressed or engendered by these ancient therapies (Ure & Ryan, 2014; Faustino, 2017). As Marta Faustino states, Nietzsche formulates 'a therapy of therapies' (Faustino, 2017), an *anti-Hellenistic* erotic pedagogy. Nietzsche's title *GS* highlights the significance of this erotic pedagogy: it is a German translation of the Provençal subtitle '*La gaya scienza*', which the twelfth-century troubadours used for their art of love poetry. Nietzsche's post-classical normative ethics and therapy attempt to re-channel all the force of love or *eros*, with all its poetic powers of idealization, into precisely those passions and drives that both ancient philosophies and Schopenhauerian asceticism conceive as incompatible with the normative goal of *ataraxia* (**8**).

In *GS* then Nietzsche's enthusiasm for the ancient Hellenistic schools turns into contempt as he begins to diagnose not only Christian asceticism and Schopenhauer's pessimistic weariness with life, but also the Hellenistic therapies as merely different versions of weakness or illness. Nietzsche still endorses the model of the philosophical physician and shares the Stoics' and Epicureans' goal of formulating a naturalistic ethics of human flourishing. But his naturalistic ethics contests their belief that the good life necessarily requires the extirpation or minimization of the passions. To put it in positive terms, in *GS* Nietzsche argues that the suffering of the passions is an integral part of his new ideal of happiness, or what he calls 'superabundant happiness' (*GS* 326). As we shall see below, Nietzsche reworks the ancient doctrine of eternal recurrence as his own 'spiritual exercise' that cultivates this new ideal of happiness.

In this light, we can see more clearly the importance of *GS* in Nietzsche's philosophical odyssey: it expresses the intoxicating recovery of health after his battle with romantic despair and his own temptation to overcome its pessimistic condemnation of the world through a retreat to the inner citadel. By contrast, in the earlier books in the trilogy, Nietzsche 'cured' himself, but only by taking on the colour of the dead, like an 'icing up in the midst of youth ... dotage at the wrong time' (*GS* P 1).[17] Nietzsche's joyful science aims at recovering from the Hellenistic insensibility, its statue-like coldness. 'Gay Science:' he writes 'signifies the saturnalia of a mind that has patiently resisted a terrible, long pressure – patiently, severely, coldly without yielding, but also without hope – and is all of a sudden attacked by hope, by hope for health, by the *intoxication* of recovery' (*GS* P 1).

10.4 Nietzsche's spiritual exercise: Eternal recurrence

Nietzsche's central project is to formulate an alternative to Schopenhauerian pessimism as a response to the discovery that 'God is dead', or that the universe has no metaphysical purpose or redemptive end. How can we love our fate ('*amor fati*') in a purposeless universe? Is it possible to wish, as Schopenhauer put it, that our lives should be of 'endless duration or of perpetually new recurrence' (*WWR* 1: 310)? Following Augustine, as we saw in the previous chapter, Schopenhauer argued that even Stoic sages would not wish for eternal life if it included all the evils that we experience.[18] If a god decreed that they must live such a life eternally, Augustine claims, the Stoics would judge life miserable. Nietzsche aims to refute the Augustinian and Schopenhauerian ascetic denial of the value of life by demonstrating that it is possible to value this life, exactly as it is, as worthy of eternity. Let us first consider Nietzsche's diagnosis of the ascetic ideal before turning to his cure.

Nietzsche argues that it was through his own struggles to cure his personal pessimism he discovered 'where thought is led and misled' when it is subject to the pressure of illness:

Every philosophy that ranks peace above war, every ethics with a negative definition of happiness, every metaphysics and physics that knows some finale, a final state of some sort, every predominantly aesthetic or religious craving for some Apart, Beyond, Outside, Above, permits the question whether it was not illness that inspired the philosopher. (*GS* P 2)

On the basis of this position, Nietzsche argues that psychologists must treat the philosophies of life of the Stoics, Epicureans, Sceptics and Platonists as symptoms of 'the body, of its success or failure, its fullness, power, high-handedness, or of its frustrations, fatigues, impoverishments, its premonitions of an end, its will to an end' (*GS* P 2). They are all variations on a paradoxical or self-defeating will to nothingness; or as Nietzsche famously put it, 'man still prefers to will *nothingness*, than *not* will' (*GM* III. 28). In most cases, as he argues in *GS* Book 5:

> the philosopher's claim to wisdom … is a hiding place in which the philosopher saves himself owing to his weariness, age, growing cold, hardening – as a wisdom of that instinct which the animals have before death – they go off alone, become silent, choose solitude, crawl into caves, become wise. (*GS* 359)

Nietzsche mockingly alludes to Socrates's conception of philosophy as learning how to die and the Stoic ideal of becoming cold and statue-like. That philosophers seek 'wisdom', he implies, is symptomatic of failing, declining, ageing life. In Nietzsche's view the highest ancient philosophical ideals have been those that suit the needs of dying animals. 'Does wisdom', he asks, 'perhaps appear on earth as a raven which is inspired by the smell of carrion?' (*TI* 'Socrates' 1)

What Nietzsche comes to call the ascetic ideal certainly works to redeem the will: it protects the species from 'suicidal nihilism' by giving suffering a meaning. 'The meaninglessness of suffering, not the suffering', as he repeats, 'was the curse that so far blanketed mankind – and *the ascetic ideal offered man a meaning!*' (*GM* III. 28) But this ideal 'saves' meaning and the will only by willing nothingness. By means of the ascetic ideal we save the will by turning against life:

> It is absolutely impossible for us to conceal what was actually expressed by that whole willing that derives its direction from the ascetic ideal: this hatred of the human, and even more the animalistic, even more of the material, this horror of the senses, of reason itself, this fear of happiness and beauty, this longing to get way from appearance, transience, growth, death, wishing, longing itself – all that means … *a will to nothingness*, an aversion to life, a rebellion against the most fundamental prerequisites of life, it is and remains a *will*.
>
> (*GM* III. 28)

Nietzsche then diagnoses how variations of the ascetic ideal have given meaning to depressed ways of life. Platonism (chapter 4), the Hellenistics (chapters 2–3), Christianity (chapter 5) and finally Schopenhauer (chapter

9), he suggests, share a strong family resemblance insofar in different ways they give meaning to and ennoble this hatred of natural life. They preserve 'diseased' life by granting the highest value to life turned against itself or life as preparation for death. They are different shades of nihilism, with Schopenhauer's radical asceticism as the culmination of the contempt for life intrinsic to our philosophical tradition (see Hatab, 2008: 31–2). Nietzsche's overriding hope is to liberate free spirits from the spell of ascetic value judgements or moralities that in one way or another identify the highest life as one that limits, paralyses or denies the expression of drives or 'spirit'. The ascetic ideal has been 'the ultimate "*faute de mieux*" par excellence', but is there a better alternative? (*GM* III. 28).

In *GS* Nietzsche identifies a crisis unique to the modern age: namely the death of God or the decline of these European ascetic moral values. However, he does not lament the death of God, but conceives it as potential historical watershed, or a 'new dawn' (*GS* 343) at least for the free spirits that he addresses. The collapse of 'our entire European morality' opens up the possibility that a few free spirits might be able to forge a new kind of 'superabundant health' (*GS* 326), or '*the great health*' (*GS* 382), which does not deny, but affirms life to the extent of willing its eternal repetition. Against the ascetic idealization of nothingness that he believes lies at the heart of European morality, Nietzsche exhorts free spirits to discover, explore and experiment with new values that facilitate the emergence of higher human or 'overhuman' types who will enjoy an as yet unknown, 'ideal human, superhuman *well-being*' (*GS* 382).[19] Nietzsche ties the realization of this ideal Dionysian pessimism of strength, which, he claims satisfies the Augustinian and Schopenhauerian test of eternity, to his ethics of self-cultivation (see Ure, 2019).

Nietzsche formulates his doctrines of *amor fati* and the eternal recurrence to elaborate a type of 'aesthetic' education that might counter the ascetic ideal in its various guises and open the way to a new affirmation of life. Let us first consider his emphatic declaration of his new love, *amor fati*:

> For the new year. – I'm still alive; I still think: I must still be alive because I still have to think. *Sum, ergo cogito: cogito, ergo sum.* Today everybody permits himself the expression of his dearest wish and thoughts: so I, too, want to say what I wish from myself today and what thought to run first crossed my heart – what thought shall be for me the reason, warranty, and sweetness of my life! I want to learn more and more to see as beautiful what is necessary in things; then I

shall be one of those who makes things beautiful. *Amor fati*: let that be my love henceforth! (*GS* 276)

Amor fati requires a certain state of the soul or type of love that makes it possible to bestow value on our lives and then to internalize this value.[20] 'What means', he asks, 'do we have for making things beautiful, attractive and desirable when they are not? And in themselves I think they never are!' (*GS* 299) Nietzsche in fact argues that we should learn (or re-learn) the artistic capacity to lend or endow value-less objects with value. Against the Stoics and Schopenhauer, Nietzsche's aesthetic education aims to achieve just this end. He suggests we should learn from artists to 'look [at things] through coloured glass or in the light of the sunset, or to give them a skin that is not fully transparent', and that we should become the 'poets of our lives, starting with the smallest and most commonplace details' (*GS* 299). Love, as he conceives it, is not learning about the object as it is 'in itself'; rather, it is learning a particular disposition towards the object that transforms our experience and valuation of it (*GS* 334). Nietzsche does not conceive the love of fate a matter of grace, but as a matter of education,[21] as a skill or technique which we can gradually develop and perfect so that eventually we will be only 'Yes-sayers'. Nietzsche illustrates this aesthetic training by way of analogy with our reception of new music:

One needs effort and good will to bear it despite its strangeness ... Finally comes a moment when we are used to it; when we expect it ... and now it continues relentlessly to compel us and enchant us until we have become its humble and enraptured lovers who no longer want anything better from the world than it and it again ... this happens to us not only in music: it is just in this way that we have learned to love everything we now love. We are always rewarded in the end for our good will, our patience, our fairmindedness and gentleness with what it strange, as it gradually casts off its veil and presents itself as a new and indescribable beauty. (*GS* 334)

Nietzsche gives beauty great importance in his anti-Hellenistic, anti-Schopenhauerian ethics because he assumes that it is closely connected with and motivates a strongly 'eternalizing' love. Creating a beautiful life makes it possible to affirm or celebrate its perpetual recurrence. Love creates this beautiful object, and in doing so makes us prefer this object to all other possibilities and to will its eternal return. In sharp contrast to Schopenhauer, who argued that beauty is an experience of contemplative detachment from will or desire (*WWR* 1: 219–24), Nietzsche argues that it incites will or desire. Nietzsche keys into the idea that the experience of beauty stimulates or even requires the act of replication or repetition (Scarry, 2001: 3). Beautiful objects solicit the desire for their repetition. What defines the love of the beautiful is the desire for the eternal return of the object of love. Learning how to see or hear beauty in one's fate or oneself, Nietzsche implies, is the key to willing the eternal recurrence. If *amor fati* requires learning how to see what is necessary in things as beautiful (*GS* 276), Nietzsche implies, this also applies to how we see ourselves. We can learn to love ourselves such that we become 'humble and enraptured lovers who no longer want anything better from the world than it and *it again*' (*GS* 334 emphasis added).

Eternal recurrence is, as it were, the wish fulfilment of those who have created their own lives. Nietzsche's ethics of self-cultivation idealizes creating a life for ourselves that we would wish to live again and again such that we also wish that eternal recurrence was *literally* true. What kind of life must we create to engender this desire for its recurrence? Nietzsche suggests that it requires individuals to harmonize all the accidents of existence so that they become essential or necessary parts of a beautiful and singular whole. Nietzsche's ethics values above all else the cultivation of the self as a unique, immortal artwork. The great work of art is his model of the affirmative life. Only those who artistically fashion a unique, unrepeatable life, he implies, will wish for its eternal repetition. Nietzsche conceives the idea of an eternally desirable life by analogy to the experience of a work of art: 'We want to experience a work of art over and over again! We should *fashion our life* in this way, so that we have the same wish for each of its parts! This is the main idea!' (*KSA* 11 [165]; see also Nehamas, 1985) We should create ourselves as works of art worthy of eternity:

> Let us etch the image of eternity upon *our* life. This thought contains far more than all those religions, which hold our present lives in contempt as being ephemeral, and which have taught us to raise our sights towards some dubious *other* life. (*KSA* 9: 503)

However, Nietzsche suggests that the thought of eternal recurrence is not simply an expression of a wish, it is also a practice or spiritual exercise that cultivates the self as an artwork. 'If you incorporate this thought within you, amongst your other thoughts', he maintains, 'it will transform you. *If for everything you wish to do you begin by asking yourself:* "Am I certain I want to do this an infinite number of times?", this will become for you the greatest weight' (*KSA* 9:11 [143]). Nietzsche links together the thought of eternity and self-transformation in the famous penultimate section of *GS*[22]:

> *The heaviest weight.* – What if some day or night a demon [Dämon] were to steal into your loneliest loneliness and say to you: 'This life as you now live it and have lived it you will have to live once again and innumerable times again; and there will be nothing new in it, but every pain and every joy and every thought and sigh and everything unspeakably small or great in your life must return to you, all in the same succession and sequence – even this spider and this moonlight between the trees, and even this moment and I myself. The eternal hourglass of existence is turned over again and again, and you with it, speck of dust!' Would you not throw yourself down and gnash your teeth and curse the demon who spoke thus? Or have you once experienced a tremendous moment when you would have answered him: 'You are a god, and never have I heard anything more divine.' If this thought gained power over you, as you are it would transform and possibly crush you; the question in each and every thing, 'Do you want this again and innumerable times again?' would lie on your actions as the heaviest weight! Or how well disposed would you have to become to yourself and to life *to long for nothing more fervently* than for this ultimate eternal confirmation and seal? (*GS* 341)

Nietzsche frames the thought of recurrence not only such that you must suppose that your present self-will re-experience the same life again and again, but also that you must assess this prospect in light of what he calls just three sections prior your 'ownmost conscience' (*GS* 338). Nietzsche's demon challenges you to assess your present life and actions in light of your 'ownmost', or what in *SE* (1874), he identified as your 'secret bad conscience' (*SE* 1). He identifies the law or principle of this conscience in the imperative: 'You should become who you are' (*GS* 270). Our 'ownmost conscience', as he explains it, impels us to follow our own '*path*', a trajectory we follow independently of, and oblivious to anything other than the realization and perfection of our own distinctive set of possibilities (*GS* 338). One of his key objections to Kantian and Schopenhauerian morality is that they both entail 'losing myself *from my path*' by compelling us to follow generalizable rules or to live for others (*GS* 338). Nietzsche's ownmost conscience censures us for betraying our own unique individuality. Nietzsche observes that this morality says, 'Live in seclusion so that you *are able* to live for yourself!' (*GS* 338) Nietzsche's *Dämon* creates this moment of seclusion and separation by stealing into your loneliest loneliness to announce the doctrine of recurrence. He stages the demon's challenge in such a way that we cannot take 'refuge in the conscience of the others' and we must therefore consider the prospect of recurrence strictly in terms of whether our present lives realize our 'personal infinity', an immeasurable gulf between our own individuality and others (*GS* 291).

The thought of eternal repetition is crucial to Nietzsche's ethics of self-cultivation because answering the question 'do you want it again and again?' is the means by which we can disclose our ownmost conscience. Nietzsche assumes that when we examine our lives through the lens of eternity (or eternal repetition) we will judge that only a life that bears the monogram of our own existence, of what is singular or particular to ourselves is worthy of repetition. Eternity makes us hone in upon our singularity. Or to put the point another way, Nietzsche supposes that if we take the view from recurrence we must despair if we discover that our lives are merely replications or minor variations on a common theme. For Nietzsche, what evokes a despairing response to the thought of our own recurrence is not the return of our *suffering*, but the return of a life that is not our *own* (Cf. Reginster, 2006: 217). The thought of recurrence arouses the dread, ultimately, of failing to become who one is.

Nietzsche also stresses that for the thought of recurrence to function as instrument of self-cultivation we must employ it as an experiment or spiritual exercise (Hadot, 1995: 82–109): namely a repeated meditation on the significance of the idea of recurrence. It is an exercise through which we transform our present life so that it becomes such that we would desire its eternal repetition. Following a classical analogy, we can conceive eternal recurrence as a spiritual gymnastic that makes us more adept at imposing the image of eternity on our lives. In this sense, as Hadot recognized, Nietzsche's philosophy follows in the footsteps of the ancient schools idea of philosophy as an art of living (Hadot, 1995: 83, 108; see also Nehamas, 1998). We therefore miss something essential about his doctrine if we conceive it as imagining or believing in recurrence as a logical or theoretical possibility. Nietzsche does not ask us to contemplate recurrence as a theoretical doctrine, but to incorporate the thought of recurrence into our lives as a practice of self-cultivation. Rather than contemplating or imagining recurrence, he asks how you might be transformed if 'this thought gained power over you' (*GS* 341). Nietzsche stresses that thought of recurrence must exercise the force of conscience. As Nietzsche conceives it, the thought of recurrence transforms or crushes us only if it exercises this mastery over our judgement and does so in the sense that 'the question in each and every thing: "Do you want this again and again and innumerable times again?" would lie on [our] actions as the heaviest weight!' (*GS* 341) Nietzsche implies that thought of repetition is only cultivating insofar as it is overpowering, applies to all of our actions and becomes incorporated into our lives as a repeated practice. His ethics of philosophical self-cultivation entails trying to see whether we can live in accordance with the thought of recurrence.

Yet even as Nietzsche conceives eternal recurrence on the ancient conception of philosophy as a technique of self-cultivation, he believes it achieves the opposite of the ancient exercises. According to Hadot, the goal of the ancient exercises is to enable individuals to transcend their individual, passionate subjectivity and ascend to an impersonal, universal perspective (Hadot, 1995: 97). 'Seneca', as he explains, 'finds joy not in Seneca, but in the Seneca identified with universal Reason. One rises from one level of the self to another, transcendent level' (Hadot, 2009: 136). The goal of Nietzsche's exercise, on the other hand, is to rise from the level of a common, collective self to a higher, singular level. If Stoics are necessarily uniform and unvaried, Nietzscheans must be varied and irregular. The Hellenistic idea, as Long puts it, 'is that an understanding of this nature can and should serve as the technologist of the self, shaping our innate potentialities in more life-enhancing ways than cultural norms themselves offer to us. This is not a project of making one's life into an artwork' (Long, 2006: 27–8). By contrast, Nietzsche maintains that the ideal life requires constructing ourselves as unique artworks. Nietzsche assumes then that thought of recurrence is a technique or exercise that can help us to identify and cultivate our unrealized, yet potential singularity. Nietzsche's exercise motivates the desire to create an uncommon life because it implicitly draws on one of the most powerful modern ethical ideals. 'Artistic creation', as Charles Taylor observes, has become 'the paradigm mode in which people can come to self-definition. The artist becomes in some way the paradigm case of the human being, as agent of original self-definition' (Taylor, 1992: 62). Nietzsche's belief that this exercise will cultivate our singularity is contingent on it mobilizing background values, specifically the Romantic value of the self as artwork.

10.5 Conclusion

Like Schopenhauer, then, Nietzsche drew on the ancient model of PWL to challenge the modern professionalization of philosophy. Drawing on his philological studies of the ancient philosophies, especially Diogenes Laertius's *Live of Famous Philosophers*, he maintained that philosophy itself is mode of living and he reprimanded his peers for failing to realize this ideal. In his untimely meditations Nietzsche sought to restore the ancient figure of the philosophical physician, diagnosing the illnesses of modern culture and experimenting with the ancient philosophical therapies to sketch potential cures. In his free-spirit trilogy, Nietzsche sought to apply these philosophical therapies to himself in order to cure himself of his Schopenhauerian pessimism. Nietzsche drew on Cynic, Epicurean and Stoic practices and discourses to restore his equanimity in the face of suffering and misfortune.

However, in *GS*, the culminating text of his trilogy, Nietzsche argued that the classical and Hellenistic normative ideals of *ataraxia* and *apatheia* are merely symptoms of the illness he later called the ascetic ideal. For this reason, he sought to identify and circumscribe a new post-classical philosophical therapy shaped in terms of alternative normative ideal that embraced the suffering of the passions as constitutive of the good life. Nietzsche called this alternative ideal 'Dionysian pessimism'. Like the ancient philosophers, Nietzsche sought to identify spiritual exercises and practices that might enable free spirits to realize this way of life. In doing so, he formulated an anti-Hellenistic, anti-Schopenhauerian philosophical pedagogy. In this context, Nietzsche conceived the thought of eternal recurrence not as a theoretical doctrine that we simply need to understand, but as a 'spiritual exercise', a meditation on the idea of our recurrence that incorporates this prospect into the way we conduct our lives. Nietzsche assumed that if we meditate on the imagined prospect of our own recurrence we will be compelled to cultivate ourselves as singular, immortal works of art. Against Schopenhauer, Nietzsche claimed, it is not the return of suffering that makes the prospect of our recurrence intolerable, but the risk that the lives we repeat will not bear the monogram of our existence. As a philosophical physician, Nietzsche recommends that the cure for pessimism lies not in the denial of life or the realization of equanimity, but in creating ourselves as singular artworks worthy of eternity.

CHAPTER 11
FOUCAULT'S REINVENTION OF PHILOSOPHY AS A WAY OF LIFE

In the last few years of his life, Michel Foucault unexpectedly changed his research focus from the history of modern sexual discourses to ancient Graeco-Roman sexuality and, in turn, to the techniques of the self or spiritual exercises that were central to ancient philosophy. In this chapter, we explore the significance of his 'trip' to antiquity for the tradition of PWL. In the first section, we survey the itinerary of his journey to the ancient world. We show how he challenges conventional histories of philosophy by conceiving ancient philosophies as practices of the self or ways of life rather than simply as theoretical doctrines. Like Ilsetraut and Pierre Hadot, Foucault contributes to modern ethical reflection by rediscovering this ancient philosophy as an ethical work of the self on itself. On this view, as we have stressed throughout, ancient philosophy is meant to form rather than merely inform the subject.[1] Foucault adds an important qualification to this claim. Ancient philosophy, he suggests, also invented a new cultural type: namely the philosophical hero (**10**). In doing so, he implies, it sublimated the archaic ideal of a beautiful existence exemplified by Greek heroes like Achilles and Odysseus. We will focus on Foucault's final lecture series published in English under the title *The Courage of Truth* (1983–4) since it is here that he claims Cynicism epitomized this ancient philosophical heroism. Foucault shows how ancient Cynics aimed to realize the beauty of invulnerability or sovereignty, but through the new means of living the truth. Cynics, as he conceives them, linked together the beautiful existence and the true life by publically displaying and boldly proclaiming their total sovereignty. Living the truth made the Cynic the true sovereign.

In the second section, we briefly examine why Foucault aims to reinvent PWL. Foucault argues that from roughly the sixteenth century onwards, this model of ancient philosophy was practised only on the margins of academic philosophy. Despite its marginality, he nevertheless claims that ancient philosophy, especially Cynicism and Roman Stoicism, constitutes a decisive moment in the history of thought that is 'still significant for our modern mode of being' (Foucault, 2005: 9). One of Foucault's central claims about the significance of ancient philosophy is that it may help us address what he sees as a contemporary problem: the absence of a principle of ethics in the context of scepticism about founding our actions on religious decrees or allegedly scientific notions of normality.[2] Foucault, we might say, looks to antiquity to develop a contemporary ethics without absolute obligations or sanctions. This is a relatively uncontroversial description of Foucault's late work, even if his ambition of reconstituting the ancient philosophical model remains deeply controversial.

In the final section, we explore whether Foucault's own philosophical ethos reclaims 'the living substance of ancient philosophy' (Foucault, 1987: 9). It shows that he conceives Nietzschean genealogy as his own philosophy's 'spiritual exercise' (3). Genealogy, as he puts it, aims to introduce discontinuity into our being. We suggest that Foucault's genealogical practice of self-dissolution necessarily opposes the basic goal of ancient ethics: self-sufficiency or sovereignty. Taking this slant on his philosophical ethos suggests that it does not refashion the ancient practices of the self. Rather, we argue that Foucault's trip to antiquity unintentionally brings to light how contemporary subjectivity is partly constituted by a 'chiastic' crossing of the ancient ethics of self-completion and the modern ethics of self-dissolution.

11.1 Philosophical Heroism: Foucault's Cynics

Foucault's intellectual histories apply what he calls a genealogical knowledge or effective history, which, as he defines it, 'is not made for understanding, but for cutting' (Foucault, 1986: 88). 'Knowledge', as he explains:

> even under the banner of history, does not depend on 'rediscovery', and it emphatically excludes the 'rediscovery of ourselves'. History becomes 'effective' to the degree that it introduces discontinuity into our very being ... 'Effective' history deprives the self of the reassuring stability of life and nature ... It will uproot its traditional foundations and relentlessly disrupt its pretended continuity. (Foucault, 1986: 88)

Foucault's genealogy lacerates our subjectivity by exposing these ontological discontinuities. In his late works, Foucault applies this genealogical method specifically to the history of ancient philosophy.

In contrast with other major interpretive traditions, by adopting a genealogical approach to the history of philosophy, Foucault aims to show that what counts as 'philosophy' is historically variable. In the early 1980s Foucault characterized his overarching research program as the history of "'the games of truth'", through which 'being is historically constituted as experience' (Foucault, 1987: 6–7). Foucault distinguishes among different philosophical practices in terms of the different relationships they established between truth and subjectivity. Foucault therefore rejects the idea we can treat ancient philosophies as early stages in the progressive development of universal reason, or analyse their arguments as answers to perennial philosophical questions. He eschews what we might broadly call these Hegelian and contemporary 'analytic' approaches to the history of philosophy. Foucault's goal is to circumscribe the historically specific forms and practices of ancient philosophies rather than seeing them through the lens of these modern models of philosophy.

Following Pierre Hadot, Foucault distinguishes ancient philosophies as practices of the self or as ways of life (**3, 7**).[3] Foucault affirms Hadot's central claim that 'philosophy in antiquity was a spiritual exercise' (Hadot, 1995: 104).[4] In his 1980s lectures at the Collège de France, he brings into sharp relief how the schools deployed both philosophical doctrines and spiritual exercises as means of giving form to life. Foucault identifies ancient philosophy itself as a kind of bio-technique, or a work ancient philosophers undertook on themselves to transform their own mode of being. As he conceives it, ancient philosophy is a voluntary and deliberate form of self-cultivation; the goal of the ancient philosophical schools is not theoretical knowledge alone, but the transformation or conversion of the self to realize a higher or 'other' mode of existence (e.g. Foucault, 2011: 244–5, 287). For this reason, Foucault does not formulate a history of philosophical *theories* or *doctrines*, nor does he focus on analysing the validity of the arguments of ancient logic, physics or ethics. Rather, he seeks to sketch 'a history of forms, modes, and styles of life, a history of the philosophical life … as a mode of being and as a form both of ethics and heroism' (Foucault, 2011: 210).

We can begin to unpack the significance Foucault attributes to his research for modern ethics by briefly sketching how this ancient model of philosophy as technology of the self or spiritual exercise recast fundamental aspects of archaic, pre-philosophical culture. In *The Hermeneutics of the Subject* (1981–2) lecture series, Foucault argues that we can conceive ancient philosophy as a synthesis of the philosophical goal of delimiting what makes it possible for the subject to access the truth and what he identifies as the 'pre-philosophic theme' of 'spirituality' (Foucault, 2005: 15; see **7.3** above). How is 'spirituality' woven into the fabric of ancient philosophy? Foucault identifies two distinct elements of pre-philosophic 'spirituality': (a) the conditions of access to truth and (b) the effects of obtaining truth.

In the first case, he defines spirituality as 'the search, practice and experience through which the subject carries out the necessary transformations on himself in order to have access to the truth' (Foucault, 2005: 46). Spirituality establishes a particular relationship between truth and subjectivity: namely 'there can be no truth without a conversion or transformation of the subject' (Foucault, 2005: 15). 'Spirituality', he explains, 'postulates that the truth is never given to the subject by right … [or] by a simple act of knowledge … that for the subject to have the right of access to the truth he must be changed, transformed, shifted, and become … other than himself' (Foucault, 2005: 15). Ancient philosophy took up the archaic practice of 'spirituality' by assuming 'that a subject could not have access to the truth if he first did not operate upon himself a certain work which would make him susceptible to knowing the truth – a work of purification, conversion of the soul by contemplation of the soul itself' (Foucault, 1986: 371). Here Foucault embroiders Pierre and Ilsetraut Hadot's account of ancient philosophy and its 'spiritual exercises' (**3**).

As we have seen [**Introduction, 3.3**], both Hadots take the view that spiritual exercises or technologies of the self make possible 'a profound transformation of the individual's mode of seeing and being. The object of spiritual exercises is precisely to bring about this transformation' (Hadot, 1995: 83 (**3**)). According to Ilsetraut Hadot, as saw in **Chapter 3**, Stoic philosophy has two parts: the doctrinal and the paraenetic (or hortatory), including its spiritual exercises. Stoicism requires both parts, because it is not enough to know its doctrines: 'one must digest them, assimilate them, let oneself be transformed by them with the help of incessant spiritual exercises' (Hadot, 2014: 40).

We can see in Seneca's depiction of philosophy as a self-transformative practice, the second aspect of spirituality Foucault entwined in ancient philosophy, namely, the self-transfiguration that flows from the ascent to truth. 'Spirituality', as he explains:

> postulates that once access to truth has really been opened up, it produces effects that are, of course, the consequence of the spiritual approach taken in order to achieve this, but which at the same time

are something quite different and much more: effects which I will call 'rebound' effects of the truth on the subject. (Foucault, 2005: 16)

By accessing the truth, ancient subjects did not 'merely' acquire knowledge, they underwent a profound ontological transformation. As Foucault explains, in the ancient context, 'the truth enlightens the subject; the truth gives beatitude to the subject; the truth gives the subject tranquility of the soul ... in access to the truth, there is something that fulfils the subject himself, which fulfils or transfigures his very being' (Foucault, 2005: 16).

In his final lecture series, *The Courage of Truth* (1983–4), Foucault extends his account of how ancient philosophy transmuted archaic culture. To live philosophically, in the ancient sense, as he conceives it, is to embody truth in a certain style of life. Foucault claims that the Cynics embodied the purest distillation of ancient philosophy insofar as they distinguished themselves precisely by their mode of life rather than by their theoretical discourse (Foucault, 2011: 165, 173–4). As Schopenhauer observed, the Cynics 'were exclusively *practical* philosophers' who gave 'no account of their theoretical philosophy' (*WWR* 2: 155). Schopenhauer and Foucault's treatment of the Cynics also overlaps in their identification of a fundamental difference between 'the spirit of Cynicism' and religious asceticism (WWR 2: 155; see **9.3** above). If humility is essential to religious asceticism, they suggest, heroic 'pride and disdain for all other men' are essential to Cynicism. Schopenhauer quotes the Roman lyric poet Horace's opening *Epistle* dedicated to the study of philosophy to capture the Cynic's heroic pride: 'It is true that the sage is second only to Jupiter, rich and free and honoured and beautiful and a King of kings' (Epist. I.1 107–08).[5]

Similarly, Foucault suggests that the Cynics are paradigmatic of ancient philosophy insofar as they sought to realize the heroic ideal of sovereignty by scandalously living the truth. Cynicism, he claims, expressed ancient philosophy's signature motif: namely 'the philosophical life as heroic life' (Foucault, 2011: 210). Let us consider these two points in turn.

In transferring Cynicism from the margins to the centre of ancient philosophy, Foucault defaces the widespread post-Hegelian representation of Cynicism as philosophically irrelevant compared with Plato and Aristotle's systematic theoretical discourses. In sharp contrast, far from dismissing Cynicism as a marginal, theoretically impoverished ancient school, Foucault sees it as 'a sort of essence ... of any possible [ancient] philosophy, the form of philosophical heroism in its most general, rudimentary, and also demanding aspect' (Foucault, 2011: 210). While the philosophical mode of life varied across the ancient schools, Cynicism, as a manifestation and act of truth, he asserts, contained the matrix for all these schools. By stripping back theoretical doctrine to the bare minimum and 'practicing the scandal of truth in and through one's life', he argues, the Cynic distilled the essence of ancient PWL (Foucault, 2011: 174). Cynicism, as he explains, makes 'truth itself visible in one's acts, one's body, the way one dresses, and in the way one conducts oneself and lives … Cynicism makes life, existence, *bios*, what could be called an alethurgy, a manifestation of truth' (Foucault, 2011: 172).

Foucault argues that the Cynics are the *quintessential* ancient philosophers in the way that they placed their stamp on the new philosophical kind of heroism that circumscribed the whole of ancient philosophy. All ancient philosophical school aimed to radically transform their practitioners' and students' ordinary selves and ways of relating to conventional values (**9**). This is one larger stake in Socrates's critiques of the ancient sophists, who traded in the currency of convention, and who taught citizens to use reason as weapon for wielding power over others and achieving immortal fame for themselves. Indeed, as we saw in **Chapter 1.6**, Socrates sought to turn the tables on his Athenian accusers by repudiating traditional conceptions of honour as shameful or deficient. Socrates defended philosophy as the true heroism against its corrupt Homeric version; he wants the philosopher to supplant Achilles and Pericles as the new Greek hero. In his apology, as we saw in **Chapter 1**, Socrates put his fellow Athenians' honour code on trial: 'Are you not ashamed to give attention to acquiring as much money as possible, and similarly reputation and honour, and giving no attention or thought to truth and the perfection of your soul?' The 'mad Socrates', Diogenes put into practice an extreme version of the Graeco-Roman philosophers' radical criticism of honour ethics. This is the force of the Cynic motto 'deface the currency'. Because of their deeply unconventional manner of living independently of, or, as in the case of the Cynics, with scandalous contempt for these worldly values and practices, many of their contemporaries saw ancient philosophers as estranged from human affairs (**9**).

However, it is too simplistic to suggest that ancient philosophers simply repudiated their own culture's ethics of honour. Rather more accurately we might say that they sought a new basis for achieving what Hannah Arendt called 'the classical ideal of uncompromising self-sufficiency' or 'sovereignty' (Arendt, 1958: 234). By contrast with the Homeric heroes, the ancient philosophers followed a novel, unconventional means of attaining sovereignty or self-sufficiency: they sought to exercise rational self-control rather than wield political power or master fickle fortune. In this sense, ancient philosophy sublimates rather than denies the pagan ethics of honour.

In his lectures on the Cynics, Foucault conceives this new philosophical heroism then as a transmutation of the archaic Greek aesthetics of existence. He argues that Cynicism sublimates the desire for glorious sovereignty that distinguished pre-philosophic heroic culture. Foucault observes that the 'aesthetics of existence', the concern for a beautiful existence, was already completely dominant in Homer and Pindar (Foucault, 2011: 162). In this pre-Socratic tradition, 'the care of the self', he writes, was 'governed by the principle of a brilliant and memorable existence' (Foucault, 2011: 163). Foucault suggests that ancient philosophy did not replace, but recast the archaic 'principle of existence as an oeuvre to be fashioned in all perfection' (Foucault, 2011: 163). Following Socrates, he claims, the Cynics too 'inflected, modified, and re-elaborated' the archaic Greek concern 'for a beautiful, striking, memorable existence' (Foucault, 2011: 163). What the Cynic aims to stake out is exactly the relationship between this 'beautiful existence and the true life' (Foucault, 2011: 163); his is 'the search for a beautiful existence in the form of the truth and the practice of truth-telling' (Foucault, 2011: 165).

How should we understand the *aesthetic* element of the art of living Foucault identifies as central to Cynicism (and ancient philosophy as a whole)? Nietzsche gives us a line on Foucault's thinking. 'The Greek philosophers', he claimed, 'went through life feeling secretly that there were far more slaves than one might think – meaning that everybody who was not a philosopher was a slave. Their pride overflowed at the thought that even the most powerful men on earth belonged among their slaves' (*GS* 18).[6] In the context of Foucault's analysis of ancient philosophy, the notion of the 'aesthetics of existence' encompasses the creation of a specifically noble or sovereign life sharply opposed to an enslaved life. Ancient philosophy, as he sees it, proposes to achieve such a beautiful, noble existence and challenges the dominant Homeric *paideia* for misleading citizens about how to achieve it (see Gouldner, 1967).

Foucault's claim that ancient philosophy recalibrated Homer's and Pindar's celebration of the archaic and Olympian hero's brilliant and memorable existence entails qualifying the 'technical' conception of ancient philosophy's aesthetics of existence (see Sellars, 2020). In the ancient sense of the term, *technē* is a skill or craft like those of rhetoric, medicine or navigation. As Foucault sees it, the Cynics' (and ancient philosophers') art of living certainly required the application of techniques of the self or spiritual exercises. Ancient philosophers deployed techniques of living analogous to those of ordinary, skilled technicians, but they did so only for the sake of shaping a life whose beauty lay in its nobility or sovereignty. Ancient philosophy, Foucault explains, is one of the aesthetic forms Graeco-Roman culture gave to 'man's way of being and conducting himself, the aspect his existence reveals to others and himself, the trace also that this existence ... will leave in the memories of others after his death' (Foucault, 2011: 162). Foucault's sketch of the way ancient philosophy recalibrated Homeric glory highlights how the ancient philosophical life was shot through with, and set out to transform the heroic, pre-Socratic dream of immortality. On Foucault's view, that is, the ancient Cynics made their lives objects of aesthetic elaboration for the sake of creating a life far more exalted than the greatest Greek heroes.[7]

We can see this rivalry between archaic and philosophical heroism writ large in the famous mythical encounter between Diogenes the Cynic and Alexander the Great:

As he was sunning himself in the Craneion, Alexander stood over him and said, 'Ask whatever you wish of me', and he replied, 'Stand out of my light'. (DL VI, 38)

Foucault's analysis of this Cynic *chreia* illuminates how ancient philosophy challenged standard Greek conceptions of heroism (Foucault, 2011: 275–7). It stages an apocryphal confrontation between symbolic opposites: the greatest political ruler who possesses an insatiable desire for worldly glory and the naked Cynic beggar who finds perfect serenity in his impoverished, bare life. In this celebrated confrontation, we witness an extraordinary role reversal: the true king is not the political king, who enjoys worldly sovereignty, but the philosopher king, who enjoys nothing other than sovereignty over himself. The Cynic poses as the King of kings. Since through Cynic *askēsis* Diogenes has made himself entirely self-sufficient, he needs nothing from Alexander and can treat him with sublime indifference. Crowned, visible sovereigns like Alexander, as Foucault explains, 'are only the shadow of true monarchy. The Cynic is the only true king. And at the same time, vis-à-vis kings of the world ... he is the anti-king who shows how hollow, illusory, and precarious the monarchy of kings is' (Foucault, 2011: 275). Diogenes claims true sovereignty because unlike Alexander, he exercises sovereignty without depending on anything external; he has defeated his internal enemies, his faults and vices; and he is invulnerable to all reversals of fortune (Foucault,

2011: 276–7). By contrast, even the sovereignty of the greatest king is intrinsically vulnerable to external and internal enemies, to misfortune and vice. Alexander is not a true king, but a slave to fortune. Only the Cynic attains unwavering sovereignty or invulnerability. Only philosophy delivers true sovereignty.

11.2 Foucault's reinvention of PWL

To what end does Foucault recall this ancient model of philosophy as a way of life and rehabilitate the ancient Cynic as the quintessence of its philosophical heroism? In the first instance, comparably to one of Pierre Hadot's preoccupations [see 5.1, 6.1, 7.1, 8.4], Foucault simply aims to chart and explain its gradual eclipse in modern culture. From antiquity through to the sixteenth century, he maintains, philosophers had continued to address the ancient question: 'What is the work which I must effect upon myself so as to be capable and worthy of acceding to the truth?' (Foucault, 1986: 371). Though Foucault is wary of identifying a specific moment when philosophy rejected the necessity of practices of self-transformation or spiritual exercises, we saw in 7.4 how he nevertheless loosely deploys the phrase 'Cartesian moment' to mark this break in the history of the relation between the truth and the subject (Foucault, 2005: 14, 17).[8] With Descartes's claim that direct evidence is sufficient to know the truth, and that therefore *any* subject who can see what is self-evident can attain knowledge, modern culture, he argues, largely jettisoned the ancient notion that one must work on the self to get to the truth. 'I think the modern age of the history of the truth', as he explains:

> begins when knowledge itself and knowledge alone gives access to the truth. That is to say when the philosopher ... or scientist ... can recognize the truth and have access to it in himself and solely through his activity of knowing, without anything else being demanded of him and without him having to change or alter his being as subject. (Foucault, 2005: 17 [see 7.1, 7.3 above])

After this 'moment', Foucault claims, for the most part philosophers held that asceticism is unnecessary to know the truth. 'Knowledge of intellectual knowledge', or knowledge for its own sake, he argues, 'gradually limited, overlaid, and finally effaced the "knowledge of spirituality"' (Foucault,

2005: 308). Of course, Foucault recognizes that even with the demise of this ancient conception of the relationship between truth and subjectivity, subjects still needed to satisfy certain conditions to access knowledge, including formal, cultural and 'moral' conditions (e.g. a commitment to truth over self-interest). Yet none of these conditions, he observes, concern the transformation of the subject's being, 'they only concern the individual in his concrete interest, and not the structure of the subject as such' (Foucault, 2005: 18). After the Cartesian moment, he argues, the ancient techniques of the self – purifications, ascetic exercises, conversions and so on – became epistemically superfluous. According to Foucault, therefore, we have arrived at a fundamentally different form of the experience of the relation between the subject and truth. At this point, he argues 'the relationship to the self no longer needs to be ascetic to get into relation to the truth ... Thus I can be immoral and know the truth. I believe that this is an idea which, more or less explicitly, was rejected by all previous cultures. Before Descartes one could not be impure, immoral and know the truth' (Foucault, 1986: 372). Philosophers now accede to the truth without fundamentally altering their subjectivity and without this acquisition of knowledge producing any ontological transformation, or enlightenment, beatitude or tranquillity. 'We can no longer think that access to the truth', as he puts it, 'will complete in the subject, like a crowning reward, the work or sacrifice, the price paid to arrive at it' (Foucault, 2005: 19). 'As such', he explains, 'henceforth the truth cannot save the subject' (Foucault, 2005: 19).

Foucault recognizes, however, that modern philosophy never completely effaced ancient philosophy. In fact, he draws attention to Schopenhauer and Nietzsche (among others) as illustrative of a nineteenth-century European protest against the eclipse of ancient philosophy (Foucault, 2005: 251). As we have seen, Schopenhauer and Nietzsche did not conceive the demise of the ancient model of PWL, and the partitioning of truth and transformation, as a cognitive gain that properly respects the limits of philosophy. Rather they claimed that this modern severance of truth from transformation, knowledge from spirituality was a historically contingent cultural, institutional and pedagogical shift and one that modern philosophers can and ought to reverse (see Schopenhauer, 2014: 149–213). Drawing on Schopenhauer as his exemplar, as we saw in **Chapter 10**, Nietzsche waged an untimely campaign against modern academic philosophy precisely for the sake of reviving the model of ancient PWL. Nietzsche did not conceive PWL as theoretically bankrupt or historically moribund. Rather he sought to reinvent it. Like Schopenhauer and Nietzsche, Foucault identifies the severance of philosophy from spirituality, truth from transformation, as a theoretical shift, the so-called Cartesian moment that became deeply entrenched in philosophical practice partly because of its institutionalization as a university discipline. 'When philosophy becomes a teaching profession', as he puts it, 'the philosophical life disappears' (Foucault, 2011: 211).

However, Nietzsche saw it as his task not simply to explain its demise, but to reclaim philosophy conceived as an art of living (Ure, 2019). Foucault, it seems, also seeks to reconstitute philosophy as practice of self-transformation and he identifies this as plausible option for developing an ethic that does not turn on metaphysical, theological, legal or scientific claims. He draws a parallel between our struggle to establish an ethics and the situation of the ancients that makes their model of philosophy seem like a viable contemporary option. Ancient citizens, he claims, practised an 'aesthetic of existence' independently of religious dogmas or legal constraints (Foucault, 1986: 343). Foucault wonders whether we might reinvent this aesthetics of existence in which rule-following is advocated and practised for the sake of giving style to one's life. Significantly, he also claims that his own philosophical ethos is continuous with the living substance of ancient philosophy. Yet, as we shall see in the next section, it is far from clear that Foucault's Nietzschean-inspired *askēsis* is compatible with ancient practices of the self.[9] On closer inspection, we discover in Foucault's work two discordant, yet equally compelling ethical practices of the self.

11.3 Genealogy as a spiritual exercise

How does Foucault's alternative philosophical ethos compare with the ancient practices of the self? We can begin to answer this question by examining his use of the genealogical method as a spiritual exercise. Foucault contrasts his own philosophical practice with what he derides as an illegitimate type of 'philosophical discourse' that presumes to 'dictate to others, to tell them where their truth is and how to find it'. His own reinvented ancient model of a 'philosophical exercise', differently, would involve the subject working on and changing itself in the game of truth (Foucault, 1987: 9). For Foucault, self-transformation is the point and purpose of philosophy, if we assume, as he does, that philosophy still is what it was for the ancients: namely an *askēsis* or an exercise of oneself in the activity of thought:

What is philosophy today ... if it is not the critical work that thought brings to bear on itself? In what does it consist, if not in the endeavor to know how and to what extent it might be possible to think differently instead of legitimating what is already known? ... philosophical discourse ... is entitled to explore what might be changed, in its own thought, through the practice of a knowledge that is foreign to it. The 'essay' – which should be understood as the assay or test by which, in the games of truth, one undergoes changes ... is the living substance of philosophy. (Foucault, 1987: 8–9)

Nevertheless, as Hadot sometimes does, Foucault seeks to distinguish between what he sees as still remaining alive for us in ancient philosophy and what has fallen into desuetude. In modern culture, Foucault assumes, the metaphysical aspects of ancient philosophy are dead. Foucault hence shows no interest in analysing the validity of the great metaphysical constructions of ancient philosophy like Plato's theory of ideas, Epicurean atoms and void, and the all-pervading fiery Stoic *pneuma* or *logos*. Yet he nonetheless asserts that its practices of the selfremain alive. Foucault identifies ancient philosophy's vital element with its foundational premise that one plays the game of truth for the sake of self-transformation.

Foucault defines his genealogical 'philosophical exercise' as exemplifying this kind of game of truth. The object of this exercise, as he puts it, 'was to learn to what extent the effort to think one's own history can free thought from what it silently thinks, and so enable it to think differently' (Foucault, 1987: 9). The living substance of ancient philosophy, he implies, continues to flourish precisely in his own genealogical research. In his reinvention of ancient philosophy, Foucault accords genealogy a position analogous to the ancient spiritual exercises of 'conversion'. Genealogy is Foucault's spiritual exercise.

We can see how through his genealogical exercise he seeks to reinvent the ancient philosophical ethos in a brief, yet remarkable passage in which he declares that he does not conceive the self-transformation that takes place through the practice of 'games of truth' as superfluous or irrelevant backstage drama to the main philosophical act. In one of the rare moments that he addresses his readers in the first-person singular, Foucault elaborates his personal motivation for investigating the ancient practices of the self. 'It was curiosity', he explains, 'the only kind of curiosity ... that is worth acting upon with any degree of obstinacy: not the curiosity that seeks to assimilate what it is proper for it to know, but that which enables one to get free of oneself' (Foucault, 1987: 8). After all, he asks rhetorically, 'what would be the value of the passion for knowledge if it resulted only in certain amount of knowledgeableness and not ... in the knower's straying afield of himself?' (Foucault, 1987: 8) Foucault clearly implies here that his own practice of genealogical investigation is a form of 'spirituality', the conversion or transformation of the self, and identifies it as an expression of what he calls the passion for knowledge.

What sense can we give to Foucault's strange locution 'the passion for knowledge'?[10] His use of this phrase is not incidental or accidental: it alludes to Nietzsche's analysis of the drive to knowledge, which he (Foucault) had directly addressed in a 1971 lecture on Nietzsche (Foucault, 2013: 202–19) and his more polished essay from the same year 'Nietzsche, Genealogy, History' (Foucault, 1986: 76–101). It is worth dwelling on the significance of Foucault's allusion since it illuminates the nature of the conversion of the self that he believes results from the Nietzschean passion for knowledge.

In his 1971 lecture, Foucault observes that Nietzsche distinguished free-spirited philosophers as having renounced the happiness that subjects derive from strong, enchanting illusions (see *D* 429). Instead these free spirits, Nietzsche suggested, pursue knowledge to the point of maliciously violating the basic inclination of our spirit to delight in beautiful appearances (*BGE* 229, 230). 'Knowledge', as he put it, 'has in us been transformed into a passion which shrinks at no sacrifice' (*D* 429). Nietzsche identifies this passion for knowledge as the source of certain kind of sublimity, which, like all things sublime, constitutes a confrontation with mortal vulnerability. 'This will to appearance, to simplification, to mask, to the cloak, in short to the superficial', he asserts, 'is *counteracted* by that sublime inclination in the man of knowledge which takes a profound, many sided and thorough view of things and will take such a view: as a kind of cruelty of the intellectual conscience' (*BGE* 230).[11] According to Nietzsche, free-spirited philosophers, who sacrifice their own beautiful illusions, do so in the belief that they derive a much higher form of exaltation under the 'compulsion and suffering of *this* passion for knowledge' (*D* 429). In his notes, he implicitly contrasts this heroically sublime willingness to sacrifice oneself in the service of the passion for knowledge with the ancient ethics of knowledge:

People have warbled on to me about the serene happiness of knowledge – but I have not found it, indeed, I despise it, now I know the bliss of unhappiness of knowledge. Am I ever bored? Always anxious, heart throbbing with expectation or disappointment! I bless this misery, it enriches the world thereby! In doing so, I take the slowest of strides and slurp down these bittersweet delicacies. I no longer want any knowledge without danger: let there always be the treacherous sea or the merciless high mountains around the seeker of knowledge. (*KSA*: 9, 7 [165])

In his 1971 lecture Foucault develops the implications of Nietzsche's account of the passion for knowledge for his own account of the relationship between knowledge and subjectivity. Glossing *GS* 333, Foucault observes how Nietzsche conceives the passion for knowledge as allied

with malice – mockery, contempt, hatred. It does not involve recognizing oneself in things but keeping one's distance from them, protecting oneself from them (by laughing), differentiating oneself by deprecating them (despising), wanting to repulse or destroy them (*detestari*). Murderous, deprecatory, differentiating – knowledge is neither of the order of *homoiōsis*, nor of the good. (Foucault, 2013: 204–5)

Foucault suggests that this 'murderous' knowledge of ourselves does not aim to free us from conventions or contingencies so that we can return to ourselves, or to pure being. Rather, we should understand Nietzsche's passion for knowledge as a 'malice' specifically 'turned also towards *the one* who knows' (Foucault, 2013: 205). Foucault recounts how Nietzsche identifies the malice of the new passion for knowledge as the will to transgress our heart's desire to affirm, love or worship beautiful appearances or illusions. In this sense, Nietzsche suggests that the knower is an artist of self-cruelty (*BGE* 141). As Foucault understands it, this passion for knowledge is a malicious will to go:

Behind the surface of things to seek out the secret, to try to extract an essence behind the appearance, a power behind the elusive flickering, a mastery … But it is also what can recognize that there is still only appearance in this secret finally broken open, that there is no ontological foundation. And that man himself, who knows, is still and always appearance. (Foucault, 2013: 205)

Unlike the Christian and modern hermeneutics of desire that Foucault made the object of genealogical analysis in the *History of Sexuality* [see

5.2 above], this Nietzschean passion for knowledge does not discover an ontological foundation, which one can either liberate or repress. It dissolves every appearance of a stable, permanent self, an ontological foundation. In place of any deep foundations, Nietzsche's genealogy of the subject identifies irreconcilable discord among competing drives. Unlike Descartes or Spinoza [**7.3**], Nietzsche discovers nothing divine or 'eternally resting in itself' in the subject, only the *'heroism'* we might discover in our 'warring depths' (*GS* 333). Nietzsche held that an unconscious war among its drives accounts for most of the subject's activity. Foucault approvingly quotes (in truncated form) *GS* 333's penultimate line: 'In all knowledge there may be something heroic, but nothing divine' (Foucault, 2013: 204).

If, then, we conceive Foucault's genealogical spiritual exercise as an expression of this passion for knowledge, then this *askēsis* takes on a more problematic appearance than we might otherwise think, if we take at face value his suggestion that he revitalizes ancient philosophy. First, Foucault conceives his genealogical practice of the self as an exercise of malice towards oneself that is required in order to tear oneself away from oneself. In order to introduce discontinuity into our being, as we noted, Foucault practices a genealogical exercise that 'deprives the self of the reassuring stability of life and nature' (Foucault, 1986: 88). Foucault's metaphorical description of the change one undergoes through the exercise of this passion for knowledge pictures the subject as led astray from predictable paths and wandering with no fixed route or known destination. Foucault stresses that for him philosophical curiosity only has value to the extent that it is a work on oneself, and that this practice is not a return to (*epistrophe*) or rebirth of oneself (*metanoia*), as in the ancient and Christian models,[12] but the paradoxical practice of freeing oneself from oneself. To follow Foucault's metaphor, this *askēsis* cultivates a permanently straying subject.

Foucault's earlier use of Nietzschean language and figures to describe the effects of the passion of knowledge dramatizes this change as a break of the self with itself rather than a return to the self. Foucault's description of the passion for knowledge that motivates his genealogical spiritual exercise highlights the 'price' the subject pays for playing this particular game of truth. In his earlier analysis of Nietzsche, Foucault suggests that 'the murderous relentlessness of knowledge' sets itself against 'the welcoming mildness of a phenomenon', or, in other words, against consoling appearances or illusions (Foucault, 2013: 206). In this sense, Foucault's exercise entails that the price for playing this game of truth is a type of self-sacrifice. He implies that this exercise introduces permanent discord into our being. If the passion for knowledge relentlessly 'murders' all phenomenon or appearances, as he puts it, 'this work … is never rewarded with access to being or the essence, but gives rise to new appearances, sets them against one another and beyond one another' (Foucault, 2013: 206). What this work on the self discovers beneath appearances is not a permanent, eternally self-sufficient subject, rather it unleashes a war among the drives analogous to the competition for supremacy among heroic warriors.

Foucault's genealogical exercise, as he conceives it, then, entails a 'systematic dissociation of identity', which reveals not 'a forgotten identity, eager to be reborn', but a complex system of distinct, competing elements (Foucault, 1986: 94). 'The purpose of history, guided by genealogy', as he puts it, 'is not to discover the roots of our identity, but to commit itself to its dissipation' (Foucault, 1986: 94). Indeed, Foucault suggests that this genealogical exercise not only dissolves the unity of the subject into competing forces and drives, it also risks the destruction of the subject of knowledge. As a genealogical exercise, Foucault maintains, 'the will to knowledge does not achieve universal truth; man is not given a serene mastery of nature'. Rather, it 'multiplies the risk, creates dangers in every area; it breaks down illusory defenses; it dissolves the unity of the subject; it releases those elements of itself that are devoted to its subversion and destruction' (Foucault, 1986: 96). 'Knowledge', as he explains this point, 'does not slowly detach itself from its empirical roots … to become pure speculation subject only to the demands of reason; its development is not tied to the constitution of and affirmation of a free subject; rather it creates a progressive enslavement to its instinctive violence' (Foucault, 1986: 96). Foucault conceives genealogical exercises as a call 'for experimentation on ourselves' that risks the 'destruction of the subject who seeks knowledge in the endless deployment of the will to knowledge' (Foucault, 1986: 96, 97).

We can now begin to take the measure of the break Foucault's genealogical *askēsis* effects with the ancient practices of the self that we surveyed in earlier chapters. Foucault maintains, as we have seen, that ancient philosophies presuppose that access to the truth 'will complete in the subject, like a crowning reward, the work or sacrifice, the price paid to arrive at it' (Foucault, 2005: 19) insofar as the truth 'fulfils the subject himself … fulfils or transfigures his very being'. Foucault summarizes the Hellenistic and Roman conversion of the self in terms of the idea of the movement towards the self, 'the subject must advance towards something that is himself' (Foucault, 2005: 248). In Hellenistic and Roman antiquity, Foucault argues, the 'self basically appeared as the aim, [and] end of an uncertain and possibly circular journey – the dangerous journey of life' (Foucault, 2005: 250). In this context, he writes, 'the path towards the self will always be something of an Odyssey' (Foucault, 2005: 249). Foucault picks out 'this prescriptive figure of the return to the self' as a singular event in the history of Western culture. He identifies this 'theme of the return to the self' as what in a 'complicated, ambiguous and contradictory way' a whole section of nineteenth century thought (and we can think of Hegel's Odyssey of the world Spirit) sought to reconstitute (Foucault, 2005: 251).

By contrast, Foucault's own philosophical *askēsis* does not complete the subject, rather it tears the self from itself without rewarding the subject with access to being or essence. This *askēsis* then has no crowning reward; access to genealogical truth does not grant the subject beatitude or tranquility (8). Instead, Foucault generates an ethics of permanent self-dissolution and discord, which he conceives as a condition of freedom. Genealogical diagnosis identifies 'virtual fractures' within the self 'which open up … a space of concrete freedom, that is, of possible transformation' (Foucault, 1996: 449–50). Through Foucault's philosophical *askēsis* the subject becomes different from itself or goes astray from itself, and does so over and over again. Freedom, as he conceives, is not realized by coming into alignment with nature or the cosmos, the fulfilment of a telos or essence, but through an exercise in the creation or invention of the new. The ethical question is not "How can I model myself on eternal being (e.g. Plato/neo-Platonism) or live according to nature (e.g. Cynic, Stoic and Epicurean) or create myself as an artwork worthy of eternity (e.g. Nietzsche)?' but 'What new game can we invent?' (Foucault, 1996: 312). To this extent, Hadot's famous critique of Foucault's return to the ancients as enshrining a distinctly modern, aestheticist vision, or a new dandyism, is not unmotivated.

In Foucault's 'philosophical ethos', which he describes as a '*limit-attitude*', freedom is a continuous, infinitely renewable exercise of inventing new norms, and pathology is the inability to transgress the limits of present norms (Foucault, 1986: 45). That is to say, Foucault conceives his genealogical critique of the present as an exercise of the self on itself that aims at generating new norms of practice and new modes of living. 'It is true', he asserts:

> that we have to give up the hope of ever acceding to a point of view that could give us access to any complete or definitive knowledge of what may constitute our historical limits. And from this point of view the theoretical and practical experience that we have of our limits

and of the possibility of moving beyond them is always limited and determined; thus we are always in the position of beginning anew. (Foucault, 1986: 47)

Foucault's *askēsis* is a practice of constant self-dissolution in the absence of any eternal horizon (see also Ure & Testa, 2018). In contrast to the ancient models, by casting the self adrift from any identification with nature, life or being, Foucault's *askēsis* stands in principled opposition to the classical ideal of a transformation of the self that brings it to completion, beatitude or tranquillity. If we view this new philosophical way of life through the lens of the Stoic philosophical *askeses*, for example, it can only appear as pathological. Ironically, Foucault's analysis of the Stoic goal of self-completion and self-sufficiency reveals exactly how his own version of *askēsis*, which makes a virtue of constantly seeking to become other to oneself, is at odds with Stoicism's fundamental normative and therapeutic orientation (Ure, 2007). From the Stoic perspective, Foucault's *askēsis* of going astray from oneself is symptomatic of a failure to care for oneself. Foucault himself recognizes that the Roman care of the self was 'not a way of marking an essential caesura in the subject' (Foucault, 2005: 214). As he observes, the Stoics deployed a series of terms to refer to a break between the self and everything else, but these terms did not refer to a 'break of the self *with* the self' (Foucault, 2005: 212, emphasis added). Foucault's own notion of *askēsis*, in other words, seems to take up the Hellenistic and Stoic conception of philosophy as a work on the self, yet he severs it from its normative ideal of rational self-sufficiency and the analysis and critique of the emotional pathologies that it seeks to cure. Viewed through the lens of Stoicism, Foucault's celebration of limit experiences that create radical caesuras within the self can only be seen as symptomatic of a failure to understand, analyze and treat the emotional agitations which compel the subject to constantly seek out another place, another time or another self.

We do not have to endorse a classical or Hellenistic perspective to recognize the troubling, difficult implications of Foucault's *askēsis*. Foucault's critics have focused on the alleged normative deficit in his philosophy, and even contemporaries who defend his ethics recognize its practical and psychological risks. Beatrice Han-Pile, for example, suggests that there is a 'threat' in his support for a practice of the self that is an exercise in self-displacement and self-estrangement. Rather than fostering an identification with a set of core features or desires, she suggests, Foucault's *askēsis* is practice of 'self-dehiscence' (Han-Pile, 2016: 99). She conceives genealogy as an exercise that might cut open and introduce discontinuities within our being, but in doing so risk creating permanent wounds. 'In its most radical form', she contends, 'Foucault's conception of critique as practice of the self would prevent identification with any aspect of the self and most likely result in a personality disorder' (Han-Pile, 2016: 99).

11.4 Conclusion

How are we to assess the significance of Foucault's reinvention of philosophy as a way of life? In studying ancient Greek and Roman philosophy, Foucault saw himself as continuing a practice 'fundamental to Western philosophy': namely 'to examine both the differences that keep us at a remove from a way of thinking in which we recognize our origin, and the proximity that remains in spite of that distance which we never cease to explore' (Foucault, 1987: 7). By means of this chiasmus, Foucault suggests that we cannot understand ourselves unless we examine our origins in ancient practices that are both distant and near, familiar and foreign.

This chapter has nevertheless stressed the ethical distance between Foucault's genealogical spiritual exercise and the ancient practices of the self. Foucault's exercise aims to create radical discontinuities between the self and itself so that it can ceaselessly experiment with new ways of living, whereas the ancient exercises aim to return the self to its true, universal form or being so that it can realize divine self-sufficiency. From the vantage point of the ancient perspective, Foucault's *askēsis* constitutes a pathological dissolution of the subject, while from his perspective, ancient ethics must be an exercise in the stagnation rather than emancipation of the subject.

We are perhaps today the inheritees of both types of spiritual exercises, exercises of ceaselessly getting free of oneself and of returning to oneself. Foucault's genealogy serves to illuminate this ethical tension between ancient and modern versions of philosophy as a way of life. Because we have inherited these two incompatible practices of the self, we can discover freedom in constant self-dissolution and imprisonment in permanent self-completion, and yet also experience enslavement in infinite ontological discord and freedom in harmonization with our true nature or being. Perhaps Nietzsche's image of modern free spirits as akin to Odysseus, but without his hope of returning to Ithaca, beautifully renders the ethical chiasma that Foucault's work bespeaks, and which we must each navigate:

In the horizon of the infinite – We have forsaken land and have gone to sea! We have burned our bridges behind us, indeed – we have destroyed the very land behind us! Now, little ship, look out! Besides you lies the ocean: it is true that it does not always roar and from time to time it lies spread out like silk and gold and reveries of goodness. But hours will come when you will realize that it is infinite and that there is nothing more terrible than infinity. Oh, the poor bird that has felt free and now strikes against the walls of this cage! Woe, when homesickness for the land overcomes you, as if there had been more *freedom* there – and there is no longer any 'land'! (*GS* 124)

CONCLUSION: PHILOSOPHY AS A WAY OF LIFE TODAY AND IN THE FUTURE

1 PWL today

The question of 'what is philosophy?' has been contested for as long as the word has been in circulation, apparently beginning with Pythagoras. Its signification remains disputed amongst those concerned to claim it. Many of the confusions hail from philosophy's ancient status as the cradle of all of what we now call the social and natural sciences, and before them, what were dubbed the 'liberal arts' throughout the medieval period [**5.4**]. In the mid-seventeenth century, for example, Descartes (at Overgaard, Gilbert, & Burwood, 2013: 19) was still able to claim that philosophy 'encompasses everything which the human mind is capable of knowing', 'both for the conduct of life and for the preservation of health and the discovery of all manner of skills'. More recently, with hardly less generality, Wilfred Sellars has claimed that philosophy has as its aim 'to understand how things in the broadest possible sense of the term hang together in the broadest possible sense of the term', where 'under "things in the broadest possible sense", I include such radically different items as not only "cabbages and kings", but numbers and duties, possibilities and finger snaps, aesthetic experience and death' (Overgaard, Gilbert, & Burwood, 2013: 21).

Of course, for some time now, biologists and horticulturalists have claimed epistemic jurisdiction over cabbages and kindred fauna; as political scientists have claimed the same authorities concerning kings and duties, and mathematicians concerning numbers. Philosophy as it has been institutionalized in modern universities has seen its ancient extension gradually shrinking. First, the 'natural philosophies' (physics, biology, chemistry); and then disciplines like psychology, sociology, anthropology and political science (the human or social sciences) have declared their disciplinary independence. Given these developments, a radically deflationary scepticism is possible. This would hold that 'philosophy', as per one of Quine's formulations, is merely an administrative category: 'one of a number of blanket terms used by deans and librarians in their necessary task of grouping the myriad topics and problems of science and scholarship under a manageable number of headings', so the fact that two scholars' respective researches are labelled philosophical 'makes neither man responsible for the other's topic' – nor, presumably, any woman (Overgaard, Gilbert, & Burwood, 2013: 20).

Philosophy departments nevertheless continue to operate, and to lay claim to relatively well-defined disciplinary object domains. With some variations, including complexities arising from the ungainly twentieth-century 'continental-analytic divide' (e.g. Prado, 2003), a number of core sub-disciplines are generally taught in Western and Western-shaped philosophy curricula: logic, epistemology, metaphysics, ethics, political philosophy, the philosophies of language and of mind, and the history of philosophy. Academic philosophers continue to teach new generations of students specialized ways of thinking and speaking, and to introduce them into long-standing traditions of debate, with canonical texts and thinkers looking back to Plato or his Socrates. We set our charges what Hadot calls intellectual exercises (2), in essays and examinations, with the hope of fostering meaningfully 'philosophical' epistemic virtues: an independence of mind tempered with due respect for tested authorities, curiosity tempered with scepticism, a breadth of vision bounded by conceptual precision, and the abilities to analyse, synthesize, organize and express complex ideas and systems of ideas in written forms. We ourselves research and write philosophy, as well as teach, although increasingly we write only in a small number of genres (refereed articles and chapters, monographs and book reviews) in a historically very limited number of sanctioned methods and styles.

It is not the place here to rehearse the anxieties about the future of academic or 'disciplinary' philosophy which have been notably expressed in Robert Frodeman and Adam Briggle's (2016) study, *Socrates Tenured*. We write and teach as philosophers today in a situation in which such anxieties are multiplying. Philosophy, like other academic disciplines, finds itself in a context in which the institution of the Western university itself, looking all the way back to Plato's Academy [4.1], is being profoundly challenged by the ascendancy of 'market imperatives' in conceiving and administering higher education. The emergence after the 1970s of, firstly, Hadot's works on PWL, then the growing number of studies on or using this approach to philosophy and its history after 1990, has coincided with the period in which these challenges to philosophy and traditional scholarship have gathered momentum. It is therefore inevitable to see the two contemporary phenomena as related in significant ways. Everything happens as if the growing interest sparked by Hadot's work in excavating the different manners in which philosophy has been conceived in the past speaks to a growing contemporary sense of the need to radically reconceive what philosophers do, and which goods it might serve, in the new millennium. If we know what philosophy has been, and the different social, intellectual, spiritual and pedagogical conditions in which it has been undertaken in the past, we can also weigh different possibilities for what it might become, as well as different models to critique and reform what we presently do. Contra a well-known *mal mot*, there may be alternatives.

We will return to these kinds of critical, reflective considerations to close the book. But first, we want to take stock of the alternative history of philosophy that our PWL approach has enabled us to write, and second to address recurrent criticisms of the idea of PWL.

2 History, declines and rebirths

Our aim in this book has been to present a history of the developments of the ancient idea of PWL identified by Pierre Hadot, with premier reference to Stoic and Epicurean sources, but looking back iconically to the *atopia* of Socrates. We flagged in the introduction how adopting a PWL perspective, by reshaping our conception of philosophy, also enables the historian of philosophy to pose and explore different questions than those which occupy other historiographies. What exactly were the stages, if there were stages, that had to unfold for Western philosophical thought to pass from Socrates's pursuit of the examined life to the life of the academic professional today? When exactly did the conception of PWL cease to be the predominant one in the West? And because of what reasons or combination of intellectual, institutional, social, political or religious conditions did this change occur? What modulations of the idea of PWL are possible, and have been explored in the history or histories of philosophy?

As a means to gain analytic purchase in addressing these (admittedly huge) questions, we introduced two innovations in the present PWL literature.

- The first was a division of some eleven species of spiritual and intellectual exercises, as a way to try to bring unity to a subject upon which scholars, following Hadot's own equivocations (1995: 79–125; 2020, 55–62), continue to differ (Sorabji, 2000: 211–42; Foucault, 2006: 425–6; Fiordalis, 2018; Harter, 2018; Sharpe & Kramer, 2019) – namely if ancient philosophers prescribed and practised spiritual exercises or 'technologies of self', just how many and what kinds of exercises did these include?

- Our second heuristic innovation was a larger division of some ten different components of philosophical activity (pictured in the 'tennead' figure) which the meta-philosophical idea of PWL asks us to attend to when we consider old philosophers. As we have proceeded, we have been signalling the places and ways that different philosophers have spoken of or embodied these ten *topoi*: (**1**) the institutional, pedagogical aspects of philosophizing, the intellectual (**2**) and (**3**) spiritual exercises; (**4**) the conceptions of parts of philosophy and philosophy's relations to other disciplines; (**5**) the turn inwards; (**6**) the plurality of written (and spoken) genres; (**7**) meta-philosophical metaphors, and visions of the good (**8**), of the many; (**9**), and of the sage or saint (**10**). In the course of our accounts, again, we have been careful to distinguish the intellectual and spiritual exercises practised and recommended by the different philosophers, from Socrates to Nietzsche.

So, let us consider the tables in Appendixes 1 and 2, which present what has emerged from our history of PWL using these respective heuristics. What do they tell us concerning the history of PWL we have charted here? The red thread running through the two tables is the dedicated subject of **Table 1**, and of column 3 in **Table 2**: *that of the spiritual exercises*. The presence of recommendations concerning these exercises, and of philosophical activities carried out in accordance with them, is the preeminent mark of the difference between academic philosophy today and the ancient Hellenistic and Roman schools. **Table 2** also allows us to point to the increasing disappearance of accounts of the good life (column 8), depictions of the sage (column 10) and especially the medicinal-therapeutic meta-philosophical metaphors (column 7) in philosophers after the renaissance, notably countered by Schopenhauer's and Nietzsche's competing attempts at reviving PWL on new terrain (see **vii** below). When we arrive at Foucault's 1960–70s work (**Chapter 11**), we have post-Nietzschean genealogy as a critical intellectual exercise bearing on history alone. The ancient exercises of meditation, attention, premeditation, examination of conscience, taming of passions and the view from above or eternity are all absent, to become in Foucault's later work the object of critical historical research (2006).

However, our account here suggests at least seven reasons to carefully qualify any simplistic 'decline of PWL' narratives. This, whether we identify the decisive 'fall' moment with the patristics (see Foucault, 2018), the scholastics (Domański, 1996), Bacon (Gaukroger, 2001), Descartes (Foucault, 2006) or the advent of the Napoleonic and Humboldtian universities in the first decades of the nineteenth century.

i. Firstly, within antiquity, the sceptical tradition already operates a narrowing of the scope of philosophical exercises within the PWL paradigm [**4.2**]. The sceptics take the Socratic turn inwards; they assign priority to the examination of one's representation; they aspire to achieve *ataraxia* and to tame the passions. But their singular focus on the assessment and critique of one's inner representations, and the barrage of the *procheiron* tropes, removes the grounds and need for meditation, attention, contemplation and reframing ways of seeing. This is especially historically portentous, given the enormous significance of the recovery of ancient scepticism in the renaissance, and its role in shaping the conceptions of both the experimental and mathematical-rationalist lineages of early modern natural philosophy [**6.3, 7.2–7.4**].

ii. Secondly, as Hadot (1995) and Domański (1996) detail, the medieval period sees a splitting off of the spiritual exercises, which are Christianized within forms of monasticism (in which the holy life of the Saint supplants the ideal of a sage [**5.2**]), from the intellectual exercises of the ancient schools, which are integrated into the pedagogy and syllabi of the scholastic universities [**5.3–5.4**]. When the two are looked at alongside or each other, as in **Table 1**, we see that the full range of ancient philosophical exercises was present within medieval Christendom. However, the pagan forms of philosophy which had presaged them were subordinated to Christian forms of life and theological inquiry.

iii. Thirdly, as Domański and Ruedi Imbach have convergently shown, in certain dissident scholastic thinkers like Boethius of Dacia, there is a recovery of the ancient notion of philosophy as the highest form of life [5.4]. But the table underscores that this recovery, based on the reading of Aristotle, was itself partial. A form of metaphysical contemplation modelled on that delineated in *Nicomachean Ethics* X, 7 is the only spiritual exercise, even as the philosophical *vita contemplativa* is heretically valorised (**Table 2**). The range of meditative, premeditative, passion-taming and attention-directing exercises prescribed in Epicureanism and Stoicism is not recovered.

iv. Fourthly, as Celenza (2013) and Domański (1996) have underscored, there was a more or less complete recovery of the idea of PWL in the Italian and then Northern Renaissance [**6.1**]. This was based in the largescale recovery of lost Hellenistic and Roman sources, and involved competing attempts to render sceptical, Stoic and even Epicurean discourse consistent with different Christian professions. Given the nearly complete disappearance of figures like Petrarch [**6.2**]), Erasmus, Montaigne [**6.3**] and Lipsius [**6.4**], figures at the heart of renaissance humanism, from nineteenth- and twentieth-century philosophy syllabi, this renaissance of PWL deserves underlining. This recovery of humanism as less a 'metaphysics' than a pedagogical and meta-philosophical programme is arguably one of the most significant results of the new perspectives on the history of philosophy shaped by PWL.

v. Fifth, in the wake of this humanistic recovery of PWL, the Baconian and then Cartesian moments represent a second, decisive but in no way final (see below) moment in the decline of this meta-philosophical paradigm. **Table 1** shows that we can indeed find almost all of the spiritual and intellectual exercises in Bacon's encyclopaedic philosophical productions. Nevertheless, care is needed here. When Bacon recommends the spiritual exercises of 'custom, exercise, habit, education, example, imitation, company, friends, praise, reproof, exhortation' (*Adv.* II, XXII, 7), it is under the heading of the 'Georgics of the mind' [**7.2**]. These exercises are not identified with philosophy per se, but as one subpart of a division of philosophy, that of morality. At the same time, as we see played out in the royal society *virtuosi*, the forms of attention and self-examination which in the Stoics or Epicureans (for instance) were intended to engender ethical transformation in the ancients, become directed in his work towards the formation of new cultures of collective experimental inquiry into (pre-eminently) the natural world [**7.4**]. By contrast, scholars continue to disagree with how to interpret Descartes's recourse to the literary genre of the meditations, with the later Foucault the most famous voice assigning epochal significance to Descartes's new method [**7.3**]. Even if we grant with the earlier Foucault, Hadot, Rorty and others that this recourse, as well as Descartes's famous adaptation of ancient sceptical arguments, marks out Descartes's continuity with premodern practices of philosophy, his reconception of philosophy involves an avowedly anti-humanistic project of re-founding inquiry on putatively more certain, systematic foundations. In the royal society thinkers [**7.4**], the *virtuoso* is pre-eminently a particular kind of inquirer, whose philosophically cultivated virtues are pre-eminently epistemic, serving to temper his intellectual more than his practical judgement.

vi. Sixth, as we have seen, the remarkable figure of the enlightenment *philosophe*, as pre-eminently exemplified by Voltaire [**8.2**] and Denis Diderot [**8.3**], reflects an eclectic familiarity with and uptake of classical meta-philosophical ideas. Diderot devotes his last work to a passionate apologetic reconstruction of Seneca's life and philosophical works. Nevertheless, if philosophy is a way of life for these figures, it is the life of the eclectic, humane critic, *litterateur* and thinker; a figure whose preeminent ancient avatar is in fact the ancient sceptic, or Cicero, whom Voltaire tellingly declared was worth more than the philosophers of Greece (Voltaire, 2004: 335; Sharpe, 2015). The view from above emerges at key moments, especially in Voltaire. But it is not prescribed as part of a larger regimen for life. Both Voltaire and Diderot are differently critical of the efficacy or goals of Hellenistic thought. The view from above is instead advertised to readers in fictions and philosophical *aperçus*, as a literary means to shake readers' theological and metaphysical presumption, in Voltaire, and to give vivid force to a dynamic, materialistic vision of the world in Diderot. For all of their literary *elan*, and their effortless spanning of genres from poetry to dialectic, the *philosophes*, unlike many of the ancients they admired, did not write handbooks, *hypomnemata* or meditations.

And most of their best lines are given to a farrago of fictional characters.

vii. Finally, **Table 1** highlights the extent to which Schopenhauer (**Chapter 9**) and Nietzsche (**Chapter 10**) operate a second 'renaissance' of PWL. Their works reanimate the medicinal metaphor for philosophizing (**Table 2**). They renovate a range of spiritual exercises which in Nietzsche's middle period are explicitly celebrated as being drawn from the Hellenistics, and which include, in his case, the pivotal 'eternal recurrence'. Nevertheless, we have seen at the same time how this rebirth of PWL operates under quite different conditions than the renaissance of PWL which we saw in Petrarch, Montaigne and Lipsius (**Chapter 6**), and against the background of fundamentally different, post-Kantian intellectual presuppositions, than PWL's first renaissance. Both Schopenhauer and Nietzsche adopt comparable meta-philosophical aspirations and prescriptions to Socrates, the Stoics and Epicureans. However, they radically call into question the wisdom and sufficiency of the ancients' conceptions of the goal of philosophy. Schopenhauer posits a kind of post-Christian ideal of Sainthood, in place of the apathic ancient sage [**9.3**]. Nietzsche, striking out against Schopenhauer, embraces forms of tragic suffering as the means, at least among the few, to forge a new or 'higher' man [**10.4–5**].

3 Criticisms

Our first aim in this book has been reconstructive, not critical. As we began by saying, we have tried to bring together the insights of the growing number of scholars globally working on different figures and periods of PWL. In many cases, we have proposed insights of our own. This Primer aims to bear out the extent to which PWL represents a revolutionary approach to the history of philosophy, with potentially radical implications for how we consider philosophy in this troubled moment. Nevertheless, like any radical prospect, PWL has not failed to attract its share of criticisms and, arguably, misunderstandings as well. We cannot address all of these here. It is however worthwhile to address four kinds of such criticisms which, in our experience, recur with great frequency whenever research inspired by Hadot's work is discussed, and as such merit a dedicated assessment.

i. The loss of philosophy – as a specific way[s] of thinking?

The first of these kinds of criticisms hails especially from philosophers and scholars of ancient philosophy trained in the analytic tradition (but cf. Aubry, 2010). It argues that Hadot's vision of ancient philosophy as involving the prescription of spiritual exercises, and hence a form of self- or other-transformation meaningfully describable as a kind of 'conversion', is misguided in both historical fact and philosophical principle. One of us has addressed these criticisms in greater detail elsewhere, so we need only lay out the key stakes of the disputes (Sharpe, 2014; 2016; 2021). John M. Cooper in particular claims (2012: x, 17–22, 402–3, n. 4–5) that Hadot's vision of ancient philosophy per se wrongly extrapolates out from an account of philosophy at the end of antiquity, once it had become contaminated by religion. The first accounts of spiritual exercises, he argues, are to be found in Roman Stoicism, which as such has a liminal place in his reconstruction of the ancient 'pursuits of wisdom'. In making this claim, Cooper negates the ample evidence in doxographies concerning the *atopia* of philosophers, before and after Socrates, and therapeutic works, now lost, written by the ancient Stoics, as well as the many ancient consolations looking back to the classical sophists. He is moreover forced, we believe indefensibly, to question the 'mainline' philosophical *bona fides* of Epicurus, the author of the letter on Menoeceus and the epitomes, as well as the Cynics and Pythagoreans (Cooper, 2012: 17, 31, 62, 226–7; cf. Nussbaum, 1994: 137–8; Sharpe, 2021). Any account of ancient 'philosophy' which reshapes how the ancients saw the extension of the term is an exercise in understanding them better than, not as they understood themselves.

Underlying Cooper's historical claim, in any case, is the *de jure* claim that any account of philosophy which sees its role as extending beyond 'logical, reasoned argument and analysis' – by proposing that students also undertake mnemonic, imaginative or physical exercises with the aim of self-transformation – cannot truly *be* 'philosophy' (Cooper, 2012: 17).[1] In her comments in *Therapy of Desire* on Michel Foucault's work on the 'technologies of the self' advocated in the Stoics and Epicureans, Martha Nussbaum (1994: 5–6) makes a nearly identical claim about the later Foucault's reconstructions of ancient philosophy. Ancient Hellenistic philosophy was intended to be therapeutic, Nussbaum documents. But its therapies, as philosophical, can have involved forms of argumentation alone.

The problem here is in fact acknowledged by Nussbaum's favoured ancient philosopher, Aristotle, when he comments:

> But the mass of mankind, instead of doing virtuous acts, have recourse to discussing virtue, and fancy that they are pursuing philosophy and that this will make them good men. In so doing they act like invalids who listen carefully to what the doctor says, but entirely neglect to carry out his prescriptions. That sort of philosophy will no more lead to a healthy state of soul than will the mode of treatment produce health of body. (*Nic. Eth.* II 4, 1105b)

What Aristotle is acknowledging here is the insufficiency of being theoretically persuaded as to the desirability of some transformed, elevated state of being like *ataraxia*, for actually *achieving* such *ataraxia*. What will be required is a work of *ethismos*, involving forms of repeated meditation upon the truths one has accepted, and their practical corollaries, as well as trying, then failing, then trying again to become better at living according to these principles, 'the way in which men train themselves for some contest or pursuit; they practice continually' (Aristotle, *NE*: 1114 a11–12). One way we might persuade analytically trained readers of this point would be to point to accounts of the learning of skills or *technai* in the work of someone like Julia Annas (2011); if for the ancient Stoics, philosophy is the exercise of a *technê* for living, we can understand that its intellectual component must shape and be shaped by constant practice, until Stoicism becomes as a second nature (Sharpe, 2021a).

These are issues of philosophical psychology, and competing accounts of human motivation. The more basic problem is with the implied argument here. This is the contention that:

(a) since some spiritual exercises involve non-rational components (such as memorization, habituation, imaginative visualization, abstinences or the taming of passions); but

(b) philosophy is (truly) a pre-eminently rational form of inquiry, analysis and reflection;

(c) philosophers, as philosophers, can never have prescribed such spiritual exercises.

The basic problem with this argument is that philosophers, like psychologists today, can give accounts of non-rational behaviours, without these accounts themselves becoming thereby 'irrational', any more than someone who describes badness well does not thereby speak badly (Plato, *Euthyd.* 284c-285d; Aristotle, *Soph. Ref.* 20, 177b12–13). Plato and Aristotle write philosophically about the passions as belonging to the sub-rational parts of our *psychai*. Rightly, no one claims that such accounts are 'not philosophical'. The moment one realizes that convincing people through argument to accept a course of life is not sufficient for them to do this successfully, it becomes *pre-eminently* rational to prescribe extra-rational means for them to try to transform themselves, so that over time they do become more philosophical, not simply in their theoretical talk, but in their everyday lives.

It is hence unsustainable to propose that, by showing that many ancient philosophers reasoned in just this manner, PWL disempowers us to distinguish philosophy from religion, rhetoric or banal egoistic 'self-help' (see **iii.** below). It is closer to the truth to say that by advocating regimens of spiritual exercise, these philosophers wanted to extend, not diminish, the hold of reasoned philosophical positions on our lives.

ii. To contextualize, to relativize?

A second form of criticism of PWL argues that the post-Hadotian attempt to reread ancient or other philosophical texts as documents shaped by philosophers' situation within different spiritual traditions, institutions or forms of life necessarily relativizes their claims to truth. This criticism supposes an unmediatable opposition. There is reading a philosophical text as the bearer of truth-claims about language, ethics, physics or metaphysics. Or, there is reading it as an historical document, embodying and representing the presuppositions or outlook of a given school, culture or period. The latter approach lays out all philosophical texts on an equal, agnostic footing, as so many 'perspectives' or 'representatives' of different historical moments. In doing so, such historicism tacitly forecloses the idea that philosophy, as philosophy, lays claim to transcultural, transhistorical truth claims about language, ethics and nature.

Some historians of ideas, led by Ian Hunter (2007), have drawn on the contextualist aspects of Hadot's work to suggest that PWL can be used to take what we might call a 'global' approach to Western thought, with relativistic implications. Hunter has written striking analyses of Kant's metaphysics of morals as the product of a certain conception of the spiritual formation of the philosopher (2002), and of post-Heideggerian 'theory' as a work of cultivating certain kinds of intellectual personae (Hunter, 2006; 2008; 2010; 2016). Followers of figures like Derrida, Deleuze, Badiou or Heidegger, Hunter contends, adopt different ways of seeing the world. As theorists, they lay claim to privileged (ultra-) transcendental insights into the bases of the social and physical sciences, as well as the world more widely. In order to ascend to this perspective, they learn recondite practices of phenomenological bracketing, textual deconstruction or set-theoretical mathematics. Each of these, Hunter says, is its own kind of persona-forming 'spiritual exercise'. It is simply not the task of the intellectual historian to adjudicate between the different first-order validity claims presented by the philosophical personae he anatomizes. Indeed, Hunter exercises his own form of ethico-politically motivated scepticism about the historical claims of metaphysicians and theologians to access and teach higher truths, as one ongoing source of civil disagreement.

It is important to stress that, while Hunter's position is explicitly based upon the contextualizing component of Hadot's post-Wittgensteinian approach to 'old books' (Hunter, 2002: 908), that the latter approach is decisively different. Hadot thinks that the work of contextualization is important to avoid the kinds of mistakes that can be fostered by the recently fashionable, laissez faire idea that a text can mean whatever readers wish, since the author her/himself is not in control of its meanings (cf. Hadot, 2019a). As such, for him as also for Juliusz Domański (1996), it is decisive that we can only talk of PWL when a philosopher announces the idea(s) that philosophy should cultivate the virtues, wisdom, or a certain way of life or preparing for death, etc. This is not the case in Hunter's work. Underlying this difference is an epistemically prior contrast. *For Hadot, the work of contextualization aims at understanding philosophers as they understood themselves.* His grounding concern is that, faced with the apparent strangeness of ancient texts, moderns wrongly project their own expectations onto these texts, thereby mistaking why they were written, with which audiences in mind, and with what goals. As Hadot writes (1995: 61), with the italics being ours:

> It seems to me, indeed, that *in order to understand the works of the philosophers of antiquity* we must take account of all the concrete

conditions in which they wrote, all the constraints that weighed upon them: the framework of the school, the very nature of *philosophia*, literary genres, rhetorical rules, dogmatic imperatives, and traditional modes of reasoning. One cannot [accurately] read an ancient author the way one does a contemporary author.[2]

Such an approach in no way forecloses the possibility that, once we have discerned the validity claims the ancient texts make about logic, ethics, physics or metaphysics, we might not be persuaded that they are true – not simply as performances of some persona, or representative statements of a given historical moment, but as philosophical claims about the way the world is. Here in fact we approach what Hadot sometimes describes as the esoteric, protreptic dimension of his writings on the ancients, whereby he seeks not only to describe but quietly recommend as possibilities the philosophical forms of thinking and living (Hadot, Ilsetraut & Pierre, 2004: 232–2; Sharpe, 2016). At least one Foucaultian commentator (Irrera, 2010) has hence criticized Hadot for his stress on the conception of a universal '*conscience cosmique*' as an essential dimension of ancient philosophy, which he so often seems to sponsor as veridical, as well as describe as historical. Hadot's works on the ancients have even been widely interpreted as pointing the way to new generations retaking up ancient philosophical ideas and practices for themselves, an interpretation which he encouraged in several places (1995: 282–3; 2020, 232).

Yet, we must concede, there is a sense in which Hadot's interpretation of PWL flirts with relativism. In decisive places, Hadot claims that ancient philosophers' 'choice of life' was prior to, and independent of their theoretical reflection. It is '*never* a purely theoretical reflection that determines the choice of life' (Hadot, 2014: 104 [italics added]). Ancient philosophers, he sometimes suggests, formulated theoretical discourses to rationalize their specific 'choice of life' rather than because they were satisfied by the arguments in favour of these discourses. 'Philosophical discourse', as Hadot explains, '*originates* in a choice of life and an existential option – not vice versa … The existential option … implies a certain vision of the world, and *the task of philosophical discourse will therefore be to reveal and rationally justify this existential option*' (2002: 3 [italics added]). The choice of life comes first, independently of reason, and then philosophical discourse comes afterwards as a means to confirm and support this pre-theoretical choice.

Or, as Hadot explains, philosophers begin with a 'fundamental orientation of inner life' and then guide and cultivate their orientation with the help of a specific philosophical discourse (2014: 104). We adopt and defend a specific philosophical discourse only because and to the extent that it enables us to practise and perfect our pre-existing choice of life. Hadot will sometimes talk, in a way which is ambiguous, of the 'reciprocal causality between theoretical reflection and choice of life' (2011: 104). Philosophical discourse does not decide on the goal we set for ourselves, this is set by our inner orientation; it simply helps us see more clearly the path we must follow to get to this goal. 'In other words', as Hadot explains, 'theoretical reflection already supposes a certain choice of life, but this choice of life can progress and specify itself only as a result of theoretical reflection' (Hadot, 2011: 104). It seems to follow from Hadot's perspective that a person with an inner orientation towards pleasure will adopt Epicureanism because it allows this orientation to flourish, independently of an assessment of the larger validity of the theoretical doctrines; and Stoics already possess statue-like indifference to the passions, so they choose Stoicism because it is conducive to and justifies their character (see Nietzsche, *KSA* 9, 15[55]; **9.3**). Philosophical discourse, it is implied, is necessarily an *ex post facto* rationalization of an ungrounded choice of life. Any contemporary return to PWL must address the issue of whether philosophical discourse is simply an instrument of our choice of life, or whether, as its critics insist, this view itself constitutes a betrayal of reason.

iii. Care of the ego?

'To take care of oneself may seem egocentric', as Hadot puts it succinctly (2009: 107). 'In the mentality of modern historians', he comments:

> there is no more cliché more firmly anchored, and more difficult to uproot, than the idea according to which ancient philosophy was an escape mechanism, an act of falling back upon oneself. In the case of Platonists, it was an escape into the heaven of ideas, into the refusal of politics in the case of Epicureans, into the submission to fate in the case of the Stoics. (Hadot, 1995: 27)

Critics assail PWL's commitment to an ethics of self-cultivation as a form of egoism, whose ideal of godlike self-sufficiency encourages withdrawal and social disengagement. Hegel's philosophy of history developed perhaps the most widely influential criticism of the Hellenistic philosophers' conceptions of inner freedom. Hegel reads the Socratic 'turn inwards' at the heart of PWL (5) as a pathological symptom of the Roman Empire's lack of moral unity. The decay of political freedom under the Roman Empire, which granted the emperor absolute sovereignty and individuals only abstract, 'lifeless' private rights, compelled the latter to render themselves indifferent to the real world: 'the whole state of things urged them to yield themselves to fate, and to strive for a perfect indifference to life – an indifference which [one] sought … in freedom of thought' (Hegel, 1900: 329). This Hegelian criticism suggests that the emergence and popularity of PWL, in the Roman Empire and again today, is symptomatic of an experience of an inhospitable socio-political world that motivates individuals to relinquish active citizenship and withdraw into themselves.[3]

A cognate criticism is also raised here. In striving to become akin to serene, untroubled gods, this criticism goes, ancient philosophers risk becoming emotionless statues, 'inhumanly' indifferent to the things of this world.[4] Is the ancient ideal of *ataraxia* or *apatheia* an intelligible or tolerable ideal for us, today? As we have seen, Bacon, Diderot, Schopenhauer and Nietzsche all ask whether Socrates's or the Stoics' wisdom is less the epitome than the antithesis of the good life. Surveying the various ancient expressions for the philosophical principle of the care of the self, Foucault observes that to our ears they can sound like a 'melancholy … expression of the withdrawal of the individual who is unable to hold onto and keep firmly before his eyes … a collective morality (that of the city-state, for example), and who, faced with the disintegration of this collective morality, has naught else to do but to attend to himself' (Foucault, 2005: 13).

Hadot acknowledges that the question whether the ancient philosophical life promotes elevated forms of egoism is a 'complicated problem' (2011: 107). He concedes that there is 'a *permanent danger of egoism* in the efforts one makes to perfect oneself, *especially from the ancient perspective*, where one seeks *ataraxia* or peace of mind' (2011: 106 [italics added]). Nevertheless, both he and the later Foucault argue that these accusations rest on anachronisms and misunderstandings. In the ancient philosophies, Hadot repeatedly stresses, the goal of the ancient exercises was nothing if not to enable individuals to ascend beyond their individual, passionate, egoistic subjectivity to a more impersonal, universal, 'superior' perspective (Hadot, 1995: 97; 2009: 107; 2020, 199–201, 230–1). Philosophical care of the self, he emphasizes, is not 'at all a concern for well-being, in the modern sense of the term … it consists in becoming aware of what one really is, that is finally, of our identity with reason, and even, with the Stoics, with reason considered as God' (2011: 107). 'Seneca', as he put it, 'finds joy not in Seneca, but in the Seneca identified with universal Reason. One rises from one level of the self to another, transcendent level' (Hadot, 2011: 136; 2020, 199–201, 230–1).

One can always nevertheless query whether PWL does not therefore instate a 'higher' egoism of ascending to divine wisdom and serenity in place of the 'lower' egoism of gratifying our desires; Socrates's philosophic pride rather than Callicles's worldly pride, and also, as Lucian and other satirists have perennially wondered, whether encouraging youths to attempt such self-elevation does not inescapably risk producing forms of worded, pretentious vanity (Lucian, 1959: 261–79). Against this, PWL's emphasis on matching deeds to words seems better placed to combat this vocational hazard than other forms of solely discursive philosophy.

Nor are the self- and other-transformative philosophies we have studied in this book necessarily symptomatic or supportive of political quietism or disengagement, Hadot and Foucault argue. On the contrary, all the ancient schools, including Epicureanism, Hadot claims, sought to have an 'effect on their cities, transforming society, and serving their citizens' (1995: 274; 2020: 50–1). The ancient ethics of self-transformation each took shape through collective social practices, not just individual practices, he stresses (see Testa, 2016; McClintock, 2018). We have repeatedly shown throughout this book, in **Chapter 2** through **5**, how ancient PWL was a collective endeavour enacted through various types of institutional practices, so there is no need to dwell any further this point. Moreover, Hadot claims that the 'concern for living in the service of the human community, and for acting in accordance with justice is an *essential* element of every philosophical life' (1995: 274, italics added).

On the basis of the previous points, it seems to us that we can reasonably reject the view that equates the ancient models of happiness with a narrowly egocentric ethos. Yet, Hadot's claims also require qualification, since the ancient schools had very different theories of justice and evaluations of political action. Once we take cognizance of these differences, it is not clear that we can accept the blanket statement that living in the service of the human community is an essential element of every philosophical life. In ancient PWL, in fact, we can identify a political continuum from the Socratic gadfly and Stoicism's dutiful citizen through to Epicureanism's purely instrumental evaluation of politics and Scepticism's tranquil, non-dogmatic apolitical quietism.

At one end of the spectrum, we have Socrates who, according to his contemporary defenders, aimed to educate his fellow citizens in a new form of what we might call critical or philosophical citizenship (see Villa, 2001: esp. 53).[5] As we saw, in **Chapter 1**, Socrates's philosophical life in fact entailed a fundamental revaluation of the Homeric Greek conception of justice, or the *lex talionis*. Ancient Stoic self-fashioning aimed to motivate citizens to perform their natural and public duties. Unlike the Epicureans, the Stoics claimed that living as a citizen is a natural outgrowth of '*oikeiosis*' or our natural impulse towards affiliation, which begins with an attachment to oneself and proceeds outwards in concentric circles to family, community and eventually to the cosmos as a whole. The true Stoic sage then must spurn the life of solitary contemplation to devote himself to civic life, which required not only performing duties owed to fellow citizens, but recalling that he is a citizen of the cosmos with obligation to all rational creatures (see Cicero, *De fin.* III 65, 68). 'The person who takes care of himself properly', as Foucault comments of the Stoics, 'will at the same time know how to fulfil his duties as part of the human community' (Foucault, 2005: 197; see also Lampe, 2020: 26–7; Ure, 2020).

However, at the other end of the political spectrum, we find the ancient Epicureans.[6] The Epicureans, as we have seen, counselled that for the sake of attaining the good life one should avoid politics, assigning it a merely instrumental value. Rather than theorizing justice as a metaphysical reality, which Plato's expressed in his image of perfectly harmonious *Kallipolis*, or as natural law, which the Stoics identified with cosmopolitan community of rational beings, the Epicureans conceived it as merely a changeable set of conventions that citizens endorsed purely for the sake of their own protection. 'For the associates within the Garden of Epicurus', as Melissa Lane explains:

> laws are simply … humanly made conventions, to be judged coolly on the basis of their utility for promoting secure pleasure and avoiding unnecessary pain. Politics may be helpful in helping humans to survive, but it is not the result of a natural impulse to sociability privileging either a local or cosmic *politeia*. It is merely an artificial contrivance, and one that should be designed not to inspire virtuous self-sacrifice, but rather to promote quotidian pleasures … politics may well be useful in achieving a secure tranquillity. (Lane, 2014: 228; see *KD* 33, 37, 38)

If the Epicureans praised a particular form of community, it was only at what Lane calls the 'infra-political level', 'within or below the level of the political community', namely the community of friends within the Epicurean garden (Lane, 2014: 230). It is possible to identify a utopian impulse in this Epicurean ideal of friendship rather than law as the model of community, which envisages the withering away of politics as sphere of contract and coercion. Diogenes of Oeneanda, for example, envisioned that with the spread of Epicureanism 'there will come to be no need of city walls or laws' (21.1.4–14). It remains the case, however, that the political community was peripheral to the Epicurean good life and that adherents to this school have remained subject to criticisms of an egoism that places *ataraxia* over onerous civil service.

Furthermore, while it is historically true that many ancient Stoics, led by Cato the Younger, gave their lives for political liberty, it remains an open question whether in doing so they acted consistently with their ethical doctrine, or that its ethics provides robust motivation for such action. Following Nussbaum, we might call this '*the problem of watery motivation*' or '*the problem of death within life*' (Nussbaum, 2003: 20). Notoriously, as we have seen, the Stoics claimed that the sage is sovereign even on the rack, and Epicureans that he is happy even when roasted alive in the Phaleric Bull. What rational motive can the Stoic or the Epicurean have then for contesting 'abuses' of power or challenging injustices, when they judge that these are indifferent to their freedom or happiness? In other words, if they are committed to the view that happiness is entirely independent of external goods, then these theories, as Nussbaum puts it, '[have] real problems justifying difficult or risky courses of action, which seem to require a greater investment in the world than the letter of the theory can deliver' (Nussbaum, 2001: 374). If virtue alone is sufficient for happiness, we have no reason to lament the loss of freedom, wealth, health or life itself, let alone such externals as republican freedom, or the right to freedom from arbitrary condemnation or imprisonment. Rather than throwing off their chains, the Stoic reasons that they do not matter: 'My leg you will fetter but my moral purpose not even Zeus himself has power to overcome' (*Disc.* I, 1, 25).[7] As Diderot worried [**8.4**], by making the principle of sovereignty or self-sufficiency the regulating component of political action, Stoicism can seemingly easily be appealed to, give priority to this inner freedom over political action that challenges political domination; and to eschew resistance to political tyranny for the sake of maintaining inner purity or sovereignty (see Lampe, 2020;

Ure, 2020). 'What is the straight road to liberty?', Seneca can ask of those facing political oppression: 'any vein in your body' (*De Ira*. 3.15). For critics such as Paul Veyne, Seneca's defence of suicide as an act of liberty:

> reveals Stoicism's profoundest truth, which is to see life from death's point of view and to make its followers live as though dead. Nothing is of significance but the disembedded self, just barely personal, whose existence can be snuffed out without disadvantage because this self is not waiting for anything ... Jean-Marie Guyau ... put it well: 'Death, release from tension, the endless, aimless toil that is life, this is Stoicism's final word'. (2003: 114)

In the words of the advice Zeno allegedly received from Delphic oracle, Stoicism seems to require that citizens 'take on the colour of the dead' (*DL* 7.1).

iv. Death within life?

At this point, we have arrived at the fourth critique of PWL, critics' fears that key forms of PWL's extirpation of the troubling passions or unnatural desires that express a high valuation of worldly goods undermine our motivations, not only for political action, but for full human, life-enriching relationships with others. Advocates of Stoicism attempt to avoid this charge by means of its doctrine of preferred indifferents. Stoics argue that we have a natural elective affinity ('*oikeiosis*') for health, life, family and so on, which make such things naturally valuable to us, and therefore that they are 'preferred' rather than 'dispreferred' indifferents ((*DL* VII 105–107; *Stob*. II 79–85; Cicero, *De fin*. III 20, 52–6). Yet, critics respond, does it really make sense to describe external goods as preferred *and* indifferent, and is this more than a terminological dodge (see Vlastos, 1991: 225; Cicero, *De fin*. IV, 9)? In any case, if such external goods never have any real value, as they maintain, then their highest and constant commitment can only be to the only thing that they believe has absolute value, their own reason or virtue, and they can lose or dispense with preferred indifferents without emotional agitation (see [**1.6**]; Vlastos, 1991: 215–16).

Persistent questions surround whether such an account of preferred indifferents, which seemingly include the well-being and flourishing even of loved ones rob us of the language and motivations to inform the kinds of erotic or passionate investments the good person will have to their family, friends and lovers. As Epictetus famously exhorts:

> In the case of everything that delights the mind, or is useful, or is loved with find affection, remember to tell yourself what sort of thing it is, beginning with the least of things. If you are fond of a jug, say. 'It is just a jug that I am fond of'; then if it is broken, you will not be disturbed, If you kiss your child, or your wife, say to yourself that it is a human being that you are kissing; and then you will not be disturbed if either of them dies. (*Ench.* §3, see §26)

From such a godlike, detached perspective, we should evaluate the loss of our own child as equivalent to the death of a stranger's child, that is, as a matter of indifference (*Ench.* §26). 'Death', Epictetus proclaims, 'is outside the sphere of choice. Throw it aside' (*Disc.* III, 3, 15). Characteristically, Hadot attempts to mitigate the potentially shocking nature of Stoicism's detachment from life. Despite the chilling appearance of indifference, Epictetus, he observes, 'emphasised family affections' (Hadot, 2009: 107). Stoic ethics requires that we exercise 'appropriate actions' (*kathêkonta*), including duties to family members. However, at least as its critics insist, for the Stoics these appropriate actions are not motivated by their love for particular mortals, but only by their aim of maintaining their reason or capacity for making choices consistent with nature (*Ench.* §30). It is only their capacity for virtue that matters to the Stoic, the rest is strictly speaking a matter of indifference (*Disc.* IV, 4, 39).

For its critics, then, Stoic *apatheia*, and by implication the ideal of philosophical tranquillity that continues to inspire philosophers up to Montaigne and Lipsius, comes at too high a price: namely the radical extirpation of the passions that express our attachments to life and to others. Against the Stoics, as Descartes declares, he 'is not one of those cruel philosophers who wish their sage to be insensible' (Descartes, 2015: 25).[8] As we have seen, Schopenhauer claimed the ideal of the ancient sage is unintelligible on the grounds that humans are essentially passionate, embodied creatures. Ancient philosophers, especially the Stoics, he argued, were unable to present the sage 'as a living being with inner poetic truth', as against a 'stiff and wooden … mannequin that no one can engage with' (*WWR* 1: 16). 'If the chilling ritual of reminding oneself, when embracing one's loved ones, that they are mortal beings is somehow supposed to cheer one up', Bernard Williams agrees, then 'we can scarcely find such an outlook either intelligible or tolerable' (Williams, 1997: 2013). Williams's criticism resonates with ancient satires of the 'atopos' Greek sage, an *atopia* which Williams suggests 'always was, in the eyes of most people a foolish and barely intelligible conception, which ministered to a picture of philosophers as strange beings on the boundaries of humanity' (Williams, 1997: 213). In the post-Romantic period, Williams claims, we tend to endorse the view that the variety and power of emotional experience contributes to the value of life, a position which we have seen Nietzsche in particular embracing ([**10.3–10.4**]; Williams, 1997: 213). Erich Auerbach shows how this new conception of the value of passions, especially sublime passions, emerged in secular forms such as the courtly love-poem and climaxed in seventeenth-century French tragedies. Racine's tragedies, Auerbach maintains, crystallize the modern conception and evaluation of the passions:

> The passions ... are the great human desires, and what is particular about them is the clear inclination to regard them as tragic, heroic, sublime and worthy of admiration. At the beginning of the century, the pejorative Stoic judgment is still sounded quite frequently, yet it soon changes into a dialectic combination in which the terrible and the noble unite in the sublime ... it reaches its high point in the tragedy of Racine, whose goal it is to excite and glorify the passions. ... *for the ... spectator the torment and rapture of the passions becomes the highest form of life.* (Auerbach, 2001: 302 emphasis added)[9]

We saw in the previous four chapters how this fundamental shift in the evaluation of the ancient schools unfolded in key modern philosophers. Diderot pitted 'strong passions' against Stoic *apatheia*, and praised Seneca the man despite his conception of the goal of life [**8.4**]. In response to Schopenhauer's lament that the ancient goal of freeing the self from the passions is impossible, Nietzsche celebrated the cultivation of the passions as the source of creative self-transformation [**10.3–10.4**]. Nietzsche firmly identifies his ethics with an explicitly anti-classical ideal of joy, one that demands pursuing 'the path to one's own heaven ... through the voluptuousness of one's own hell' (*GS* 338). Yet by 'the voluptuousness of hell' as Nietzsche puts it, 'no sage has yet gone' (*KSA* 13:20[103]; cf. *GS* 359). As we saw in our chapters on Nietzsche and Foucault, one central reason for this modern revaluation of the passions was the belief that they are essential to realizing the modern, post-Romantic ideal of living a creative, original life.

Nietzsche's dramatic repudiation of the ancient ideal of rational self-possession marks a pivotal cultural shift that any reinvention of PWL must take into account. Indeed, Hadot himself acknowledged that the positive evaluation of intense or sublime passions is integral to the modern conception of the good life. 'One does not', he observed, 'aim to eliminate the anxiety of death, as in Antiquity. I think this is characteristic of the modern world ... an aspect, to my mind, appears first in Goethe, Schelling, Nietzsche' (Hadot, 2011: 106). 'The idea', as he explains,

> that the consciousness of existing is tied to an anxiety ... that *the value of life* comes precisely from ... the chill (frisson) before the *Ungeheure* – the terrible, the prodigious, the monstrous ... This is something that is found in all modern thought ... I believe that this nuance of anxiety does not exist at all ... in Epicurus, in the Stoics, or in Plato. (Hadot, 2011: 106, emphasis added)

Whether or how we might accommodate our distinctively modern ethos in a renewed PWL, as Hadot conceded, would require its own, separate treatment. At a minimum, we suggest, any contemporary reinventions of PWL must find ways to navigate the tension between the ancient ideal of rational self-completion and its extirpation of the passions and the modern ideal of artistic self-creation and its affirmation of grand passions.

4 PWL of the future?

With this question of the requirements for any PWL 'of the future', we arrive at the end of our itinerary. The last query many critics within academic scholarship raise about PWL concerns its allegedly solely historical relevance. 'PWL was how philosophy was once done, even done for a long time', these voices chorus, 'but that is all in the past. We should be grateful to Hadot et al. for allowing us to better understand what philosophy has been, and for providing new directions for further historical research. But we can draw no lessons from what was concerning what might or should be. How, after all, could one exactly teach PWL in conditions of mass higher education? One can hardly be a Seneca to several hundred Lucilius for the eleven-to-twelve-week span of a standard university term. How could one assess a student's ethical or spiritual progress, or their meditative practices, their self-control and serenity in the face of adversity? Isn't the role of spiritual director that ancient pedagogy supposed no longer possible, respecting alike our pupils' privacy, and the limitations of the time-pressed modern adjunct who increasingly typifies the really-existing professional? At the same time, how else might we institute a meaningful study of PWL which went beyond a course in the history of philosophy, and tried to in some way inculcate the kinds of philosophical ethos that we find in the Epicureans, Stoics, sceptics, or renaissance *humanisti*?'

On the one hand, if our book has served to show just how fruitful an approach PWL forms to the history of philosophy, and as such, just how rewarding its systematic study will be in existing academic programmes, we can be satisfied. On the other hand, we cannot close this book without proffering several comments in response to these hard questions concerning the future of PWL, and its relationship to academic philosophy.

It is exciting, in this troubled moment of mid-2020, to be able to report that, de facto, many philosophers globally, gathered around the Mellon project based at Notre Dame in the United States, are exploring the possibilities for teaching PWL, as more than a hermeneutic or historiographical approach to philosophy (cf. Horst, 2020).[10] Outside of the academy, in a way which would have twenty years ago sounded far more outlandish, the modern Stoicism movement continues to go from strength to strength, led by work by figures such as Massimo Pigliucci (2017) and Donald Robertson (2020). This is a movement bringing together psychologists, counsellors, academics, with members of the wider community devoted to reanimating PWL, including drawing inspiration from Hadot (esp. 1995, 1998). It is at least premature to prejudge all such attempts as misguided, and far more liberal-minded (or even 'philosophical', in some post-sceptical sense) to remain open to the pedagogical possibilities that are presently being explored, mindful also of the increasing 'legitimation crisis' facing non-PWL philosophy in public discourse today. At the very least, we hope to have shown here that PWL's approach to philosophy, by speaking again to problems of non-philosophers surrounding life, meaning, death, the virtues and the good life, can afford philosophers a protreptic language to speak to non-philosophers, including providing rich normative justifications for the importance of philosophy in wider culture.

With this much said about academic futures for PWL, it will not have escaped readers that, with the exception of several scholastics, none of the thinkers we have considered here lastingly belonged to the medieval and modern universities (Schopenhauer, who was a dissident, excepted), and the discipline of philosophy or its medieval Arts and Theology Faculty forebears. One could make a case for ancient schools, notably the Academy and Lyceum, as forebears of the medieval corporations, but one thing Hadot et al. have shown that we should recall is that they were equally forbears of the coenobitic monasteries [5.2]. PWL, in short, has never exactly been a universitized affair. We have seen here how, in thinkers from Petrarch or Montaigne to Schopenhauer or Nietzsche, its claims to philosophical value have been staked on sometimes-acerbic criticisms of medieval scholasticism, or its modern legatees (4, 8). The issues the academic critic above raises about its possible institutionalization into modern regimes of assessment ironically reflect these criticisms, albeit from inside the institutions Petrarch et al. critiqued. Perhaps PWL's future does not depend on its fate in being incorporated or not into academic curricula. Perhaps we cannot ask students, as students, to undertake a regimen of Epicurean or Stoic exercises. Perhaps as professional philosophers, or teachers of philosophy, we can only practice PWL 'off the clock', and in our professional lives in no more direct ways than if we were pursuing other gainful things.

But human beings, as rational animals, are never solely students or administrators, professors or professionals, however often we play at convincing ourselves, and everyone else, that things are otherwise. There are real and difficult questions as to whether the growing numbers of non-academics who are turning to Stoicism as a way of life can authentically do this, without an intellectually impossible reembrace of Stoic physics and theology. We note that these questions do not present the same problems for people interested in the Epicurean way of life, and its physical foundations. The question of to what extent different spiritual exercises of meditation, contemplation, attention, premeditation and taming the passions depend upon a large-scale philosophical vision, including any particular dogmatic account of nature, is one that should inspire coming considerations as PWL continues to develop as a subject of academic research. But any knee-jerk *a priori* declaration against all those people who, following one of Hadot's statements (1995: 280), feel that 'Epicureanism and Stoicism … could nourish the spiritual life of men and women of our times, as well as my own' is at least questionable. As Emerson once reminded us, the sun still shines today. We may admire past characters, times and philosophers, but we live today. As we have just indicated, the advent of 'modern Stoicism' since the turn of the millennium, and its remarkable growth in popularity in all continents and walks of life since 2010, presents an *a posteriori* rebuttal of overly cavalier dismissals that deserves to be taken seriously. Like any endeavour involving large numbers of people, we can well expect that all of the all-too-human problems that attend such endeavours will apply to such attempts to breathe new life into old lived philosophies: factionalism, dogmatism, retail and wholesale misreadings, political misappropriations (Sharpe, 2018b), passions, profiteering, a bonfire of vanities and brushfires of credulity. But then, the very promise of PWL in all of the forms we have documented in this book is that it can ideally foster awareness of these human things, ask us to avow them when we confront them or act them out, and provide philosophically informed means to undertake the difficult, perhaps never-completable work of trying to overcome them in ourselves and others. Isn't it worth asking whether philosophers, *as philosophers*, can for too long neglect such a post-Socratic orientation as proper to their calling?

APPENDIX

Appendix 1
Table 1 The spiritual exercises

	Meditation (concentration, memorization)	Attention, observation as discipline	Contemplation	Premeditation of death, of evils, of pain	Examination of conscience, of inner representations	Reframing exercises (view from above, eternity ...)
Socrates	X		X		X	
Epicureans	X		X	Death, pain as no evils	X	X
Stoics	X	X	X	Death, evils	X	X
Sceptics					X	
Cicero	X			X	X	
Plotinus	X	X	X		X	X
Boethius	X		X	X	X	X
Patristics, monastic authors	X	X	X	X	X	X
Scholastics						
Dissident scholastics			X			
Petrarch	X	X	X	X	X	X
Montaigne	X	X	X	X	X	X
Lipsius	X			X	X	X
Bacon	X			X	X	X
Descartes	X		X			
Royal Society *virtuosi*		X				
Voltaire		X				X [in context of literary-philosophical writings]
Diderot		X				X [in context of literary-philosophical writings]
Schopenhauer	X		X		X	
Nietzsche		X [physics]			X	X [eternal recurrence]
Foucault						

...ming/mastery passions (egs: ...nger, grief)	Training in fortitude, abstinence	Teaching as spiritual direction/, counselling	Dialogue or dialectic or inquiry as intellectual &/or spiritual exercise	Reading & writing exercises (prescribed or practised)	Rhetorical exercises (prescribed, cultivated)
	X	X	X		
X	X	X			
X	X	X	X	X[epitomes]	
X			X [tropes]	X [hypomnemata]	X
X	X				
X	X	X	X		
X	X	X	X		
X	X	X		X [florilegia]	
			X	X	X
			X	X	X
X	X	X		X [hypomnemata]	X
X	X		X [sceptical tropes]	X [essaying]	
X	X		X		
X	X	X	X	X	X
X [taming of epistemic arrogance]			X [experimentalism as discipline]		
			X [experimentalism as discipline, sceptical tropes]		X
			X [experimentalism as discipline, sceptical tropes]		X
X	X				
X				X	X
			X [genealogy]	X	X

Appendix

Appendix 2

Table 2 The 'Tennead', or ten features of PWL in the different philosophers

	1, Reflection on pedagogy, relation philosophy to other disciplines	2. Intellectual exercises	3. Spiritual exercises	4. Systematic discourse, divisions of parts of philosophy
1. Socrates	Philosophy v. sophistry, concerned with highest good for human beings	elenchus	Elenchus, meditation, endurance	
2. Epicureans	Philosophy v. liberal arts (*paideia*), concerned with highest good for human beings	Physics as spiritual exercise	meditation, memorisation, friendship, withdrawal, fourfold cure, remembrance of good things, contemplation	Physics, ethics, 'canonic'
3. Stoics	Philosophy v. liberal arts (Seneca, *Ep. 88*), v. sophistry, concerned with highest good for human beings	Physics, ethics, and logic as disciplines	Meditation, memorization, contemplation, premeditation evils & death, distinguishing what does/not depend on us, withholding assent to uncertain, uncritical beliefs	Physics, ethics, logic (includes dialectic and rhetoric)
4. Academic & Pyrrhonian sceptics		Elenchus, sceptical tropes, destructive arguments	Memorisation of tropes, *epochē* (suspension of assent to uncertain, uncritical beliefs)	
5. Cicero	Philosophy and its relations to rhetoric	Sceptical tropes, dialectical-rhetorical topics	Memorization of topics, meditation (in context of consolations), consolation	
6. Plotinus	Philosophy v. gnosticism, v. Christianity	Dialectical teaching	Ascetic exercises, meditation, contemplation	
7. Boethius			Meditation on arguments, consolation	[Aristotelian] speculative philosophy (including mathematics) v. practical philosophy

5. Literary genres	6. Turn inwards	7. Meta-philosophical metaphors and conceptions	8. Models of happiness	9. Critique of non-philosophers	10. Discourse on the sage
[words and deeds documented by pupils]	Philosophy as examined life, care of soul, government of self	As midwifery, sting of stingray, gadfly, philosophy as preparation for death, becoming godlike, knowledge of ignorance	The life of *zetēsis*, inquiry into virtue	The many as unthinking, prone to manipulation by sophists, demagogues	Socrates himself as paradigm/ exemplar
Treatises (mostly lost), epitomes, letters	Philosophy as therapy of desires	As medicine, therapy, athletics training, wrestling training	*Ataraxia*, life free of pain and disturbance, replete with 'stable pleasures' including friendship	Civic life as 'plagued' by empty opinions, unnatural desires, and dependency on fortune	Epicurus as sage; sage as he who lives quietly, desiring only natural things
Treatises (lost), hymn (Cleanthes), therapies for passions, consolations, diatribes, letters, meditations, hypomnemata, manuals	Philosophy as exercise of *techne* of living	As medicine, therapy, inner citadel, shield (*enchieridion*), cultivation (agricultural)	*Apatheia* (*serenitas, tranquilitas*), life undisturbed by destructive passions, lived in virtue(s), selecting things according to nature	Ordinary human life involves unconditional attachments to things which don't depend on us, and cannot deliver happiness	Socrates and Cato the Younger as exemplars, the hyperbolic paradoxes of the sage (only true king, general, rich man ...), above fortune, passions, and attachment to things which 'befall good and bad men alike'
Sextus' *Hypertyposes* (outlines)	Philosophy as examined life		*Ataraxia*	Ordinary human life involves uncertain, uncritical beliefs, leading to empty desires and conflicts	Socrates; Pyrrho, for Pyrrhonians as exemplars
Speeches, treatises, dialogues, consolations	Philosophy as examined life, medicine for the soul	Philosophy as *medicina animi* (medicine for the soul), as medicine to the body	The 'mixed life' of philosophy, with friendship and civil service		Socrates, Plato, Cato the Younger as exemplars, the sage as above fortune
Biography by Porphyry, discourse or enneads' recorded by the same	Philosophy as ascent from bodily existence towards unity with One	As erotics, as ascent, as 'epoptics' (initiation to higher mysteries)	The life of contemplation	Ordinary humans are captivated by bodily desires	Plato, Plotinus as exemplars; the sage as he who has transcended bodily desires and captation
Consolation (fictive-mythic dialogue with poetry)	Philosophy as medicine for the soul	Philosophy as medicine for the soul, as (feminine) consoler and deity	The life reconciled completely with fortune, awake to God	Ordinary human lives as captive to false beliefs and desires which cause avoidable suffering	

Appendix

	1, Reflection on pedagogy, relation philosophy to other disciplines	2. Intellectual exercises	3. Spiritual exercises	4. Systematic discours divisions of parts of philosophy
8. Patristics, monastic authors	Pagan versus 'true' or 'Christian philosophy'		Meditation, memorisation, attention, contemplation, prayer, hymning	Logic, ethics, physics, epoptic (Clement, Origen)
9. Scholastics	Philosophy v. liberal arts	Dialectical reading, disputations		Platonic, Aristotelian hierarchy of disciplines based on ascent to immaterial/God, theology. Pedagogical primacy of dialectic
10. Dissident scholastics		Dialectical reading, disputations	Contemplation	Platonic, Aristotelian hierarchy of disciplines based on ascent to immaterial/God, theology.
11. Petrarch	Philosophy as a way of life v sophistry/ philosophy (also medicine) as wholly theoretical	Rhetorical exercises	meditation, memorisation, contemplation	Five 'humanities': grammar, rhetoric, poetry, history and mo philosophy in place of liberal arts, led by dialectic
12. Montaigne	Philosophy as a way of life v purely theoretical speculation	Sceptical tropes	Meditation, premeditation, attention, contemplation, remembering pleasant things (distraction) from pain/sorrow	
13. Lipsius	Philosophy as a way of life v purely theoretical speculation		Meditation, memorisation, contemplation, premeditation evils & death, distinguishing what does/not depend on us, withholding assent to uncertain, uncritical beliefs	
14. Bacon	Divisions of according to human faculty: philosophy is to reason as memory to history, and imagination to poetics	The new method in natural philosophy: exercises in observation, tabulation, remaking 'prerogative instances'	'Georgics', being 'custom, exercise, habit, education, example, imitation, emulation, company, friends, praise, reproof, exhortation, fame, laws, books, studies ... '	Natural philosophy, human philosophy (including therapeutic Georgics), civil philosophy

5. Literary genres	6. Turn inwards	7. Meta-philosophical metaphors and conceptions	8. Models of happiness	9. Critique of non-philosophers	10. Discourse on the sage
Lives [of Christian figures], florilegia for meditation, the Bible itself	Christianity as 'sole and eternal philosophy'	Philosophy as life in imitation of Christ	The holy life	Ordinary non-Christian life as sinful (seven deadly sins) and closed to God	Christ and Saints as exemplars
Summas (questions, answers, objections)		As handmaid to theology	[The holy life, but attainable only through Christianity insofar as it transcends philosophising/reason]		
Summas (questions, answers, objections)	[Aristotelian] philosophy as basis of contemplative, most contended and elevated life		Philosophy as 'the knowledge of the true and accomplishment of the good and their enjoyment … ' (Boethius of Dacia)		
Letters, dialogues, 'secret book', 'remedies'	Philosophy as medicine of soul (Ciceronian), preparation for death (Platonic)	As medicine to soul	The secular life of contemplative solitude	Ordinary life freighted with 'plague' of bodily needs, dependency on fortune, avoidable sufferings	Augustine as exemplar
Essays, hypomnemata	Philosophy as preparation for death, as medicine of the soul, as what instructs us to life	Medicinal/ therapeutic, government of self, as a 'backshop' against fortune	An examined life, aware of one's limits, awake to variety and wonder of experience, but 'ordinary and without lustre'	Human life as freighted with false opinions, presumption, and propensity to cruelty and prejudice	Socrates, Cato, Seneca the Younger, Epaminondas
Dialogue, treatise	Philosophy as remedy for false opinions, avoidable sufferings	Medicinal/ therapeutic, military	A Stoic life of constancy, reconciled to public and private evils but committed to private and public virtue	Human life as freighted with false opinions, propensity to cruelty and prejudice	Socrates, Seneca the Younger
Treatises, essays, Apothegmata, notebooks, dialogues, letters	Georgics depends on distinction between what one can and cannot control	Georgics as medicinal, ministerial (counselling) cultivation (agricultural)	An active life devoted to public service and Christian charity, fortified by philosophy	Human mind as freighted with idols of the species, or individuals, of language, and of particular dogmatisms	Alexander, Caesar, Cicero, Xenophon [learned men of action]

Appendix

	1, Reflection on pedagogy, relation philosophy to other disciplines	2. Intellectual exercises	3. Spiritual exercises	4. Systematic discourse divisions of parts of philosophy
15. Descartes		The new method of natural philosophy	Radical sceptical doubt, meditations, contemplation	
16. Royal Society *virtuosi*		Post-Baconian method of natural philosophy: a discipline of observation and experimentation		
17. Voltaire	Philosophy as living force of social critique v academic profession	Sceptical tropes, rhetorical topics	The view from above [within fictions]	
18. Diderot	Philosophy as living force of social critique v academic profession	Sceptical tropes, rhetorical topics	The view from above [within fictions]	
19. Schopenhauer	Philosophy as a metaphysical consolation vs academic profession	Metaphysical exercises (seeing sub species aeternitas)	Ascetic exercises: Self-mortification, self-deprivation, (e.g. poverty, chastity, fasting)	
20. Nietzsche	Philosophy as an art of living vs academic profession	Physics/Science as a spiritual exercise Psychological self-dissection	The view from above The view from recurrence	
21. Foucault	Philosophy as an art of self-transformation and political critique versus academic profession	Historical exercises: archaeology & genealogy		

5. Literary genres	6. Turn inwards	7. Meta-philosophical metaphors and conceptions	8. Models of happiness	9. Critique of non-philosophers	10. Discourse on the sage
Meditations, treatises, letters, discourses	The true philosophy depends on radical sceptical examination of all extant beliefs			the human mind, through freedom of will, ordinarily assents too carelessly to false and partial beliefs	
Essays, treatises	The true philosophy as grounded in observation, and awareness of inquirers' limitations			Human mind clouded by vanity, presumption, impatience, lack of discipline in observation and inferences	Bacon, the new man of science or 'cirtuosi' characterised by curiosity tempered by epistemic moderation
Essays, treatises, dialogues, dictionaries, plays, contes, polemics, fables	Philosophy as criticism of fanaticism, prejudice, interested in social reform	medicinal, critical	An active life devoted to public service and deistic charity and fellowship, fortified and informed by philosophy	Human mind ordinarily impatient, presumptuous, inclined to prejudice and fanaticism	Socrates, Marcus Aurelius, Epictetus, Cicero, Christ, Bayle, Zadig [fictional hero of conte]
Essays, treatises, dictionaries, plays, contes, polemics, fables	Philosophy as criticism of fanaticism, prejudice, interested in social reform	Medicinal, critical	An active life devoted to public service and charity, fortified and informed by philosophy	Human mind ordinarily impatient, presumptuous, inclined to prejudice and fanaticism	Diogenes the Cynic, Seneca the Younger, Voltaire as political agent
	Philosophy as medicine for the soul	Medical: Philosopher as Physician	Pure contemplative, desire free life	Human mind as hapless victim of the distortions and sufferings of the passions	Ancient sages as lifeless, unrealistic mannequins Religious ascetics & mystics as true sages
Aphorisms, Anecdotes, Maxims, Miniature dialogues, Jokes, Poetry, Notebooks, Philosophic Autobiogra-phies	Philosophy as medicine for the soulPhilosophy as art of living	Medical Philosopher as Physician Political: Philosopher as Legislator	Impassioned 'moraline' free life devoted to the creation of the self as an artwork	Human mind ordinarily conformist, utilitarian, myopic, loveless	Ancient sages as degenerate, declining forms of life Transformative artists & political legislators as true 'sages'
	Philosophy as art of self-transformation	Philosopher as experimenter with the limits of the possible	A life of perpetual self-transformation	Human mind ordinarily bound to limits of historical context	Ancient sages as useful examples of experiments in living

NOTES

Introduction

1   We debated at length whether to include a chapter on Spinoza on the grounds that some scholars see him as a neo-Stoic ethical naturalist who conceives philosophy as an art of living. However, since we cover at great length both the key ancient Stoics and discuss many later reinterpretations and recalibrations of Stoicism (see Chapters 5, 6, 8, 9 and 10), and Spinoza's assessment of, and exact relationship to Stoicism is a matter of considerable debate (see, for example, *Ethics* III pref and *Politics* 1.4; & Armstrong 2013), in the end we reluctantly decided not to cover this terrain. However, for those interested in Spinoza's place in and contribution to the history of PWL, Susan James's recent book should be especially useful. She argues that Spinoza conceives philosophizing as 'the project of learning to live joyfully' (James 2020).

2   Readers should note the link between Chapters 5 and 7; the use of predominant metaphors. When, for instance, a philosophy is conceived as a work of elevation or illumination, this speaks to a more hierarchical conception of the different parts of philosophy, or the ordering of their teaching. Metaphors of cultivation, training or even the crafts may speak to such an hierarchical division of the parts of philosophy, but are also consistent with the more 'organic' understanding of each part of philosophy as codeterminative of the others, as we find paradigmatically in Stoicism (Hadot, 2020: 105–32).

Chapter 1

1   In his lectures 'The Preplatonic Philosophers', Nietzsche calls Socrates the first philosopher of life [*Lebensphilosoph*] and his philosophy an absolutely practical philosophy: 'Thinking serves life, whereas with all earlier philosophers life served thinking and knowing' (quoted in Sallis, 1991: 123).

2   Plato represents Callicles as student of the historical sophist Gorgias. On the one hand, Callicles defends the view that conventional morality is an instrument the weak use to proscribe the actions of strong individuals. By maintaining the conventional judgement that it is wrong to do harm, he claims, the weak seek to limit the capacity of the strong to exercise power. On the other hand, he argues, a few 'better' individuals have a natural right to rule

over the lesser, and to do so purely for their own 'higher' ends (*G*. 482e-483d). What we might call Callicles's aristocratic radicalism finds a latter-day supporter in the later Nietzsche.

3   For this reason, unless he was under a strict legal obligation, Socrates famously refused to exercise the privileges and duties of Athenian citizenship such as debating and voting in the democratic Assembly or acting as juror in the popular courts. Socrates stresses that even when he was formally required to act as member of the Athenian council (406 BCE), or indeed when he was at the mercy of the thirty tyrants' decrees during their brief reign of terror (404–403 BCE), he acted according to his own rational judgement of the claims of justice even though this meant risking death (*Ap*. 31). Socrates claims that acting in accordance with reason trumps all other values.

4   In Thucydides's *History of the Peloponnesian War*, Pericles, the greatest political figure of Athenian democracy, observed that Athenians defined themselves in terms of active citizenship: 'Here each individual is interested not only in his own affairs but in the affairs of the state as well (…) this is a peculiarity of ours: we do not say that a man who takes no interest in politics is a man who minds his own business; we say that he has no business here at all' (*FO*: 40). From this Periclean perspective, by his choice of the philosophical way of life Socrates made himself a stranger in Athens.

5   For a detailed treatment of each of these sources, see Guthrie (1971: 13–35, 39–55).

6   Kenneth Lapatin gives a thorough history of the visual representations of Socrates from antiquity to modernity; see Lapatin (2006).

7   James Colaiaco gives an excellent treatment of Socrates's attack on the sophists (2001: 23–36). It is important to note that Plato's treatment of the sophists is partial and that the sophistic movement itself was internally complex, encompassing moderate relativists and 'cynical' realists. On the sophists, see M. Untersteiner (1954) and W. K. C. Guthrie (1971).

8   Observing how Aristophanes identified the danger that Socrates's critical examination of conventional definitions of virtue might undermine the validity of law and custom, Hegel endorsed the ancient comedian's judgement: 'The sole justification is that Aristophanes was correct in *The Clouds*' (Hegel, 2006: 143). In the figure of Socrates, Hegel suggests, 'the absolute right of self-consciousness' came into collision 'with the ethical life of his people': 'Socrates pits his conscience, the fact that he did not feel himself guilty, against the judicial verdict. But the Athenian people do not have to acknowledge a tribunal of conscience … The Athenian people upheld the right of law, of their custom and religion, against this attack … Socrates offended against … the ethical and juridical life of his people, and this positive offence was necessarily punished' (Hegel, 2006: 154).

9   In the *Apology* Socrates remarks that in Hades he will be 'inconceivably happy to have discussions with men *and* women' (*Ap*. 41c, emphasis added).

Notes

10   Gregory Vlastos argues that Plato develops two distinct and incompatible philosophies through the character of Socrates. In his early elenctic dialogues, he argues, Socrates is an exclusively moral philosopher, who seeks knowledge elenctically, avowing that he has none, whereas in the later dialogues Socrates is a moral philosopher *and* metaphysician, epistemologist, philosopher of science, language, religion, education and art who seeks knowledge demonstratively and is confident he finds it. See Vlastos (1991: 41–80, esp. 47–8). Vlastos also argues that the former Socrates expresses the views of the historical Socrates, whereas the latter Socrates is the mouthpiece of Plato's own views. Like nearly everything about Plato and Socrates, these views are contested by different commentators.

11   Which of Plato texts we should classify as earlier and later dialogues is also still a matter of contention. Vlastos identifies the following as early elenctic dialogues: *Apology, Charmides, Crito, Euthyphro, Gorgias, Hippias Minor, Ion, Laches, Protagoras, Republic* Book 1. If we accept the *First Alcibiades* as a genuine Platonic text, then it should also include in this list. On the authenticity of *the First Alcibiades*, see Annas (1985: 111).

12   To explain the dramatic dynamics of the elenchus further, Hadot draws on the German scholar Otto Apelt's description of the mechanisms of *Spaltung* (splitting) and *Verdoppalung* (redoubling). 'Socrates splits himself into two, so that there are two Socrates: the Socrates who knows in advance how the discussion is going to end and the Socrates who travels the entire dialectical path along with his interlocutor.' Through the aporetic work of the elenchus, drawing out the interlocutor's self-contradictions, the latter then also becomes effectively 'split': 'There is the interlocutor as he was before his conversation with Socrates, and there is the interlocutor who, in the course of their constant mutual accord, has identified himself with Socrates, and who henceforth will never be the same again' (PWL: 153).

13   See also: 'Why did god tell Socrates, in the *Theaetetus,* to be a midwife to others, but not to give birth himself? … Suppose that nothing can be apprehended and known by humans: then it was reasonable for god to prevent Socrates giving birth to bogus beliefs, false and baseless, and to force him to test others who had opinions of that kind. Argument that rids you of the greatest evil – deception and pretentiousness – is no small help, rather a major one … This was Socrates' healing, not of the body but of the festering and corrupted soul. But suppose there is knowledge of the truth, and that there is one truth then this is had not just by the person who discovers it but no less by the person who learns from the discoverer. But you are more likely to get it if you are not already convinced that you have it, and then you get the best of all, just as you can adopt an excellent child without having given birth yourself' (Plutarch, *Platonic Question* 1).

14   At times, Hadot clearly interprets Socrates's spiritual exercise in terms of a Platonic (or Neoplatonic) conversion: it induces in interlocutors the desire

to ascend beyond their embodied, mortal selves to a higher, eternal self (see **Chapter 4**)–but this is controversial. In Plato's view, as Hadot sees it, 'every dialectical exercise, precisely because it is an exercise of pure thought, subject to the demands of Logos, turns the soul away from the sensible world and allows it to convert itself towards the Good' (Hadot, 1995: 93).

15 See also *The First Alcibiades.*

16 Nietzsche's ambivalence is evident in the following famous note: 'Socrates … stands so close to me that I am practically always waging a battle with him' (*KSA* 8.97. 6[3]). Werner Dannhauser (1974) surveys Nietzsche's shifting and ambivalent relationship to Socrates. For a recent appraisal of Nietzsche's revaluation of Socrates, see Raymond (2019).

17 Vlastos is hence right to suggest then that while later renowned ethicists and moral philosophers like Aristotle, Hume and Kant set themselves the task of rationalizing conventional morality, Socrates is the greatest among those who have questioned their own culture's basic norms: 'Proceeding entirely from within the morality of his own time and place, he nevertheless finds reason to stigmatise as unjust one of most venerable, best established, rules of justice' (Vlastos, 1991: 179).

18 Recalling that Achilles slayed Hector knowing that it meant his own death, Socrates tells his Athenian judges that he pursues his philosophic mission in the certainty that by doing so, they will put him to death. And he deliberately inflames their already bitter animus towards him by declaring that he will not trade his silence in exchange for his life. Socrates prefers death to a life without philosophical examination (*Ap*. 30a). Like Achilles, he declares, that he too only considers whether he acts rightly or wrongly, regardless of personal consequences (*Ap*. 28 b-d).

19 On the gradual discovery of mind or psyche in Greek culture, see Snell (1953).

20 Nietzsche clearly has in mind the Greek view of happiness that Plato articulates through Thrasymachus's defence of tyranny as the happiest or best life. See, e.g., *Republic* (344a-c).

21 Vlastos aims to rescue Socrates from what he sees as the Cynics and Stoics' absurd version of ancient eudaimonism. He does so by softening or domesticating Socrates's thesis. On Vlastos's interpretation, Socrates argues that virtue is necessary and sufficient for happiness, but unlike the Stoics, he claims, Socrates also holds that sages will be marginally happier than others, if, for example, they sleep on a bed of roses rather than a hard camp bed, as long as sleeping on a bed of roses does not require them to compromise their virtue. For Socrates, he argues, possession of non-moral goods (e.g. health, wealth, reputation) makes a 'miniscule', or 'small, but not negligible' difference to our happiness (1991: 231). Cf. Long (1988: 169) who argues that we should prefer Zeno's strict Stoic interpretation of Socrates's eudaimonism to Vlastos's softened version.

Notes

Chapter 2

1   We return this point in the chapter's conclusion.

2   See also Erler & Schofield (1999: 646): 'Philosophy as therapy and the philosopher as a doctor of the soul: the analogy is familiar from Democritus and Plato. Yet in Epicurus' case it is carried through with particular thoroughness. His teaching is a sort of medicine and his writings a kind of prescription'; and Konstan (2008: x): 'Even more than the other philosophical schools of classical antiquity, the Epicureans conceived of their insights as providing a cure for tribulations afflicting the mind.'

3   Epicureans divide philosophy into ethics, physics and a third discipline called 'canonics', and closer to what we would term an epistemology based on the materialist premises of the physics than a logic or analytics (Hadot, 2002: 120–1).

4   For a detailed analysis of Epicurean therapeutic strategies, see Tsouna (2009: 234–48) and Tsouna (2007: 75–87), respectively.

5   This being also the second half of the fourfold cure. See **2.6**.

6   See D. Sedley, *Lucretius and the Transformation of Greek Wisdom*, chapter 3 'Epicurus' *On Nature*'.

7   Again, a comparison with Aristotle *NE* X, 7 suggests itself.

8   Diogenes Laertius briefly records Epicurus's polemical attacks on other schools and philosophers, including Plato and the Platonists, whom he called 'Dionysiokolakes', or flatterers of Dionysus II, the tyrant of Syracuse whom Plato sought to educate as a philosopher king (*DL* X. 7–8; see Plato, *Seventh Letter*). Notoriously, Dionysus II is said to have 'rewarded' Plato for his pedagogical efforts by selling him into slavery.

9   For a detailed analysis of these Epicurean arguments that it is irrational to fear death, see Warren (2004; 2009).

10 One variation on the argument in Lucretius (RN III, 899–900) addresses the worry we may have of all the good things we will lose by being dead. But then, once we are dead, there will be no 'we', so 'there now remains left over in you no yearning for these things' as well.

11 In an argument Socrates anticipates in the Platonic *Apology* (29a), Lucretius also contends that, from the first person perspective, death will be like a deep sleep, and thence to be feared only as much as we – clearly do not – fear deep, dreamless sleep (RN III 920 ff.; 978).

12 Cf. Vladimir Nabokov challenges the Epicurean symmetry argument. He argues that while we are ordinarily untroubled by our eternal, ante-natal non-existence, this is only because natural adaptation has stifled our temporal imagination. It is, he suggests, maladaptive rather than irrational to lament our ante-natal non-existence. 'Nature', as he puts it, 'expects a full-grown

man to accept the two black voids, fore and aft, as stolidly as he accepts the extraordinary visions in between. Imagination, the supreme delight of the immortal and the immature, should be limited. In order to enjoy life, we should not enjoy it too much' (Nabokov, 1989: 39–40).

13 See Clay (2009: 27): 'Epicurus' Garden was not a school … Unlike the Academy under the direction of Plato, the Peripatos under the direction of Aristotle … there was no scientific or historical research conducted in Epicurus' Garden'.

14 We should not, however, assume the early Christians unequivocally condemned Epicureanism. 'To my mind', Augustine confessed, 'Epicurus would have been awarded the palm of victory had I not believed that after death the life of the soul remain with the consequences of our acts' (*Con.* VII I [1]). Michael Erler shows that despite the common view that for the early Christians Epicurus was simply a target of polemic as an atheist who questioned the moral world order and providence, in fact in some cases the Christian interpretation and evaluation of Epicureanism was ambivalent. On the one hand, Christian thinkers like Augustine polemicized against Epicurus's materialist philosophical doctrines such as its conception of the mortal soul and its prudential justification of virtue. On the other hand, Christians also expressed appreciation of the modest Epicurean art of living. Erler demonstrates this negative evaluation of Epicurean philosophic doctrine alongside a positive appreciation of its style of life through the Middle Ages and Renaissance (see Erler, 2009: 60–4).

15 Modern secular materialists who are otherwise ethical opponents are often united in their appreciation of this aspect of Epicurean doctrine. Nietzsche, for example, cautions against the dangers of renouncing 'faith in the god of Epicurus, those carefree and unknown ones, and believing instead in some petty deity who is full of worries and personally knows every little hair on our heads and finds nothing nauseating in the most miserable small service?' (1882: GS 277).

16 Annas quotes Arius's Introduction to summarize this point: 'The Epicurean philosophers do not accept [the final end's] being said to be in activity, because of supposing the final end to be passive not active; for it is pleasure' (1999: 347).

Chapter 3

1 After Zeno's death, Cleanthes (famous for his reverential 'hymn to Zeus') became the second 'scholarch' or leader of the Stoics. After Cleanthes came the great systematizer Chrysippus of Silo, who is said to have authored some 165 books, none of which survive in complete form. The Stoic school survived in Athens, with an unbroken sequence of Scholarchs, until the late second century. This is the period of so-called 'middle Stoics', Panaetius and Posidonius. Both of these figures based themselves in Rhodes, attracting

some of the leading figures in the later Roman Republic to pay them court. According to most sources, they also brought non-Stoic, Platonic and Aristotelian elements into Stoic thought.

2   Ilsetraut Hadot, *Sénèque: direction spirituelle et pratique de la philosophie* (Paris: Librairie Philosophique J. Vrin, 2014).

3   Sextus Empiricus *Adv. math.* 11.170 (= *SVF* 3.598); trans. Bett modified; Epictetus, *Disc.* 1.15.2; see John Sellars, *Art of Living: The Stoics on the Nature and Function of Philosophy.* (Aldershot: Ashgate, 2003), 22.

4   'The Stoics said that [i] wisdom is knowledge of human and divine matters, and [ii] philosophy exercise of fitting expertise; [iii] the single and supremely fitting expertise is excellence, [iv] and excellences at their most general are three: in nature, in behaviour, in reasoning'. Plutarch, *Placita, SVF* 2.35, LS 26 A, FDS 15; Sextus Empiricus, at *Against the Professors* 9.125 (SVF 2.1017).

5   'Others defined philosophy as the exercise of fitting expertise of the best life for human beings, saying that philosophy is exercise, and calling wisdom fitting expertise, which is also a cognition of human and divine matters'. Ps.-Galen, *On the History of Philosophy*, at 5, 602.19–3.2 Diels.

6   Again, the Stoics' understandings of the technai themselves all point to these arts, as Socrates had suggested, involving both systematic, applicable understandings of their objects, as well as a transformed *hexis* in the psyche of the technician. Such a definition would be applied to the fitting craft of philosophy as well. Indeed, a further definition of the *technai* attributed to Zeno defines an art as 'a system of cognitions unified by training (σύστημα ἐκ καταλήψεων συγγεγυμνασμένων ...) towards some useful end in life'. Olympiodorus, *Commentary on the Gorgias* 12.1 (SVF 1.73, FDS 392, LS 42, at Brouwer, 2014: 51.

7   The pseudo-Platonic *Axiochus* pictures Socrates consoling the eponymous protagonist against his own imminent death, while fourth-century Platonist Crantor penned a work on grief (*Peri Penthous*), and the third-century Cynic Teles penned a work *On Exile* with the same psychotherapeutic intentionality. Later, there is Cicero's lost *Hortensius* (and, to some degree, *The Tusculan Disputations*), a consolation of (pseudo-)Plutarch, and Musonius's ninth recorded discourse, *On Exile*. See Baltussen (2009: 70–6).

8   Seneca also uses the Stoic doctrine of recurrence as a consolation (cf. **Chapter 10**). In his *Consolation to Marcia*, for example, Seneca consoles Marcia for the loss of her son Metilius by imagining that in the interim before the world repeats itself he is happy. Here, Seneca endeavours to console Marcia's grief not only by picturing her son's postmortem happiness, but also by claiming that he is happy specifically because he knows that he will return to repeat the same life. On this cosmological view, and son will be eternally reunited (*Ad Marc.* 26, 7). See Hadot (1995: 238–50): 'The View for Above'.

9   *Disc.* III 21.

10   See also several untranslated pieces in French, notably Hadot, 'Une Clé des *Pensées* de Marc Aurèle: Les Trois *Topoi* Philosophiques selon Épictète', in Hadot (2002: 165–92).

11   Simplicius, 'Preface' to *Commentary on Ench.*, 18–20; at Ilsetraut and Pierre Hadot, *Apprendre à philosopher dans l'Antiquité: L'enseignement du Manuel d'Epictète et son commentaire néoplatonicien* (Paris: proche, 2004), 53.

12   Simplicius, 'Preface', 82–7.

13   Epictetus, *Ench.* 8 start.

14   Such is the nature of the *Meditations*, that it is easy to forget that this is a document written by one of the most powerful men in history. Of the 473 sections of this text, less than forty address imperial experience. These exclusively treat imperial life as a barrier to living well, as in *Meds.* V 16, V 30; cf. I 17, 3, IX 29.

15   What has become Book I of the Meditations involves a kind of spiritual exercise in gratitude and remembrance. Marcus looks back over his upbringing, recalling his particular debts to all of his beneficiaries. Three central chapters (I 6–9) are devoted to his philosophical teachers (Diognetus, Rusticus, Apollonius, Sextus). The longest, penultimate chapter (I 16) gives an idealized portrait of his father, Antoninus Pius, as a perfect Stoic ruler. The final, seventeenth chapter, expresses gratitude to the gods for the external goods accorded him by fortune or fate. Notably, the debts Marcus expresses to the philosophers are ethical.

16   Two centuries after Marcus's death, Themistius mentions Marcus's *parragelmata* or exhortations. But it is unclear whether he had access to the 12 books we have inherited. The text resurfaces at the turn of the tenth century in Byzantium, with Bishop Arethas in a letter of 907 CE describing 'the very profitable book of the Emperor Marcus'. The first editions of the text appear in Western Europe in the early sixteenth century.

17   Compare, e.g., 'how could that which does not make a man worse, make life worse' with 'that which does not make a man worse than he is, does not make his life worse either' (*Meds.* II, 11, 4; IV, 8; cf. IV, 35; VIII, 21, 2).

18   Cf. 'Let these thoughts be at your command [*prokheiron*] by night and day: write them, read them, talk of them, to yourself and to your neighbour' (*Disc.* III.24.103).

19   Namely 'We should see to it that whatever we have absorbed should not be allowed to remain unchanged, or it will be no part of us. We must digest it: otherwise it will merely enter the memory and not the reasoning power *[in memoriam non in ingenium]*. Let us loyally welcome such foods and make them our own, so that something that is one may be formed out of many elements, just as one number is formed of several elements.'

20   There is an urgency here, as in Epictetus's *Encheiridion*, which attests to Marcus's own struggle to live up to his Stoic ideals: 'Wrong thyself, wrong

thyself, my psyche! But the time for honouring yourself will soon have gone by', *Meds.* II, 6; cf. X, 1.

Chapter 4

1   Of the highest truths at stake in philosophy, the *Seventh Letter* famously tells us: 'There neither is nor ever will be a treatise of mine on the subject. For it does not admit of exposition like other branches of knowledge; but after much converse about the matter itself and a life lived together, suddenly a light, as it were, is kindled in one soul by a flame that leaps to it from another, and thereafter sustains itself.'

2   The first four scholarchs of the Academy after Plato (Speusippus, Xenocrates, Polemo and Crates of Athens) carried forwards the metaphysical dimensions to Plato's *oeuvre*. After the sixth scholarch Arcesilaus (*c.* 320–240 BCE), nevertheless, 'Academic' forms of scepticism developed which looked back for their inspiration to Socrates, rather than Plato himself. As Cicero tells us in his *De Oratore*, Arcesilaus was: 'The first to adopt from the varied books of Plato and from Socrates' dialogues, especially the idea that there is no certainty that can be grasped either by the senses or the mind... and also to have been the first to establish the practice – although this was very characteristic of Socrates – of not revealing his own view, but of always arguing against any view that any one else would assert' (Cicero, *De Or.* 3.67; cf. Cicero, *de Fin.* 2.2; *Ac.* 1.16). In the first century before Christ, the Platonic Academy split apart a second time, when Aenesidemus (*c.* 80–10 BCE) broke with the Academy completely. He contended that the last Athenian scholarch of the Academy, Philo of Larissa (159/8–84/3 BCE)'s softened version of 'probabilistic' scepticism (maintaining that, while certainty was impossible, we could still measure the different probabilities of beliefs being true) betrayed what is decisive in Socrates's heritage. Aenesidemus instead founded Pyrrhonism, a rival, more radical form of scepticism which we will examine momentarily. At nearly the same time, a second pupil of Philo of Larissa, Antiochus of Ascalon (*c.* 125–*c.* 68 BCE), broke with Philo's academic scepticism, but in the opposite, metaphysical direction (Cicero, *Acad.* 1.46). While it is unclear what Antiochus maintained concerning the Platonic Ideas and teachings concerning the immortality of the soul, within a generation, Eudorus of Alexandria had in Alexandria initiated an increasingly 'dogmatic' species of Platonism. This is what is now known as 'middle Platonism', which maintained that the goal of philosophy was *homoiôsis theiou* (becoming godlike), rather than the suspension of all uncertain beliefs. Middle Platonism would in due course inform the later 'Neoplatonism' of Plotinus (died *c.* 265 CE), Porphyry (233–309 CE), see **4.4–4.5**.

3   One does not want to stir up a hornet's nest. But we know with great probability that the metaphysical doctrines are programmatically Platonic and not Socratic, since there is no equivalent for them in Xenophon's *Socratikoi*

Logoi. Moreover, the Stoics had little interest in Plato, while drawing heavily on the Platonic Socrates, even though Zeno had studied under Xenocrates and Polemo, the third and fourth academic scholarch. Cf. Long (1999). There is ample ancient testimony concerning Plato's *agrapha dogmata*, for example in Aristotle *Metaphysics* 1, and that these unwritten doctrines were metaphysical (concerning the relation of the One and the Good and the 'indeterminate dyad' (*aoristas dyas*), cf. Dillon (1996: 1–11) with Reale (1996) and Kramer, *Plato and the Foundations of Metaphysics*, 1990. Finally, Speusippus and Xenocrates, Plato's immediate successors in the academy, were supremely interested in these metaphysical doctrines and 'first principles', a situation which seems improbable were Plato to have only taught them 'esoterically', *ad captum vulgari*, as the Straussian school has suggested in the twentieth century. See Dillon (1996: 11–39). For a recent attempt to reconstruct the Platonic reading order, on pedagogical principles, see Altman (2012; 2016a; 2016b).

4   The academic scepticism of Arcesilaus then developed by way of an ongoing sceptical engagement with, and refutation, of the claims of the 'dogmatic' Hellenistic schools, led by Stoicism. See Cicero, *Ac.* II, 77; Thorsrud (2009: 36–58).

5   See, e.g., *De Fin.* 1.4: 'For what problem does life offer so important as all the topics of philosophy, and especially the questions raised in these volumes – What is the End, the final and ultimate aim, which gives the standard for all principles of well-being and of right conduct? What does Nature pursue as the thing supremely desirable, what does she avoid as the ultimate evil? It is a subject on which the most learned philosophers disagree profoundly; who then can think it derogatory to such esteem as each may assign to me, to investigate what is the highest good and the truest rule in every relationship of life?'

6   See **Chapter 6.1** on Petrarch's *De Remediis*, directly indebted to Cicero's account of the emotions.

7   Comparably, Cicero's eclectic liberty is evident in Book I on death, wherein he adduces Epicurean arguments against the fear of being dead ('Well, then, I … own that the dead are not miserable, since you have drawn from me a concession that they who do not exist at all cannot be miserable' [*TD* I, 5–7]); Stoicizing arguments against the fear of having to die, as against being dead [*TD* I, 8–11]); an extensive rendition of Platonic consolations contending 'that souls do exist after death' (*TD* I, 12–31); before returning to more Epicurean and Stoic arguments as to 'why, even allowing [mortality of soul], death cannot be an evil' (*TD* I, 32 ff.).

8   'The same system of instruction seems to have imparted education both in right conduct and in good speech; nor were professors in two separate groups, but the same masters gave instruction both in ethics and in rhetoric, for instance the great Phoenix in Homer, who says that he was assigned to the young Achilles by his father Peleus to accompany him to the wars in order to make him "a speaker of words and a doer of deeds."' Cicero, *De or.* III. 57; cf. *Iliad*, 9, 443.

Notes

9   *De Inv.* I 1; cf. *De Or.* III 61. If there is a villain to this piece, it is the Socrates of the Gorgias. Except, as Cicero archly argues, that if Socrates is so successful in devaluing rhetoric unguided by philosophy to being a mere 'knack', 'it was because Socrates was the more eloquent and convincing, or, as you term it, the more powerful and better orator' than Polus, Callicles or Gorgias. Cicero, *TD* III, 129.

10 Our reading of Plotinus in this section is heavily indebted to this remarkable work.

11 Hadot, *Plotinus,* 26–7; cf. Michael Chase, 'Translator's Introduction', in *Plotinus, or the Simplicity of Vision,* 2–3.

12 At issue is a kind of wonder before the fact of this order: 'Surely no one seeing the loveliness lavish in the world of sense; this vast orderliness, the Form which the stars even in their remoteness display; no one could be so dull-witted, so immoveable, as not to be carried by all this to recollection, and gripped by reverent awe in the thought of all this', *Enn.* II, 9, 16, 43–55.

13 'To be sure, if the soul remains within the Nous, it sees beautiful and venerable things', Plotinus concedes, 'but it still does not have all that it is looking for. It is as though the soul were approaching a face which, although beautiful, was not yet capable of stimulating our sight, since there did not shine forth from it that grace which shimmers on the surface of beauty', *Enn.* VI.7. 22.

14 Plotinus's abiding influence on Orthodox spirituality, and via Augustine and Ambrose on the meditative traditions within Latin Christianity, is testimony to this characteristically later antique longing for world-Transcendence which also underlay the rise and spread of Christianity.

15 We know from Porphyry that he conducted his classes through dialectical questioning. See Porphyry, *Life of Plotinus,* 13; Hadot (1998: 53, 83, 87).

16 'Withdraw into yourself and look. And if you do not find yourself beautiful yet, act as does the creator of a statue that is to be made beautiful: he cuts away here, he smooths there, he makes this line lighter, this other purer, until a lovely face has grown upon his work. So do you also: cut away all that is excessive, straighten all that is crooked, bring light to all that is overcast, labour to make all one glow of beauty and never cease chiselling your statue, until there shall shine out from you the godlike splendour of virtue, until you shall see the perfect goodness surely established in the stainless shrine', *Enn.* I, 6, 9.

17 See Hadot, *Plotinus,* esp. 82–6.

18 The Platonic origins of this conception of the virtues again come from the *Phaedo,* 82d-83c.

19 Or again: 'The novice must hold himself constantly under some image of the Divine Being and seek in the light of a clear conception; knowing thus, in a deep conviction, whither he is going- into what a sublimity he penetrates – he must give himself forthwith to the inner and, radiant with the Divine Intellections, be no longer the seer but, as that place has made him, the seen', *Enn.* V, 8, 11.

20 Also, Platonic, Odyssean metaphorics of the return homewards.

21 Compare the comparable use of the view from above to counter the desire for glory in Petrarch's *secretum*, in **Chapter 6.2**.

Chapter 5

1 See **4.3**, with the articles 'The Divisions of the Parts of Philosophy in Antiquity' and 'Philosophy, Dialectic, and Rhetoric in Antiquity', in Hadot (2020: 105–62).

2 The extent of Saint Augustine's (354–430 CE) debts to Platonic philosophy is well known. Clement's and Origen's discourses already bear deep traces of their debts to the Neoplatonic philosophical discourse: whose notions of three hypostases, emanating from the transcendent One (*Hen*), would deeply inform the emerging theological understandings of the Father, Son and Holy Spirit. Likewise, the Aristotelian distinctions integrated into these Neoplatonic philosophies – between essence, substance, nature, and hypostasis, form and matter – 'furnished concepts that were indispensable for the formulation of the dogmas of the Trinity and the Incarnation'. Hadot (2002: 256).

3 For Evagrius, more than this, the goal of monastic practice can be described as cultivating the virtues, which he conceives explicitly on the basis of the tripartite Platonic psychology: 'The rational soul acts according to nature when its desiring part (*epithymetikon*) desires virtue, its spirited part (*thymikon*) fights for virtue, and its rational part (*logistikon*) attains the contemplation of beings.' At Hadot, *What Is Ancient Philosophy?*, 245.

4 Leclercq (1935) (in our translation): 'The Latin *exercitium* appears in translations of biblical texts, led by *1 Tim. 4, 7–8*, a passage which formed the basis of a long-standing distinction between bodily and spiritual practices. It is used also in early church descriptions of the trials of the martyrs. The *Historia Monachorum* (c. 395 CE) talks of both "monastic exercises" and "spiritual exercises"; Cassian speaks of "exercises of virtue"; and the term is sometimes reserved for difficult practices like vigils, fasting, the *durae crucis exercitia*. The term us also closely associated with practices of meditation wherein, as we will see, what is at issue is "the application of the spirit, and especially this effort of repetition, memory, and of reflection which is meditation; saint Isidore, in his turn, will formulate the same equivalence: *exercitium dicitur, hoc est meditatio*" (*Origines seu Etymologiae* XV, 2, 30, *PL* 82, 539a). He equates "to think, to proclaim, to repeat in order to be penetrated by [the text]", that is to say, to meditate and to speak, memorisation implying an effort to reiterate with the lips, which repeat and "chew" the sacred text. The anonymous author of *Octo puncta perfectionis assequendae* makes purity of heart the most important of the "spiritual exercises" (*PL* 184, 1181d-1182c). … [Later] Bernard uses …, in the singular, spiritual *exercitium* to designate all the trials of the spiritual life,

in which "temptations and tribulations exercise us" (*Sermones super Cantica* 21, 10, *PL* 183, 877ab, et t. 1, p 128, 5–12; cf. *De diversis*, 16, 6, *PL* 183, 582a; *In vigilia Nativitatis* 3, 6, *PL* 183, 97cd, etc). ... Nevertheless, more and more, and especially during the 12th century, the word *exercitia*, especially when it is accompanied by the epithet *spiritualia*, is used preferably to designate the activities of prayer.'

5 As Brian Stock (2001, 14) has commented, we simply have a great deal more of the writings of the Christian monks concerning their exercises than have survived to us from the Hellenistic and Roman philosophers.

6 Indeed, via Clement and Origin, the philosophical optic shapes monastic ways of reading the Bible, with its abundant inunctions to the faithful to 'take care', 'watch', 'pay attention' and the like: 'Thus, we saw Basil of Caesarea making a connection between *prosochē* and a text from Deuteronomy. Then, in Athanasius' *Life of Antony*, and throughout monastic literature, *prosochē* was transformed into the "watch of the heart," under the influence of *Proverbs*, 4:23: "Above all else, guard your heart." Examination of one's conscience was often justified by the *Second Letter to the Corinthians, 13:5*: "Examine yourselves ... and test yourselves." Finally, the meditation on death was recommended on the basis of *First Corinthians, 15*: 31: "I die every day"' (Hadot, 1995: 139).

7 The sermon takes as its text the Septuagint version of *Deuteronomy 15:9*; see Hadot, 'Ancient Spiritual Exercises', 130.

8 Like Marcus Aurelius's *Meditations*, which if read sequentially yield little logic, the sentences of the ascetic and mystical florilegia are often only grouped associatively: 'The structure is as free as the outline for meditation. To emphasize that there is nothing systematic about it, many an author will choose an entirely conventional number of chapters: one hundred. Maximus the Confessor and Diadochus of Photike had written Centuries' (Leclerq, 1996: 183). Or else, as in the commonplace books whose importance we will return to in **Chapters 6 and 7**, apothegms and sentences are grouped under conventional headers like the different virtues. See **Chapters 6.2** and **7.1**.

9 In his influential *Grammar*, reading Boethius's *Consolation of Philosophy*, the Carolingian scholar Alcuin (735–804 CE) replaces the figure of 'Philosophy' by Christian 'Divine Wisdom', anticipating what will be the later scholastic elevation of the science of theology as 'queen of the sciences'. This figure's dismissal of the liberal arts in Boethius is however now qualified, if not overturned. The liberal arts are now to be reinstated as necessary steps towards wisdom, rather than opponents to its pursuit or consolations. Alcuin next advances an allegorical interpretation of the biblical description of Solomon's mansion from Proverbs, which is said to have been built by wisdom and supported by seven pillars (cf. *Prov.* 9.1). The pillars represent, we are told, the 'seven degrees of philosophy' that the ancient philosophers exhausted themselves upon. But then, these degrees of 'philosophy' turn out for Alcuin to be none other than grammar, rhetoric, logic, astronomy, geometry, music and arithmetic; namely the trivium and quadrivium, which would become the core of the thirteenth-century Arts curricula (Domański, 1996: 37).

10 Domański himself will note that, as early as the tenth century, Gaudier of Spire could allegorically depict three brothers (physics, ethics and dialectic) attending their six sisters, the liberal arts minus dialectic – the parts of philosophy here remaining autonomous; as in the twelfth century, the school of Chartres added physics as a separate discipline to its curriculum; whether Abelard was also advocating for ethics as a separate *scientia*, at the same time as he headed a growing chorus of voices arguing for the ascendancy of dialectic in pedagogy.

11 This being the central thesis of the magisterial I. Hadot (2005).

12 When Thomas turns his attention to the ideal teaching order of the disciplines, we find a different, Aristotelian, but still discernibly pedagogical set of concerns governs his classification. Thomas's decisive consideration in recommending that students start with logic and mathematics, and only then ascend by way of the natural and moral sciences to the study of divine things, is the need for greater experience before a student tackles physics and ethical concerns. Then, there is the need for moral rectification before approaching the subjects of theology. See Weisheipl (1965: 88–9).

13 In all the *disputationes*, there were two sessions. The opening exchange was between objector and respondent; then, in the second section of the dispute, the master would intervene. His task was to summarize the positions put by each side, before presenting his own answer to the question, together with supporting argumentation.

14 Everything about the rules and setting of these disputations, then, bespeak the continuing medieval, pedagogical debt to Aristotle's *Topics*, and the rules of the pedagogical dialectical game that 'the philosopher' set out, apparently for his own students in book VIII of that text. John of Salisbury, in his *Metalogicon*, makes clear the importance of this philosophical text, in order to understand the rules of the *disputationes*.

15 Domański, *La Philosophie*, 50.

16 As Imbach (1996: 31) has documented, nearly the same vision was in fact shared by Aubrey of Reims in his *Philosophia* of around 1260. The philosopher, as Aubrey envisages him, flees base pleasures in search of union with 'this imperial Queen' which is philosophy. 'It is beautiful to excel in her [philosophy]', Aubrey intones, 'because, through her, all men are perfect: to ignore [philosophy] is ugly, for it is only in an equivocal sense that one calls a man who ignores [philosophy] a man.'

17 Richard Kilwardy (1215–79 CE) in the *De ortu scientiarum* is the third figure Domański examines in this medieval counter-lineage of meta-philosophical discourse, at Imbach (1996: 73–4).

18 Bacon cites with approval Cicero on the ancient exercise of the Meditatio mortis as illustrating such a 'practicist' bent to philosophical learning: an exercise which we know looks back to the Platonic Phaedo, before receiving different articulations in the Stoic, Epicurean and Neoplatonic schools (Domański, 1996: 75).

Notes

19 As such, in the second Treatise, Dante likens moral philosophy to the eighth, governing sphere in the celestial harmony: the sphere which, literally, moves the heavens and thereby maintains that order that allows all life, including human life, to flourish. The seven premier celestial spheres represent or reflect the seven liberal arts with which we are familiar; whilst the ninth, quiet sphere beyond the firmament belongs to contemplation. Nevertheless, without this eighth sphere: 'Here below there would be neither generation, nor the life of animals, nor of plants; there would be no night, nor day, nor week, nor month, nor year; but the whole Universe would be disordered, and the movement of the stars would be in vain. Not otherwise, should Moral Philosophy cease to be, would the other Sciences be hidden for some time, and there would be no generation nor life of happiness, and all books would be in vain, and all discoveries of old. Therefore, it is sufficiently evident that there is a comparison between this Heaven and Moral Philosophy.' See Imbach, *Dante*, 136 ff.

Chapter 6

1 The one outlier here is Machiavelli's *The Prince*, a staple in political philosophy courses.

2 Our argument in this chapter will be especially indebted to these two scholars' work.

3 Wallis's work, like Diogenes Laertius's or Eunapius's in later antiquity, collected information on the lives and sentences of the philosophers, presenting them as models of life. Walter Burley in his popular *De vita et moribus philosophorum* (*c*. 1330–45 CE) reworks Diogenes Laertius, as translated into Latin by Henri Aristippus in twelfth century.

4 Most of their sayings and actions have been introduced in the book without taking account of the sentiment of decency in such a way that they could cause concern, Traversari apologises: 'nevertheless, the rules of translation and of respect for the truth do not authorise me to omit them.' At Domański (1996: 101–2).

5 The Northern humanist Erasmus of Rotterdam, in the sixteenth century, in his *Convivium religiosum* evokes Virgil, Cicero, Socrates and others as 'pagan saints'. In his *Sileni Alcibiadis* the Northern humanist lists Socrates, Diogenes and Epictetus alongside John the Baptist, the apostles, Saint Martin and Christ as examples of what he terms 'Silenic' lives, manifest in their teaching as well as their comportment. Domański (1996: 115).

6 'I think there has been a tendency,' Kristeller can write: 'To assign to [the humanists] an importance in the history of scientific and philosophical thought which they neither could nor did attain. ... Those scholars who read the treatises of the humanists and noticed their comparative emptiness of scientific and philosophical thought came to the conclusion that the humanists

were bad scientists and philosophers … [yet] the Italian humanists on the whole were neither good nor bad philosophers, but no philosophers at all.' Kristeller (1961: 100). Compare: 'In the field of Philosophy Humanism must be regarded, quite frankly, as a Philistine movement: even an obscurantist movement. In that sense the New Learning created the New Ignorance.' C. S. Lewis, *New Learning and New Ignorance*, cited at Perreiah (1982: 3).

7   Salutati and Bruni, for instance, were chancellors of Florence, a large component of whose role consisted in crafting official orations, letters and documentation. These men saw in the recovery of classical norms of behaviour and style the means to cultivate a new republican elite. See Baron (1966). Guarini and several others were teachers of grammar, rhetoric and poetry. See Grafton and Jardine (1986).

8   On this fivefold humanist division of rhetoric, grammar, moral philosophy, poetry and history, see, e.g. Kristeller's 'Humanist Learning in the Renaissance' and 'The Moral Thought of the Humanists', 20–68, both in Kristeller (1980). As Kristeller writes: 'The humanists continued the medieval tradition in these fields [of grammar and rhetoric], as represented, for example, by the *ars dictaminis* and the *ars arengandi*, but they gave it a new direction toward classical standards and classical studies,' Kristeller (1961: 100–1). See for a competing account than Kristeller's, Witt (2006: 21–35).

9   Kristeller (1980; 39).

10   See, e.g. Kennedy (2003: 58–74).

11   See Hadot (2020: 133–40).

12   See Long (1999b: 85–7); and the articles collected in *Advances in the History of Rhetoric* 14:1 (2011): 'Rhetorics of Reason & Restraint: Stoic Rhetoric from Antiquity to the Present' [special edition].

13   See Siegel, 'Rhetoric and Philosophy: the Ciceronian Model', 3–30.

14   See Perreiah, 'Humanist Critique', 3–5 for example.

15   See *De Or.* III. 66: 'They [the Stoics] have a manner of speaking which is perhaps subtle, and certainly acute, but for an orator, dry, strange, unsuited to the ear of the populace, obscure, barren, jejune, and altogether of that species which a speaker cannot use to a multitude … if we should adopt their notions, we should never be able to expedite any business by speaking.'

16   See Nauta (2009; 2016).

17   Petrarch, *Familiar Letters* I, 6: 'Against Aged Dialecticians'.

18   See Zak (2010: 81–2).

19   Cf.: 'for the cure of the mind you do not go to philosophers, who, if they are true philosophers are certainly doctors of minds (*animorum medici*) and experts on living. For if they are false and only puffed up with the name of philosophy, not only must they not be consulted but they must be avoided – nothing is more troublesome and insipid than such philosophers, of whom no age is more abundant than our own, since it is so lacking in good men.'

Notes

20   On this Petrarchan text, see Maggi (2012); and in the same volume, Barsella (2012). The metaphors of height we observe here (viz. the mountain, the sky) are significant, and recur across Petrarch's works. Petrarch's famous 'Ascent of Mount Ventoux' with his brother explicitly develops the analogy between this physical climb and Petrarch's search for wisdom. The 'view from above' (3) afforded by his attaining to the summit with his brother, Gherardo, provokes in Petrarch a turn inwards (5). He is moved by the spatial panorama to an urgent sense of the need to conquer a comparably unifying perspective of his own life, across the span of time: 'Thus my thoughts turned back over the last ten years and then with concentrated thought on the future, I asked myself: "If you should be chance, prolong this uncertain life of yours for another ten years, advancing towards virtue in proportion to the distance from which you departed from your original infatuation during the past two years ... could you not face death on reaching forty years of age, if not with complete assurance then at least with hopefulness, calmly dismissing from your thoughts the residuum of life that fades into old age?"' Petrarch (2000: 14–16). See Zak (2012: 499–500).

21   See McClure (1991: chapters 1–3), which deal respectively with the letters, the *Secret Book* and the *Remedies*.

22   Petrarch, *Sen.*, 16.9, at McClure, *Sorrow and Consolation*, 56: 'in which I strive to the best of my abilities to mollify or, if possible, to extirpate my own passions and those of my readers'.

23   'The third point is this: if a man expends every effort to become happy, it is in his power to do so,' Petrarch (1989: 42). Compare Seneca, *Ep. 93.2*.

24   Compare, at Petrarch (1989: 44): 'Now if it is virtue only that makes the happiness of man, which is demonstrated by Cicero and a whole multitude of weighty reasons, it follows of necessity that nothing is opposed to true happiness except what is also opposed to virtue.'

25   'You should rather turn to those studies to which you had dedicated your youth and which would have made your advanced years certainly tranquil except that your homeland which you now desire had forbidden them. However, they will certainly make your old age peaceful and venerable if it remains a despiser not only of your exile but of all casual things. I speak of liberal studies and especially of that part of philosophy which is the teacher of life.' *Fam.*, 2.4.27–9; cf. Zak (2010: 92–4).

26   On Petrarch's understanding of reading and its continuity with medieval models of *lectio*, see Carruthers (2008: 203–33) and Chapter **5.2**.

27   In his *Familiar Letters* 7.16, Petrarch can therefore even 'beg' [his addressee] to not go easy, but to 'reveal me to myself': 'turn your most eloquent pen this way; ... seize, bind, strike, burn, cut, restrain all exaggeration, cut away all that is superfluous, and do not fear that you will cause me either to blush or to grow pale. A dismal drink drives away dismal illness. I am ill, who does not know it? I must be cured by more bitter remedies than yours.'

28 Respectively, *Essays* I 37, I 40, I 50, II 32. Hereafter, in this section, we will refer to the *Essays*, as here, by book and chapter, and the pages from *The Complete Essays of Montaigne*, trans. D. Frame (Stanford, CA: Stanford University Press, 1958).

29 See: 'I cannot keep my subject still. It goes along befuddled and staggering, with a natural drunkenness. I take it in this condition, just as it is at the moment I give my attention to it. I do not portray being: I portray passing .... I may presently change, not only by chance, but also by intention. This is a record of various and changeable occurrences, and of irresolute and, when it so befalls, contradictory ideas: whether I am different myself, or whether I take hold of my subjects in different circumstances and aspects. So, all in all, I may indeed contradict myself now and then; but truth, as Demades said, I do not contradict,' *Ess.* III.2, 610–11).

30 See Jacob Zeitlin, 'The Development of Bacon's Essays: With Special Reference to the Question of Montaigne's Influence upon Them', *The Journal of English and Germanic Philology*, 27/4 (October 1928), 496–519; and Kenneth Alan Hovey, '"Mountaigny Saith Prettily": Bacon's French and the Essay', *PMLA* 106: 1 (January 1991), 71–82.

31 Compare 'It is many years now that I have had only myself as object of my thoughts, that I have been examining and studying only myself; and if I study anything else, it is in order promptly to apply it to myself, or rather within myself. And it does not seem to me that I am making a mistake ... There is no description equal in difficulty, or certainly in usefulness, to the description of oneself' (II, 6, 273); again, 'I study myself more than any other subject. That is my metaphysics, that is my physics' (III, 13, 821).

32 Let us mention the political valences of the *Essais*: a book Montaigne's cited Preface ostentatiously dates as having been completed on the eighteenth anniversary (20 June 1862) of the Massacre at Vassy, and which frequently decries the cruelties of the French religious wars. Montaigne's 'playing the fool' might well, in this register, reflect his desire to 'speak the truth, not so much as I would, but as much as I dare'.

33 *Ess.* I.20, 122.

34 Since the hour of death is unknown, we should premeditate upon it: Let us disarm him of his novelty and strangeness, let us converse and be familiar with him, and have nothing so frequent in our thoughts as death' (I, 19, 60); death removes from us all other troubles; being dead is like to before we were born; if you have lived well, be content; if badly, death will end the miseries; that our life is but a moment in eternity: 'long life, and short life, are made by death but one'; that death is natural, so to despise death is to despise the world; that nature only repeats herself, the eternal recurrence of the same; our death makes space for the next generations (per Lucretius); if you are alive, death is nothing to you; if you are dead, you are nothing (per Epicurus); it is not the length of life, but its quality (as per Epictetus's theatre metaphor: it not being

the length but the quality of the play that counts); and death is a blessing, since immortal life would be truly unbearable.

35 See Hankins and Ada Palmer, *The Recovery of Classical Philosophy in the Renaissance*.

36 Compare: the criticism of Pyrrhonism at II 12, 430. Montaigne clearly allows for levels of probability and argues that we can more safely judge concerning our own experience although the 'form and essence' of things is evidently not given to us. He would rather follow, in III.11 'the solid and the probable' rather than obscure and improbable; and compare. II 12, 421, and Montaigne's metaphor of the bears and their cubs, little by little being licked into form over time.

37 See 403: 'Let us lay aside this infinite confusion of opinions, which we see even amongst the philosophers themselves, and this perpetual and universal dispute about the knowledge of things; for this is truly presupposed, that men, I mean the most knowing, the best born, and of the best parts, are not agreed about any one thing, not that heaven is over our heads; for they that doubt of everything, do also doubt of that; and they who deny that we are able to comprehend anything, say that we have not comprehended that the heaven is over our heads, and these two opinions are, without comparison, the stronger in number.'

38 Cf. 'These transcendental humours affright me, like high and inaccessible places', as Montaigne writes in 'Of Experience', the last essay of the 1588 text: 'and nothing is hard for me to digest in the life of Socrates but his ecstasies and communication with demons; nothing so human in Plato as that for which they say he was called divine; and of our sciences, those seem to be the most terrestrial and low that are highest mounted; and I find nothing so humble and mortal in the life of Alexander as his fancies about his immortalisation', from *Ess.* III 13, 856. See Sharpe (2016b).

39 Sellars (2007: 339). We are indebted to this article in this section, as we indicated in the Introduction and as is reflected in the notes which follow.

40 As Sellars notes, the choice of such a literary form is provocative and interesting: are we to take Lipsius's submission to play the younger man's role as a matter of gracefully avoiding the position of the *subjet supposé savoir*, as a man or 'one making progress' still at this time in his thirties, or is it (also) a political guise to ensure that the text did not provoke the censors' anger? See Sellars (2017: 342–3), with 356–7. See Morford (1991: 161–4).

41 Later, we are instructed that 'the school of the philosopher is a physician's shop', as Musonius Rufus had taught (also Epictetus), at Lipsius, *Const.*, I, 10, 47.

42 Sellars sees in Lipsius's further qualification of constancy as 'a voluntary sufferance without grudging of all things whatsoever can happen to or in a man' (*Const.* 1, 4, 37) as being 'the foundations laid for the modern popular image of the Stoic heroically enduring whatever fate throws at him', as against

being someone for whom these evils are not 'truly' evils at all, and as such do not need to be 'suffered'.

43   Lipsius's typology, as in Petrarch's *De Remediis*, is that of Cicero, as Sellars notes at 2017: 345–6. Joy and desire 'puff up the mind', responding to the presence or anticipation of external things taken to be 'good'. By contrast, as we know, fear and sorrow 'press it down too much', in response to the presence or anticipation of external things taken to be, imperatively, 'evil' for us. This is especially so, to the extent that such emotions are supported by unphilosophic *endoxa*.

44   Lipsius makes it very clear which particular public affliction is presently distressing him: see how the country of Belgica is affected with sundry calamities, and swinged on every side with the scorching flame of civil wars. The fields are wasted and spoiled, defiled, virgins defloured, with such other like miseries as follow after wars. *Const.*, I, 7, 43.

45   *On Const.*, I, 8, 44. Too often, Langius presses in a 'sharp reprehension' at which Lipsius takes umbrage (I, 9, 46), people bewail their own misfortunes in their hearts. They lament public misfortunes 'in words only and for fashion's sake.'

46   Sellars considers but questions the proximity, at Sellars (2017: 356). *De Constantia* is not, in his view, a work of consolation. It is a dialogue *ad se* and a work of psychotherapy, more like the *De Remediis* of Petrarch (see **5.2**). For us, it is less the consolatory intentionality than the theological and theodical content in Lipsius's second book, and Boethius's third-through-fifth books that invites the comparison.

47   Seneca, *Consolation to Polybius*, 5, 9–11.

48   For the dog being dragged behind the cart metaphor, see Epictetus, *Ench.* 53, and Seneca, *Ep.* 107.10.

49   Cf. Lucretius, *Nature of Things*, ends of books I and II.

50   And here, in a way much more developed than in Petrarch, *On Constancy* thematizes the tension between Christian and Stoic teachings. Fate, Langius advises, is the product of God's mind and Providence, and He is not subject to fate; fate is beneath God; all creation is subject to His Will. The Stoic idea that Zeus himself is subject to fate, as an imminent, material being is directly raised and rejected (*Const.*, I, 20, 69–70). Langius instead emphasizes a distinction between God as primary cause for all events, and secondary causes for particular events, which – again now departing alike from Stoicism and some forms of contemporary Protestantism – include human free will. Lipsius's intentions here, we see, are to make Stoicism consistent with Christianity by jettisoning elements of the former's physics and theology. With that said, we should also note that in other works, he defends the full compatibility of Christianity and Stoic metaphysics. The Stoics, he notes, also distinguished between primary and secondary causes in just Langius's way in *On Constancy*, and argued for the compatibility of determinism and human freedom. It is

little wonder in any case that Lipsius's *On Constancy* I, 21, 71–2 contains a cautionary retraction: they are in perilous waters and ought not inquire too much farther. See on this issue, Sellars (2014b: 653–74); with his 2017: 348–50.

51   Certainly, ordinary human understanding may not be able to grasp that it is necessary for some transient parts of the whole to perish in order to preserve the order and beauty of the whole, just as Lady Philosophy had advised her charge in *The Consolation of Philosophy* (see **4.5**) But faith goes beyond reason.

52   It is notable that the God who is invoked in the final words seems as close to the Stoic notion of the creative fire than to the Christian deity. So Langius implores: 'Because that as fire is not forced out of the flint with one stroke, so in these frozen hearts of ours, the lurking and languishing sparks of honesty are not kindled with the first stroke of admonitions. Which, that they may at the last be thoroughly enkindled in thee, not in words or appearance, but in deed and fact, I humbly and reverently beseech that eternal and celestial fire', Lipsius, *Const.*, II, 24, 129. If this is only a figure of speech, it is a loaded figure.

Chapter 7

1   For an indicative collection, attesting to the extent of Bacon's humanistic *paideia*, see Francis Bacon, *Bacon's Essays, including his Moral and Historical Works, namely The Essays, The Colours of Good and Evil; Ornamenta Rationalia, or Elegant Sentences; Short Notes for Civil Conversation; Advancement of Learning; Wisdom of the Ancients; New Atlantis; Apophthegms; History of Henry VII, … VIII, … Elizabeth, with Memoir, Notes and Glossary* (London: Frederick Warned and Co., 1911). See also Vickers (2000).

2   Here as elsewhere, we cite the *Novum* as NO, then by book, then section or aphorism number.

3   Both Bacon's biblical language of 'idols', and his depiction of the mind as by nature proud (unhappy to countenance contradiction) and slothful (ever-ready to leap to comforting generalizations), reflect his Christian as well as pagan-philosophical heritage. See, for instance, this passage: 'The human mind resembles not a dry light, but admits a tincture of the will and passions, which generate their own system accordingly; for man always believes more readily that which he prefers. He, therefore, rejects difficulties for want of patience in investigation; sobriety, because it limits his hope; the depths of nature, from superstition; the light of experiment, from arrogance and pride … in short, his feelings imbue and corrupt his understanding in innumerable and sometimes imperceptible ways.' NO I, XLIX.

4   The Christian and pagan premeditation of death, in this vein, is held by Bacon as later by Spinoza to be 'more fearful and cautious than the nature of things

requireth. So have they increased the fear of death in offering to cure it.' *Adv.* II, XXI, 5. See 'Of Death', *Essays*.

5 Aristotle is again attacked for treating the passions only in his *Rhetoric*, while Plutarch and Seneca get some fairly muted praise: 'some particular writings of an elegant nature, touching some of the affections: as of anger, of comfort upon adverse accidents, of tenderness of countenance, and other'. *Adv.* II, XXI, 6.

6 Bacon, 'Of Nature', 'Of Custom', *Essays*.

7 With that said, there is a distinctly modern, dynamic dimension to Descartes's enjoyment which concerns not the contemplation of truths already secured, but novel discoveries: 'since every day I discovered through this method some truths which seemed to me sufficiently important and commonly unknown to other men, the satisfaction I got from it so filled my mind that nothing else affected me.' Compare Bacon on augmentation, as better than preservation, in *AL* II.20–22.

8 This, so that even he who would follow Descartes's method 'must make an effort, … must not seek to deceive our world, and the interests of financial reward, career, and status must be combined in a way that is fully compatible with the norms of disinterested research, etcetera' (Foucault, 2005: 18).

Chapter 8

1 Italics here again being ours.

2 He remains open to a plurality of possible perspectives. And while he may not assent to others' conclusions, he seeks always to comprehend their rationales. Thus, 'the philosopher understands the sentiment that he rejects, to the same extent and with the same clarity that he understands the one he adopts'.

3 The link which we saw that Montaigne suggested between cruelty and unfounded metaphysical claims is suggested here (**Chapter 7.1**).

4 As for the implied charge that the wisdom of such a man would incline him to suppose himself beyond good and evil: 'Crime would find in him too much opposition, he would have too many natural ideas and too many acquired ideas to destroy.' Like Socrates or the followers of Zeno: 'He is afraid to be off-key, to be out of harmony with himself; and this reminds me of what Velleius said of Cato of Utica. "Never," he said, "did he do good deeds in order to appear to have done them, but because it was not in him to do otherwise."'

5 It is the method of dogmatists, as against sceptical inquirers, 'not to speak soberly of the reasons of the opposite party', Bayle comments, 'to hide all weak spots of the cause they defend', and to choose or present only those adversaries and objections they can parry.

6 See Bayle, *Dictionnaire*, 'David', 'Manicheans', 'Paulicians', 'Simonides'.

Notes

7   On the great importance of travel literature from the new world and Far East in shaping the intellectual culture of the enlightenment philosophes, see Wade (2015: 361–91). See chapter 6.2 on Montaigne. There is a link between certain sceptical tropes, emphasizing the relativity of perceptions and opinions, and what the early modern free thinkers saw in the accounts of the new world and Far East: means to relativize their own and their own cultures' perceptions and opinions, by demonstrating that there were other ways of seeing and being in the world.

8   See in general the chapter 'Organic Unity in Voltaire'; *Intellectual Development of Voltaire*, esp. 367–450, with 755–67. Voltaire's *Philosophical Dictionary* of 1764 condenses this manifold into one work, with its 486 alphabetized entries on everything from metaphysical subjects like the soul, free will or God to biblical topics such as Adam, Agar or Hagar, David or Bethshemesh; from the history of the Church, like Counsels, Constantine and Universities to the lives and thought of philosophers like Aristotle, Bayle or Cicero; and from historical figures like Caesar, Gregory VII or the Franks, to apparent curios like the beard, bees, laughter, the different significations of the word '*fasti*' or the extinction of the Greek language at Marseilles. Some of these entries read like short essays. Others are longer, almost self-contained works. Others again are epigrammatic. 'On Disputations', 'Cicero' and several others include poetry. The entries on 'Nature', 'China' and a dozen others feature fictive dialogues. Many other entries contain Voltairean fables and mises-en-scènes, with the philosophe speaking through personae or placing likely speeches into the mouths of historical figures.

9   Firstly, Confucius is singled out, as 'a sage of simple manners and character, without arrogance and without imposture, who taught men how to live happy six hundred years before our era'. It is exactly the absence of any metaphysical or theological bases for his 'rule of conduct' that Voltaire admires, alongside its simple, universalizable tenets: 'Rule a state as you rule a family; a man cannot govern his family well without giving a good example … Under the good kings Yao and Xu, the Chinese were good; under the bad kings Kie and Chu, they were wicked. Do to another as to thyself; love mankind in general, but cherish those who are good; forget injuries, but never benefits.' Voltaire (2004: 334–5).

10 In his own life, Voltaire set himself up at different periods in Cirey and Ferney as a kind of monarch of the mind, to whom visitors from all Europe would come to pay court. Voltaire is also famous for his marvellous apothegms, many of which are worthy of Diogenes Laertius Lives, as when Casanova informed Voltaire that van Haller, whom Voltaire had praised to the skies, did not speak as well of the patriarch. 'Well, perhaps we are both of us mistaken,' was the reply – and we can almost see the wry smile pursing the lips of the master.

11 Again, in 'The Two Consolers', Voltaire (1807: 179–81) has fun with the ancient genre of the philosophical consolation. 'The great philosopher Citosile' sets

about consoling a young bereaved woman in Senecan vein, by adducing examples of eminent women, Mary Stuart, the daughter of Henri IV, Joan of Naples, Hecuba and Niobe, who have suffered greater calamities. 'Ah!', Voltaire has the young lady reply: 'had I lived in their time, or in that of so many beautiful princesses, and had you endeavoured to console them by a relation of my misfortunes, would they have listened to you, do you imagine?' The next day, the philosopher loses his son, and his plucky student sends him a catalogue of great men who had suffered worse losses than his. 'He read it – found it very exact – and wept nevertheless,' Voltaire tells us. The denouement comes when the two meet again after three months: 'and were mutually surprised to find each other in such a gay and sprightly humour. To commemorate this event, they caused to be erected a beautiful statue to Time, with this inscription: "TO HIM WHO COMFORTS"'.

12 See esp. Voltaire, 'Fanaticism', in 2004: 201–4.

13 Voltaire, 'Fanaticism [full text]', https://ebooks.adelaide.edu.au/v/voltaire/dictionary/chapter199.html

14 Echoing Du Marsais's stress on the philosophe's sociability, Voltaire frequently protests that, while philosophical sects have often multiplied, their votaries have never killed each other. Meanwhile, throughout history, philosophers led by Socrates have been censored, indicted, exiled or killed by people claiming to speak in the name of God or the gods.

15 The speech is put in the mouth of 'a man who had some knowledge of the human heart' by Voltaire.

16 Voltaire, 'The Questions of Zapata translated by Dr. Tamponbt of the Sorbonne', https://en.wikisource.org/wiki/The_Questions_of_Zapata, 66

17 In *Candide*, as everybody knows, it is not Christianity but Popean and Leibnizian theodicy that falls victim of Voltaire's philosophical satire. The comedic contrast here is not between two competing dimensions within Leibniz's attempts to show that this is the best of possible worlds – although Pangloss is at one point set to be burnt by the Inquisition for the heterodoxy of the teaching. The contradiction which makes the comedy bite here is between this Rationalist doctrine, articulated at the highest pitch of abstraction, and the concrete miseries, all based on historical events that beset Candide, his beloved Cunegonde and Pangloss, from the moment that Cunegonde's father evicts the *amants* from Edenic Westphalia. See on this text the classic study Wade (1959). '*If we are to believe this and actually to live it*', Voltaire is crying out in *Candide* (to use Victor Hugo's verb): '*then we must accept slaughter, greed, natural disasters, auto-da-fés, rapine, pillage, stupidity, prejudice, fanaticism, slavery, deception, lechery … Your a priori theorems have this a posteriori corollaries. However, once we exit our studies and our systems to rebecome fathers, mothers, lovers, brothers, sisters, friends, in brief, human beings, we see that this corollary is abhorrent*'.

18 Diderot characteristically admired Socrates as someone who not only 'theorized' virtue, but lived it out in action, and unto death, not as 'an affair of ostentation and parade, but of courage and practice'. After his time in Vincennes, Diderot thought of writing a play on Socrates's death. By contrast, in a pattern again presaged in Voltaire, he was as sceptical about Plato as enamoured of his teacher, whom he presents as the best of citizens, as well as men. In Diderot's entry 'Socratique' in the *Encyclopaedia*, for example, he declaims that 'Socrates saw that it was necessary to work to make men good, before starting to make them learned; that while we had our eyes attached to the stars, we did not know what happened at his feet ... that time was lost in frivolous speculation ... and he brought back to earth the philosophy lost in the regions of the sun'.

19 As Andrew (2016: 385; 2004: 294–5) puts it: 'Diderot's works on Seneca were ... an apology for his (Diderot's) life as the beneficiary of tyranny [Catherine the Great's] as well as an accusation of Satanic pride and ingratitude on the part of his former friend Rousseau'. Russo is scarcely more charitable: 'Diderot's Seneca was ... a *pis-aller*, a makeshift role model appropriate to a tainted philosopher who had several times bowed to necessity, played the game, and recanted his ideas ... ' Russo (2009: 9).

20 By contrast, Diderot can still raise encomia to Seneca's 'natural religion', and the sublimity of the Stoic's language in describing the natural world in passages that suggest Diderot's continuing proximity to the Deism of Voltaire and his own earlier *Philosophical Thoughts* (of 1745): 'Thus the soul of the great man, the virtuous man, sent from above to show us the deity more closely, stays at our side without forgetting the place of its origin. She recollects this high origin, she aspires to return there, she remains attached to this provenance ... Such are the points Seneca makes, when speaking of God, justice and the virtuous man'. In the same vein, Diderot has little patience for Stoic logic, depicting those parts of Seneca's oeuvre wherein the latter engages in renditions of the famous Stoic paradoxes as sophistical. In these aspects, he claims: 'the Stoic philosophy is a species of theology full of subtleties'. Diderot (1828: 273–4).

21 With characteristic pathos, Diderot tells us that he is moved to tears by the sociable generosity manifest in *On Benefits* – indeed one central text in his reading of Seneca, as Edward Andrew (2004) has stressed. 'One is convinced, dragged, by reading the treatise *On Anger*', Diderot writes. By contrast: 'one is softened, touched, by reading *On Benefits*. The one is full of strength; the other of finesse; in the former, it is reason that commands; in the latter, it is the delicacy of feeling that charms. Seneca speaks to the heart, and is none the less convincing: because the heart has its evidence ... ' Diderot (1828: 280–1, 296).

22 On Diderot's criticism of the contemplative life, in words he puts into Seneca's mouth, see Lojkine (2001: 107–8, 113–14).

Chapter 9

1   It is one measure of the extent to which we have seen a contemporary, popular rehabilitation of Cynic PWL that Martha Nussbaum has used Hipparchia as an exemplar of how to live in a valedictory address to law school graduate students: https://www.law.uchicago.edu/news/law-school-celebrates-new-graduates

2   We should note, though, that the Renaissance reception of ancient Cynicism was complicated and ambivalent. Hugh Roberts shows that Renaissance thinkers hardly ever questioned the status of Cynicism as a philosophy, and that Diogenes's comic, philosophical performance informed the Renaissance ideal of self-fashioning (see Roberts, 2006).

3   Compare the Roman Stoics positive appraisal of Cynicism in Epictetus's portrait of the ideal Cynic (*Diss.* 3.22.1–109).

4   It is worth recalling that not all Hegelians rejected ancient philosophy. The left Hegelian Ludwig Feuerbach, to take one example, attempted to revive the spirit of ancient philosophy. In his late unfinished treatise 'On Eudaimonism' (1867/1869), he sought to develop a new Epicurean-inspired ethics of hedonism (see Bishop, 2009).

5   Schopenhauer was well versed in Hellenistic philosophies, especially Epicureanism and Stoicism. He discusses Greek Stoics like Chrysippus, citing fragments from Diogenes Laertius, Stobaeus and Plutarch, and the main Roman Stoics, Seneca, Marcus Aurelius and Seneca. Schopenhauer drew the epigraph of *WWR* 2 from Seneca (*Ep.* 79.17). By means of his Seneca epigraph, Schopenhauer implies that he will join the ranks of great philosophers like Epicurus who was enviously ignored or silenced by his contemporaries, but who ultimately achieved posthumous fame.

6   Despite Schopenhauer's late attempt to formulate a eudaimonistic perspective or 'instructions to a happy existence' (*PP* 1: 273) in his essay 'Aphorism on the Wisdom of Life' (1850), we will not discuss it here, even though, as Janaway observes it 'owes much to Stoicism and his advice is peppered with quotations from the likes of Seneca and Epictetus' (Janaway, 2014: xxxii). We bracket Schopenhauer's late popular, eudaimonistic because it rejects *the* essential feature of PWL (**5**): namely, the idea that philosophy is transformative. In his 1850 essay, Schopenhauer argues that our measure of happiness is determined in advance by our character, which is impervious to transformation. He claims that only rare geniuses naturally endowed with an excess of intellect can enjoy godlike happiness, and only then if they are fortunate enough to live without want. 'People with superior intellectual powers', he claims, 'are capable, and in fact, in need of the most lively interest by way of mere cognition, without any interference of the will. But this interest then transports them to a region where pain is essentially alien, into the atmosphere of the lightly living gods, "of the gods who live at ease"' (*PP* 1: 295; quoting Odys. IV, 805). For Schopenhauer,

because the vast majority lack this excess of intellect they are condemned a life of insatiable desire or boredom, and they cannot alter their fate through the practice of philosophy. This is the deeply unpopular thesis of his so-called popular philosophy. Cf. Vasalou (2013: 162).

7   In attacking university philosophy, Schopenhauer was responding to aspects of the model that developed in the philosophical faculty of the 1810 University of Berlin, a model that, Christopher Celenza claims, is still with us today. Celenza argues that this model carries assumptions that do not reflect the practice of ancient, medieval or Renaissance philosophy. These include the assumption that real or professional philosophy is primarily about metaphysics and ontology, privileges epistemology, and, crucially for our purposes, 'trains the mind to become more intellectual agile rather than the person to become more morally whole, is primarily about doctrines rather than practice, is centred on the written word rather than the well-lived life' (see Celenza, 2005: 484–5).

8   Or, as Atwell nicely neatly explains Schopenhauer's key idea: 'The double-sided world [as both will and representation] is the striving of the will to become conscious of itself so that, recoiling in horror of its inner, self-divisive nature, it may annul itself and thereby its self-affirmation, and then reach salvation' (Atwell, 1995: 31).

9   This point is a matter of contention among Schopenhauer scholars. Strictly speaking, Schopenhauer maintains that reason never determines the will. Yet Schopenhauer's principle that philosophy is 'always theoretical' and can never 'become practical' or 'shape character' (*WWR* I: 297) is one that, at least in the case of his own philosophy, he honours more in the breach than the observance. Throughout *WWR* Schopenhauer directly suggests that correct, intuitive metaphysical cognition radically transforms the knower, turning him/her from the affirmation to the denial of the will to life. In this chapter, we therefore follow Julian Young's view that Schopenhauer's claim that philosophy is purely theoretical is a confused self-misrepresentation on his part (see Young, 2005: 158–68; 2008: 321, fn 2). We thank David Cartwright for urging us to clarify our interpretation of this point.

10 Schopenhauer condemns Stoicism on similar grounds to Augustine. Augustine polemicizes against the Stoics 'ungodly pride' in their reason, mocking their belief that we can realize a perfectly happy life through exercising rational, voluntary control over our passions (*civ.* 14.9; see also 19.4).

11 'Reason which is not able to control the will'. On akrasia see Aristotle, *Nicomachean Ethics* VII, chapters 1–5. For an excellent summary of modern debates on akrasia see the Stanford Encyclopaedia of Philosophy entry, 'Weakness of the Will', https://plato.stanford.edu/entries/weakness-will/index. html#ref-1

12 Cf. Epictetus *Diss.* II. 26.7 (discussed in Chapter 3): 'Socrates knew how a rational soul is moved: that it is like a balance, and if a weight is thrown in the scale, it will incline whether it wishes or not. Show the rational governing faculty a contradiction, and it will renounce it.'

13 Schopenhauer again echoes Augustine's criticism of Stoicism. Augustine identifies the failure of Stoicism to genuinely affirm life by proposing the test of eternity. Can Stoics wish for eternal life? If not, he argues, then they do not affirm life (*civ.* 19.4).

14 See *PP* 2: 170: 'Stoicism of disposition, which defies fates, is of course also a good armour against the suffering of life and useful in order to better endure the present, but it stands in the way of true salvation because it hardens the heart. How is it supposed to be improved by sufferings if, encased in a stony rind, it does not sense them? – Moreover a certain degree of this stoicism is not very rare … where it is undisguised it usually arises from mere absence of feeling, from a lack of energy, vitality, sensitivity and imagination, which are even required for great sorrow.'

15 Bernard Reginster usefully explains the difference between Stoic endurance and Schopenhauerian resignation in the following terms: 'Ordinarily, to be resigned does not mean that I cease to desire a certain object, but only that I accept that it is out of my reach and therefore renounce its pursuit. Complete resignation, by contrast, requires not only that I renounce pursuing a desire, but also that I become indifferent to whether or not it is satisfied, and this amounts to renouncing the desire itself' (Reginster, 2009: 105).

16 Schopenhauer, Nietzsche observes 'was the first admitted and inexorable atheist among us Germans … The ungodliness of existence was for him something given, palpable, indisputable; he always lost his philosopher's composure and became indignant when he saw anyone hesitate or mince matters at this point. This is the locus of his whole integrity; unconditional and honest atheism is simply the presupposition of the way he poses his problem, being a triumph achieved finally and with great difficulty by the European conscience, being the most fateful act of two thousand years of discipline for truth that in the end forbids itself the lie in faith in God' (*GS* 357).

17 Elsewhere, Schopenhauer offers a moment of dark comic relief from this pessimistic view: 'Suppose this race were transported to a fool's paradise, where everything grew on its own and the pigeons flew around already roasted, and everyone found his dearly beloved and held on to her without difficulty. There some would die of boredom, or hang themselves, but some would assault, throttle and murder each other' (*PP* 2: 293).

18 See Thomas à Kempis, *Imitation of Christ*, Book 3 Internal Consolation: 'A man's true progress consists in denying himself [*abnegatio sui ipsius*], and the man who has denied himself is truly free and secure. The old enemy, however, setting himself against all good, never ceases to tempt them, but day and night plots dangerous snares to cast the unwary into the net of deceit. "Watch ye and pray", says the Lord, "that ye enter not into temptation".'

19 'Ultimately, scientific knowledge is practical. It produces more efficient means for reshaping, responding, and manipulating the world to serve human needs' (Cartwright, 2010: 300).

Notes

Chapter 10

1   Nietzsche's 'Laertiana' trace Diogenes's sources to Diocles of Magnesia's *Summary of the Lives of Philosophers*. See Barnes (1986); Porter (2000) and Jensen and Heit (2014).

2   See also Tobias Dahlkvist (2007) on Nietzsche's relationship to contemporaneous pessimistic doctrines: Eugen Dühring's '*Der Werth des Lebens*' (1865) and particularly Eduard von Hartmann's '*Die Philosophie des Unbewussten*' (1869).

3   To the frustration of many modern philosophers and commentators, Diogenes Laertius gives a great deal of attention to how the ancient philosophers lived or practised their philosophy, but fails to examine their theoretical doctrines with critical detail. In some cases, Diogenes's anecdotal method accurately reflected the fundamental tenor of ancient philosophies, and notably the genre of the anecdote of *Chreia* most closely associated with Cynicism. 'Though thoroughly popular in form', as Burton Mack observes, 'the *chreia* was cultivated at the highest levels of intellectual life and became in fact a major means for characterizing [ancient] philosophers' (Mack, 2003: 38). On the attention paid to biographies of ancient philosophers, see **Chapter 6.1**.

4   Nietzsche's title refers to four 'meditations': 'David Strauss the Confessor and the Writer', 'On the Uses and Disadvantages of History for Life', 'Schopenhauer as Educator' and 'Richard Wagner in Bayreuth'.

5   'Even as I was celebrating Schopenhauer as my educator', he wrote, 'I had forgotten that for a long time before that none of his dogmas could withstand my mistrust ... because I revelled with gratitude in the powerful impact that Schopenhauer – *freely and bravely standing before things and against them – had had on me a decade earlier*' (quoted in Breazeale, 1997: xxxii; cf. xvii–xviii). See Nietzsche's 1868 notes on Schopenhauer, in which, as Janaway observes 'Schopenhauer appears as a philosophical opponent, and sustains, as it were, an attack on the central nervous system, an attack that should make us doubt whether Nietzsche ever seriously adhered to Schopenhauer's metaphysics of the will' (Janaway 163). 'By 1871 at the latest, he had privately rejected not only Schopenhauer's "world-negating" pessimism, but also his fundamental dualism of "appearance" ("representations") and "reality" (the "will" qua "thing in itself"). Even if one remains suspicious of Nietzsche's later claim that "I distrusted Schopenhauer's system from the start", there still can be no doubt that by the time he wrote the third *Meditation* he had long since jettisoned any allegiance he may once have had to the two most distinctive features of Schopenhauer's philosophical system' (quoted in Breazeale, 1997: xvii); see also (Janaway, 2003: 164–5).

6   On Zeller's purely theoretical conception of philosophy, see Celenza (2005).

7   See also *BGE* 6: 'I have gradually come to realize what every great philosophy so far has been: namely the personal confession (self-confession)

[*Selbstbekenntnis*] of its author and a kind of involuntary/unwanted and unconscious/unnoticed memoir [*mémoires*, N uses the French]; in short, that the moral (or immoral) intentions in every philosophy constitute the true living seed from which the whole plant has always grown. In fact, to explain how the strangest metaphysical claims of a philosopher really come about, it is always good (and wise) to begin by asking: at what morality does it (does *he* –) aim?'

8   See also Nietzsche's 1882 letter to Rohde describing the purpose of his writing from 1876 to 1882: 'Without an aim, which I thought to be indescribably important, I would not have kept myself above the black torrents! This is actually my only excuse for the kind of things which I have been writing since 1876; it is my prescription and my home-brewed medicine against weariness with life!' (15 July 1882)

9   See Robert Miner's lucid treatment of Nietzsche and Montaigne's account on the relationship between philosophy and health (Miner, 2017: 44ff.).

10 Nietzsche frames his writings as spiritual directions and exhortations in much the same way as Seneca in his *Letters*. To Lucilius Seneca writes that he is recording the stages in his self-treatment for those who 'are recovering from a prolonged spiritual sickness' and on 'behalf of later generations': 'I am writing down a few things that may be of use to them; I am committing to writing some helpful recommendations, which might be compared to formulae of successful medications, the effectiveness of which I have experienced in the case of my own sores, which may not have been completely cured but have at least ceased to spread' (*Ep.* 7). See also *Ep.* 27.1: 'I am not so shameless as to undertake to cure my fellow-men when I am ill myself. I am, however, discussing with you troubles which concern us both, and sharing the remedy with you, just as if we were lying ill in the same hospital'.

11 Nietzsche seems to gloss Seneca, *Ep.* 9. 18–19.

12 Epictetus's *Encheiridion* or manual was a primary source of Nietzsche's knowledge of Stoicism; he read this specifically during the autumn of 1880, and his reading generated at least seven notes in 1880/1881, three entries in *D*, and one in *GS*, see Brobjer (2003).

13 Martha Nussbaum (1999: 341–74) convincingly argues that in *BT* (1872) Nietzsche had already implicitly, if obscurely formulated his subversion of Schopenhauer's normative ethics of pessimism in favour of his so-called Dionysian pessimism, which, as she puts it 'urges us to take joy in life, in the body, in becoming – even, and especially, in face of the recognition that the world is chaotic and cruel'. Yet, as she acknowledges, we can only see *BT*'s anti-Schopenhauerian message if we interpret it in light of his later arguments against pessimism beginning with *GS* (see 1999: 269). It remains true then Nietzsche's first clearly articulates and develops his own normative perspective in *GS*, and, additionally, on the view we put forwards, he does so not only against Schopenhauerian pessimism, but also against the Greek and Roman philosophical therapies he had used to counter his own pessimism.

Notes

14 The Stoics themselves occasionally appear to concede it would be possible and desirable to choose Stoic philosophy not because we judge it to be true, but because we judge the outcome of doing so desirable. Epictetus, for example, appears to claim that he would follow Stoic ethics even if its philosophical basis could be proven false: 'If one had to be taught by fictions that things external and outside the sphere of choice are nothing to us, I, for my part, should wish for such a fiction as would enable me to live henceforth in peace of mind and free from perturbation. What you on your part wish for is for you yourself to consider' (*Diss*. 1.4.27). On this point, see Nussbaum (1994: 391).

15 In describing statues embracing statues Nietzsche alludes to the Cynic exercises of hardening one's body against the elements in order to resist or extirpate the desire for external goods. Diogenes was said to roll in the burning sand in summer and embrace snow-covered statues in winter to inure himself to hardship (*DL* 6.23). It is worth noting that Epictetus argues a Stoic 'ought not to be unmoved [*apathês*] like a statue, but ... should maintain [his] natural and acquired relationships, as a dutiful man and as a son, brother, father, citizen' (*Diss*. 3.2.4; see Long, 2006: 232). See **Conclusion, 3** 'Criticisms'.

16 Nietzsche implicitly identifies Stoicism as the archetype of moralities that afflict us with this disease. Stoics, he implies, suffer from the disease of self-denial: 'Whatever may henceforth push, pull, beckon, impel from within or without will always strike this irritable one as endangering his self-control: no longer may he entrust himself to any instinct or free wing-beat; instead he stands there rigidly with a defensive posture, armed against himself, with sharp and suspicious eyes, the eternal guardian of his fortress, since he has turned himself into a fortress' (*GS* 305).

17 Michel Foucault shows how Hellenistic philosophers characterized their ideal of complete, untroubled self-sufficiency as analogous to 'old age' (2005: 108). In Seneca's terms, we must complete our life before our death: '*consummare vitam ante mortem*' (*Ep*. 32.4). If the Hellenistic philosophers' ideal of self-sufficiency counsels that we achieve 'old age' even in our youth, in *GS* Nietzsche identifies his philosophical therapy with recovery from this onset of dotage at the wrong time.

18 Augustine's claim flies in the face of the actual Stoic view. Seneca, for example, argues that for the Stoic the prospect of the eternal recurrence of their own life is a consolation that can spur us to remain true to public virtues; see Ure and Ryan (2020).

19 For a thorough analysis of the different ways Nietzsche used the philosophical concept of 'superhumans' (*Übermenschen*), see Loeb and Tinsley (2019: 757–94).

20 Here I follow Guy Elgat (2016: 186): 'If we are to understand the Eternal Recurrence as a kind of test, then ... the question arises: How is one to prepare for this test? It is here that *amor fati* enters the picture, for to practice *amor fati* "from morning till evening" [*GS* 304] to learn to see the necessary and ugly as beautiful and say "Yes" to it, is, I suggest, precisely the right kind of practice that can enable one to successfully affirm the idea of Eternal Recurrence.'

21 Cf. Robert Pippin (2010: 13) argues that because of his (alleged) scepticism about self-reflective reason or consciousness, Nietzsche never presented this way of life as a recommendation or injunction However, Nietzsche in fact does present amor fati as the result of an ethical practice of self-cultivation and declares it precisely in the form of an injunction: viz., '*One must learn to love*' (*GS* 334). See also Anderson and Cristy (2017) who demonstrate that for Nietzsche self-affirmation is the result of aesthetic practice and education.

22 See also Tracy Strong (2010: 61, 63) who argues that the aim of Nietzsche's writing was to produce 'a transformation in the self ... such is, after all, the oldest purpose of philosophy' and that eternal return 'is the mode of transformation or transfiguration'.

Chapter 11

1 We gloss Victor Goldschmidt's statement that the goal of the Platonic dialogue is more to form than to inform, which Hadot used to characterize all of ancient philosophy; see Hadot (2002: 73).

2 Foucault also claims that reconstituting ancient ethics 'is an urgent, fundamental and politically indispensable task' (Foucault, 2005: 252). Here, I bracket his claims about the political significance of reinventing ancient ethics. I discuss this issue in Ure (2020). On the genealogy of normality, see Cryle and Stephens (2017).

3 Arnold Davidson reports that Foucault indicated that his discussion of the relation between spirituality and philosophy was the fruit of his encounter with the work of Hadot on the tradition of spiritual exercises (2005: xxix). Foucault explicitly discusses Hadot in *The Hermeneutics of the Subject* (2005: 216–17).

4 To circumscribe ancient philosophy, Foucault occasionally uses Hadot's expression 'spiritual exercises' (e.g. Foucault, 2005: 292–4, 306–7), or more frequently the cognate term 'spirituality' (e.g. Foucault, 2005: 15–19, 25–30), though he prefers his own terminology of techniques and technologies of the self. As John Sellars observes, Foucault's own notion of 'technologies of the self' shares much in common with Hadot's 'spiritual exercises' (Sellars, 2020).

5 Schopenhauer edits out Horace's punchline, which deflates the Stoic ideal of the sage: 'Sane, above all, sound, unless he's a cold in the head!' (109)

6 See: 'Stoics ... declare that [the sage] alone is free and bad men are slaves' *DL* VII, 121–2.

7 Cf. Foucault (1986: 350–1): 'What strikes me is the fact that in our society, art has become something which is related only to objects and not to individuals, or to life ... But couldn't everyone's life become a work of art? Why should the lamp or the house be an art object, but not our life?' From the perspective of the Homeric and ancient philosophic conception of the art of living, Foucault's

thumbnail sketch of a potential contemporary reinvention of the art of living appears contentious. For Homer, Plato and Diogenes, the value of the art of living turns not simply on successfully crafting a beautiful existence, but an existence whose beauty resides specifically in its sovereignty or self-sufficiency.

8   See Hadot (2002: 263–5) and **Chapter 7.3**. Hadot criticizes Foucault's claim that Descartes's philosophy marked a break with these ancient practices. By contrast, Christopher Davidson agrees with Foucault that Descartes's *Meditations* requires no *ethical* transfiguration of subject as such (Davidson, 2015: 139).

9   As we shall see, Foucault especially focused on Nietzschean genealogy, treating it as a spiritual exercise. On the comparison and differences between Nietzsche and Foucault's ethics, see Ure and Testa (2018).

10 See Ansell-Pearson (2018) on Nietzsche and Foucault's analysis of the passion for knowledge.

11 As many commentators observe, Nietzsche struggles to come to terms with the tension between the unconditional will to truth and the need for artistic illusion. For a brief survey of this debate, see Ure (2019: 208–20).

12 See Hadot (2020) ('chapter 5: Conversion').

Conclusion

1   See Cooper (2012: 17 [italics ours]): 'In speaking of ancient philosophy I have been assuming that for the ancients with whom I am concerned, *exactly as with us, the essential core of philosophy is a certain, specifically and recognisably philosophical, style of logical, reasoned argument and analysis. Anyone who has read any philosophy at all* is familiar with this style, whether it takes the form we find in the question-and-answer dialectic of the character Socrates in Plato's Socratic dialogues, ... *or, again, in the writings of a contemporary analytic philosopher.*' This seems to us an exercise in begging the question (cf. Aristotle, *Soph. Ref.* 15, 174b39).

2   Hadot, 'Forms of Life', 61.

3   In *The Human Condition*, one of the most influential, yet controversial twentieth-century accounts of the nature of the political, Hannah Arendt makes a similar claim, dismissing Stoicism and Epicureanism as philosophies that exhorts the individual to withdraw from politics 'as the only safeguard to one's sovereignty and integrity as a person' (1958: 243). She elaborates this criticism in her 1968 essay 'What Is Freedom?' (Arendt, 1968).

4   See **Chapter 3**; see also Epictetus *H* 24.

5   For his political critics, however, Socrates's ethics appears profoundly unworldly, if not anti-political. Hannah Arendt expresses this worry: 'To the philosopher the ethical proposition about doing and suffering wrong is

compelling ... But to man insofar as he is a citizen, an acting being concerned with the world and the public welfare rather than his own well being – the Socratic statement is not true at all. The disastrous consequences for any community that began in all earnest to follow ... Socratic [precepts] have been frequently point out' (Arendt, 2000: 559).

6   The Sceptics, here as elsewhere, are the jokers in the pack. If the Epicureans conceived politics instrumentally as a set of conventions justified only the basis of expediency, the Sceptics suspend or bracket judgements about whether laws or conventions are true or false. As we commented in [**4.2**], they hence end by simply following local conventions, whatever they are. 'With no doctrinaire reason to flout convention', as Lane explains, 'the Sceptic will live in accordance with the customs of the land in which he finds himself ... he will withhold judgement as to whether these customs and laws are truly right or wrong. Thus the path of a Sceptic will look outwardly like those of their ordinary unphilosophical neighbours. Live without full commitment to any claim about how things are by nature, and you can live in peace and quiet. The Sceptic will be no provocateur or provocatrice' (Lane, 2014: 237).

7   In *The Phenomenology of Spirit* Hegel develops the fullest and most sophisticated modern version of this critique of ancient eudaimonism (Hegel, 1997). See also Paul Veyne (2003): 'As for what political line to take, the Stoics never gave it a thought, never grew impassioned over it, and had no theoretical position on the matter. Without any possibility of imagining a concrete politics, along with the reduction of every problem to a question of the morality of an individual whose capacity to exercise reason had been restored, one could justify – or contest – anything, from building a rational utopia to living reasonably and docilely according to the status quo. As far as individual liberty or national independence went the Stoics had only one thing to say: true liberty is not being enslaved to one's passions' (2003: 142).

8   Cf. Deborah Brown (2006: 196, 207) on Descartes's criticisms of the Stoic sage.

9   Auerbach suggests that ancient terms, including *pathos* as well as terms such as *epithymia* and *mania*, 'lack the possibility of the sublime. Modern passion is more than desire, craving, or frenzy. The word always contains as a possibility, often as its dominant meaning, the noble creative fire ... and next to which temperate reason at times appears contemptible' (Auerbach, 2001: 290). Against PWL's normative ideal of the untroubled life, in this newly emerging romantic view the good life required the transfiguration rather than extirpation of the passions that betray our high valuation of the transient, uncontrollable things of this world.

10   For the Mellon project, see https://philife.nd.edu/

BIBLIOGRAPHY

Primary texts, including texts by Pierre & Ilsetraut Hadot

D'Alembert, Jean-Baptiste le Rond. 1751 [2009]. 'Preliminary Discourse'. In R.
    N. Schwab and W. E. Rex (trans.), *The Encyclopedia of Diderot & d'Alembert
    Collaborative Translation Project*. Ann Arbor: Michigan Publishing, University
    of Michigan Library. Web 16 July 2018. Online at http://hdl.handle.net/2027/
    spo.did2222.0001.083. Trans. of 'is course Préliminaire', *Encyclopédie ou
    Dictionnaire raisonné des sciences, des arts et des métiers*, vol. 1. Paris, 1751.
Anderson, Ranier and Rachel Cristy. 2017. 'What is "The Meaning of Our
    Cheerfulness"? Philosophy as a Way of Life in Nietzsche and Montaigne'.
    European Journal of Philosophy 25, no. 4: 1514–49.
Aristotle. *Nic. Eth.* = *Nicomachean Ethics*. Translated by H. Rackham. Loeb
    Classical Library, no. 19.
Aristotle. '*Soph. Ref.* = *On Sophistical Refutations*'. In E. S Forster et al. (trans.),
    *Aristotle: On Sophistical Refutations. On Coming-to-be and Passing Away. On the
    Cosmos*. Loeb Classical Library, no. 400.
Bacon, Francis. 1591 [1753]. 'VII. To My Lord Treasurer Lord Burghley, 1591'. In
    Works of Francis Bacon, Volume II, 413. London: D. Midwinter et al.
Bacon, Francis. 1841. 'Sir Francis Bacon: His Letter of Request to Doctor Playfer,
    to Translate the Book of Advancement of Learning into Latin'. In B. Montagu
    (eds.), *The Works of Francis Bacon. A New Edition: with a Biography by Basil
    Montagu. Volume III*. 27. Philadelphia: A Hart.
Bacon, Francis. 1863. 'Preparative for a Natural and Experimental History
    [*Parasceve*]'. In J. Spedding et al. (ed. and trans), *The Works of Francis Bacon*, vol.
    VIII. 351–72. Boston, MA: Houghton, Mifflin & Co.
Bacon, Francis. 1869. '*Novum Organum*'. In J. Spedding, R. L. Ellis and D. D. Heath
    (trans. and ed.), *The Works of Francis Bacon: Volume VIII*. New York: Hurd &
    Houghton.
Bacon, Francis. 1873 [1973]. *Advancement of Learning*. Edited by Henry Morley
    [1893]. London: J.M. Dent & Sons.
Bacon, Francis. 2008. 'Advice to the Earl of Rutland on His Travels. First Letter'. In
    Francis Bacon: The Major Works, 69–76. Oxford: Oxford World's Classics.
Bacon, Francis. 2008b. 'A Letter and Discourse to Sir Henry Savill, Touching Helps
    for the Intellectual Powers'. In *Major Works*. 114–19.
Bayle, Pierre. 2006. *Dictionnaire historique et critique*. Paris: Elibron Classics [16
    vols.], XV.
'Boethius. *Cons.* = *Consolation of Philosophy*'. In H. F. Stewart (trans.), *Theological
    Tractates. The Consolation of Philosophy*. Loeb Classical Library, no. 74.

Brouwer, René. 2014. *The Stoic Sage: The Early Stoics on Wisdom, Sagehood and Socrates*. Cambridge: Cambridge University Press.

Cassian, John. 1894. 'Institutes of the Coenobia'. In E. C. S. Gibson (trans.), *A Select Library of Nicene and Post-Nicene Fathers of the Christian Church*. Second Series, vol. 11, New York.

Cicero, Marcus Tullius. 1933. *De ac.* = *De academica I* and *II*. Translated by H. Rackham. Loeb Classical Library, no. 268.

Cicero, Marcus Tullius. 1914. *De fin.* = *De finibus/On Moral Ends*. Translated by H. Rackham. Loeb Classical Library, no. 40.

Cicero, Marcus Tullius. 1933. *De nat. deo.* = *De natura deorum*. Translated by H. Rackham. Loeb Classical Library, no. 268.

Cicero, Marcus Tullius. 1939. *De or.* = *On the Orator/De oratore*. Translated by E. W. Sutton and H. Rackham. Loeb Classical Library, nos. 348,349.

Cicero, Marcus Tullius. 1942. 'Sto. par. = Stoic Paradoxes'. In H. Rackham (trans.), *Cicero: On the Orator: Book 3. On Fate. Stoic Paradoxes. On the Divisions of Oratory: A. Rhetorical Treatises*. Loeb Classical Library, no. 349.

Cicero, Marcus Tullius. 1945. *TD* = *Tusculan Disputations*. Translated by J. E. King. Loeb Classical Library, no. 141.

Dante. 1923. *The Banquet (Il Convito)*. Translated by E. Sayer. Ulan Press. 1923. Online at http://www.online-literature.com/dante/banquet/

Descartes, René. 1952. *Meditations on First Philosophy*. Translated by Elizabeth S. Haldane and G.R.T. Ross, 1–40. Chicago, IL: University of Chicago, The Great Books.

Descartes, René. 1952a. 'Discourse on Method', 41–68.

Descartes, René. 2015. *The Passions of the Soul and Other Late Philosophical Writings*. Oxford: Oxford University Press.

Diderot, Denis. 1765 [2003]. 'Pyrrhonic or Skeptical Philosophy'. In N. S. Hoyt and T. Cassirer (trans.), *The Encyclopedia of Diderot & d'Alembert Collaborative Translation Project*. Ann Arbor: Michigan Publishing, University of Michigan Library. Web 16 July 2018. Online at http://hdl.handle.net/2027/spo.did2222.0000.164. Trans. of "Pyrrhonienne ou Sceptique Philosophie," *Encyclopédie ou Dictionnaire raisonné des sciences, des arts et des métiers*, vol. 13. Paris, 1765.

Diderot, Denis. 1765 [2009]. 'System'. In Stephen J. Gendzier (trans.), *The Encyclopedia of Diderot & d'Alembert Collaborative Translation Project*. Ann Arbor: Michigan Publishing, University of Michigan Library. Web 15 July 2018. Online at http://hdl.handle.net/2027/spo.did2222.0001.321. Translation of 'ystème', *Encyclopédie ou Dictionnaire raisonné des sciences, des arts et des métiers*, vol. 15. Paris, 1765.

Diderot, Denis. [1782] 1792. *Essai sur les regnes de Claude et de Néron et sur la vie et les écrits de Séneque pour servir d'introduction a la lecture de ce philosophe*. Paris: L'Imprimerie de J.J. Smith et al.

Diderot, Denis. [1798] 1828. *Essai sur la vie de Sénèque le philosophe, sur ses écrits et sur les règnes de Claude et de Néron*. Paris: J. L. J. Bbière, Libraire.

Diderot, Denis. 1875. 'Regrets for My Old Dressing Gown, or a Warning to Those Who Have More Taste than Fortune'. In Mitchell Abidor (trans.), from *Oeuvres*

Complètes, vol. IV. Paris: Garnier Fréres, 1875. Online at https://www.marxists.
org/reference/archive/diderot/1769/regrets.htm

Diderot, Denis. 1967. *The Encyclopedia*. Edited by Stephen J. Gendzier. New York:
Harper.

Diogenes Laertius. *DL = Lives of Eminent Philosophers*. Translated by R. Hicks.
Loeb Classical Library, nos.184–5.

Du Marsais, César Chesneau. 2002. 'Philosopher'. In Dena Goodman (trans.), *The
Encyclopedia of Diderot & d'Alembert Collaborative Translation Project*. Ann
Arbor: Michigan Publishing, University of Michigan Library. Web 15 July
2018. Online at http://hdl.handle.net/2027/spo.did2222.0000.001. Trans. of
'philosophe', *Encyclopédie ou Dictionnaire raisonné des sciences, des arts et des
métiers*, vol. 12. Paris, 1765.

Epictetus. *Disc. = Discourses*. Loeb Classical Library, nos. 131, 218.

Epictetus. *'Ench. = Encheiridion'*. In *Discourses III-IV, Encheiridion*. Loeb Classical
Library, no. 218.

Epicurus. 2018. U = *Selected Fragments by Epicurus* (Επίκουρος). Translated by
Peter, Saint-André. Enumeration of Hermann Usener, 1887. Online at http://
monadnock.net/epicurus/fragments.html

Foucault, Michel. 1983. 'Self-Writing'. Online at https://foucault.info/documents/
foucault.hypomnemata.en/. Translated from *Corps écrit* 5 (February 1983): 3–23.

Foucault, Michel. 1984. *The Foucault Reader*. Edited. by P. Rabinow. New York:
Pantheon Books.

Foucault, Michel. 1987. *The Use of Pleasure: Volume 2 of The History of Sexuality*.
Translated by R. Hurley. Harmondsworth: Penguin Books.

Foucault, Michel. 1996. *Foucault Live: Collected Interviews, 1961–1984*. Edited by S.
Lotringer, trans. L. Hochroth and J. Johnston, New York: Semiotext(e).

Foucault, Michel. 1997. 'Technologies of the Self'. In P. Rabinow, trans. R. Hurley
and others (eds.), *Ethics, Subjectivity and Truth*. New York: New Press.

Foucault, Michel. 1998. 'This Body, This Paper, This Fire'. In James D. Faubion
(ed.), *Aesthetics, Method, and Epistemology*. Translated by Robert Hurley et al.,
393–418. New York: New Press.

Foucault, Michel. 2005. *The Hermeneutics of the Subject: Lectures at the Collège
de France 1981–1982*. Edited by F. Gros. Translated by G. Burchell. New York:
Palgrave Macmillan.

Foucault, Michel. 2011. *The Courage of Truth (The Government of Self and Others
II): Lectures at the Collège de France 1983–1984*. Edited by F. Gros. Translated by
G. Burchell. Basingstoke: Palgrave Macmillan.

Foucault, Michel. 2013. *Lectures on the Will to Know: Lectures at the Collège de
France 1970–1971*. Edited by D. Defert. Translated by G. Burchell. Basingstoke:
Palgrave Macmillan.

Hadot, Ilsetraut. 1986. 'The Spiritual Guide'. In A. H. Armstrong (ed.), *Classical
Mediterranean Spirituality: Egyptian, Greek, Roman*. 436–59. New York: Crossroad.

Hadot, Ilsetraut. 2005. *Arts libéraux et philosophie dans la pensée antique:
contribution à l'histoire de l'éducation et de la culture dans l'antiquité*. Paris: Vrin.

Hadot, Ilsetraut. 2014. *Sénèque: direction spirituelle et pratique de la philosophie*.
Paris: Librairie Philosophique J. Vrin.

Hadot, Ilsetraut. 2014a. 'Getting to Goodness: Reflections on Chapter 10 of Brad Inwood's Reading Seneca'. In J. Wildberger and M. L. Colish (eds.), *Seneca Philosophus*. 9–41. Berlin: Walter de Gruyter.

Hadot, Ilsetraut and Pierre. 2004. *Apprendre a philosopher dans l'Antiquité: L'enseignement du Manuel d'Epictete et son commentaire néoplatonicien*. Paris: Proche.

Hadot, Pierre. 1973. 'La physique comme exercise spirituel ou pessimisme et optimisme chez Marc Aurèle'. In P. Hadot (ed.), *Exercice spirituels et philosophie antique*, 145–64. Paris: Éditions Albin Michel.

Hadot, Pierre. 1981. 'Pour une préhistoire des genres philosophiques médiévaux'. In *Les genres litteraires dans les sources theologiques et philosophiques médiévales: définition, critique, et exploitation, Actes du Colloque international de Louvain-la-Neuve*. 25: 7 May 1981.

Hadot, Pierre. 1995. *Philosophy as a Way of Life*. Edited by A. Davidson. Translated by M. Chase. Oxford: Blackwell.

Hadot, Pierre. 1998. *Plotinus, or the Simplicity of Vision*. Translated by Michael Chase. Chicago, IL and London: University of Chicago Press.

Hadot, Pierre. 2002. *What Is Ancient Philosophy?* Translated by Michael Chase. Cambridge, MA: Belknap Press [Harvard].

Hadot, Pierre. 2002a. *Exercises spirituels et philosophie antique*. Préface d'Arnold Davidson. Paris: Éditions Albin Michel.

Hadot, Pierre. 2004. *Wittgenstein et les limites du langage*. Paris: Vrin.

Hadot, Pierre. 2006. *The Veil of Isis: An Essay on History of the Idea of Nature*. Translated by M. Chase. Cambridge, MA: Harvard University Press.

Hadot, Pierre. 2008. *N'Oublie pas de vivre: Goethe et la tradition des exercices spirituels*. Paris: Albin Michel.

Hadot, Pierre. 2009. *The Present Alone Is Our Happiness: Conversations with Jeannie Carlier & Arnold I. Davidson*. Translated by M. Djaballah. Stanford, CA: Stanford University Press.

Hadot, Pierre. 2019a. 'Préface à Ernst Bertram, *Nietzsche: Essai de Mythologie'*. In P. Hadot, *Philosophie comme education des adultes: textes, perspectives, entretiens*. Paris: Vrin.

Hadot, Pierre. 2019b. *La philosophie comme education des adultes: Textes, perspectives, entretiens*. Paris: Vrin.

Hadot, Pierre. 2020. *Selected Writings of Pierre Hadot: Philosophy as Practice*. Translated by M. Sharpe and F. Testa. London: Bloomsbury.

Horst, Steven. 2020. "Philosophy as Empirical Exploration of Living: An Approach to Courses in Philosophy as a Way of Life." *Special Issue: Philosophy as a Way of Life* 51, no. 2–3: 455–471.

Irrera, Orazio. 2010. 'Pleasure and Transcendence of the Self: Notes on "a Dialogue Too Soon Interrupted" between Michel Foucault and Pierre Hadot'. *Philosophy & Social Criticism* 36, no. 9: 995–1017.

Justin the Martyr. 1885. '*First Apology'*. In Marcus Dods and George Reith (eds.), *Ante-Nicene Fathers*, vol. 1. ed. A. Roberts, James Donaldson, and A. Cleveland Coxe. Buffalo, NY: Christian Literature Publishing Co. Revised and edited for New Advent by Kevin Knight. Online at http://www.newadvent.org/fathers/0126.htm

Bibliography

Lipsius, Justus. 2006. *On Constancy*. Edited by J. Sellars, with an Introduction, Notes and Bibliography. Exeter: University of Exeter Press, 2006.

Lucian. 1959. *Hermotimus, or Concerning the Sects*, Translated by K. Kilburn. Cambridge, MA: Harvard [Loeb Classical Library 430].

Marcus Aurelius. 1958. *Ess. = The Complete Essays*. Translated by D. Frame. Stanford, CA: Stanford University Press.

Marcus Aurelius. *Meds. = Meditations*. Translated by C. R. Haines. Loeb Classical Library, no. 58.

Montaigne, Michel de. *The Complete Essays of Michel de Montaigne*. Translated by Donald Frame. Stanford: Stanford University Press.

Montesquieu, Charles-Louis le Secondat. 2002. 'Discourse on Cicero." Translated by David Fott, *Political Theory* 30, no. 5: 733–7.

Musonius Rufus, Gaius. 1947. *Lectures and Sayings*. Introduction and Translation by Cora E. Lutz. Yale Classical Studies: Yale University Press [vol. X].

Nietzsche, Friedrich. 1967. *The Birth of Tragedy or Hellenism and Pessimism*. Edited and translated by W. Kaufmann. Toronto: Random House.

Nietzsche, Friedrich. 1967. *Sämtliche Werke: Kritische Studienausgabe*. Edited by G. Colli and M. Montinari. Berlin: Walter de Gruyter.

Nietzsche, Friedrich. 1967. *The Will to Power*. Translated by Walter Kaufmann and R. J. Hollingdale. New York: Random House.

Nietzsche, Friedrich. 1968. *Twilight of the Idols*. Translated by R. J. Hollingdale. Harmondsworth: Penguin Books. Sections abbreviated 'Maxims,' 'Socrates,' 'Reason,' 'World,' 'Morality,' 'Errors,' 'Improvers,' 'Germans,' 'Skirmishes,' 'Ancients,' 'Hammer'.

Nietzsche, Friedrich. 1979. *Ecce Homo: How One Becomes What One Is*. Translated by. R. J. Hollingdale. Harmondsworth: Penguin Books. Sections abbreviated 'Wise,' 'Clever,' 'Books,' 'Destiny,'; abbreviations for titles discussed in 'Books' are indicated instead of 'Books' where relevant.

Nietzsche, Friedrich. 1979. *Philosophy and Truth: Selections from Nietzsche's Notebooks of the Early 1870s*. Translated by D. Breazeale. Atlantic Highlands, Nj: Humanities Press.

Nietzsche, Friedrich. 1982. *Daybreak: Thoughts on The Prejudices of Morality*. Translated by R. J. Hollingdale. Cambridge: Cambridge University Press, 1982.

Nietzsche, Friedrich. 1983. *On the Uses and Disadvantages of History for Life*, in *Untimely Meditations*. Translated by R. J. Hollingdale. Cambridge: Cambridge University Press.

Nietzsche, Friedrich. 1983. *Schopenhauer as Educator*. Untimely Meditations.

Nietzsche, Friedrich. 1985. *The Anti-Christ*. Translated by R. J. Hollingdale. Harmondsworth: Penguin Books.

Nietzsche, Friedrich. 1986. *Human, All Too Human: A Book for Free Spirits, Vol. 1*. Translated by R. J. Hollingdale. Cambridge: Cambridge University Press.

Nietzsche, Friedrich. 1986. *Human, All Too Human: A Book for Free Spirits, Vol. 2, Part One*. Translated by R. J. Hollingdale. Cambridge: Cambridge University Press.

Nietzsche, Friedrich. 1986. *The Wander and His Shadow*, in *Human, All Too Human, Volume 2, Part Two*.

Nietzsche, Friedrich. 1988. *Thus Spoke Zarathustra: A Book for Everyone and No One*. Translated by R. J. Hollingdale. London: Penguin Books.

Nietzsche, Friedrich. 1996. *Beyond Good and Evil: Prelude to a Philosophy of the Future*. Edited and translated by W. Kaufmann. New York: Vintage.

Nietzsche, Friedrich. 1997. *On the Genealogy of Morality*. Edited by K. Ansell-Pearson and translated by C. Diethe. Cambridge: Cambridge University Press, 1997.

Nietzsche, Friedrich. 2001. *The Gay Science*. Edited by B. Williams, trans. J. Nauckhoff and poems by A. Del Caro. Cambridge: Cambridge University Press, 2001.

Nietzsche, Friedrich. 2002. *Philosophy in the Tragic Age of the Greeks*. Translated Marianne Cowan. Washington, DC: Regnery Gateway.

Petrarch. 1898. 'Letter to Posterity'. In J. H. Robinson (ed.), *Petrarch: The First Modern Scholar and Man of Letters*. 59–76. New York: G.P. Putnam.

Petrarch. 1948. *On His Own Ignorance and That of Many Others*. trans. Hans Nachod. In E. Cassirer, P. O. Kristeller and J. H. Randall Jr. (eds.), *The Renaissance Philosophy of Man*. Chicago, IL: University of Chicago Press.

Petrarch. 1989. *Petrarch's Secret Book*. Edited by Davy A. Carozza and H. James Shey, with Introduction, Notes and Critical Anthology. New York: Peter Lang.

Petrarch. 1991. *Petrarch's Remedies for Fortune Fair and Foul: A Modern English Translation of De remediis utriusque fortuna, with a Commentary*. Translated by C. H. Rawski. Indianapolis and Bloomington: Indiana University Press [5 vols.].

Petrarch. 2000. 'Ascent of Mount Ventoux'. In *Selections from the Canzioniere and Other Works*. 14–16. Oxford: Oxford University Press.

Pigliucci, Massimo. 2017. *How to Be a Stoic: Ancient Wisdom for Modern Living*. London: Penguin.

Plato. 'Apo. = Apology'. In Christopher Emlyn-Jones and William Preddy (eds.), *Plato: Euthyphro. Apology. Crito. Phaedo*. Loeb Classical Library, no. 36.

Plato. 'Gorg. = Gorgias'. In R. M. Lamb (ed.), *Plato: Lysis. Symposium. Gorgias*. Loeb Classical Library, no. 166.

Plato. *Pha. = Phaedo*. In *Plato: Euthyphro. Apology. Crito. Phaedo*.

Plato. *Rep. = Republic*. Translated by Christopher Emlyn-Jones and William Preddy. Loeb Classical Library, nos. 237, 276.

Plotinus. *Enn. = Enneads*. Translated by L. Gerson. Cambridge: Cambridge University, 2019.

Schopenhauer, Arthur. 1966. *The World as Will and Representation, vol. II*. Translated by E. F. J. Payne. New York: Dover Publications.

Schopenhauer, Arthur. 2010. *The World as Will and Representation, vol. 1*. Translated and edited by J. Norman, A. Welchman and C. Janaway. Cambridge: Cambridge University Press.

Schopenhauer, Arthur. 2014. *Parerga & Paralipomena vol. 1*. Translated and edited by S. Roehr and C. Janaway. Cambridge: Cambridge University Press.

Schopenhauer, Arthur. 2015. *Parerga & Paralipomena vol. 2*. Translated and edited by A. Del Caro and C. Janaway. Cambridge: Cambridge University Press.

Sextus Empiricus. *Hyp. = Outlines of Pyrrhonism [Hypertyposis]*. Translated by R. B. Bury. Loeb Classical Library, no. 273.

Bibliography

Voltaire. 1807. 'Memnon the Philosopher, or Human Wisdom'. In *Voltaire, Classic Tales*. London: John Hunt et al.

Voltaire. 1901. 'Philosopher [full entry]'. In William F. Fleming (ed.), *Philosophical Dictionary*, derived from *The Works of Voltaire, A Contemporary Version*. New York: E.R. DuMont, 1901.

Voltaire. 1977. '*Candide*'. In B. Redman (ed.), *The Portable Voltaire*, 229–328. London: Penguin.

Voltaire. 2004. *Philosophical Dictionary*. Translated by T. Besterman. London: Penguin.

Xenophon. 1979. *Apo. = Apology. Xenophon in Seven* Volumes, *4*. Harvard University Press. Cambridge, MA; William Heinemann, Ltd., London. Online at http://www.perseus.tufts.edu/hopper/text?doc=Perseus:text:1999.01.0212

Secondary texts

Altman, William H. F. 2012. *Plato the Teacher: The Crisis of the Republic*. Lanham, MD: Lexington.

Altman, William H. F. 2016a. *The Guardians in Action: Plato the Teacher and the Post-Republic Dialogues from Timaeus to Theaetetus*. Lanham, MD: Lexington.

Altman, William H. F. 2016b. *The Guardians on Trial: The Reading Order of Plato's Dialogues from Euthyphro to Phaedo*. Lanham, MD: Lexington.

Altman, William H. F 2016c. *The Revival of Platonism in Cicero's Late Philosophy*. Lanham, MD: Lexington.

Annas, Julia. 1985. "Self-Knowledge in Early Plato" in D. J. O'Meara (ed.) Platonic Investigations (Washington: Catholic University Press), 11–138.

Annas, Julia. 1999. *The Morality of Happiness*. Oxford: Oxford University Press.

Annas, Julia. 2008. 'The Sage in Ancient Philosophy'. In F. Alesse and others, volume in memory of Gabriele Giannantoni (eds.), *Anthropine Sophia*. Naples: Bibliopolis.

Annas, Julia. 2011. *Intelligent Virtue*. Oxford: Oxford University Press.

Andrew, Edward. 2004. 'The Senecan Moment: Patronage and Philosophy in the Eighteenth Century'. *Journal of the History of Ideas* 65, no. 2.

Andrew, Edward. 2016. 'The Epicurean Stoicism of the French Enlightenment'. In John Sellars (ed.), *Routledge Handbook of the Stoic Tradition*, 395–411.

Anheim, Etienne. 2008. 'Pétrarque: l'écriture comme philosophie'. *Revue de synthèse* 129, no. 4: 587–609.

Ansell-Pearson, Keith. 2013. 'True to the Earth: Nietzsche's Epicurean Care of Self and World'. In H. Hutter and E. Friedland (eds.), *Nietzsche's Therapeutic Teaching*, 97–116. London: Bloomsbury.

Ansell-Pearson, Keith. 2014. 'Heroic-Idyllic Philosophizing: Nietzsche and the Epicurean Tradition'. *Royal Institute of Philosophy Supplement* 74: 237–63.

Ansell-Pearson, Keith. 2018. '"We Are Experiments": Nietzsche, Foucault, and The Passion for Knowledge'. In J. Westfall and A. Rosenberg (eds.), *Nietzsche and Foucault: A Critical Encounter*. London: Bloomsbury, 79–98.

Arendt, Hannah. 1958. *The Human Condition*. Chicago, IL and London: University of Chicago Press.

Arendt, Hannah. 1968. 'What Is Freedom?' In *Between Past and Future: Eight Exercises in Political Thought*. New York: Viking Press.

Arendt, Hannah. 2000. 'Truth and Politics'. In Peter Baeher (ed.), *The Portable Arendt*, 545–75. New York: Penguin Press.

Atwell, John. 1995. *Schopenhauer on the Character of the World: The Metaphysics of the Will*. Berkeley: University of California Press.

Aubry, Gwenaëlle. 2010. 'Philosophie comme manière de vivre'. In A. Davidson and F. Worms (eds.), *Pierre Hadot, l'enseignement antiques, l'enseignement moderns*. 81–94. Paris: Rue d'Ulm.

Auerbach, Erich. 2001. 'Passio als Leidenschaft'. *Criticism* 43, no. 3: 285–308.

Baltussen, Han. 2009. 'Personal Grief and Public Mourning in Plutarch's Consolation'. *American Journal of Philology* 130, no. 1 (Spring): 70–6.

Baltussen, Han. 2013. 'Cicero's *Consolatio ad se*: Character, Purpose and Impact of a Curious Treatise'. In Han Baltussen (ed.), *Greek and Roman Consolations: Eight Studies of a Tradition and Its Afterlife*, 67–91. Wales: Classic Press of Wales.

Baraz, Yelena. 2012. *A Written Republic: Cicero's Philosophical Politics*. Princeton, NJ and Oxford: Princeton University Press.

Barnes, Jonathon. 1986. 'Nietzsche and Diogenes Laertius'. *Nietzsche-Studien* 15: 16–40.

Baron, Hans. 1966. *Crisis of the Early Italian Renaissance*, rev ed. Princeton, NJ: Princeton University Press.

Barsella, Susanna. 2012. 'A Humanistic Approach to Religious Solitude'. In *Petrarch: A Critical Guide*, 197–209.

Beckwith, Christopher. *Greek Buddha: Pyrrho's Encounter with Early Buddhism in Central Asia*. Princeton, NJ: Princeton University Press.

Bishop, Paul. 2009. 'Eudaimonism, Hedonism and Feuerbach's Philosophy of the Future'. *Intellectual History Review* 19, no. 1: 65–81.

Blanchard, W. Scott. 2001. 'Petrarch and the Genealogy of Asceticism'. *Journal of the History of Ideas* 62, no. 3: 401–23.

Bourgault, Sophie. 2010. 'Appeals to Antiquity: Reflections on Some French Enlightenment Readings of Socrates and Plato'. *Lumen* 29: 43–8

Bousma, William. 2002. *The Waning of the Renaissance, 1550–1640*. New Haven, CT: Yale University Press.

Brakke, David. 2001. 'The Making of Monastic Demonology: Three Ascetic Teachers on Withdrawal and Resistance'. *Church History* 70: 19–48.

Breazeale, Daniel. 1979. 'Introduction'. In D. Breazeale (trans.), *Philosophy and Truth: Selections from Nietzsche's Notebooks of the Early 1870s*, xiii–xlix. Atlantic Highlands, NJ: Humanities Press.

Brooke, Christopher. 2012. *Philosophic Pride. Stoicism and political thought from Lipsius to Rousseau*. Princeton, NJ: Princeton University Press.

Brown, Deborah J. 2006. *Descartes and the Passionate Mind*. Cambridge: Cambridge University Press.

Brown, Peter. 1970. 'Sorcery, Demons, and the Rise of Christianity from Late Antiquity into the Middle Ages'. In M. Douglas (ed.), *Witchcraft, Confessions and Accusations*, 17–45. London: Tavistock.

Brunschwig, Jacques. 1986. 'The Cradle Argument in Epicureanism and Stoicism'. In Malcolm Schofield and Gisela Striker (eds.), *The Norms of Nature: Studies in Hellenistic Ethics*. Cambridge: Cambridge University Press.

Butler, E. M. 2012. *The Tyranny of Greece over Germany*. Cambridge: Cambridge University Press.

Cabane, Frank. 2004. 'D'un Essai l'autre, métamorphoses d'un texte'. *Recherches sur Diderot et sur l'Encyclopédie* 36: 21–4.

Caddan, Joan. 2013. 'The Organisation of Knowledges: Disciplines and Practices'. In David C. Lindberg and Michael H. Shank (eds.), *Medieval Science*. Cambridge: Cambridge University Press.

Carruthers, Mary. 2008. *The Book of Memory: A Study of Memory in Medieval Culture*. Cambridge: Cambridge University Press.

Cartwright, David. 2010. *Schopenhauer: A Biography*. Cambridge: Cambridge University Press

Cassirer, Ernst. 1955. *The Philosophy of the Enlightenment*. Boston, MA: Beacon Press.

Cavaillé, Jean-Pierre. 2012. 'Libertine and Libertinism: Polemic Uses of the Terms in Sixteenth- and Seventeenth-Century English and Scottish Literature'. *Journal for Early Modern Cultural Studies* 12, no. 2: 12–36.

Celenza, Christopher S. 2005. 'Lorenzo Valla and the Traditions and Transmissions of Philosophy'. *Journal of the History of Ideas* 66: 483–506.

Celenza, Christopher S. 2013. 'What Counted as Philosophy in the Italian Renaissance? The History of Philosophy, the History of Science, and Styles of Life'. *Critical Inquiry* 39, no. 2: 367–401.

Celenza, Christopher S. 2017. *Petrarch: Everywhere a Wanderer*. Chicago, IL: University of Chicago Press.

Chadwick, H. 1981. *Boethius: The Consolations of Music, Logic, Theology, and Philosophy*. Oxford: Clarendon Press.

Chase, Michael. 1998. 'Translator's Introduction'. In Pierre Hadot (ed.), *Plotinus, or the Simplicity of Vision*.

Checchi, Paulo. 2012. 'The Unforgettable *Book of Things to Be Remembered* (*Rerum memorandarum libre*)'. In *Petrarch: A Critical Guide*, 151–63.

Clay, Diskin. 1998. *Paradosis and Survival: Three Chapter in the History of Epicurean Philosophy*. Ann Arbor: University of Michigan Press.

Clay, Diskin. 2007. 'The Philosophical Inscriptions of Diogenes of Oenoanda'. *Bulletin of the Institute of Classical Studies*. Supplement 94: 283–91.

Clay, Diskin. 2009. 'The Athenian Garden'. In James Warren (ed.), *The Cambridge Companion to Epicureanism*, 9–28. Cambridge: Cambridge University Press.

Colaiaco, James. 2001. *Socrates against Athens: Philosophy on Trial*. New York: Routledge

Cooper, John M. 2004. 'Moral Theory and Moral Improvement: Seneca'. In *Knowledge, Nature, and the Good: Essays on Ancient Philosophy*, 309–34. Princeton, NJ: Princeton University Press.

Cooper, John M. 2012. *Pursuits of Wisdom: Six Ways of Life in Ancient Philosophy from Socrates to Plotinus*. Princeton, NJ: Princeton University Press.

Corneanu, Sorana. 2011. *Regimens of the Mind: Boyle, Locke, and the Early Modern Cultura Animi Tradition*. Chicago, IL: University of Chicago Press.

Cornford, F. M. 1965. *Before and After Socrates*. London: Cambridge University Press.

Crane, Ronald S. 1968. 'The Relation of Bacon's *Essays* to the Program of the Advancement of Learning'. In *Essential Articles for the Study of Francis Bacon*, 272–92. Hamden, CT: Archon Books.

Cryle, Peter and Stephens, Elizabeth. 2017. *Normality: A Critical Genealogy*. Chicago, IL and London: University of Chicago Press.

Curtis, Cathy. 2011. 'Advising Monarchs and Their Counsellors: Juan Luis Vives on the Emotions, Civil Life and International Relations'. *Australian and New Zealand Association of Medieval and Early Modern Studies* 28, no. 2: 29–53.

Dahlkvist, Tobias. 2007. *Nietzsche and the Philosophy of Pessimism: A Study of Nietzsche's Relation to the Pessimistic Tradition. Schopenhauer, Hartmann, Leopardi*. Stockholm: Elanders Gotab.

Danielou, Jean. 1935. 'Demon'. In *Le Dictionnaire de Spiritualité ascétique et mystique. Doctrine et histoire*. Tome III – cols. 142–89.

Dannhauser, Werner. 1974. *Nietzsche's View of Socrates*. Ithaca, NY: Cornell University Press.

Davidson, Arnold I. 2006. 'Introduction'. In F. Gros (ed.), G. Burchell (trans.), *The Hermeneutics of the Subject: Lectures at the Collège de France 1981–1982*, xix–xxx. New York: Palgrave Macmillan.

Davidson, Christopher. 2015. 'Spinoza as an Exemplar of Foucault's Spirituality and Technologies of the Self'. *Journal of Early Modern Studies* 4, no. 2: 111–46.

Davie, William. 1999. 'Hume on Monkish Virtues'. *Hume Studies* 25: 139–53.

Dealy, Ross. 2017. *The Stoic Origins of Erasmus' Philosophy of Christ*. Toronto: University of Toronto Press.

De la Charité, Raymond. 1968. *The Concept of Judgment in Montaigne*. The Hague: Martinus Nijhoff.

De Vries, Hent. 2009. '*Philosophia Ancilla Theologiae*: Allegory and Ascension in Philo's *On Mating* with the Preliminary Studies (*De congress quaerendae eruditionis gratia*)'. J. Ben-Levi (trans.), *The Bible and Critical Theory* 5, no. 3: 1–19.

De Mowbray, Malcolm. 2004. 'Philosophy as Handmaid of Theology: Biblical Exegesis in the Service of Scholarship'. *Traditio* 59: 1–37.

Desmond, William. 2006. *Cynics*. Stocksfield: Acumen.

Desmond, William. 2010. 'Ancient Cynicism and Modern Philosophy'. *Filozofia* 65: 571–6.

Dillon, John. 1996. *The Middle Platonists*, 1–11. Ithaca, NY: Cornell University Press.

Dodds, E. R. 1963. *The Greeks and the Irrational*. Berkeley: University of California Press.

Domański, Juliusz. 1996. *La Philosophie, théorie ou manière de vivre?: les controverses de l'Antiquité à la Renaissance*. avec une préface de Pierre Hadot. Paris, Fribourg (Suisse): Cerf Presses Universitaires Fribourg.

Dreyfus, Hubert and Paul Rabinow. 1983. *Michel Foucault: Between Structuralism and Hermeneutics*. Chicago, IL: University of Chicago Press.

Bibliography

Duflo, Calas. 2003. *Diderot, Philosophe*. Paris: Honoré Champion.

Durant, Will and Ariel Durant. 1950. *The Age of Faith*. New York: Simon & Schuster.

Durant, Will and Ariel Durant. 1965. *The Age of Voltaire*. New York: Simon & Schuster.

Edelman, Christopher. 2010. 'Essaying Oneself: Montaigne and Philosophy as a Way of Life'. Emery University, PhD Thesis. Online at https://legacy-etd.library.emory.edu/view/record/pid/emory:5d028

Elgat, Guy. 2016. '*Amor Fati* as Practice: How to Love Fate'. *Southern Journal of Philosophy* 54, no. 2: 174–88.

Erler, Michael. 2009. 'Epicureanism in the Roman Empire'. In James Warren (ed.), *The Cambridge Companion to Epicureanism*, 46–64. Cambridge: Cambridge University Press.

Erler, Michael and Schofield, Malcolm. 1999. 'Epicurean Ethics'. In Keimpe Algra, Jonathan Barnes, Jaap Mansfeld and Malcolm Schofield (eds.), *The Cambridge History of Hellenistic Philosophy*, 642–74. Cambridge: Cambridge University Press.

Ettinghausen, Henry. 1972. *Francesco de Quevedo and the Neostoic Movement*. Oxford: Oxford University Press.

Evans, G. R. 1993. *Philosophy and Theology in the Middle Ages*. London and New York: Routledge.

Faustino, M. 2017. 'Nietzsche's Therapy of Therapy'. *Nietzsche-Studien* 46, no. 1: 82–104.

Ferry, Luc and Alain Renaut. 1979. 'Université et système: Réflexions sur les théories de l'Université dans l'idéalisme allemand'. *Archives de Philosophie* 42, no. 1 (January–March): 59–90.

Fiordalis, David. ed. 2018. *Buddhist Spiritual Practices: Thinking with Pierre Hadot on Buddhism, Philosophy, and the Path*. Berkeley, CA: Mangalam Press.

Fish, Jeffrey and Sanders, Kirk. eds. 2011. *Epicurus and the Epicurean Tradition*. Cambridge: Cambridge University Press.

Force, Pierre. 2009. Montaigne and the Coherence of Eclecticism 70, no. 4: 523–44.

Franco, Paul. 2011. *Nietzsche's Enlightenment: The Free-Spirit Trilogy*. Chicago: University of Chicago Press.

Frede, Michael. 1986. 'The Stoic Doctrine of the Affections of the Soul'. In *The Norms of Nature: Studies in Hellenistic Ethics*, 93–110. Cambridge: Cambridge University Press.

Frodeman, Robert and Adam Briggle. 2016. *Socrates Tenured. The Institutions of 21st-Century Philosophy*. Lanham, MD: Rowman & Littlefield.

Gaukroger, Stephen. 2001. *Francis Bacon and the Transformation of Early-Modern Philosophy*. Cambridge: Cambridge University Press.

Gaukroger, Stephen. 2008. 'The Académie des Sciences and the Republic of Letters: Fontenelle's Role in the Shaping of a New Natural-Philosophical Persona, 1699–1734'. *Intellectual History Review* 18, no. 3: 385–402.

Gay, Peter. 1995a. *The Enlightenment: An Interpretation. Volume I: The Rise of Modern Paganism*. New York: W. W. Norton.

Gay, Peter. 1995b. *The Enlightenment: An Interpretation. Volume II: The Science of Freedom*. New York: W. W. Norton.

Gernet, Louis, 1981. *The Anthropology of Ancient Greece*. Baltimore, MD: Johns Hopkins University Press.

Gill, Michael B. 2018. 'Shaftesbury on Life as a Work of Art'. *British Journal for the History of Philosophy* 26, no. 6: 1110–31.

Glasscock, Allison. 2009. 'A Consistent Consolation: True Happiness in Boethius' *Consolation of Philosophy*'. *Stance* 2: 42–8.

Gontier, T. and S. Mayer. eds. 2010. *Le Socratisme de Montaigne*. Paris: Classiques Garnier.

Goodman, Dena. 1989. 'Enlightenment Salons: The Convergence of Female and Philosophic Ambitions'. *Eighteenth Century Studies* 22, no. 3: 329–50.

Goulbourne, Russell. 2007. 'Voltaire's Socrates'. In M. Trapp (ed.), *Socrates from Antiquity to the Enlightenment*. 229–48. Aldershot and Burlington, VT: Ashgate.

Goulbourne, Russell. 2011. 'Diderot and the Ancients'. In N. Fowler (ed.), *New Essays on Diderot*. 13–30. Cambridge: Cambridge University Press.

Gouldner, Alvin. 1967. *Enter Plato: Classical Greece and The Origins of Social Theory*. New York and London: Basic Books.

Grafton, Anthony and Lisa Jardine. 1986. *From Humanism to the Humanities: Education and the Liberal Arts in Fifteenth and Sixteenth Century Europe*. London: Duckworth.

Graver, Margaret. 2007. *Stoicism and Emotion*. Chicago, IL: University of Chicago Press.

Greenblatt, Stephen. 2011. *The Swerve: How the World Became Modern*. New York: W. W. Norton.

Guthrie, W. K. C. 1971. *Socrates*. Cambridge: Cambridge University Press.

Habermas, Jurgen. 1989. *The Structural Transformation of the Public Sphere*. Translated by T. Burger with the assistance of F. Lawrence. Polity Press, Cambridge.

Hadot, Ilsetraut. 1969. 'Épicure et l'enseignement philosophique hellénistique et romain', In *Actes du Vlll congrès de l'Association Guillaume Budé*. Paris, 347–54.

Hadot, Pierre. 2020a. "The Figure of the Sage". In *The Selected Writings of Pierre Hadot*, 185–206.

Hadot, Pierre. 2020b. "The Ancient Philosophers". In *The Selected Writings of Pierre Hadot*, 43–54.

Hadot, Pierre. 2020c. "Physics as Spiritual Exercise, or Pessimism and Optimism in Marcus Aurelius". In *The Selected Writings of Pierre Hadot*, 207–26.

Hackforth, R. (1933). 'Great Thinkers 1: Socrates'. *Philosophy* 8: 259–72.

Haldane, John. 1992. '*De Consolatione Philosophiae*'. *Philosophy* Supplement 32: 31–45.

Hankins, James. 2006. 'Socrates in the Italian Renaissance'. In S. Ahbel-Rappe and R. A. Kamtekar (eds.), *Companion to Socrates*. Malden, MA and Oxford: Blackwell Publishing.

Hankins, James. 2008. 'Manetti's Socrates and the Socrateses of Antiquity'. In Stefano U. Baldassarri (ed.), *Dignitas et excellentia hominis: Atti del convegno internazionale di studi su Giannozzo Manetti*. Florence: La Lettere.

Hankins, James and Ada Palmer. 2008. *The Recovery of Classical Philosophy in the Renaissance. A Brief Guide*. Florence: Leo S. Olschki.

Han-Pile, Beatrice. 2016. 'Foucault, Normativity and Critique as a Practice of the Self'. *Continental Philosophy Review* 49: 85–101.

Hard, Robin. 2012. *Diogenes the Cynic: Sayings and Anecdotes*. Translated by R. Hard. Oxford: Oxford University Press.

Harrison, Peter. 2006. 'The Natural Philosopher and the Virtues'. In C. Condren, S. Gaukroger and I. Hunter (eds.), *The Philosopher in Early Modern Europe: The Nature of a Contested Identity*. Cambridge: Cambridge University Press.

Harrison, Peter. 2007. *The Fall of Man and the Foundation of Science*. Cambridge: Cambridge University Press.

Harrison, Peter. 2015. *Territories of Knowledge and Science*. Chicago, IL: University of Chicago Press.

Harter, Jean-Pierre. 2018. 'Spiritual Exercises and the Buddhist Path: An Exercise in Thinking with and against Hadot'. In David Fiordalis (ed.), *Buddhist Spiritual Practices. Thinking* with *Pierre Hadot on Buddhism, Philosophy, and the Path*, 147–80. Berkeley, CA: Mangalam Press.

Hatab, Lawrence. 2008. *Nietzsche's Genealogy of Morality: An Introduction*. Cambridge: Cambridge University Press.

Hatfield, Gary. 1985. 'Descartes's Meditations as Cognitive Exercises'. *Philosophy and Literature* 9: 41–58.

Hegel, G. W. F. 1900. *The History of Philosophy*. Translated by J. Sibree. London: George Bell and Sons.

Hegel, G. W. F. 1977. *Phenomenology of Spirit*. Translated by A. V. Miller. Oxford: Oxford University Press.

Hegel, G. W. F. 2006. *Lectures on the History of Philosophy, 1825–1826, Vol. 2 Greek Philosophy*. Edited by R. Brown, translated by R. Brown and J. M. Stewart. Oxford: Oxford University Press.

Heidegger, Martin. 2008. 'Modern Science, Metaphysics, and Mathematics'. In David Farrell Krell (ed.), *Basic Writings*, 267–306. New York: Harper & Row.

Heidegger, Martin. 2008b. 'Letter on Humanism'. In *Basic Writings*, 213–66.

Heit, Helmut and Anthony Jensen. eds. 2014. *Nietzsche as a Scholar of Antiquity*. London: Bloomsbury.

Henrichs, Albert. 1968. 'Philosophy, the Handmaiden of Theology'. *Greek, Roman and Byzantine Studies*: 437–50.

Hope, Valerie M. 2017. 'Living without the Dead: Finding Solace in Ancient Rome'. In F. S. Tappenden and C. Daniel-Hughes (eds.), with Bradley N. Rice, *Coming Back to Life: The Permeability of Past and Present, Mortality and Immortality, Death and Life in the Ancient Mediterranean*, 39–70. Montreal, QC: McGill University Library.

Hovey, Kenneth Alan. 1991. '"Mountaigny Saith Prettily": Bacon's French and the Essay'. *PMLA* 106, no. 1: 71–82.

Hughes, Frank Witt. 1991. 'The Rhetoric of Reconciliation: 2 Corinthians 1.1-2.13 and 7.5-8.24'. In Duane Frederick Watson (ed.), *Persuasive Artistry: Studies in New Testament Rhetoric in Honor of George A. Kennedy*. Michigan: JSOT Press.

Hunter, Ian. 2001. *Rival Enlightenments: Civil and Metaphysical Philosophy in Early Modern Germany*. Cambridge: Cambridge University Press.

Hunter, Ian. 2002. 'The Morals of Metaphysics: Kant's Groundwork as Intellectual Paideia'. *Critical Inquiry* 28, no. 4 (Summer 2002): 908–29.

Hunter, Ian. 2006. 'The History of Theory'. *Critical Inquiry* 33, no. 1 (Autumn 2006): 78–112.

Hunter, Ian. 2007. 'The History of Philosophy and the Persona of the Philosopher'. *Modern Intellectual History* 4, no. 3: 571–600.

Hunter, Ian. 2008. 'Talking about My Generation'. *Critical Inquiry* 34, no. 3 (Spring 2008): 583–600.

Hunter, Ian. 2010. 'Scenes from the History of Poststructuralism: Davos, Freiburg, Baltimore, Leipzig'. *New Literary History* 41: 491–516.

Hunter, Ian. 2016. 'Heideggerian Mathematics: Badiou's *Being and Event* as Spiritual Pedagogy'. *Representations* 134 (Spring 2016): 116–56.

Imbach, Ruedi. 1996. *Dante, la philosophie et les laics*. Paris, Éditions du Cerf; Fribourg, Éditions Universitaires de Fribourg.

Imbach, Ruedi. 2015. '*Virtus Illiterata*: Signification philosophie de la critique de la scholastique dans le *De sui ipsius et multorum ignoranta* de Pétrarque'. In Ruedi Imbach and Catherine König-Pralong (eds.), *Le défi laïque*, 167–92. Paris: Vrin.

Inwood, Brad and Pierluigi Dononi. 1999. 'Stoic Ethics'. In K. Algra et al. (eds.), *Cambridge History of Hellenistic Philosophy*, 699–717. Oxford: Oxford University Press.

Israel, Jonathan. 2013. *Democratic Enlightenment: Philosophy, Revolution and Human Rights 1750–1790*. Oxford: Oxford University Press.

Jacob, Margaret. 2001. 'The Clandestine Universe of the Early Eighteenth Century'. Online at http://www.pierre-marteau.com/html/studies.html

Janaway, Christopher. 1998. 'Schopenhauer as Nietzsche's Educator'. In Christopher Janaway (ed.), *Willing and Nothingness: Schopenhauer as Nietzsche's Educator*. Oxford: The Clarendon Press.

Janaway, Christopher. ed. 1999. *Cambridge Companion to Schopenhauer*. Cambridge: Cambridge University Press.

Janaway, Christopher. 2003. 'Schopenhauer as Nietzsche's Educator'. In Nicholas Martin (ed.), *Nietzsche and the German Tradition*. Oxford: Peter Lang, 155–85.

Janaway, Christopher. 2014. 'Introduction'. In S. Roehr and C. Janaway (eds.), *Parerga & Paralipomena*. Cambridge: Cambridge University Press.

Jaegar, Hasso. 1935. 'Examen de conscience'. *Le Dictionnaire de Spiritualité ascétique et mystique. Doctrine et histoire*, Tome 4 – Colonne 1789.

Kennedy, George. 2003. *Classical Rhetoric and Its Christian and Secular Tradition*, 2nd ed. Chapel Hill and London: University of North Carolina Press.

Keohane, Nannerl O. 1980. *Philosophy and the State in France: The Renaissance to the Enlightenment*. Princeton, NJ: Princeton University Press.

Ker, James. 2009. *Deaths of Seneca*. Oxford: Oxford Scholarship.

Kirham, V. and A. Maggi. eds. 2012. *Petrarch: A Critical Guide to the Complete Works*. Chicago, IL: University of Chicago Press.

Konstan, David et al. 1998. 'Introduction'. In David Konstan, Diskin Clay, Clarence E. Glad, Johan C. Thorn and James Ware (eds.), *Philodemus on Frank Criticism*, 1–24. Atlanta: Georgia: Scholars Press.

Konstan, David et al. 2008. *A Life Worthy of the Gods: The Materialist Psychology of Epicurus*. Las Vegas: Parmenides Publishing.

Konstan, David et al. 2011. 'Epicurus on the Gods'. In J. Fish and K. Sanders (eds.), *Epicurus and the Epicurean Tradition*, 53–71. Cambridge: Cambridge University Press.

Konstan, David et al. 2014. 'Crossing Conceptual World: Greek Comedy and Philosophy'. In Mike Fontaine and Adele Scafuro (eds.), *The Oxford Handbook of Ancient Comedy*, 278–95. New York: Oxford University Press.

Kramer, Hans-Joachim. 1990. *Plato and the Foundations of Metaphysics*. New York: SUNY.

Kristeller, Paul Otto. 1961. *Renaissance Thought*. New York: Harper Torch.

Kristeller, Paul Otto. 1980. 'The Moral Thought of Renaissance Humanists'. In *Renaissance Thought and the Arts: Collected Essays*. Princeton, NJ: Princeton University Press.

Lampe, Kurt. 2015. *The Birth of Hedonism: The Cyrenaic Philosophers and Pleasure as a Way of Life*. Princeton, NJ: Princeton University Press.

Lampe, Kurt. 2020. 'Introduction: Stoicism, Language, and Freedom'. In K. Lampe and J. Sholtz (eds.), *French and Italian Stoicisms*. London: Bloomsbury.

Lane, Melissa. 2014. *Greek and Roman Political Ideas*. London: Pelican Books.

Lange, Friedrich Albert. 1925. *The History of Materialism*. London: Kegan Paul.

Lapatin, Kenneth. 2006, 'Picturing Socrates'. In S. Ahbel-Rappe and R. A. Kamtekar (eds.), *Companion to Socrates*. Malden, MA and Oxford: Blackwell Publishing.

Lebreton, John. 'Contemplation'. In *Le Dictionnaire de Spiritualité ascétique et mystique. Doctrine et histoire*. Tome 2 – Colonne 1643.

Leclercq, Jean. 1935. 'Exercises Spirituels'. *Le Dictionnaire de Spiritualité ascétique et mystique. Doctrine et histoire*. Beauchesne, 1935–26. Tome 4 – Colonne 1902.

Leclercq, Jean. 1952. 'Pour l'histoire de l'expression "philosophie chrétienne"'. In *Mélanges de Science Réligieuse*. Lille: Facultes Catholiques.

Leclercq, Jean. 1996. *The Love of Learning and the Desire for God: A Study of Monastic Culture*. New York: Fordham University Press.

Leff, Gordon. 1992. 'The Trivium and the Three Philosophies'. In Hilde de Ridder-symoens (ed.), *A History of the University in Europe, Vol. I: Universities in the Middle Ages*, 307–36. New York: Cambridge University Press.

Lerer, Seth. 1985. *Boethius and Dialogue: Literary Method in the Consolation of Philosophy*. Princeton, NJ: Princeton University Press.

Limbrick, Elaine. 1973. 'Montaigne and Socrates'. *Renaissance and Reformation/ Renaissance et Réforme* 9, no. 2: 46–57.

Loeb, Paul and David Tinsley. 2019. 'Translator's Afterword'. In *Nietzsche, Unpublished Fragments from the Period of Thus Spoke Zarathustra*. Stanford, CA: Stanford University Press.

Loeb, Paul and Matthew Meyer. 2019. *Nietzsche's Metaphilosophy: The Nature, Method, and Aims of Philosophy*. Cambridge: Cambridge University Press.

Lojkine, Stéphane. 2001. 'Du détachement à la révolte: philosophie et politique dans l'Essai sur les règnes de Claude et de Néron'. *Lieux littéraires/La Revue*. Dir. Alain Vaillant, 3 (June).

Long, A. A. 1988. 'Socrates in Hellenistic Philosophy'. *Classical Quarterly* 38, no. i: 150–71.

Long, A. A. 1999. 'Socrates in Hellenistic Philosophy'. In *Stoic Studies*, 1–34. Berkeley: University of California Press.

Long, A. A. 1999b. 'Dialectic and the Stoic Sage'. In *Stoic Studies*, 85–87.

Long, A. A. 1999c. 'The Socratic Legacy'. In K. Algra, J. Barnes, J. Mansfield and M. Schofield (eds.), *The Cambridge History of Hellenistic Philosophy*, 617–41. Cambridge: Cambridge University Press.

Long, A. A. 2002. *Epictetus: A Stoic and Socratic Guide to Life*, 67–96. Oxford: Oxford University Press.

Long, A. A. 2006. *From Epicurus to Epictetus: Studies in Hellenistic and Roman Philosophy*. Oxford: Oxford University Press.

Lorch, Maristella de. 2009. 'The Epicurean in Lorenzo Valla's *On Pleasure*'. In Margaret J. Osler (ed.), *Atoms and Pneuma*. Cambridge: Cambridge University Press.

MacCulloch, Diarmaid. 2014. *Silence: A Christian History*. London: Penguin.

Mack, Burton. 2003. *The Christian Myth: Origins, Logic, Legacy*. London: Continuum International.

Mack, Peter. 1993. 'Rhetoric and the Essay'. *Rhetoric Society Journal* 23, no. 2: 41–9.

Maggi, A. 2012. '"You Will Be My Solitude": Solitude as Prophecy (*De Vita Solitaria*)'. In *Petrarch: A Critical Guide to the Complete Works*, 179–96.

Magnard, Pierre. 2010. 'Au tournant de l'humanisme: Socrate humain, rien qu'humain'. In *Le Socratisme de Montaigne*, 267–74.

Marenbon, John. 1991. *Later Medieval Philosophy*. London: Routledge.

Marenbon, John. 2003. *Boethius*. Oxford: Oxford University Press.

Marx, Karl. 2000. *The Difference between the Democritean and Epicurean Philosophy of Nature*. Online at https://marxists.catbull.com/archive/marx/works/1841/dr-theses/. Accessed February 2020.

Mason, H. T. 1963. *Voltaire and Bayle*. Oxford: Oxford University Press.

McClintock. 2018. 'Schools, Schools, Schools – Or, Must a Philosopher Be Like a Fish?' In David Fiordalis (ed.), *Buddhist Spiritual Practices. Thinking with Pierre Hadot on Buddhism, Philosophy, and the Path*, 71–104. Berkeley, CA: Mangalam Press.

McClure, George. 1991. *Sorrow and Consolation in Italian Humanism*. Princeton, NJ: Princeton University Press.

Merton, Thomas. 1970. *The Wisdom of the Desert: Sayings from the Desert Fathers of the Fourth Century*. New York: New Directions.

Miner, Robert. 2017. *Nietzsche and Montaigne*. New York: Palgrave Macmillan.

Moreau, Isabelle. 2007. '*Guérir du sot*'. *Les stratégies d'écriture des libertins à l'âge Classique*. Paris: Honoré Champion.

Moss, Ann. 1996. *Printed Commonplace Books*. Oxford: Oxford University Press.

Nabokov, Vladimir. 1989. *Speak, Memory*. New York: Vintage.

Nauta, Lodi. 2009. *In Defense of Common Sense: Lorenzo Valla's Critique of Scholastic Philosophy (I Tatti Studies in Italian Renaissance History)*. Cambridge, MA and London: Harvard University Press.

Nauta, Lodi. 2016. 'The Critique of Scholastic Language in Renaissance Humanism and Early Modern Philosophy'. In C. Muratori and G. Paganini (eds.), *Early Modern Philosophers and the Renaissance Legacy*, 59-79. International Archives of the History of Ideas, vol. 220: Springer International Publishing.

Bibliography

Nehamas, Alexander. 1985. *Nietzsche: Life as Literature*. Cambridge, MA: Harvard University Press.

Nehamas, Alexander. 1998. *The Art of Living: Socratic Reflections from Plato to Foucault*. Berkeley: University of California Press.

Niehues-Pröbsting, Heinrich. 1996. 'The Modern Reception of Cynicism'. In R. Bracht Branham and Marie-Coile Goulet-Gaze (eds.), *The Cynics*, 329–65. Berkeley: University of California Press.

Nussbaum, Martha C. 1994. *The Therapy of Desire*. Princeton, NJ: Princeton University Press.

Nussbaum, Martha C. 1999. 'Nietzsche, Schopenhauer, and Dionysus'. In C. Janaway (ed.), *Cambridge Companion to Schopenhauer*, 344–74.

Nussbaum, Martha C. 2001. *Upheavals of Thought: The Intelligence of the Emotions*. Cambridge: Cambridge University Press.

Nussbaum, Martha C. 2003. 'Compassion and Terror'. *Daedalus* 132: 10–26.

Ong, R. 2007. 'Between Memory and Paperbooks: Baconianism and Natural History in Seventeenth-Century England'. *History of Science* 45, no. 2007: 1–46.

Overgaard, Søren, Paul Gilbert, and Stephen Burwood. 2013. *An Introduction to Metaphilosophy*. Cambridge: Cambridge University Press.

Pagden, Anthony. 2013. *The Enlightenment, and Why It Still Matters*. Oxford: Oxford University Press.

Palmer, Ada. 2016. 'The Recovery of Stoicism'. In John Sellars (ed.), *Routledge Handbook of the Stoic Tradition*, 196–218. London: Routledge.

Panizza, Letizia A. 2009. 'Stoic Psychotherapy in the Middle Ages and Renaissance: Petrarch's *De remediis*'. In Margaret J. Graver (ed.), *Atoms and Pneuma*, 39–66.

Papy, Jan. 2010. 'Lipsius' Neostoic Views on the Pale Face of Death: From Stoic Constancy and Liberty to Suicide and Rubens' Dying Seneca' *LIAS* 37, no. 1.

Pekacz, Jolanta T. 1999. 'The *Salonnières* and the Philosophes in Old Regime France: The Authority of Aesthetic Judgment'. *Journal of the History of Ideas* 60, no. 2: 277–97.

Perreiah, Alan. 1982. 'Humanistic Critiques of Scholastic Dialectic'. *Sixteenth Century Journal* 13: 3.

Pippin, Robert. 2010. *Nietzsche, Psychology, and First Philosophy*. Chicago, IL: University of Chicago Press.

Popkins, Richard. 2003. *The History of Scepticism: From Savonarola to Bayle*. Revised and expanded. Oxford: Oxford University Press.

Porter, James. 2000. *Nietzsche and the Philology of the Future*. Stanford, CA: Stanford University Press.

Prado, C. G. ed. 2003. *A House Divided: Comparing Analytic and Continental Philosophy*. New York: Humanity Books.

Rasmussen, Dennis. 2013. *The Pragmatic Enlightenment: Recovering the Liberalism of Hume, Smith, Montesquieu, and Voltaire*. Cambridge: Cambridge University Press.

Raymond, Christopher. 2019. 'Nietzsche Revaluation of Socrates'. In Christopher Moore (ed.), *Brill's Companion to the Reception of Socrates*. Leiden: Brill.

Reginster, Bernard. 2006. *The Affirmation of Life: Nietzsche on Overcoming Nihilism*. Cambridge, MA: Harvard University Press.

Reginster, Bernard. 2009. 'Knowledge and Selflessness: Schopenhauer and the Paradox of Reflection'. In A. Alex Neil and Christopher Janaway (eds.), *Better Consciousness, Schopenhauer's Philosophy of Value*, 98–119. Malden, MA: Blackwell.

Reale, Giovanni. 1996. *Towards a New Interpretation of Plato*. Edited and translated by J. R. Caton. Washington, DC: Catholic University of America Press.

Rée, Jonathan. 1978. 'Philosophy as an Academic Discipline: The Changing Place of Philosophy in an Arts Education'. *Studies in Higher Education* 3, no. 1: 5–23.

Reeve, Christopher D. C. 2012. 'Aristotle's Philosophical Method'. In Christopher Shields (ed.), *The Oxford Handbook of Aristotle*. Oxford: Oxford University Press.

Roberts, Hugh. 2006. *Dogs' Tales: Representations of Ancient Cynicism in French Renaissance Texts*. Amsterdam, New York: Rodopi.

Robinson, Richard. 1971. 'Elenchus'. In G. Vlastos (ed.), *The Philosophy of Socrates*. 78–93. London: Palgrave Macmillan.

Rorty, Amelie Oksenberg. 1983. *Critical Inquiry* 9, no. 3: 545–64.

Rosenberg, Daniel. 1999. 'An Eighteenth-Century Time Machine: The "Encyclopedia" of Denis Diderot'. *Historical Reflections/Réflexions Historiques, Postmodernism and the French Enlightenment* 25, no. 2: 227–50.

Ruch, Michael. 1958. *Le Préambule dans les oeuvres philosophiques de Cicéron (Essai sur la genèse et l'art du dialogue)*. Paris: Broché.

Ruch, Michael ed. 1958. *L'Hortensius de Ciceron: Histoire et reconstitution*. Paris: Belles Lettres.

Russo, Elena. 2009. 'Slander and Glory in the Republic of Letters: Diderot and Seneca Confront Rousseau'. *Republic of Letters* 1.

Sallis, John. 1991. *Nietzsche and the Space of Tragedy*. Chicago, IL: University of Chicago Press.

Sargent, Rose-Mary. 1996. 'Bacon as an Advocate for Cooperative Scientific Research'. In Markku Peltone (ed.), *The Cambridge Companion to Bacon*. 147–71. Cambridge: Cambridge University Press.

Scarry, Elaine. 2001. *On Beauty and Being Just*. Princeton, NJ: Princeton University Press.

Schaeffer, David L. 1990. *The Political Philosophy of Montaigne*. Ithaca, NY: Cornell University Press.

Sellars, John. 2011. 'Is God a Mindless Vegetable? Cudworth on Stoic Theology'. *Intellectual History Review* 21, no. 2: 121–33.

Sellars, John. 2014. *The Art of Living: The Stoics on the Nature and Function of Philosophy*. 2nd ed. London: Bloomsbury.

Sellars, John. 2016. 'Shaftesbury, Stoicism, and Philosophy as a Way of Life'. *Sophia* 55, no. 3 (2016): 395–408.

Sellars, John. 2017. 'What Is Philosophy as a Way of Life?' *Parrhesia* 28: 40–56.

Sellars, John. 2019. 'The Early Modern Legacy of the Stoics'. Online at https://www.academia.edu/37646446/The_Early_Modern_Legacy_of_the_Stoics. Accessed February 2019.

Bibliography

Sellars, John. 2020. 'Self or Cosmos: Foucault *versus* Hadot'. In M. Faustino and G. Ferraro (eds.), *The Late Foucault*. London: Bloomsbury.

Shapin, Stephen. 1994. *The Social History of Truth: Civility and Science in Seventeenth Century England*. Chicago, IL: University of Chicago Press.

Sharpe, Matthew. 2014. 'It's Not the Chrysippus You Read: On Cooper, Hadot, Epictetus and Stoicism as a Way of Life'. *Philosophy Today* 58, no. 3 (Summer 2014): 367–92.

Sharpe, Matthew. 2014b. 'The Georgics of the Mind and the Architecture of Fortune: Francis Bacon's Therapeutic Ethics'. *Philosophical Papers* 43, no. 1: 89–121.

Sharpe, Matthew. 2015. 'Cicero, Voltaire, and the Philosophes in the French Enlightenment'. In W. H. F. Altman (ed.), *The Brill Companion to the Reception of Cicero*, 329–56. Leiden: Brill.

Sharpe, Matthew. 2015a. *Camus, Philosophe. To Return to Our Beginnings*. Leiden: Brill.

Sharpe, Matthew. 2016. 'Socratic Ironies: Reading Hadot, Reading Kierkegaard'. *Sophia* 55, no. 3: 409–35.

Sharpe, Matthew. 2016a. 'There Is Not Only a War: Recalling the Therapeutic Metaphor in Western Metaphilosophy'. *Sophia*, no. 1: 31–54.

Sharpe, Matthew. 2016b. 'Guide to the Classics: Michel de Montaigne's Essays'. *The Conversation*, 2 November. Online at https://theconversation.com/guide-to-the-classics-michel-de-montaignes-essays-63508

Sharpe, Matthew. 2017. 'Fearless? Peter Weir, The Sage, and the Fragility of Goodness'. *Philosophy and Literature* 41, no. 1: 136–57.

Sharpe, Matthew. 2018. 'Ilsetraut Hadot's Seneca: Spiritual Direction and the Transformation of the Other'. In Matthew Dennis et al. (eds.), *Ethics and Self-Cultivation: Historical and Contemporary Perspectives*, 104–23. London: Routledge.

Sharpe, Matthew. 2018a. 'The Topics Transformed: Reframing the Baconian Prerogative Instances'. *Journal of the History of Philosophy* 56: 429–54.

Sharpe, Matthew. 2018b. 'Into the Heart of Darkness or: Alt-Stoicism? Actually, No … ' *Eidos: A Journal of the Philosophy of Culture* 2, no. 4(6): 106–13.

Sharpe, Matthew. 2019. 'Home to Men's Business and Bosoms: Philosophy and Rhetoric in Francis Bacon's *Essayes*'. *British Journal of the History of Philosophy* 27, no. 3: 492–512.

Sharpe, Matthew. 2021. 'Drafted into a Foreign War? On the Very Idea of Philosophy as a Way of Life'. *Rhizomata* 8, no. 2: 183–217.

Sharpe, Matthew. 2021a. 'Between Too Intellectualist and Not Intellectualist Enough'. *Journal of Value Inquiry*, online first (April 2021): 1–19.

Sharpe, Matthew. 2021. 'Drafted into a Foreign War? On the Very Idea of Philosophy as a Way of Life.' *Rhizomata* [in press].

Sharpe, Matthew and Kirk Turner. 2018. 'Bibliopolitics'. *Foucault Studies*, no. 25: 146–74.

Sharpe, Matthew and Eli Kramer. 2019. 'Hadotian Considerations on Buddhist Spiritual Practices'. *Eidos* 3, no. 4(10): 157–69.

Shea, Louisa. 2010. *The Cynic Enlightenment: Diogenes in the Salon*. Baltimore, MD: Johns Hopkins Press.

Siegel, James. 1968. *Rhetoric and Philosophy in Renaissance Humanism*. Princeton, NJ: Princeton University Press.

Smith, Jonathan. 1978. 'Towards Interpreting Demonic Powers in Hellenistic and Roman Antiquity'. *ANRW* 16, no. 1: 425–39.

Smith, Plínio J. 2013. 'Bayle and Pyrrhonism: Antinomy, Method, and History'. In S.J. Charles and P. Smith (eds.), *Scepticism in the Eighteenth Century: Enlightenment, Lumières, Aufklärung*. International Archives of the History of Ideas Archives internationales d'histoire des idées, vol. 210, 19–30. Springer: Dordrecht.

Snell, Bruno. 1953. *The Discovery of the Mind: The Greek Origins of European Thought*. Translated by T. G. Rosenmeyer. Oxford: Basil Blackwell.

Snell, Bruno. 2011. *The Discovery of Mind in Greek Philosophy and Literature*. Dover Publications.

Sorabji, Richard. 2000. *Emotion and Peace of Mind: From Stoic Agitation to Christian Temptation*. Oxford: Oxford University Press, 2002.

Spinoza, Baruch de. 1982. *The Ethics and the Emendation of the Intellect*. Edited by Seymour Feldman, translated by Samuel Shirley. Indianapolis: Hackett Publishing.

Stephens, William O. 2002. *Marcus Aurelius: A Guide for the Perplexed*. London: Continuum.

Stirner, Max. 1995. *The Ego and Its Own*. Edited by David Leopold. Cambridge: Cambridge University Press.

Stock, Brian. 2001. *After Augustine: The Meditative Reader and the Text*. Philadelphia: University of Pennsylvania Press.

Striker, Gisela. 1994. 'Plato's Socrates and the Stoics'. In Paul A. Vander Waerdt (ed.), *The Socratic Movement*. Ithaca, NY: Cornell University Press, 241–51.

Streuver, Nancy S. 1992. *Theory as Practice: Ethical Inquiry in the Renaissance*. Chicago, IL: University of Chicago Press.

Strong, Tracy B. 2010. 'Philosophy of the Morning'. *Journal of Nietzsche Studies* 39: 51–65.

Taylor, Charles. 1979. *Hegel and Modern Society*. Cambridge: Cambridge University Press.

Taylor, Charles. 1992. *The Ethics of Authenticity*. Cambridge, MA: Harvard University Press.

Testa, Federico. 2016. 'Towards a History of Philosophical Practices in Michel Foucault and Pierre Hadot'. *PLI: the Warwick Journal of Philosophy*, 168–90. Special Volume. Self-Cultivation: Ancient and Modern.

Thorsrud, Harold. 2009. *Ancient Scepticism*. Berkeley and Los Angeles: University of California Press.

Trinkhaus, Charles. 1965. *Adversity's Noblemen: The Italian Humanists on Happiness*. London: Octagon.

Trinkhaus, Charles. 1971. *The Poet as Philosopher: Petrarch and the Formation of Renaissance Consciousness*. New Haven, CT and London: Yale University Press.

Tsouna, Voula. 2007. *The Ethics of Philodemus*. Oxford: Oxford University Press.

Tsouna, Voula. 2009. 'Epicurean Therapeutic Strategies'. In James Warren (ed.), *The Cambridge Companion to Epicureanism*, 249–65. Cambridge: Cambridge University Press.

Ure, Michael. 2007. 'Senecan Moods: Foucault and Nietzsche on the Art of the Self'. *Foucault Studies* 4: 19–52.

Ure, Michael. 2016. 'Stoicism in Nineteenth Century German Philosophy'. In John Sellars (ed.), *Routledge Handbook of Stoicism*, 287–302. London and New York: Routledge.

Ure, Michael. 2018. 'Nietzsche's Ethics of Self-Cultivation & Eternity'. In Sander Werkhoven and Matthew Dennis (eds.), *Ethics & Self-Cultivation: Historical and Contemporary Perspectives*, 84–103. London: Routledge.

Ure, Michael. 2019. *The Gay Science: An Introduction*. Cambridge: Cambridge University Press.

Ure, Michael. 2020. 'Stoic Freedom: Political Resistance or Retreat? Foucault and Arendt'. In K. Lampe and J. Sholtz (eds.), *French and Italian Stoicisms*. London: Bloomsbury.

Ure, Michael and Thomas Ryan. 2014. 'Nietzsche's Post-Classical Therapy'. *PLI: Warwick Journal of Philosophy* 25: 91–110.

Ure, Michael and Federico Testa. 2018. 'Foucault and Nietzsche: Sisyphus and Dionysus'. In J. Westfall and A. Rosenberg (eds.), *Nietzsche and Foucault: A Critical Encounter*, 127–49. London: Bloomsbury.

Ure, Michael and Thomas Ryan. 2020. 'Eternal Recurrence: Epicurean Oblivion, Stoic Consolation, Nietzschean Cultivation'. In V. Acharaya and R. Johnson (eds.), *Epicurus and Nietzsche*. London: Bloomsbury.

Vasalou, Sophia. 2013. *Schopenhauer and the Aesthetic Standpoint: Philosophy as a Practice of the Sublime*. Cambridge: Cambridge University Press.

Vendler, Zeno, 1989. 'Descartes' Exercises'. *Canadian Journal of Philosophy* 19, no. 2: 193–224.

Verbeke, Gerard. 1983. *Presence of Stoicism in Medieval Thought*. Washington, DC: Catholic University of America Press.

Vernant, J-P. 1982. *The Origins of Greek Thought*. Ithaca, NY: Cornell University Press.

Vernay, Robert. 1935. 'Attention' *Le Dictionnaire de Spiritualité ascétique et mystique. Doctrine et histoire*. Tome 1 – Colonne O.

Veyne, Paul. 2003. *Seneca: The Life of a Stoic*. New York: Routledge.

Vickers, Brian, 2000. 'The Myth of Bacon's Anti-Humanism'. In Jill Kraye et al. (eds.), *Humanism and Early Modern Philosophy*, 135–58. London: Routledge.

Vickers, Brian. 2008. 'Philosophy and Humanistic Disciplines: Rhetoric and Poetics'. In C. B. Schmitt, Quentin Skinner, Eckhard Kessler and Jill Kraye (eds.), *The Cambridge History of Renaissance Philosophy*, 713–45. Cambridge: Cambridge University Press.

Villa, Dana. 2001. *Socratic Citizenship*. Princeton, NJ: Princeton University Press.

Villey, Pierre. *Les Sources et l'évolution des Essais de Montaigne* [2 vols.]. Paris: Hachet.

Vlastos, Gregory. 1983. 'The Socratic Elenchus'. *Oxford Studies in Ancient Philosophy* 1: 27–58.

Vlastos, Gregory. 1991. *Socrates: Ironist and Moral Philosopher*. Cambridge: Cambridge University Press.

Voltaire. 1725 [2007]. *Philosophical Letters or Letters Regarding the English Nation*. Translated by Prudence L. Steiner. Indianapolis: Hackett Publishing.

Von Severus, Emmanuel and Aimé Solignac. 1935. 'Meditation'. In *Le Dictionnaire de Spiritualité ascétique et mystique. Doctrine et histoire*. Tome 10 – Colonne 906.

Wade, Ira. 1959. *Voltaire and Candide. A Study in the Fusion of History, Art, and Philosophy. With the Text of the La Vallière Manuscript of Candide*. Princeton, NJ: Princeton University Press.

Wade, Ira. 1977a. *The Structure and Form of the French Enlightenment, Volume 1: Esprit Philosophique*. Princeton, NJ: Princeton University Press.

Wade, Ira. 1977b. *The Structure and Form of the French Enlightenment, Volume 2. Esprit Révolutionnaire*. Princeton, NJ: Princeton University Press.

Wade, Ira. 2015. *Intellectual Origins of the French Enlightenment*. Princeton, NJ: Princeton University Press.

Warren, James. 2004. *Facing Death: Epicurus and His Critics*. Cambridge: Cambridge University Press.

Warren, James. 2009. 'Removing Fear'. In James Warren (ed.), *The Cambridge Companion to Epicureanism*, 234–48. Cambridge: Cambridge University Press.

Weisheipl, James A. 1965. 'Classification of the Science in the Mediaeval Thought'. *Mediaeval Studies* 27, no. 1: 54–90.

Williams, Bernard. 1994. 'Do Not Disturb: Review of Martha Nussbaum, *Therapy of Desire*'. *London Review of Books* 16, no. 20: 25–6.

Williams, Bernard. 1997. 'Stoic Philosophy and the Emotions'. In R. Sorabji (ed.), *Aristotle and After, Bulletin of the Institute of Classical Studies*, suppl. 68., 211–13.

Wilson, Catherine. 2008. 'The Enlightenment Philosopher as Social Critic'. *Intellectual History Review* 18, no. 3: 413–25.

Wilson, Catherine. 2009. 'Epicureanism in Early Modern Philosophy'. In James Warren (ed.), *The Cambridge Companion to Epicureanism*, 266–86. Cambridge: Cambridge University Press.

Wilson, Catherine. 2019. *The Pleasure Principle: Epicureanism A Philosophy for Modern Living*. London: HarperCollins.

De Witt, Norman W. 1936. 'Organization and Procedure in Epicurean Groups'. *Classical Philology* 31, no. 3 (July 1936): 205–11.

De Witt, Norman W. 1954. *Epicurus and His Philosophy*. Minneapolis: University of Minnesota Press.

Witt, Ronald G. 2006. 'Kristeller's Humanists as Heirs to the Medieval *Dictatores*'. In Angello Mazzocco (ed.), *Interpretations of Renaissance humanism*. Leiden: Brill.

Young, Julian. 1997. *Willing and Unwilling: A Study in the Philosophy of Arthur Schopenhauer*. Dordrecht: Nijhoff.

Young, Julian. 2005. *Schopenhauer*. London and New York: Routledge.

Young, Julian. 2008. 'Schopenhauer, Nietzsche, Death and Salvation'. *European Journal of Philosophy* 16, no. 2: 311–24.

Young, Julian. 2010. *Nietzsche: A Philosophical Biography*. Cambridge: Cambridge University Press.

Bibliography

Zak, Gur. 2010. *Humanism and the Care of the Self*. Cambridge: Cambridge University Press.

Zak, Gur. 2012. 'Modes of Self-Writing from Antiquity to the Later Middle Ages'. In R. J. Hexter and D. Townsend (eds.), *The Oxford Handbook of Medieval Latin Literature*. Oxford: Oxford University Press.

Zak, Gur. 2014. 'Humanism as a Way of Life: Leon Battista Alberti and the Legacy of Petrarch'. I *Tatti Studies in the Italian Renaissance* 17, no. 2 (Fall): 217–40.

Zeitlin, Jacob. 1928. 'The Development of Bacon's Essays: With Special Reference to the Question of Montaigne's Influence upon Them'. *The Journal of English and Germanic Philology* 27 no. 4: 496–519.

Zim, Rivkah. 2017. *The Consolations of Writing: Literary Strategies of Resistance from Boethius to Primo Levi*. Princeton, NJ: Princeton University Press.

INDEX OF PROPER NAMES OF PRIMARY SOURCES

Index of Proper names of primary sources

INDEX OF CONCEPTS